# Macroeconomics for Business

Interpreting and applying macroeconomic analysis to the global economic environment and understanding the tools used to do so is fundamental to making good managerial decisions. Presuming no background in economic theory and prioritizing international application, this textbook introduces macroeconomics to business students. It explains how to understand domestic and global macroeconomic developments, policies, and data, and makes extensive use of case studies and data sets to present modern macroeconomics in a globalized world. Each chapter has several specific data exercises and practices as well as an international application focusing on the global perspective. By providing a host of international material, this book is useful for instructors and students around the globe.

**Lawrence S. Davidson** is Professor Emeritus of Business Economics and Public Policy at the Kelley School of Business, Indiana University, Bloomington, with a PhD in economics from the University of North Carolina. He was the Founding Director of the Indiana Center for Global Business and the Global Business Information Network and received the John Ryan Award for Distinguished Contributions to International Programs and Studies at Indiana University. He was the Founding Director of the Kelley Center for the Business of Life Sciences and W. Michael and William D. Wells Life Sciences Faculty Fellow. Davidson worked as a visiting professor in Finland, Germany, the Netherlands, and South Korea.

**Andreas Hauskrecht** is Clinical Professor of Business Economics and Public Policy at the Kelley School of Business, Indiana University, in Bloomington, with a PhD in economics from the Free University of Berlin. He has published two monographs and more than forty papers in journals and books. He has taught courses at universities in the US, Germany, Bulgaria, Bolivia, Ecuador, Croatia, Thailand, Vietnam, and Lao, and served as adviser to governments and central banks in Europe, Latin America, and Asia. He has worked as policy adviser for the Vietnamese government for more than two decades.

Jürgen von Hagen is Professor of Economics, University of Bonn, Germany, and Visiting Professor, Department of Business Economics and Public Policy, the Kelley School of Business, Indiana University, with a PhD from University of Bonn and teaches MBA macroeconomics at Indiana University. He taught economics at Indiana University, the University of Mannheim, and the University of Bonn. Von Hagen has worked for the Federal Reserve Bank of St. Louis and the European Central Bank and has been a consultant to the IMF, the World Bank, the Inter-American Development Bank, the European Commission, the Federal Reserve Board of Governors, the Deutsche Bundesbank, the Bank of Japan, and governments in Europe and beyond. Von Hagen's publications include over ninety articles in refereed professional journals and over forty monographs.

# Macroeconomics for Business

## The Manager's Way of Understanding the Global Economy

**Lawrence S. Davidson**

Indiana University

**Andreas Hauskrecht**

Indiana University

**Jürgen von Hagen**

University of Bonn and Indiana University

CAMBRIDGE
UNIVERSITY PRESS

# CAMBRIDGE
## UNIVERSITY PRESS

University Printing House, Cambridge CB2 8BS, United Kingdom

One Liberty Plaza, 20th Floor, New York, NY 10006, USA

477 Williamstown Road, Port Melbourne, VIC 3207, Australia

314-321, 3rd Floor, Plot 3, Splendor Forum, Jasola District Centre, New Delhi - 110025, India

79 Anson Road, #06-04/06, Singapore 079906

Cambridge University Press is part of the University of Cambridge.

It furthers the University's mission by disseminating knowledge in the pursuit of
education, learning and research at the highest international levels of excellence.

www.cambridge.org
Information on this title: www.cambridge.org/9781108470858
DOI:10.1017/9781108557221

© Lawrence S. Davidson, Andreas Hauskrecht, and Jürgen von Hagen 2020

First published 2020

*A catalogue record for this publication is available from the British Library*

*Library of Congress Cataloging in Publication data*
Names: Davidson, Lawrence S., author. | Hauskrecht, Andreas, Jürgen von Hagen, author.
Title: Macroeconomics for business : the manager's way of understanding the global economy / Lawrence
    S. Davidson, Indiana University, Andreas Hauskrecht, Indiana University, Jürgen von Hagen, University of
    Bonn and Indiana University.
Description: First Edition. | New York : 2019. | Summary: "This book was developed as a text for business
    school courses in macroeconomics. It has been used in the Core MBA and Kelley Direct Programs at the
    Indiana University Kelley School of Business, the German International Graduate School of Management
    and Administration in Hanover, the German Graduate School for Law and Management in Heilbronn,
    Germany, the Helsinki School of Economics, and the Sungkyunkwan University MBA Program in Seoul,
    Korea. This book is a different kind of macroeconomics textbook. Because it was written for business
    students specifically, it focuses on their needs to interpret and apply macroeconomic analysis and tools.
    It uses very little mathematics and it shuns the model-building general equilibrium approach taken in most
    textbooks. Rather, the book is organized around topics - those topics that are written about daily in the
    business press like inflation, government deficits, international trade imbalances, exchange rates, and
    more" – Provided by publisher.
Identifiers: LCCN 2019021299 | ISBN 9781108456753 (paperback) | ISBN 9781108470858 (hardback)
Subjects: LCSH: Macroeconomics.
Classification: LCC HB172.5 .D3778 2019 | DDC 339–dc23
LC record available at https://lccn.loc.gov/2019021299

ISBN 978-1-108-47085-8 Hardback
ISBN 978-1-108-45675-3 Paperback

# Brief Contents

# Contents

# Figures

# Tables

# Boxes

# A Note to the Reader

This book was developed as a text for business school courses in macroeconomics. It has been used in the Core MBA and Kelley Direct Programs at the Indiana University Kelley School of Business, the German International Graduate School of Management and Administration in Hanover, the German Graduate School for Law and Management in Heilbronn, Germany, the Helsinki School of Economics, and the Sungkyunkwan University MBA Program in Seoul, Korea.

This book is a different kind of macroeconomics textbook. Because it was written for business students specifically, it focuses on their needs to interpret and apply macroeconomic analysis and tools. It uses very little mathematics and it shuns the model-building general-equilibrium approach taken in most textbooks. Rather, the book is organized around topics – those topics that are written about daily in the business press like inflation, government deficits, international trade imbalances, exchange rates, and more.

As such, this book is less about economic modeling techniques and more about understanding the macroeconomic environment in which businesses and their leaders operate. It is, however, impossible to understand all that without a firm grasp of concepts like aggregate supply and aggregate demand. Therefore, the book spends much effort developing these concepts and giving them a diagrammatical exposition in the form of AS and AD curves and how they interact with one another to explain changes in employment, unemployment, inflation, and national output.

The business executive is essentially a planner or decision maker who integrates a broad set of information into a decision-making process. Some of that information is economic, while some of it is not. Some of it is specific to his or her business and industry, or microeconomic, while some of it relates to national, regional, or global economic circumstances and developments, or macroeconomic. It is sometimes said that business executives deal with internal and external factors. The national and global macroeconomic picture forms the external environment in which businesses operate and executives make decisions.

Business students come to business school to learn marketing, finance, accounting, supply chain and other specialties that will advance their business careers. And while we would never downplay the importance of learning these specialties, it is also clear that the better a business executive understands how to anticipate and react to changes in the external environment, the better he or she will be at making marketing, finance, and other decisions. When local or global economic circumstances and developments change, executives that have an informed appreciation of macroeconomics make better decisions than those who do not.

Business executives are continually bombarded with many kinds of macroeconomic information and analyses. Very few weeks or months go by during which some analyst is not predicting a change in, say, consumer confidence, central bank interest rates, government policy, or exchange rates that could bring major changes in the financial and economic environment. This book provides a framework for understanding how macroeconomic shocks and trends impact the external environment, and how monetary and fiscal policies affect the future courses of output, employment, unemployment, inflation, interest rates, exchange rates, and international trade and capital flows.

The book emphasizes applications. Readers will see a lot of macroeconomic data and learn how to find and to interpret them. It is one thing to be able to say that "the model predicts higher inflation"; it is another thing to know where to find inflation data and to know what the latest inflation report means. A second aspect of application is to know what professional economists and other experts are saying about domestic and global macroeconomic changes. All chapters have sections devoted to the interpretation of such changes. Knowing that many issues in macroeconomics and economic policy are controversial, we have included in each chapter sections explaining "differences of opinion" that reflect different viewpoints in the debates over such issues.

This book is also quite international. Each chapter has one or more sections that extend the general ideas to other countries. Chapters 8 and 9 are devoted to the balance of payments, exchange rates, international trade, international capital flows, and international organizations.

All three of us have enjoyed teaching macroeconomics to current and future business executives. We think that macroeconomics is exciting and fun. That is the spirit in which we have written this book. We hope that you will enjoy it and get excited about macroeconomics as a result.

In writing this book, we have benefitted enormously from the critical comments and questions of countless students in our classes. We are very grateful to them and invite future readers to provide us with similar comments and remarks to help improve the book and the teaching based on it.

# 1 Macroeconomic Concepts and Indicators

This chapter is all about a nation's macroeconomy – it introduces the key concepts and indicators business managers, policymakers, and analysts look at and talk about when they describe the state of a nation's economy and diagnose whether or not it is healthy, provides new business opportunities, or needs some policy intervention for improvement. To understand the macroeconomic environment you and your business operate in, you want to know the relevant terms, understand the concepts, and know what indicators to look at.

A firm's revenue in any given year is a result of a combination of forces that are directly related to the company, its industry, and the domestic and international macroeconomic environment. Depending on the firm and the year, these factors might alternate in importance. In some years, macroeconomic factors might not be very important; but in others – particularly at the beginning or end of a recession – changes in macroeconomic conditions can be very important. Furthermore, firm and industry-specific forces tend to lose and macroeconomic factors tend to gain prominence the more one looks into the future. For investment projects with time horizons of five, ten, and even more years, information about whether the general economy is going to grow or not, whether interest rates will be high or low, whether prices in general will be rising at a fast or a low pace is crucial.

It is, therefore, important for a successful business manager to understand the macroeconomic environment his or her business is operating in. He or she must be able to interpret current and past data and developments, to understand current and past government policies, and to form expectations about future developments as an input to his or her business strategy. The purpose of this book is to enable you to do that.

As you will see, some of the material you are going to read sounds pretty technical. Macroeconomics is filled with jargon. This jargon is necessary, however, because the economy is complex and we need to be precise with our language and our thinking to deal with that complexity without getting confused. The people who write about the economy break their stories down by using specific terminology. If you are to understand what these experts are saying, you must master the terminology.

Good business managers continuously monitor the development of the markets for their products, observing prices and quantities of their own and competing products. We usually divide up the analysis of such markets into supply components and demand components. Supply-and-demand components convey different meaning. For example, cell phones are bought and sold at a certain price. That price and the quantity of cell phones sold can vary over time, depending on demand and supply factors. Demand factors determine how many people want to buy cell phones and how much they are willing to spend on them. Supply factors determine how many cell phones firms decide to produce at given production costs and sales prices. The number of cell phones actually traded in the market during a particular year stems from the interactions of demand and supply factors. We might say that cell phone sales increased this year because some new apps made them more attractive to the consumer. That would be a demand story. Or we could say that cell phone prices fell because of the decline in the prices of rare earth metals used for their production. That would be a supply tale.

We do the same in macroeconomics. Here, however, we are not concerned with the quantity and price of an individual good or service, but with the quantities of all the goods and services produced on the territory of a nation and their average price, the nation's price level. At the heart of macroeconomics is aggregation. Instead of the demand for an individual good or service, we are interested in *aggregate demand* (AD), i.e., the demand for all goods and services produced. Similarly, we are interested in the *aggregate supply* (AS) of all goods and services produced on the territory of a nation. It might be helpful to note that very much, though not all, of the discussion about changes in a country's economy tends to focus on AD factors, because these are what drives the economy in the short run. Many of us are so busy with the short run that we never think much about the long run. That means that we often think that all of macroeconomics is about aggregate demand. But that isn't true and we hope to explain why in this book. AS factors tend to be more important in the long run. As the late Paul Samuelson, winner of the Nobel Prize in economics in 1970 once said: "God gave economists two eyes, one to watch demand, one to watch supply."[1]

In macroeconomics, we ask these kinds of questions: Why did the economy slow down this year? Why did the recovery begin? How strong will the recovery be? What can monetary and fiscal policy do to achieve better outcomes? What are the prospects for growth of the economy as a whole over the next few years?

In order to answer these and similar questions, we begin with the most comprehensive measure of a nation's economic activity, gross domestic product (GDP). We look at GDP from three different perspectives: GDP as aggregate demand, as aggregate supply, and as aggregate income (AI). The *economic circuit* shows why these three have to be the same. Next, we decompose GDP into its quantity component, called *real* GDP, and its price component. Real GDP is the main vehicle we use to talk about economic growth. We will then consider real GDP as an indicator of a nation's overall wellbeing. Considering the price component will lead us to various measures of the nation's price level and inflation. Finally, we look at various indicators of the nation's labor force and the state of the labor market.

## 1.1   GDP: Aggregate Demand, Supply, and Income

Macroeconomics ignores the specific attributes of particular goods or services so that it can concentrate on all of a nation's production. Instead of the markets for steel or consulting services, we think of the market for all the goods and services produced by the nation taken together. Goods are tangible things such as cars, computers, and umbrellas, or intangible things such as a piece of music down-loadable from the internet. Goods are produced and they satisfy the wants and desires of consumers or producers. They are often described as being durables (e.g. cars, washing machines) or non-durables (e.g. food, clothing). They can also be referred to as follows:

### Types of goods

| Final consumer | Intermediate | Raw material | Fixed asset |
|---|---|---|---|
| A good intended for final use by a consumer. Can be durable or non-durable (example: dish washer and breakfast cereals) | A good intended as an input into the production of another good (example: steering wheel) | A material extracted from the earth or an agricultural product that will be further transformed by a producer (example: crude oil) | A durable good that will be repeatedly or continuously used by businesses to produce other goods (example: printing machine) |

Fixed assets include structures such as commercial or residential buildings or highways, equipment, and intellectual property products.

A service is an intangible which is consumed as it is rendered. Sure, you look beautiful for days after your haircut – but we think of the act of giving the haircut as over when you leave the hair salon. Consumers enjoy lots of personal services like travel, banking, education, medical services, and many more.

Aggregate demand is the total demand for all of a nation's newly produced final consumer goods and services and fixed assets. Aggregate supply is the total supply of all the nation's newly produced final consumer goods and services and fixed assets. Okay – we want to talk about the sum or aggregate of all these goods and services. How do we get from the thousands of different goods and services to talking about all of them? Al Capp, the famous cartoonist, had some fun with this idea – he talked about *smooshing* together all these goods and services into one unit; so he called the sum total of all goods and services a SHMOO.[2] It turns out that most countries do not publish statistics on the price or quantity of SHMOOs – but they do use a concept called GDP. What is that?

GDP is the aggregate market value of all final goods and services produced within a nation's borders during a given period (usually a year or a quarter).

By multiplying the quantities of the goods and services included in GDP by their market prices, we obtain dollar values for all of them, which we can then aggregate, i.e., sum up. For the US, GDP is expressed in dollars. For Japan, GDP is expressed in yen, and for the euro area (the European Union (EU) countries using the euro as their currency), GDP is expressed in euros.

## 1.1.1   The Economic Circuit

The key to understanding macroeconomics is the economic circuit. The economic circuit describes the circular flow of goods and services and monetary payments through the economy during a given period. In the simplest version of the economic circuit, we divide a country's entire economy into two sectors: households and firms or businesses. We abstract from the existence of the government sector and the international sector for a moment. The household sector consumes the final goods and services produced by the firm sector. It is also the ultimate owner of all labor, capital, and land in the economy. *Capital* in this context consists of the stock of fixed assets businesses use in the process of production. That households are the ultimate owners of the firms' capital is obvious in the case of a hairdresser who owns his own shop and equipment. It is less obvious in the case of a common stock company, but shareholders do own a share in its capital. The firm sector produces final goods and services and new fixed assets using the labor, capital, and land that the household sector makes available to it through the markets for labor, land, and capital. Note that the firm sector includes all production activities from the extraction or production of raw materials to the assembly of the finished products. Thus, all production takes place in the firm sector, while the household sector makes use of the goods and services produced. Note that the distinction between "firms" and "households" is a functional one. An individual person can belong to both sectors at the same time. For example, a private consultant is a "firm" producing consulting services and a consumer at the same time.

The economic circuit describes the flow of labor, capital-use, and land-use services from households to firms and the flow of final goods and services produced by the firms to households. It represents a basic insight from macroeconomics, namely that every buyer on one market is also a seller on another market, and every seller on one market is also a buyer on another market. This is the essence of an exchange economy: Everybody gives something to obtain something else. For example, employees work for their companies in order to receive a salary which they spend on consumer goods sold by these and other companies.

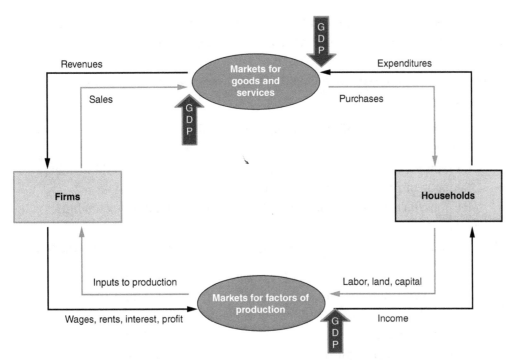

Figure 1.1 The economic circuit

Consider Figure 1.1, which illustrates the economic circuit. Blue arrows indicate flows of goods and services between households and firms in one direction. Black arrows indicate flows of payments between households and firms in the opposite direction. The upper half shows the flows of final goods and services from firms to households. These flows are intermediated through markets for goods and services. The lower half of the circuit shows the flows of labor, land-use, and capital-use services from households to firms. These flows are intermediated through markets for labor, capital, and land. Firms use them as inputs to production. They compensate households for making these factors of production available by paying wages for labor, rents for the use of land, and interest and profits for the use of capital. These payments constitute the household sector's income in any given period. Household expenditures for goods and services become the revenues of the firms. Firms use their revenues to pay wages, rents, interest, and profits to the households.

Households use their incomes to finance their expenditures for goods and services. If they spend less than their current incomes, they save, i.e., they increase their net wealth. If they spend more than their current incomes, they dis-save and reduce their net wealth. Financial markets and institutions serve to intermediate income flows between those households who save and those who dis-save. But how can the household sector as a whole save? If the country's total stock of land is fixed, all households together can save only by buying additional fixed assets which they then make available to the firm sector. Remember that the households are the ultimate owners of all capital in the economy. The household sector may, in any given period, increase the stock of capital available for production. We call this investment.

The essence of the economic circuit is that these flows must be equal in value in any given period. That is:

- total firm sales (value of production) equals total household expenditures (value of purchases);
- total remuneration of inputs to production equals total household income;
- total value of production equals total income paid to households;
- total household income equals total household consumption expenditures plus saving;
- total household saving equals total purchases of capital goods or investment.

These are accounting identities, i.e., they must always be true. It cannot be otherwise. But, you will say, what about unsold goods that have been produced? We treat them as changes in inventories and include them in investment, because they can be sold in future periods.

The economic circuit indicates that any increase in household income must lead to an increase in household expenditures, which must lead to an increase in firm revenues and to an increase in wages, rents, interest, and profit paid to households. Thus, one household's expenditure ultimately becomes another household's income. For example, if the price of apples goes up, the income of apple farmers usually increases. This implies that, while the demand for apples by nonfarm households may fall due to the increase in price, aggregate household expenditures on all final goods and services will increase. Understanding this is key to understanding macroeconomics.

While the flows represented by the blue arrows are flows of goods and services, the flows represented by black arrows are payment flows, which are executed using the economy's means of payment, money. Each unit of money may be used in multiple payments during a period. For example a dollar note can be used during a period first by a customer to buy bread, and then by the baker to pay the wages of the baker's employee, and then by the employee to buy an apple for the employee's family. We call the average number of times each unit of money is used in payments during a period the velocity of money. Thus, another identity from the economic circuit is that

(Number of units of money) ∗ (velocity of money) = total value of expenditures for final goods and services.

Figure 1.1 indicates the fundamental identities by showing that one can measure the total value of output, or GDP, of an economy at three points. GDP can be regarded as the total value of expenditures for final goods and services. This is aggregate demand. GDP can be regarded as the total value of goods and services produced. This is aggregate supply. GDP can be regarded as the total of all incomes paid to the household sector. This is aggregate income. Because of the economic circuit, it must be true that aggregate demand equals aggregate supply, and aggregate supply equals aggregate income, and, therefore, aggregate demand equals aggregate income.

Now, when we say that these identities are accounting identities, we say that they must be true *ex post*, i.e., when all market transactions have been executed, all goods and services have been produced, delivered, consumed, or invested (think of this as at the end of a period). This is how we measure GDP statistically.

*Ex ante*, before this has happened (think of this as at the beginning of a period), these identities are not necessarily true. This is because aggregate demand is planned and decided by the households, while aggregate supply is planned and decided by the firms. Wages, rents, interest, and profits are paid by firms, while incomes are received and expended by households. Since there are different decision makers involved, nothing guarantees that their plans are compatible with each other. For example, suppose that firms plan to produce less at current prices than households desire to buy and to employ less capital and labor than households wish to make available at current wages and interest rates. As a result, incomes are lower than desired and households cannot finance their expenditure plans. At the same time, there is idle capital and unemployed labor. The fundamental identities do not hold *ex ante* in that case. Alternatively, suppose that some households put the money they do not spend on consumption under their mattresses instead of buying new capital goods. This is called *hoarding* rather than saving. At given prices, wages, and interest rates, planned savings are lower than planned investment. Again, the fundamental identities do not hold in an *ex ante* sense.

*Ex ante*, the equality of aggregate demand, aggregate supply, and aggregate income defines what we call a *macroeconomic equilibrium*. An important feature of a market economy is that prices, wages, and interest rates adjust every period to achieve such an equilibrium. This gives us a hint for predicting how prices, wages, and interest rates co-move with output, consumption, investment, and employment each period. Analyzing these co-movements will be the topic of the later chapters in this book.

Figure 1.2 gives us an expanded view of the economic circuit. It includes the government sector and the international sector. The government collects taxes from households and firms; it buys goods and services from private firms and employs government workers and civil servants. It can also be an owner of land and capital and receive income from these. The government, in fact, has a hybrid function in the economy, because it uses labor, land, and capital to produce "public goods and services" such as national defense, internal security, law and order, maintenance of infrastructure like roads, etc. Such public goods and services are not traded on markets, and, therefore, cannot be evaluated at market prices. In GDP accounting,

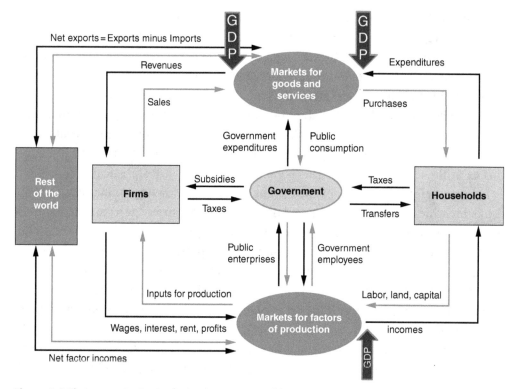

**Figure 1.2** The economic circuit of an open economy with government sector

we represent their value by the cost of producing them. Government spending on wages and salaries, capital-use, and land-use services thus become part of aggregate demand, aggregate supply, and aggregate income all at the same time.

Once we recognize the existence of the government in the economic circuit, our fundamental identities must be adjusted. This is because the government can spend more than it receives in tax revenues and finance the difference by issuing government bonds. This gives the household sector another way of saving, namely by buying government bonds. Furthermore, we have to take into account that households have to pay taxes out of their incomes. Thus, we consider total disposable income, which is household income net of taxes. Abstracting from the international sector for now, our fundamental identities are as follows:

- total value of production (firms and government) equals total household consumption expenditures plus government consumption;
- total remuneration of inputs to production equals total household disposable income plus total tax revenue;
- total value of production equals total household disposable income plus tax revenues;
- total household disposable income equals total household consumption expenditures plus saving;

- total tax revenues equals total government spending plus government saving;
- total household saving plus government saving equals total investment.

Next, we turn to the international sector. Firms sell output produced in the country to other countries (exports) and foreign firms sell goods and services and new fixed assets produced abroad to domestic households and the government (imports). As a result, the total demand for domestically produced goods and services now includes the demand from abroad, i.e., exports, and domestic consumption, government expenditures, and investment contain goods and services produced by foreign firms. Since GDP is the value of domestically produced goods and services, we have to subtract imports from the sum total of domestic consumption, government expenditures, and investment. The difference between exports and imports, or net exports, thus becomes part of aggregate demand.

Foreign firms may employ domestic workers, land, and capital for production and pay wages, rents, interest, and profits to domestic households, while domestic firms may use foreign labor, land, and capital for their production and pay incomes to foreign households. Thus, there is also a net flow of factor incomes between the domestic and the foreign economies.

Once again, there are some fundamental identities, and we can measure GDP as aggregate demand, aggregate supply, and aggregate income. We look at these identities in more detail in the next section.

## 1.1.2 National Accounting

The economic circuit is the foundation of national accounting, the statistical measurement of economic activity. In the US, national accounting is a job done by the Bureau of Economic Analysis (BEA) (www.bea.gov), which is part of the federal government. BEA's accounting system is called National Income and Product Accounts (NIPA). It is the analogue of an income and expense statement for the entire economy.

There are a few important accounting principles behind NIPA. The first is double-entry bookkeeping. Every economic transaction recorded in NIPA must appear in two different places, once as a source of revenue and once as an expenditure of resources. These different places may well be in the accounts of two different sectors. For example, wages paid by firms will be recorded as an expense in the business sector's production account and as a revenue in the household sector's income account. Double-entry bookkeeping conforms with the principle of the economic circuit that one agent's purchase must be another agent's sale.

The second important principle behind NIPA is accrual accounting. This means that a transaction is recorded at the time when the commitments to deliver and to pay are incurred and regardless of when the pertinent transactions are actually executed. This is in contrast to cash accounting, where transactions are recorded at the time of their execution. For annual national accounts, the difference between accruals and cash accounting plays no big role for consumer purchases of food or clothing, for example. But it does play a role for transactions that involve significant gestation periods, e.g., a government's purchase of a new submarine.

The third important principle is that NIPA includes some imputations of the value of goods and services produced for own use or for non-market transactions. Cases of own use include farm production for consumption by the farm household, and the value of the services provided by owner-occupied housing. The value of the service provided by the use of a tenant-occupied house is measured by the rent paid. If the same house is owner-occupied, no rent is paid although the same service is being produced and consumed. In order to assure that changes in ownership do not affect the measurement of economic activity, the rent paid for a comparable house is imputed for the use of an owner-occupied house.

The most important case of non-market transactions is the government's production of public goods and services. Their value is accounted for by the cost of production. Illegal activities such as drug dealing or prostitution are not included in NIPA at all. In contrast, the 2010 European System of National and Regional Accounts (ESA) published by the EU's statistical office, Eurostat, allows governments to include estimates of such activities in their national accounts.

The final accounting principle is periodicity and territoriality. NIPA is compiled and published in two versions, quarterly and annually based on the calendar year. It measures economic activities on the territory of the US.

Without going into too much detail, we show how US national accounting works and how it is linked to the concept of the economic circuit. We recognize productive activities in two sectors of the economy: the firm or business sector and the government sector.[3] Domestic firms produce goods and services for sale to domestic and foreign households, firms, and governments. We begin with the production account of an individual domestic business (Table 1.1). For the sake of brevity, we write "goods" instead of the more proper "goods and services." On the right-hand side, the account reports all payment inflows to the business from selling final and intermediate goods to domestic households, other domestic businesses, and the domestic government as well as foreign firms.

The left-hand side reports all the expenses incurred by the firm. These consist of the payment for purchases of intermediate goods, the compensation of employees, i.e., wages and salaries including any supplements, rents paid for buildings, interest paid on loans, taxes on production and imports such as payroll taxes or sales taxes, non-personal property taxes, federal excise taxes, and import and export tariffs, less production subsidies such as farm subsidies. Note that all purchases of foreign goods are considered purchases of intermediate goods, since the domestic business as a minimum provides the services of bringing the imported goods to the domestic retailer or consumer. The difference between all revenues and all expenses is called gross operating surplus. It is split up into the consumption of fixed capital or

**Table 1.1** Production account of an individual domestic business

| Expenses | Revenues |
| --- | --- |
| Purchases of intermediate goods from other domestic businesses | Sales of final goods to domestic households |
| Purchases of intermediate goods from domestic government | Sales of final goods to other domestic businesses |
| Rent paid for buildings | Sales of final goods to domestic government |
| Interest paid on loans | Sales of intermediate goods to other domestic businesses |
| Compensation of employees | Sales of intermediate goods to domestic government |
| Purchases of intermediate goods from foreign businesses | Sales of final goods to foreign businesses |
| Taxes on production and imports less subsidies | |
| Consumption of fixed capital | |
| Net operating surplus | |

**Table 1.2** Production account domestic business sector

| Expenses | Revenues |
| --- | --- |
| Purchases of intermediate goods from domestic government | Sales of final goods to domestic households |
| Compensation of employees | Sales of final goods to other domestic businesses |
| Taxes on production less subsidies | Sales of final goods to domestic government |
| Consumption of fixed capital | Sales of intermediate goods to domestic government |
| Net operating surplus | Sales of final goods to foreign businesses less purchases of intermediate goods from foreign businesses |

depreciation, i.e., the loss of value of the firm's fixed assets due to their use in production, and net operating surplus or profits.

Next, we aggregate the production accounts of all domestic firms in the country (Table 1.2). By doing so, revenues from sales of intermediate goods to domestic businesses and expenses for purchases of intermediate goods from domestic businesses cancel each other out. Since we treat the renting of buildings and the granting of loans as a business activity, rents and interest paid also cancel out. Thus we are left with business-sector expenses and revenues as shown in Table 1.2.

Net operating surplus consists of a large variety of types of incomes paid to households owning businesses or shares in them and profits retained in the business sector. This includes proprietors' incomes, dividends, net interest payments, e.g., on corporate bonds held by households, rental incomes, corporate profits, and undistributed profits.

The production account of the domestic government sector reports primarily the transactions of all parts of the government (local, state, and federal) related to the production of public goods and services (Table 1.3). Note that, by definition, there is no net operating surplus in the government sector. This is because the government's consumption expenditures represent the value of the nation's consumption of the public goods and services produced by the government, and this value is measured by the cost of production.

Finally, we aggregate the production accounts of the domestic business and government sectors to arrive at the national product and income account. This is the first of seven tables which form the skeleton of BEA's NIPA system.[4] For illustration, we report the numbers for the US economy in 2016.

We can now see that GDP is the total of all net value added in domestic production during a given period. The right-hand side of Table 1.4 reports the total revenues from private business and government production and the different uses of the goods and services produced during that year, namely personal or household

**Table 1.3** Production account of domestic government sector

| Expenses | Revenues |
|---|---|
| Purchases of intermediate goods from domestic businesses | Sales of intermediate goods to domestic businesses |
| Compensation of employees | Government consumption expenditures and gross investment |
| Consumption of fixed capital | |

**Table 1.4** National income and product account (US 2016, USD trillions)

| Expenses | | Revenues | |
|---|---|---|---|
| Compensation of employees | 9.99 | Personal consumption expenditures (C) | 12.82 |
| Taxes on production and imports less subsidies | 1.22 | Gross private domestic investment (I) | 3.06 |
| Consumption of fixed capital | 2.92 | Government consumption expenditures and gross investment (G) | 3.27 |
| Net operating surplus | 4.65 | Exports (2.2) less imports (2.7) of goods and services (X-Im) | −0.50 |
| Gross domestic income = GDP | 18.62 | Total net value added = GDP | 18.62 |

*Source*: BEA NIPA Account 1.

**Table 1.5** Private enterprise income account (US 2016, USD trillions)

| Expenses | | Revenues | |
|---|---|---|---|
| Income payments on assets | 2.78 | Net operating surplus of private enterprises | 4.65 |
| Current transfer payments (net) | 0.16 | Interest receipts on assets | 2.42 |
| Proprietors' incomes after depreciation | 1.34 | | |
| Household rental incomes after depreciation | 0.71 | | |
| Corporate profits after depreciation | 2.07 | | |
| Uses of private enterprise income | 7.07 | Sources of private enterprise income | 7.07 |

*Source*: BEA NIPA Account 2.

consumption, private investment, government consumption and investment, and net exports. The left-hand side tells us how these revenues were used. It is clear now that the total value added equals the value of all incomes generated from domestic production in the same period, gross domestic income (GDI). Subtracting the consumption of fixed capital from GDP, we obtain net domestic product (NDP). This is also called net domestic income at market prices because all goods and services are valued at their sales prices. Subtracting taxes on production less subsidies from NDP, we obtain NDP at factor prices.

Next, we turn to the income accounts of the business sector, the household sector, and the government sector. The private enterprise income account shown in Table 1.5 reports the sources and uses of private enterprise income. Income comes from net operating surplus and interest receipts on assets owned by enterprises. Uses of income comprise income payments on assets, transfer payments such as company pensions, proprietors' incomes net of depreciation, household rental incomes, and corporate profits. The latter include corporate profit taxes paid, net dividends paid, and undistributed profits.

Table 1.6 reports the household or personal income and outlay account. On the right-hand side we recognize the compensation of employees from Table 1.4, and proprietors' income and household rental income after depreciation from Table 1.5. Personal transfer receipts include government transfers such as social security benefits and business transfers such as corporate pensions.

The left-hand side of Table 1.6 reports the uses of personal income, beginning with personal taxes on income and property. Subtracting personal taxes from personal income gives disposable personal income, USD 13.9 trillion in 2016. The largest item is PCEs, also recorded on the right-hand side of Table 1.4. Personal savings amounted to USD 0.8 trillion in 2016.

**Table 1.6** Personal income and outlay account (US 2016, USD trillions)

| Expenses | | Revenues | |
|---|---|---|---|
| Personal taxes | 1.96 | Compensation of employees | 9.99 |
| PCEs | 12.82 | Proprietors' income | 1.34 |
| Personal interest payments | 0.28 | Household rental income after depreciation | 0.71 |
| Personal transfer payments | 0.19 | Personal income on assets | 2.38 |
| Personal savings | 0.68 | Personal transfer receipts net | 1.51 |
| Personal income | 15.93 | Personal income | 15.93 |

*Source*: BEA NIPA Account 3.

**Table 1.7** Government receipts and expenditures account (US 2016, USD trillions)

| Expenses | | Revenues | |
|---|---|---|---|
| Consumption expenditures | 2.66 | Current taxes | 3.73 |
| Current transfer payments | 2.79 | Social insurance contributions | 1.25 |
| Interest payments | 0.67 | Interest receipts on assets | 0.13 |
| Subsidies | 0.06 | Current transfer receipts | 0.22 |
| Government savings net | −0.86 | Current surplus of government enterprises | −0.01 |
| Total current expenses | 5.31 | Total current receipts | 5.31 |

*Source*: BEA NIPA Account 4.

Table 1.7 reports the Government Receipts and Expenditures Account. Current taxes and social insurance contributions are the main revenue items of the government. Government consumption expenditures of USD 2.7 trillion are from the right-hand column of Table 1.4. Current transfer payments are partly included in personal transfer receipts in Table 1.6 and partly paid to the rest of the world (RoW), e.g., as foreign aid. Net government savings were negative in 2016 indicating that the government needed to borrow from domestic and foreign households and foreign governments to cover its expenses.

Table 1.8 records the current transactions between the US and the RoW. Exports and imports of goods and services are from Table 1.4. Income payments to and from the RoW include wages and asset incomes paid to foreign residents by domestic businesses and by foreign businesses to domestic residents. The former are included in incomes paid in Tables 1.4 and 1.5, the latter in incomes received in Table 1.6. The balance on the current account shows that in 2016 the US paid USD 0.5 trillion more to the RoW than it earned from it, a result of larger imports than exports of goods and services.

The domestic capital account, Table 1.9, shows how the US economy used the gross savings of domestic households and governments. Consumption of fixed

**Table 1.8** Foreign transactions current account (US 2016, USD trillions)

| Current receipts from the RoW | | Current payments to the RoW | |
|---|---|---|---|
| Exports of goods and services | 2.21 | Imports of goods and services | 2.74 |
| Income payments from the RoW | 0.84 | Income payments to the RoW | 0.65 |
| Taxes and transfers from the RoW | 0.14 | Taxes and transfers paid to the RoW | 0.28 |
| | | Balance on current account | −0.46 |
| Total current receipts | 3.20 | Total current payments | 3.20 |

*Source*: BEA NIPA Account 5.

**Table 1.9** Domestic capital account (US 2016, USD trillions)

| Investment | | Saving | |
|---|---|---|---|
| Gross domestic private investment | 3.02 | Net personal saving and undistributed profits | 1.31 |
| Gross domestic public investment | 0.61 | Net government saving | −0.86 |
| Capital account transactions (net) | 0.00 | Consumption of fixed capital | 2.92 |
| Net lending or borrowing (−) | −0.46 | Statistical error | −0.15 |
| Total gross investment | 3.21 | Total gross saving | 3.21 |

*Source*: BEA NIPA Account 6.

**Table 1.10** Foreign transactions capital account (US 2016, USD trillions)

| Balance on current account | −0.46 | Capital account transactions (net) | 0.00 |
|---|---|---|---|
| | | Net lending or borrowing (−) | −0.46 |

*Source*: BEA NIPA Account 7.

capital from Table 1.4 is the largest amount. Net savings come from Table 1.6 (personal) and Table 1.7 (government). Since gross domestic private and public investment (USD 3.7 trillion) exceeded gross domestic personal and public saving (USD 3.2 trillion including the statistical discrepancy), the US economy as a whole needed to borrow an amount of USD 0.5 trillion from the RoW. This equals the net borrowing reported in the foreign transactions capital account in Table 1.10 and corresponds to the balance on the current account from Table 1.8.

Subtracting the consumption of fixed capital from gross domestic private and public investment in Table 1.9 gives the value of newly acquired fixed assets used in future production by the US economy, or the increase in the US capital stock, USD 0.8 trillion in 2016, USD 0.5 trillion of which was financed by borrowing from abroad. As a result, US net foreign assets decreased by USD 0.5 trillion that year.

Here is a final caveat. When you look at BEA data, you notice two things which you may never have in your company's income statement: *statistical discrepancies* and *revisions*. In national accounting, you find statistical discrepancies because the data are compiled from different sources such as business income and sales reports to the government, tax reports, and customs reports. These are produced by different entities and not necessarily consistent in practice, although in theory they should be. Revisions reflect the fact that GDP data are initially estimated by the BEA. That is, when they are first published, the BEA does not have all the information about all items included in GDP. Rather than wait until all information is in – which would take a couple of years – the BEA estimates the missing information based on past experience and statistical methods. As time goes by and more information comes in, the GDP numbers are revised and become more precise.

### 1.1.3   GDP as Aggregate Demand

We now look at GDP in more detail from the AD side. Once again, it is the aggregate market value of all the newly produced final goods and services and fixed assets produced within the borders of a country during a given period of time, usually a quarter or a year. It is very typical to discuss aggregate demand in terms of its key components listed below. In interpreting these components, remember that we are only interested in final goods and services and fixed assets produced within the current period, which means we are not thinking about demand for goods that are already in existence like houses that were built a year ago or used cars.

- *Personal consumption expenditures*, C: This consists of the final goods and services purchased by households. This does not include newly built homes.
- *Gross domestic private investment*, I: This consists of fixed domestic private investment and changes in inventories (ΔINV). Fixed domestic private investment falls into fixed residential investment (I-R), the purchases of new homes, condos, apartments, etc.; and fixed non-residential investment (I-NR), the purchases of new fixed assets like machinery, equipment, and buildings by businesses.
- *Government expenditures*, G: This consists of government consumption, the public services delivered by the government, and gross public investment, the purchases of new fixed assets by the government.
- *Net exports*, X-Im: Exports are domestically produced final goods and services purchased by foreign businesses and governments. Imports are intermediate goods and services purchased abroad by domestic businesses and sold as final goods and services to domestic households, businesses, and the government.

Note that the goods and services bought by domestic households for final consumption include goods and services produced within the borders of other countries: Toys made in China, or consulting services rendered by phone from India, for instance. Similarly, non-residential investment includes machinery and equipment produced within the borders of other countries, such as printing machines made in Germany. To compute US GDP (the aggregate market value of all final goods and services and fixed assets produced within the borders of the US) correctly, we have to subtract imports, Im, from consumption, non-residential investment, and government purchases. All legal imports to a country must go through some form of customs and in that way all imports can be calculated.

Once you can remember the abbreviations, we can write the definition of GDP more simply as:

$$GDP = C + I + G + X - IM$$

So now consider the following (trick) question: If US imports increase, what happens to US GDP? Yes, most people are tempted to say that GDP falls, because imports appear with a minus sign in the equation above. But that's wrong! When imports increase, either personal consumption, or gross domestic private investment or government spending or perhaps all three also increase, reflecting the fact that the imported goods are used for consumption, investment or by the government. Therefore, the correct answer is: GDP remains the same!

A country's net exports (NX) is the difference between the exports (X) and the imports (Im), so we can write the GDP expression one more time

$$GDP = C + I + G + NX$$

Okay – so now we know what GDP is and how you can talk about it or calculate it by taking the AD approach. Let's do that for 2016. To find these data, go to www.BEA.gov, click on "interactive tables GDP and the national income and product accounts" and select "begin using the table."

From the AD side, shown in Table 1.11, a little more than two-thirds (68.8 percent) of US GDP consists of personal consumption. The US is a consumer society! Two-thirds of personal consumption (67.8 percent) is consumption of services. Gross domestic private investment made up 16.4 percent of GDP, government expenditures 17.5 percent; 81 percent of government expenditures are government consumption and this includes the making available of public services. In 2016, the US exported 11.9 percent of its GDP. This shows that, despite all the talk about foreign trade and globalization, the US economy is still relatively *closed*. Compare that to Germany, where exports make up 46 percent of GDP!

## 1.1.4 GDP as Aggregate Supply

What are the kinds of things the US economy produces? We can answer that question by looking at GDP from the AS perspective. Here, we distinguish different production sectors of the economy such as manufacturing, construction, or farming, and ask how much each of these contributes to GDP. The numbers in Table 1.12 come again from the BEA.

**Table 1.11** US GDP as aggregate demand (2016, USD billions)

| | |
|---|---:|
| PCEs | 12,821 |
| Goods | 4,121 |
| Services | 8,699 |
| Gross domestic private investment | 3,057 |
| Fixed Residential | 706 |
| Fixed Nonresidential | 2,316 |
| Changes in inventories | 35 |
| Government expenditures | 3,268 |
| Government consumption expenditures | 2,658 |
| Gross public investment | 610 |
| Net exports | −521 |
| Exports | 2,215 |
| Imports | 2,736 |
| GDP | 18,625 |

*Source*: BEA table 1.1.5.

**Table 1.12** US GDP as aggregate supply (2016, USD billions)

| | |
|---|---:|
| Private industries | 16,225 |
| Agriculture, fishing, forestry, hunting | 178 |
| Mining | 261 |
| Utilities | 287 |
| Construction | 793 |
| Manufacturing | 2,183 |
| Wholesale trade | 1,103 |
| Retail trade | 1,097 |
| Transportation and warehousing | 563 |
| Information | 904 |
| Finance, insurance, leasing, real estate, renting | 3,884 |
| Professional and business services | 2,252 |
| Educational services, healthcare, social assistance | 1,556 |
| Arts, entertainment, recreation | 752 |
| Other services | 416 |
| Government | 2,400 |
| GDP | 18,625 |

*Source*: BEA, GDP by industry.

Of US GDP, 87.1 percent is produced by private industries; the rest is the government's production of public services. It is common to distinguish between three large sectors of private industries. The primary sector consists of agriculture, fishing, forestry, hunting, and mining. The secondary sector consists of construction and manufacturing. The tertiary sector includes all the rest, which is utilities and all the types of services listed in Table 1.12. From this point of view, the primary sector contributes a mere 2.3 percent to GDP. The secondary sector contributes 16 percent and the tertiary sector 81.7 percent. Viewed from the supply side, the US is very much a service economy. Compare that to Germany, where the tertiary sector makes up 69 percent of GDP and the secondary 30.5 percent. Generally, in the process of economic development, the secondary sector has become less and the service sector more important.

## 1.1.5   GDP as Aggregate Income

From the AI perspective, we can see how GDP is divided up into various types of incomes. From Table 1.13, we see that there is a slight statistical discrepancy between GDP and GDI, the sum of all incomes earned in the process of domestic production.

Of GDI, 54 percent consists of the compensation of employees. Taxes on production and imports less subsidies account for 6.5 percent, roughly 25 percent is operating surplus, 15.5 percent is the consumption of fixed capital. Subtracting the latter from GDI we obtain net domestic income, which represents the amount of goods and services that the economy can consume in a year without running down its capital stock.

Comparing the tables in sections 1.3.3, 1.3.4, and 1.3.5, we see that the fundamental accounting equations hold: AD = AS = AI. Wow! The US has good statisticians!

## 1.1.6   GDP and Gross National Income

GDP is the value of all final goods and services and fixed assets newly produced within the borders of a country during a given period of time. In a country with no

**Table 1.13** US GDP as aggregate income (2016, USD billions)

| | |
|---|---|
| Compensation of employees | 9,992 |
| Taxes on production and imports less subsidies | 1,226 |
| Net operating surplus | 4,637 |
| Interest payments by domestic industries | 755 |
| Business current transfers (net) | 164 |
| Proprietors' income after depreciation | 1,342 |
| Rental income after depreciation | 707 |
| Corporate profits after depreciation | 1,679 |
| Consumption of fixed capital | 2,917 |
| Gross domestic income | 18,772 |
| Statistical discrepancy | −147 |
| GDP | 18,625 |

*Source*: BEA table 1.10.

economic ties to any other countries – a "closed economy" – it is also the sum of all incomes earned by all its residents during that period.

In general, this is not true, because some of the residents of the country may receive wages or profits from firms and businesses residing in other countries, while some of the businesses of the country may pay wages and profits to residents of other countries. An example for the former would be a resident of Detroit, an MBA student, who does a paid internship at Mercedes in Stuttgart, Germany. An example of the latter would be a resident of Mexico who works for GM during the summer.

Gross *national* (not Domestic) *income* (GNI) is the sum of all incomes earned by domestic residents in a given period. The keyword here is *residents*. A citizen of a foreign nation residing in the US is counted as a US resident for statistical and national accounting purposes. While GDP represents the value of domestic output, GNI represents the amount of goods and services domestic residents can afford to purchase during a given period. To define GNI, we add incomes domestic residents earn abroad to GDP and we subtract the incomes domestic firms pay to foreign residents. Thus, we have

$$GNI = GDP + \text{incomes earned abroad by domestic residents} - \text{incomes paid to foreign residents.}$$

Note that older texts and statistical publications call GNI "gross national product" (GNP). This is a misnomer, since GNI is an income, not a product!

For the US, the difference between GDP and GNI is minimal, because relatively few US residents work abroad and relatively few foreign residents work in the US. We already know that US GDP was USD 18.625 trillion. According to the BEA table 1.17.5, for January 2018, US GNI was USD 18.969 trillion in the same year. This indicates that the total incomes earned abroad by domestic residents exceeded the total incomes paid to foreign residents by USD 344 billion – a large number for every one of us but small relative to US GDP.

## 1.1.7   From GNI to Personal Income

Subtracting the consumption of fixed capital from GNI we obtain national income, USD 16,052 billion in 2016. Whose income is this? It is distributed between three sectors: businesses, the government, and households. To get from there to the income US households have at their disposal, we need a few more adjustments (see Table 1.14).

Thus, out of a GNI of USD 18,969 billion in 2016, US households received USD 15,969 billion or about 84 percent. Subtracting personal income taxes from this yields personal disposable income, USD 13,969 billion. This is the income they can freely dispose of. Personal savings is what is left over after accounting for consumption expenditures, interest paid on personal loans and personal transfer payments (such as financial gifts US residents send to their families abroad). US households thus saved a little under 5 percent of their disposable incomes.

**Table 1.14** US national income at factor prices (2016, USD billions)

| | |
|---|---:|
| GNI | 18,969 |
| Less consumption of fixed capital | 2,917 |
| **National income (at market prices)** | 16,052 |
| Less corporate profits after depreciation | 2,074 |
| Less taxes on production and subsidies | 1,226 |
| Less business transfer payments (net) | 164 |
| Less contributions to government social insurance | 1,245 |
| Less net interest payments on assets | 571 |
| Less current surplus of government enterprises | −11 |
| Plus personal income receipts on assets | 2,378 |
| Plus personal transfer receipts | 2,768 |
| **Equals personal income** | 15,929 |
| Less personal income tax | 1,960 |
| **Equals personal disposable income** | 13,969 |
| Personal consumption | 12,821 |
| Personal interest payments | 278 |
| Personal transfer payments | 189 |
| Personal saving | 681 |

*Source*: BEA tables 1.7.5. and 2.1.

## 1.2    Real GDP

As we have seen, GDP is a concept very much like revenue. Revenue is the product of two things – prices and quantities. So, when the revenue of a company increases from USD 100 to USD 120, without further study you would not know how much of that USD 20 increase was the result of selling more units of goods (quantity) and how much was the result of higher prices. Revenue is useful to you, but it doesn't tell you everything you might want to know. Similarly, when GDP goes up, the increase may be due to larger quantities of final goods and services produced or to higher prices with the same quantities, or a mixture of both.

### 1.2.1    Separating Quantity from Price Changes

We use *real GDP* in order to tell price from quantity changes for the economy as a whole. To do that would be very simple if all prices increased by the same rate and if all quantities increased by the same rate. In practice, however, there is a myriad of prices and they can all change by different rates of increase and the same is true for a myriad of quantities. Real GDP is a measure of the average change in the quantity component in GDP. Note that real GDP is a *relative* concept. We use it only to disentangle aggregate quantity from aggregate price changes in the economy. While the level of real GDP is not informative, since it is an index number, growth rates of real GDP or cross-country comparisons carry important information. In order to compute real GDP, we use the quantities of final goods and services from one period and the prices of these same quantities of final goods and services from a different period.

Here is an example. The BEA tells us that US GDP in 2009 was USD 14,419 billion and US GDP in 2016 was USD 18,625 billion. The market value of all final goods and services and fixed assets newly and domestically produced increased by USD 4,206 billion, or 29.2 percent between 2009 and 2016. How much of that is price and how much is quantity increase? To find out, we take the 2009 prices of all final goods and services included in 2009 GDP and we multiply them by the 2016 quantities of the same final goods and services. The result is called "2016 GDP in prices of 2009" or "2016 real GDP with base period 2009" and it amounts to USD 16,716 billion. This is now a measure of the quantity component of GDP. It gives us the value of US GDP with 2016 quantities and 2009 prices of final goods and services produced. Measured in prices of 2009, US real GDP increased by USD 2,297 billion between 2009 and 2016. We will also say that "the US economy grew by 15.9 percent" over this period. The quantity of final goods and services produced in the US increased by 15.9 percent.

Sounds complicated? Table 1.15 presents a simple example. Consider an economy producing only apples and oranges. We compare its GDP in year 1 and year 2.

Apple production grew by 10 percent, while orange production increased by 6.67 percent. GDP increased by 12.3 percent, but that increase is a mixture of price and quantities rising. Year 2 real GDP in prices of year 1 is 430. The economy as a whole grew by 7.5 percent.

Real GDP statistics are often presented as index numbers. For example, the real GDP index for 2016 is calculated as

$$\text{2016 Real GDP Index} = 100 * (\text{2016 real GDP})/(\text{2009 GDP}) = 115.93$$

The index is a quick way of showing how much larger real GDP was in 2016 compared to 2009 – 15.93 percent.

**Table 1.15** Real GDP example

| Year 1 | | Year 2 | |
|---|---|---|---|
| Apples produced | 100 | Apples produced | 110 |
| Price of apples | 1.0 | Price of apples | 1.03 |
| Oranges produced | 150 | Oranges produced | 160 |
| Price of oranges | 2.0 | Price of oranges | 2.1 |
| GDP | $1 * 100 + 2 * 150 = 400$ | GDP | $1.03 * 110 + 160 * 2.1 = 449.3$ |
| | | Real GDP | $1 * 110 + 2 * 160 = 430$ |

Until 2017, the BEA calculated real GDP as GDP in prices of 2009; 2009 was called the base year. In 2018, they changed the base year to 2012. Why 2009 and then 2012? In principle, the choice of the base year is not important. It is just a decision of the BEA. When you look for longer time series of real GDP, you will see that the statisticians change the base year from time to time. This is because the composition of GDP changes and there are things included in today's GDP that did not even exist years ago. Changes in the base year assure that our measures of real GDP are not biased by such changes. Longer time series are then *chained together*, meaning that they combine series using different base years.

### 1.2.2  Working with Data

The change in real GDP between any two years tells us how aggregate economic activity has changed in the country. A country's economic growth is measured by the growth rate of real GDP. As we will see later in more detail, the difference between the growth rate of GDP and the growth rate of real GDP is a measure of the average rate of price change in the economy; 13.1 percent for US GDP between 2009 and 2016, 4.8 percent in the example.

Figure 1.3 is a chart which shows recent changes in US GDP and real GDP. The black bars in this figure are annual growth rates of GDP for each year. The blue bars

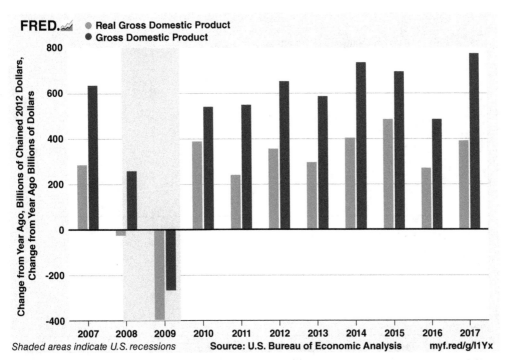

**Figure 1.3** Growth rates of GDP and real GDP

*Source*: US Bureau of Economic Analysis, real GDP [A191RO1Q156NBEA], and GDP [A191RP1A027NBEA], retrieved from FRED, Federal Reserve Bank of St. Louis; https://fred.stlouisfed.org/series/A191RO1Q156NBEA, August 29, 2018.

are annual growth rates of real GDP. For example, GDP grew by a little over 4 percent in 2007. Real GDP grew by less than 2 percent. Generally, because of inflation, the black bars are larger than the blue bars.

### BOX 1.1  Point of Interest: FRED

This and many of the following graphs are taken from FRED, the Federal Reserve Bank of St. Louis Economic Database. In many of these graphs, shaded areas mark periods of recession. Make yourself familiar with FRED at www.stlouisfed.org. FRED will become an indispensable source of macroeconomic data for you.

Figure 1.4 plots annual real GDP growth rates over the eighty-six years from 1930 to 2016. Real GDP growth was generally positive but with uneven cycles. That period began with the *Great Depression* during which the US economy shrank dramatically and millions of Americans were unemployed. Another sharp recession occurred immediately after World War II. In the 1950s and 1960s, the US economy

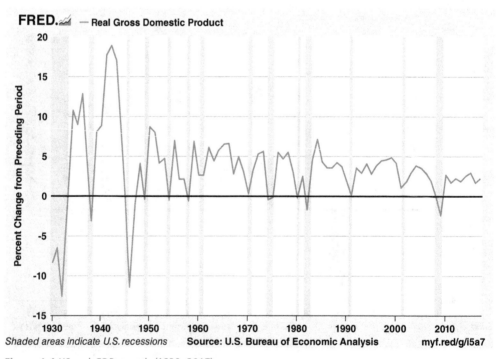

**Figure 1.4** US real GDP growth (1930–2017)

*Source*: US Bureau of Economic Analysis, real GDP [A191RL1A225NBEA], retrieved from FRED, Federal Reserve Bank of St. Louis; https://fred.stlouisfed.org/series/A191RL1A225NBEA, August 29, 2018.

would grow by 5 percent or more in a good year. This has become quite rare for the US since then. Since 1990, growth rates between 2.5 and 3.0 percent have become typical.

Periods of a pronounced decline in real GDP (negative growth rates) are called *recessions*. Technically speaking, a recession is a period beginning with two consecutive quarters of negative growth. A recession ends when the National Bureau of Economic Research (NBER) declares it to be over. The NBER is an economic think tank in Cambridge, MA. In this graph and many subsequent ones, recessions are marked by gray bars. This allows us to divide time into different *business cycles*, where each cycle begins with a recession and ends when the next recession begins. The notion of a business cycle comes from the observation that real GDP growth rates tend to increase when the economy comes out of a recession, then peak and then come down again. Note that, even taking into account the *Great Recession* of 2008–9, business cycles have become generally milder since the 1990s.

## 1.2.3   Potential Real GDP and the GDP Gap

Potential real GDP is the amount of final goods and services that a country can produce, if all its resources (labor, capital, and land) are fully utilized, i.e., the economy is operating at full capacity. This may or may not be true in any given quarter. For example, part of the labor force may not be employed or a part of the economy's capital stock may be idle. It is sometimes useful to know how large potential real GDP is. Unfortunately, however, potential real GDP cannot be observed directly. It must be estimated by statistical methods. Government statistical services provide such estimates.

In order to see whether or not the country is operating at full capacity, we compare real GDP with potential real GDP and calculate that the

$$\text{Real GDP Gap} = \text{Real GDP} - \text{Potential Real GDP}$$

or

$$\%\text{Real GDP Gap} = 100 * (\text{Real GDP} - \text{Potential Real GDP})/(\text{Potential Real GDP})$$

The %real GDP gap is also known as the output gap. A negative output gap tells you that the amount of real GDP being produced is less than what the economy could produce if all its resources were fully used – the economy is operating at less than full capacity. A negative output gap is often used as a reason to advocate a stronger AD policy, i.e., a government policy causing aggregate demand to increase. The rationale of such an argument is that if policy can move the economy to a higher level of aggregate demand, firms would want to produce more and they would hire more inputs to do so.

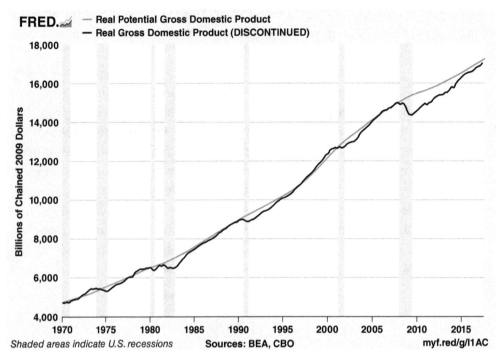

Figure 1.5 Real GDP and potential real GDP

*Source*: US Bureau of Economic Analysis, real GDP [GDPC96] and US Congressional Budget Office, Real Potential GDP [GDPPOT], retrieved from FRED, Federal Reserve Bank of St. Louis; https://fred.stlouisfed.org/series/GDPPOT, August 30, 2018.

A positive output gap means the country is producing more than potential real GDP. In this case resources are being stretched or overutilized. Too many people work overtime, and the capital stock is being used too intensively, implying that there is more wear and tear than usual. This may call for a reduction in aggregate demand through appropriate policy.

Figure 1.5 shows real GDP and potential real GDP from 1970 to 2016. You can see that recessions tend to coincide with periods where the output gap is growing more negative. Notice also that after the recession of 2008–9, US real GDP took a very long time to return to potential output. One interpretation of this observation is that potential output actually fell together with actual output in the recession and that the estimate of potential output shown in the figure did not take that into account.

## 1.3   Working with Data: GDP Statistics

National accounts are put together and published by national governments. International organizations like the *United Nations* (UN) and the *Organisation for*

*Economic Co-operation and Development* (OECD) coordinate and harmonize the accounting frameworks of national governments in an attempt to make them internationally comparable. The UN have developed accounting rules and standards for all their member states known as the *System of National Accounts* (SNA).[5] EU countries use the *European System of Accounts* (ESA), currently in its 2010 version.[6] In the US, national accounting rules are defined by the BEA.[7] Nevertheless, comparing national accounts of different countries can be tricky and must always be regarded with caution.

For most developed countries, national accounts are published on a quarterly and annual basis. In the US, the BEA (www.bea.gov) is responsible for this task; in Japan, it is the *Economic and Social Research Institute* (ESRI), of the government's Cabinet Office (www.esri.cao.go.jp); in the EU, it is *Eurostat* (ec.europa.eu/eurostat). National accounting data are gathered from a large variety of sources such as sales and employment figures reported by businesses to various government agencies, tax and customs records, business, and household surveys. Many of these data are not originally produced for the purposes of national accounting and have to be translated into a suitable format before they can be used for that purpose. This is why national accounts are *estimates* rather than precise figures. They contain statistical errors which can be kept small but not avoided. Because parts of the necessary data come in with considerable time lags, national accounts are revised over time. As a result, data for the same variable, period, and country, say, US GDP in the first quarter of 2017, taken from the same publishing agency, can differ if they were published at different points in time. In developed countries, the revision process takes up to two years before the estimates are considered final; in developing countries and emerging markets, it can take even longer.

The OECD is a Paris, France, based club of the main developed countries around the world. It produces reports on important economic developments for each member country (called Country Reports) and a forecast of the member economies for the next couple of years. This forecast is published biannually as the OECD Economic Outlook. Each Outlook has a section for each member country, including the US, and a discussion of the main risks associated with that forecast – i.e., what could go wrong and why.[8]

The *International Monetary Fund* (IMF) also produces a biannual *World Economic Outlook* in which it discusses global economic developments and provides forecasts for some key macroeconomic variables for its member countries.[9] The IMF also publishes important reports on economic outlooks, global financial stability and more. These sources have the great advantage for comparing international developments that they use the same statistical methodology for all countries. Note that, therefore, OECD and IMF statistics are not necessarily the same and can differ from statistics provided by national institutions. Because of the different membership compositions of these two world organizations, the coverages of the two publications differ. For example, the IMF will have regular reports on many Asian countries that are not generally found in OECD publications.

## 1.4   Real GDP per Capita around the World

If one divides a nation's real GDP by its population, this yields *real GDP per person* or *per capita*. A rising per-capita real GDP is a good thing: It means rising average incomes, rising employment, and rising amounts of goods and services available to the average person for consumption and investment. Governments, therefore, generally aim at achieving rising levels of real GDP per capita.

Table 1.16 provides you with estimates of real GDP per capita of several countries and country groups in 1990 and 2016 along with the relative increase

**Table 1.16** International comparison of real GDP per capita

| Country | 1990 | 2016 | Increase (%) | Country/group | 1990 | 2016 | Increase (%) |
|---|---|---|---|---|---|---|---|
| Luxembourg | 57,618 | 94,765 | 64 | Ethiopia | 652 | 1,608 | 147 |
| Singapore | 34,340 | 81,443 | 137 | Gambia | 1,506 | 1,555 | 3 |
| United Arab Emirates | 111,067 | 67,133 | −40 | Madagascar | 1,653 | 1,397 | −16 |
| Norway | 42,814 | 64,179 | 50 | Togo | 1,350 | 1,382 | 2 |
| Ireland | 21,453 | 62,992 | 194 | Sierra Leone | 1,251 | 1,369 | 9 |
| Switzerland | 48,182 | 57,430 | 19 | Mozambique | 379 | 1,128 | 198 |
| US | 37,062 | 53,342 | 44 | Malawi | 744 | 1,084 | 46 |
| Saudi Arabia | 42,457 | 50,458 | 19 | Niger | 894 | 914 | 2 |
| Netherlands | 32,090 | 47,303 | 47 | Liberia | 875 | 754 | −14 |
| Sweden | 30,934 | 46,662 | 51 | Congo | 1,280 | 744 | −42 |
| Denmark | 33,786 | 45,966 | 36 | Burundi | 1,087 | 721 | −34 |
| Australia | 28,583 | 44,414 | 55 | Central African Republic | 932 | 648 | −31 |
| Germany | 31,287 | 44,260 | 41 | OECD | 26,941 | 38,807 | 44 |
| Canada | 31,300 | 43,088 | 38 | Euro area | 28,120 | 38,335 | 36 |
| UK | 26,828 | 39,230 | 46 | Upper middle income | 6,067 | 15,794 | 160 |
| Japan | 30,447 | 38,252 | 26 | Middle income | 4,470 | 10,678 | 139 |
| France | 29,528 | 38,059 | 29 | Lower middle income | 2,787 | 6,316 | 127 |
| Malta | 16,156 | 35,743 | 121 | Low income | 1,149 | 1,574 | 37 |
| New Zealand | 24,161 | 35,271 | 46 | Least developed | 1,314 | 2,427 | 85 |
| Korea | 11,633 | 34,986 | 201 | HIPC | 1,472 | 2,102 | 43 |

*Note*: HIPC: highly indebted poor countries.
*Source*: World Bank, https://data.worldbank.org/indicator/NY.GDP.PCAP.PP.KD

between these two years. These data are produced by the World Bank. Real GDP is calculated on the basis of *purchasing power parities* or *international dollars*. That is, instead of using market exchange rates to convert GDP denominated in national currencies into USD, they use exchange rate estimates taking into account that a dollar has different purchasing power in different countries and that these differences are not adequately reflected in market exchange rates. To compute real GDP, the data in Table 1.16 are based on *constant international dollars* in prices of 2011. The countries are ranked in order of their 2016 per-capita real GDP.

Of the countries chosen, Luxembourg, Singapore, the United Arab Emirates, Norway, Ireland, and Switzerland stand at the top. All top-six countries are quite small. The US has the largest real GDP per capita among the medium-sized and large countries in the world. The countries with the lowest real GDP per capita are all African countries. The table shows that the OECD is a club of relatively rich countries.

The table shows that, in 2016, an average person in Luxembourg had almost 78 percent more final goods and services available to himself or herself than an average person in the US. In contrast, an average person in the Central African Republic had merely 1.4 percent of the amount of final goods and services a typical American had available to himself. Such differences indicate significant differences in standards of living or national welfare.

Real GDP is, therefore, more than a gauge of business activity – it has become a relative measure of country economic success – some go so far as to say a measure of wellbeing or happiness. If, for example, the real GDP per capita of a country exceeds that of another country, the residents and the government of the former country would take that as a positive. Governments often refer to the growth rate of both absolute and per-capita real GDP since they came into office as an indication of the success of their policies and to support their bids for reelection.

But this might be taking things too far. While real GDP does contain a lot of useful information, it is not a perfect measure of national wellbeing or happiness. Real GDP is noticeably silent on several important scores. If production "chews up" the environment, most of that loss is not subtracted or netted out properly, because environmental goods like clean air and fresh water are not traded on markets and their use does not come with an explicit market price. Furthermore, real GDP does not include the value of most of home production and it misses most of the informal (illegal, gray, or simply unmeasured) economy. Real GDP most clearly does not measure one's happiness derived from a sunny day in the spring or the presentation of the first grandchild to a happy grandmother. Two countries might have the same real GDP per capita, but in one country incomes are evenly distributed while in the other they are not. One country might have a high literacy or low crime rate while the other does not.

## BOX 1.2 DIFFERENCE OF OPINION: REAL GDP AND NATIONAL WELLBEING

Following the onset of the Great Recession, French President Nicolas Sarkozy created the Commission on Measurement of Economic Performance and Social Progress headed by former World Bank chief economist and Nobel laureate Joseph Stiglitz. The Commission, which became known as the *Stiglitz Commission*, was asked to discuss the quality of real GDP as an indicator of economic wellbeing. The US government under Barack Obama and the German government under Angela Merkel liked the idea and joined the project.[10]

Similar discussions had been ongoing for a while already in various think tanks. For example, the California-based organization Redefining Progress presents a provocative discussion of these issues and has proposed the *Genuine Progress Indicator* as an alternative to real GDP.[11] The indicator is meant to take into consideration how the goods and services produced affect the "wellbeing of the population." The *Happy Planet Index* is another measure of economic wellbeing taking into account a broader range of statistics than real GDP.[12] It aims at including indicators of the quality of the environment in measures of wellbeing. In 1972, the King of Bhutan, a small Asian nation, declared that his government should aim at increasing *Gross National Happiness* (GNH) rather than real GDP. In addition to real GDP, GNH includes measures of health, psychological wellbeing, spiritual and cultural development, and environmental quality.[13] In a similar vein, the 2008 Constitution of Ecuador declares the *sumak kawsay* or *good living* to be the supreme goal of the country's society. *Good living* emphasizes the harmony among people of diverse cultures and religions and a life in harmony with nature.

The Stiglitz Commission made five recommendations:

- Governments should use measures of income and consumption rather than production as indicators of material wellbeing.
- Governments should regard the economy from the perspective of households rather than businesses.
- Indicators of wellbeing should include measures of wealth in addition to income, since wealth represents future wellbeing.
- Indicators of wellbeing should take into account the distribution of income and wealth.
- Measures of income should take into account non-market activities to a greater extent and, in particular, include the value of leisure.

The Commission criticized the use of a measure of production as an indicator of wellbeing on the grounds that some production only serves to repair the damage caused by natural disasters or diseases without raising the wellbeing of the population. For example, the reconstruction of New Orleans after Hurricane Katrina added positively to real GDP and made the US look like being better off in the year after the flood than the year before even though people's wellbeing was generally down. This, however, is false logic, because it takes the wrong point of reference for comparison. Given that Hurricane Katrina had hit New Orleans, the subsequent clean-up activities certainly made its citizens better off. Since real GDP is embedded in the concept of the economic circuit, it seems odd to criticize it for a business rather than a household perspective. In a circuit, what goes around comes around.

Including measures of wealth and the distribution of income and wealth as proposed by the Stiglitz Commission raises additional problems. Obviously, the relevant measures of wealth should refer to net rather than gross wealth, since otherwise a country with a lot of government and other debt would seem to be better off than a country with low debt, since one person's debt is another person's asset. Even if the necessary data were available, it is not clear how assets should be valued. Taking the distribution of income into consideration seems more straightforward, but it raises the question of what is a good income distribution – one where all incomes are the same? One where the difference between the highest and the lowest income does not exceed a certain limit? Democratic countries organize elections to have the people decide on such contentious issues.

That the wellbeing of a population does not depend on its provision with material and immaterial goods and services alone is obvious. But the introduction of other criteria and considerations raises new problems. Suppose that we all agree that, apart from the availability of final goods and services, health is an important part of national wellbeing. We can use indicators like life expectancy or child mortality to measure the health status of the population. But this raises an immediate question: How should we weigh real GDP compared to health to come up with a comprehensive measure of wellbeing. Different people have different values and preferences. One of the nice characteristics of real GDP is that we aggregate final goods and services with market prices, which are thought to reflect society's valuation of these goods and services adequately. But there is no market price for life expectancy. How then can we aggregate? Any weights used to combine indicators of health with real GDP would be arbitrary and, therefore, controversial. But without aggregating the different indicators, we cannot compare two years or two countries and say that welfare was better in one than in the other, unless real GDP and life expectancy have both moved in the same direction. Obviously, this problem becomes worse, the more dimensions and indicators we add to measure national wellbeing.

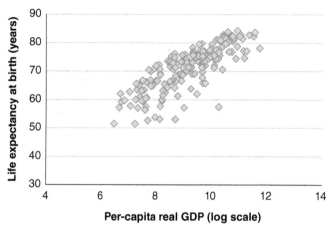

**Figure 1.6** Per-capita real GDP and life expectancy
*Note*: GDP per capita in USD (horizontal axis) and life expectancy in years (vertical axis), 2015.
*Source*: World Bank.

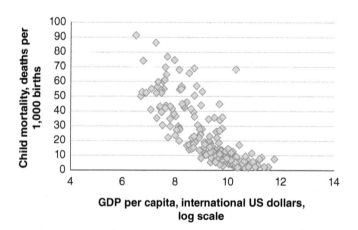

**Figure 1.7** Per-capita real GDP and child mortality
*Note*: GDP per capita in USD (horizontal axis) and child mortality (deaths per 1,000 births) 2015.
*Source*: World Bank.

One way around this problem is to note that real GDP per capita is closely related to other dimensions of wellbeing that we value highly. Figure 1.6 plots per-capita real GDP against life expectancy in an international comparison for the year 2015. Each dot marks a country. Clearly, the two are positively correlated. Figure 1.7 plots real GDP per capita against child mortality. Clearly, real GDP per capita and child mortality are negatively correlated.

These correlations suggest that we can generally expect that countries with higher real GDP per capita are also countries with a better state of health in their populations. This does not mean that every increase in real GDP per capita leads to a health improvement of the population. But it does suggest that anyone who seeks a country with good health should seek a country with high real GDP. Similar comparisons over time show that the provision of the population with final goods and services and its health tend to move in the same direction and that pursuing economic growth is compatible with improving general health. In the end, keeping in mind its imperfections, using per-capita real GDP as a measure of wellbeing is perhaps the best we can do.

## 1.5   International Application: Millennium Goals and Better Life

In September 2000, the United Nations Millennium Summit adopted the Millennium Declaration. The Declaration defined eight Millennium Goals of world development to be achieved by 2015. These goals are

- to eradicate extreme poverty and hunger;
- to achieve universal primary education;
- to promote gender equality and empower women;
- to reduce child mortality;
- to improve maternal health;
- to combat HIV, malaria, and other diseases;
- to ensure environmental sustainability;
- to promote a global partnership for development.

Progress toward reaching these goals is measured in terms of twenty-one sub-targets and a total of sixty statistical indicators. The UN did not agree on a weighting scheme of these indicators.

So, have we made progress in achieving the Millennium Goals? You can judge for yourself by looking at the UN's progress reports.[14] The quick answer is: We don't know. Considering all indicators together, the world is now worse off than in 2000, because there are a few indicators which look worse today. But it doesn't seem reasonable to judge the world based on those few exceptions. If you don't want to do that, define your own weights based on what you think are the most important goals and indicators. But don't expect anybody else to agree.

The Paris-based OECD has proposed a similar approach, measuring the quality of life in eleven dimensions: housing, income, job, community, education, environment, civic engagement, health, life satisfaction, safety, life–work balance. On its website, the OECD allows you to define your own weights for each dimension and then calculate your own *Better Life Index*.[15] It's actually fun to go there to see how happy you can be at home and in other places around the world. Try it out with your friends to see whether you would all want to live in the same country!

## 1.6    Measuring the Price Level and Inflation

A nation's *price level* is an average of all prices of final goods and services produced during a given period. *Inflation* refers to a relatively permanent increase in the price level. It is measured as the percentage change in the price level. Although statistical offices and the media call every increase in the price level inflation, we use this specific definition, because we want to differentiate price changes that have lasting macroeconomic impacts from less important blips that come and go.

*Disinflation* refers to a time when the inflation rate is positive but declining. For example, when the inflation rate goes from 3 to 2 percent, we would call this disinflation. Notable disinflation periods include the 1980s before 1987, 1991–2, 1997–8, and 2001–2. A rise in the rate of inflation following a period of disinflation is often called *reflation*.

*Hyperinflation* is a very high rate of inflation. To be called hyperinflation it has to exceed 50 percent a month. History has some spectacular examples of hyperinflation. In Germany, inflation exceeded one million percent in 1923. At that time it took about a trillion marks to buy one dollar. It was said that a wheelbarrow of money would not buy a newspaper . . . unless the wheelbarrow came with the money! In 2018, the rate of inflation in Venezuela exceeded 1,000,000 percent per year. That means prices were increasing by 2.55 percent every day or 19 percent every week. You should note that this does not imply that everybody becomes very poor and there is mass starvation during hyperinflation. Generally, wages keep up with prices. It is money that loses its value and if you keep your savings in assets of fixed money value like bank notes or government bonds, you lose your savings. But as prices of real estate, equity, and foreign currency, for example, increase, too, your savings are protected if you hold them in those forms.

*Deflation* refers to an extended period of time when the index of prices is falling – the calculated inflation rate is negative. By some measure, US inflation was negative in 2009, but we would not call that deflation because the episode was very short-lived.

### 1.6.1    The GDP Implicit Price Deflator

The *GDP implicit price deflator* is the broadest measure of the price level and inflation for the US economy. It is a relative concept made to compare price levels in different periods. Technically, it is one hundred times the ratio of GDP and real GDP:

$$\text{GDP Implicit Price Deflator} = 100 * \text{GDP/Real GDP}$$

For example, we know from section 1.4.1 that GDP in 2016 was USD 18,625 billion. Above, we calculated US real GDP for the same year as USD 16,716 billion. The GDP implicit price deflator for 2016 with base period 2009 is $100 * 18,625/16,716 = 111.42$.

**Table 1.17** Implicit price deflators for GDP and its components

|                                              | 2015  | 2016  | Rate of change |
|----------------------------------------------|-------|-------|----------------|
| GDP                                          | 110.0 | 111.4 | 1.27           |
| PCEs                                         | 109.5 | 110.8 | 1.19           |
| Gross private domestic investment            | 106.5 | 107.0 | 0.47           |
| Net exports                                  |       |       |                |
|    Exports                    | 106.5 | 104.5 | −1.88          |
|    Imports                    | 104.4 | 101.1 | −3.16          |
| Government consumption and gross investment  | 111.8 | 112.7 | 0.81           |

*Source*: BEA table 1.1.4.

This says that the US price level as measured by the GDP implicit price deflator was 11.42 percent higher in 2016 than in 2009. US inflation between 2009 and 2016 was 11.42 percent or 1.63 percent per year. Table 1.17 shows that the GDP implicit price deflator for 2015 was 110.0. US inflation in 2016 based on this measure was 1.27 percent.

Implicit deflators can be defined and calculated for all components of GDP as shown in Table 1.17. For example, if you work in the consumer goods industry, you may want to know how the average price of consumer goods and services developed in the US economy, but you do not care about the average price of investment goods. In that case, you might look at the personal consumption expenditure (PCE) implicit price deflator (PCE deflator for short). If you work in the capital goods industry, you may feel the reverse and be interested in the GDPI implicit price deflator. Note that the prices of PCEs, GDPI, and government consumption and gross investment include prices of imported goods and services. GDP as a whole does not. From Table 1.17, you can see that investment goods prices increased only by 0.5 percent between 2015 and 2016, while the prices of final consumer goods and services increased by 1.19 percent.

## BOX 1.3 **Formal Analysis: Price Level Changes**

We can express the relationship between the price level in 2016 and the price level in the base year, 2009, as

$$\%\Delta \text{ GDP Implicit Price Deflator} = \%\Delta \text{GDP} - \%\Delta \text{real GDP}$$
$$- \%\Delta \text{GDP} * \%\Delta \text{real GDP}$$

Here, $\%\Delta$ means percentage change in the following variable. If each growth rate is small, the product of the two rates even smaller and the difference between the

growth rate of GDP and the growth rate of real GDP is a good approximation of
the rate of inflation:

$$\%\Delta \text{ GDP Implicit Price Deflator} \approx \%\Delta GDP - \%\Delta \text{real GDP}$$

Let's see if you can apply this idea flexibly: Suppose we tell you that next year GDP
will increase by 3 percent and that prices will increase by 4 percent. What is your
conclusion about the percentage change in real GDP? Answer – real GDP will
decrease by 1 percent. Did you just forecast a recession? Answer – not
necessarily! A recession starts with two consecutive quarters of negative real GDP
growth. Suppose that real GDP fell by 1 percent in the first quarter of next year
and then remained constant. That would not be a recession!

## 1.6.2   Other Price Indexes

The consumer price index (CPI) is an index of prices of goods and services purchased
by consumers. It is the price index most relevant for households. It is used to measure
the development of the "cost of living" and to calculate adjustments to government
pensions, social security benefits, and other transfer payments to changes in the price
level, assuring that their purchasing power is not eroded over time. Since different
types of consumers have different consumption habits, there exists a whole host of
CPIs, for example a CPI for urban households and a CPI for households in rural areas.
CPI data are published by the Bureau of Labor Statistics (www.BLS.gov).

The PCE deflator and the CPI both measure inflation from the point of view of
consumers, but they are based on different statistical conventions. First, the underlying weights used for individual prices are different. Second, while the CPI includes
sales taxes and import duties, the PCE deflator does not. Third, the CPI uses a
different method of comparison. Recall that real GDP is the answer to the question:
What would 2016 GDP have been using 2009 prices? Similarly, real PCEs is
the answer to the question: What would 2016 PCEs have been in 2009 prices? The
2016 PCE deflator with base year 2009 is the answer to the question: What is the
weighted average consumer price in 2016 relative to the weighted average consumer
price in 2009, taking the 2016 quantities of final goods and services consumed as
weights? In contrast, the 2016 CPI with base year 2009 is the answer to the question:
What is the weighted average consumer price in 2016 relative to the weighted
average consumer price in 2009, taking the 2009 quantities of final goods and
services consumed as weights? These differences explain why inflation measured by
the PCE implicit price deflator and the CPI are often different; see Figure 1.9.

The producer price index is an index of prices of domestically produced, finished
industrial goods. Its weights reflect the structure of US manufacturing industries
rather than consumption habits. The producer price index is typically more volatile
than the CPI; see Figure 1.8.

Because the prices of some goods are notoriously volatile, we sometimes use more sophisticated measures of inflation in order to get a better picture of the trend movement underlying all prices. One such measure is *core inflation*. It takes the prices of oil and food out of the price index, because these prices often rise or fall for reasons which have little to do with macroeconomic developments. Core inflation is meant to give a better impression of the underlying trend in the rate of inflation. Figure 1.8 shows you measures of inflation (the black line) and core inflation (the light blue line) – based on the PCE deflator and PCE deflator with food and energy prices removed, respectively. Notice that most of the time inflation measured by the PCE deflator lies above core inflation. Exceptions are the mid-1980s, 2009, and 2015. Who cares? The Fed cares, because it formulates its inflation targets and assessments in terms of core inflation. Therefore, all *Fed watchers* care, too. Fed watchers are analysts working mostly in financial institutions trying to figure out what the Fed will do in the near future. If actual inflation was increasing, one would ordinarily expect the Fed to worry about that and change its policies. But, if core inflation did not move as much, as was the case in the late 1990s and after 2002, and the rise in inflation was mainly due to food and energy prices, the Fed might be less worried and be less prone to starting policies designed to reduce the inflation rate.

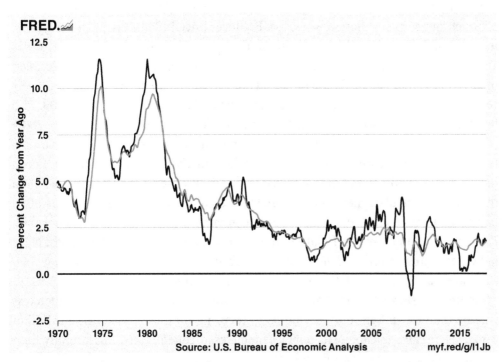

**Figure 1.8** Personal consumption price indexes

*Source*: US Bureau of Economic Analysis, PCE Price Index [PCEPI],PCE and Price Index Less Food and Energy [JCXFE], retrieved from FRED, Federal Reserve Bank of St. Louis; https://fred.stlouisfed.org/series/JCXFE, August 30, 2018.

Chris Giles's article in the September 13, 2006, *Financial Times* laments that "differences on the goods and services chosen, various formulas for calculating price changes, and divergent views on the types of households to be included render international comparisons a hazardous business."[16] One big difference in price indexes of different countries is how they treat housing prices. One approach is that a home is an asset and shouldn't be included in a price index. Another approach is that owner-occupied homes render services, just as rental units. Since rents paid for the latter are included in GDP and the GDP implicit deflator, the price of the services of the former should be included. Another issue concerns core inflation. While measures of core inflation are interesting and attempt to get more directly at macroeconomic inflation, they eliminate important price changes. You can't have it both ways. Giles recommends ignoring observed inflation and instead focusing on forecasts of future inflation. But many forecasts rely on the analysis or extrapolation of past observed inflation. So one cannot get away from measurement problems by using forecasts. Possibly better advice is to admit that inflation is not one single thing! It has many faces. We should evaluate and interpret all of the ones that are relevant.

### 1.6.3   Working with Data: Price Indexes

Figure 1.9 shows annual inflation rates based on the PCE deflator, the CPI, and the producer price index. Note the long, gradual decline of inflation after 1980, regardless of which measure of inflation is chosen. Producer price inflation is the most volatile measure of inflation. Its highest value during the period from 1970 to 2016 was 16.1 percent in August 2008, the lowest value (−12.7) percent in the Great Recession of 2009. Consumer price inflation peaked at 10.3 percent in 1980 and again at 11.3 percent in 2008. It was negative only for one short period in the summer of 2009. PCE inflation peaked at 4 percent also in 1980 and dipped under zero only slightly in 2009.

Median consumer price inflation and trimmed mean consumer price inflation are two other measures used by the Fed to get at the underlying trend of inflation. Recall that a median is the data point such that half of all observations are smaller than this point. To calculate median inflation, the Fed computes the rates of change of all individual prices contained in the CPI and then takes the median rate in each period. To compute trimmed-mean inflation, the Fed takes the lowest and the highest eight individual rates of price change out of all observations for each period and then calculates the average inflation rate from the remaining price changes.

Figure 1.10 shows that median and trimmed-mean inflation are indeed much less volatile than CPI inflation. A central bank focusing on these measures of inflation would see reasons to change its policies much less frequently and less strongly than a central bank focusing on CPI inflation.

### 1.6.4   International Application: Inflation

Figure 1.11 shows the CPI rates of inflation for four major advanced economies, Germany, Japan, the UK, and the US.

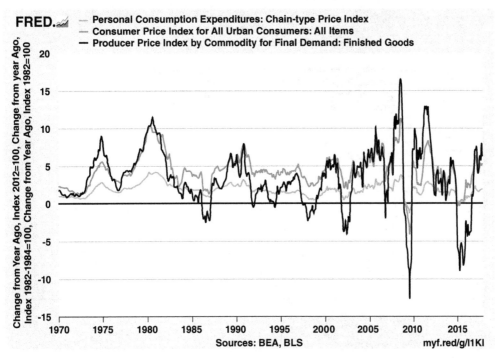

**Figure 1.9** Price indexes for consumption and producer prices

*Source*: US Bureau of Economic Analysis, PCE Price Index [PCEPI], US Bureau of Labor Statistics, CPI for All Urban Consumers: All Items [CPIAUCSL], and PPI for Final Demand: Finished Goods [WPUFD49207], retrieved from FRED, Federal Reserve Bank of St. Louis; https://fred.stlouisfed.org/series/PCEPI, August 30, 2018.

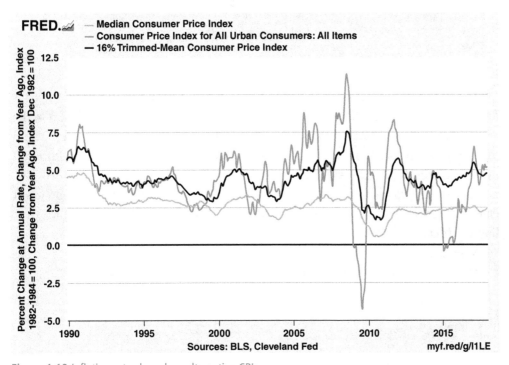

**Figure 1.10** Inflation rates based on alternative CPIs

*Source*: Federal Reserve Bank of Cleveland, Median CPI [MEDCPIM159SFRBCLE], US Bureau of Labor Statistics, CPI for All Urban Consumers: All Items [CPIAUCSL], Federal Reserve Bank of Cleveland, 16% Trimmed-Mean CPI [TRMMEANCPIM094SFRBCLE] retrieved from FRED, Federal Reserve Bank of St. Louis; https://fred.stlouisfed.org/series/MEDCPIM159SFRBCLE, August 30, 2018.

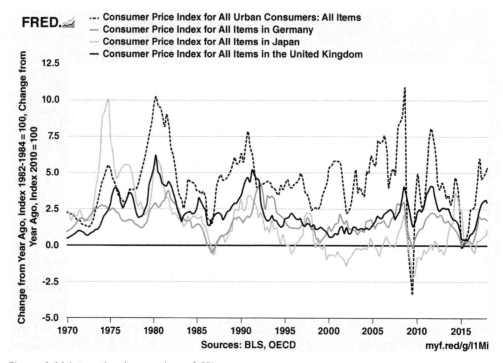

**Figure 1.11** International comparison of CPIs

*Source*: US Bureau of Labor Statistics, CPI for All Urban Consumers: All Items [CPIAUCSL], OECD, CPI of All Items in Germany [DEUCPIALLMINMEI], CPI of All Items in Japan [JPNCPIALLMINMEI], CPI of All Items in the United Kingdom [GBRCPIALLMINMEI], retrieved from FRED, Federal Reserve Bank of St. Louis; https://fred.stlouisfed.org/series/CPIAUCSL, August 30, 2018.

We can see that all four had their highest inflation rates in the 1970s, with peaks around the two oil price hikes of 1973 and 1978. Inflation came down quickly in the 1980s and remained much more moderate afterwards – generally between 1 and 5 percent. Japan stands out as the country experiencing persistent negative inflation rates – deflation, in fact – since the late 1990s.

Figure 1.12 provides us with a picture of CPI inflation rates in five important *emerging economies*, i.e., fast-growing developing countries, China, Brazil, Mexico, South Africa, and India.

These countries generally experienced higher inflation in the 1990s than the advanced economies and their inflation rates are more volatile, too.

## 1.7   Employment, Unemployment, and Productivity

People like to consume the final goods and services the economy produces, and they like free time to spend with their families and friends, watching football games or going on bicycle rides. Most of us, however, have to work in order to afford the

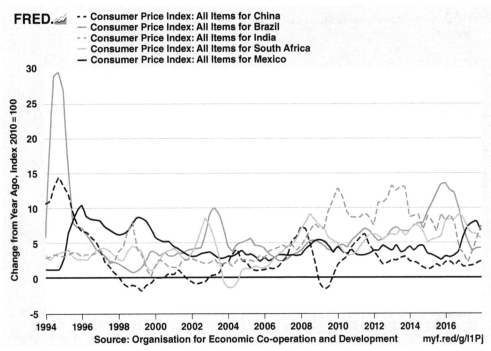

**Figure 1.12** CPIs in major emerging economies

*Source*: OECD, CPI All Items for China [CHNCPIALLMINMEI], CPI All Items for Brazil [BRACPIALLMINMEI], CPI All Items for India [INDCPIALLMINMEI], CPI All Items for South Africa [ZAFCPIALLMINMEI], CPI All Items for Mexico [MEXCPIALLMINMEI], retrieved from FRED, Federal Reserve Bank of St. Louis; https://fred.stlouisfed.org/series/CHNCPIALLMINMEI, August 30, 2018.

consumption we desire. One of the main tasks of the macroeconomy is to provide plenty of good jobs to keep the labor force employed. Policymakers watch employment closely and praise their policies when the number of jobs is increasing, and they try their best to keep unemployment low. In this section, you get to know the main concepts and indicators relating to the labor market.

## 1.7.1   Employment and Unemployment

A nation's *civilian non-institutional population* is the number of persons residing in its territory who are of age 16 and above who do not actively serve in the military and who are not inmates in institutions such as prisons, mental health clinics, or homes for old persons. Think of this as the number of persons who, based on their age, are available in principle for work of some form. Not all of these people choose to work or seek employment, however. Some are in the process of being trained or educated. Some prefer to care for their families. Some have chosen to retire and work no more.

Figure 1.13 shows the development of the US civilian non-institutional population from 1970 to 2016. Over this period, the civilian non-institutional population

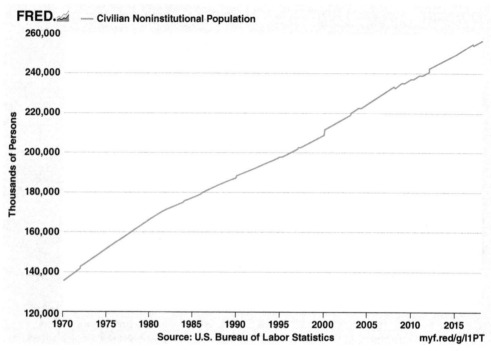

**Figure 1.13** US civilian noninstitutional population

*Source*: US Bureau of Labor Statistics, Civilian Noninstitutional Population [CNP16OV], retrieved from FRED, Federal Reserve Bank of St. Louis; https://fred.stlouisfed.org/series/CNP16OV, August 30, 2018.

increased steadily from 135 million to 255 million people. It amounts to 79 percent of the total 2016 resident population of the US, which the US Bureau of Census estimated to be 323 million persons.

The nation's *labor force* is the number of persons in the civilian non-institutional population that are either employed or unemployed. The labor force is estimated by surveys done by the US Department of Labor. A person is counted as employed in these surveys if, during the reference week, she did any work at all for pay or profit, worked for her own business, did at least fifteen hours of unpaid work in an enterprise of a family member, or held a job from which she was temporarily absent due to illness, vacation, bad weather, or similar circumstances. A person is counted as unemployed in these surveys if, during the reference week, she had no employment, was available for work, and was actively seeking employment or waiting to be recalled to a job from which she was temporarily laid off. Note that this is different from the definition of unemployment in many countries outside the US. There, to be unemployed means to be registered as unemployed with the national unemployment insurance or labor agency in order to receive unemployment benefits. This is regardless of whether or not the person seeks work or actually does work. Any person who is neither employed nor unemployed is regarded as not being in the labor force.

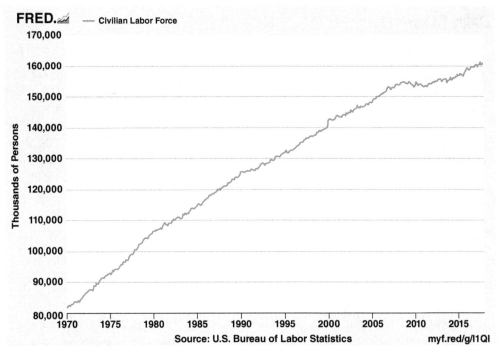

**Figure 1.14** US civilian labor force

*Source*: US Bureau of Labor Statistics, Civilian Labor Force [CLF16OV], retrieved from FRED, Federal Reserve Bank of St. Louis; https://fred.stlouisfed.org/series/CLF16OV, August 30, 2018.

The US government conducts two different surveys to estimate employment and unemployment. The household survey includes persons working in agriculture. The payroll survey does not include agricultural establishments and counts every individual job, so that a person holding two jobs is counted twice. There was much discussion about these different measures following the 2001 recession, when the household survey was showing much faster employment growth than the payroll survey. Because of its larger sample size, most economists attribute more reliability to the payroll survey. However, because the household survey covers a wider number of industries and since it covers the many start-ups, small enterprises, and self-employed persons, some experts believe it gives the most accurate reading of employment changes.

The *labor force participation rate* is the ratio of the labor force and the non-institutional civilian population. The employment population ratio is the number of employed persons relative to the civilian non-institutional population. The *unemployment rate* is the number of unemployed persons divided by the number of persons in the labor force.[17] Table 1.18 summarizes the BLS data for October 2017.

Almost 63 percent of the civilian non-institutional population participated in the labor force during these two months and about 60 percent of the civilian

**Table 1.18** Labor force statistics

| Employment status | October 2016 | October 2017 |
|---|---|---|
| Civilian non-institutional population (1,000 persons) | 254,3211 | 255,7666 |
| Civilian labor force (1,000 persons) | 159,6433 | 160,3711 |
| Participation rate (percent) | 62.88 | 62,77 |
| Employed (1,000 persons) | 151,9022 | 153,8641 |
| Employment–population rate (%) | 59.77 | 60.22 |
| Unemployed (1,000 persons) | 7,7400 | 6,5240 |
| Unemployment rate (%) | 4.88 | 4.11 |
| Not in the labor force (1,000 persons) | 94,6788 | 95,3955 |

*Source*: BLS, *The Employment Situation* December 2016 and December 2017.

non-institutional population were employed. The unemployment rate came down from 4.8 to 4.1 percent of the labor force.

Labor market analysts and policymakers often refer to different types of unemployment. *Frictional* unemployment is the number of unemployed persons who are thought to be in transition from one job to the next or who are moving and looking for work at their new place of residence. A transition of this kind naturally takes time and it is part of the normal functioning of an economy. However, frictional unemployment is considered to be quite short for each individual frictionally unemployed person. The existence of frictional unemployment implies that unemployment will be positive even if the economy is operating at full employment. Government can reduce frictional unemployment by offering information services on job openings that improve the transparency of the labor market.

*Structural* unemployment refers to people who have lost their jobs in industries or regions which are economically declining and need to move to a new industry or region in order to find a new job. Structural unemployment is considered to last longer for each individual finding himself in that condition, because moving from one industry or region to another can be more difficult and it can involve additional schooling or training to acquire new skills.

The *natural rate of unemployment* refers to the rate of unemployment that prevails when the economy operates at full capacity, or when the output gap is zero. In a boom, the actual rate of unemployment is below the natural rate; in a recession, it is above the natural rate. Note that *natural* does not mean that this is a level or rate of unemployment that cannot change over time. As mentioned above, government policies can try to reduce it.

*Full employment* is the level of employment in normal times, i.e., when the economy is neither in a boom nor in a recession. Thus, it is the level of employment associated with the natural rate of unemployment. In a boom, employment is above full employment, while in a recession, employment is below unemployment. Similar to natural unemployment, full employment can change over time. For example, it might differ in the 1990s from what it was in the 1980s. Below we discuss more why it might change.

## 1.7.2   Working with Data: the Labor Market

Figure 1.15 shows the aggregate labor force participation rate together with the male and female participation rates. The total participation rate peaked at about 67 percent in the late 1990s. It was up from about 64 percent in 1979. After 2000, the labor force participation rate shows a slight downward trend to about 63 percent in 2016.

Behind this general trend, however, two distinct developments are hidden. One is a general and steady decline in the male participation rate from 80 percent in 1970 to 69 percent in 2016. The other is a strong and steady increase in the female participation rate from 43 percent in 1970 to 57 percent in 2016. It reflects the general change in attitudes toward women working outside the home in the US population. But note also that the Great Recession affected male labor market participation (−3.2 percent) more strongly than female labor market participation (−2.7 percent).

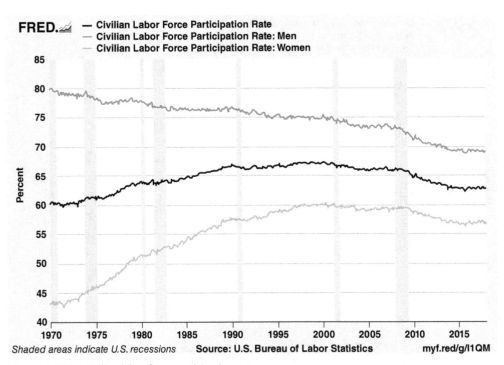

**Figure 1.15** US civilian labor force participation rates

*Source*: US Bureau of Labor Statistics, Civilian Labor Force Participation Rate [CIVPART], Civilian Labor Force Participation Rate: Men [LNS11300001], Civilian Labor Force Participation Rate: Women [LNS11300002], retrieved from FRED, Federal Reserve Bank of St. Louis; https://fred.stlouisfed.org/series/CIVPART, August 30, 2018.

Figure 1.15 looks at the civilian employment population ratio. It confirms the general tendencies from the participation rates, but it also shows that employment rates are strongly affected by recessions. The overall employment population ratio stood at 58 percent in 1970 and 60 percent in 2016. It increased to 65 percent at the turn of the century but has come down since then. The employment population ratio for men came down from almost 80 percent in 1970 to a little under 70 percent in 1980, to hover around that value until the onset of the Great Recession. In 2016, it stood at 65 percent.

In contrast, the female employment–population ratio was just above 40 percent in 1970. It increased steadily to peak at 57 percent in 1999. Since then, it has declined again to 55 percent. The difference between male and female employment rates is today much smaller than in 1970.

Figure 1.17 looks at unemployment rates. In 1970, the civilian unemployment rate was about 4 percent. In the wake of the oil price hikes of the mid and late 1970s it increased dramatically. In mid 1975, it peaked at 9 percent. It fell in the following years, but the recession of 1979 brought a new increase and the recession of the early 1980s made things even worse. In December 1982, it peaked at 10.8 percent. Apart from the recession in the early 1990s, there was then a general tendency for

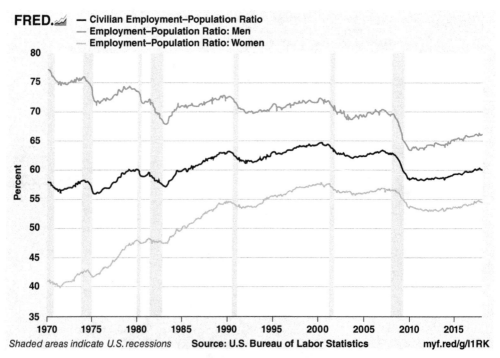

**Figure 1.16** US civilian employment–population ratios

*Source*: US Bureau of Labor Statistics, Civilian Employment–Population Ratio [EMRATIO], Employment–Population Ratio: Men [LNS12300001], Employment–Population Ratio: Women [LNS12300002], retrieved from FRED, Federal Reserve Bank of St. Louis; https://fred.stlouisfed.org/series/EMRATIO, August 30, 2018.

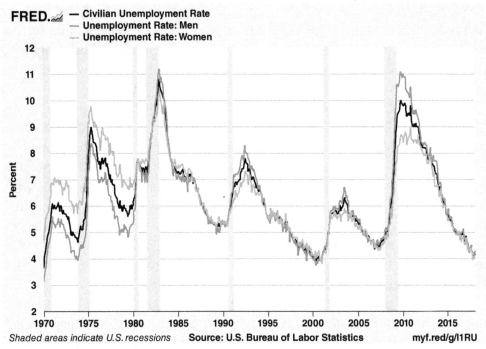

**Figure 1.17** US civilian unemployment rates

*Source*: US Bureau of Labor Statistics, Civilian Unemployment Rate [UNRATE], Unemployment Rate: Men
[LNS14000001], Unemployment Rate: Women [LNS14000002], retrieved from FRED, Federal Reserve Bank of
St. Louis; https://fred.stlouisfed.org/series/UNRATE, August 30, 2018.

the unemployment rate to fall and it bottomed out again at 4 percent at the turn of
the century.

It also shows what appears to be a downward trend – with the successive peaks
and valleys getting smaller and smaller. Cycles revolve around this trend but the
overall direction has been toward a lower unemployment rate in the US. What might
be considered a "normal" unemployment rate in the early 1980s would be higher
than a "normal" unemployment rate in 2000. However, the Great Recession brought
a huge increase in the unemployment rate again. It reached almost 10 percent in
December of 2009. At the end of 2016, the unemployment rate had come down to
just above 4 percent again. Obviously, unemployment rates are supersensitive to the
swings of the business cycle.

Figure 1.17 also confirms the impression that there has been a long-lasting
structural change in the US labor market. In a 1970s or earlier recession, female
unemployment increased more strongly than male unemployment. That is, women
were relatively more affected by economic downturns and subsequent upturns
than men. Those differences disappeared in the 1990s and in the Great Recession
we see that the opposite was true. Men had a greater likelihood of losing their jobs
than women.

### 1.7.3 International Application: European Unemployment Rates

The performance of national labor markets depends strongly on institutions such as unemployment insurance and welfare systems. This is visible from comparing national unemployment rates in different countries. Figure 1.18 shows unemployment rates in four major European economies.

Like the US, European economies started with low unemployment rates in the 1970s. As in the US, these rates increased due to the oil price hikes in the 1970s. But there is a major difference between these countries and the US. This is that unemployment rates kept creeping upward over the long haul. Consider Germany. The unemployment rate was almost zero in 1970. Due to the mid-1970s recession it went up to 3.5 percent. Then it came down somewhat during the subsequent recovery, but the next recession sent it up to over 7 percent. The recovery from 1985 to 1990 helped again, but then the unemployment rate reached almost 10 percent by 1997. The recession of the early 2000s made it peak at over 11 percent. Similar observations hold for France, Italy, and the UK in the 1970s to mid 1980s.

Labor market analysts speak about *ratchet effects* to describe these observations. Unemployment rates are pushed up by adverse macroeconomic developments, but they do not come down when the macroeconomy performs better afterwards. Why not? The general explanation is that generous unemployment insurance and welfare programs allow people to stay in unemployment and do not provide sufficiently strong incentives to actively seek and find work.

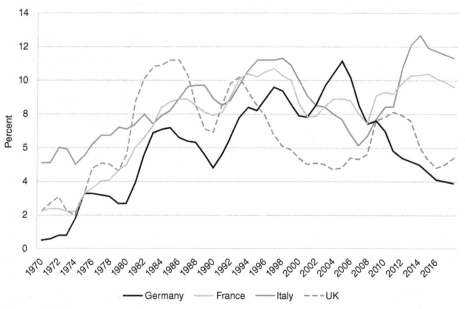

**Figure 1.18** European unemployment rates
*Source*: European Commission, AMECO Database.

This argument is corroborated by the UK experience following the mid 1980s and the German experience after 2000. Both countries instituted labor market reforms making welfare programs less generous and strengthening incentives to seek and find employment. *Workfare* was an element in both. This is the idea that people get government support conditional on working even for low pay rather than conditional on not being employed at all. The reforms seemed to have worked in both cases in the sense that the growing trend of unemployment rates was broken.

Youth unemployment rates are interesting to compare across countries, too, because they also tell us much about labor market institutions. Youth unemployment refers to the age group from 16 to 25. Figure 1.19 shows that there are marked differences in youth unemployment rates across countries.

Even in relatively normal times like 2005–6, youth unemployment rates were significantly higher in France and Italy than in Germany and the US. Following the onset of the Great Recession, however, the differences became much stronger. The graph suggests that young people bear a much larger burden of the economic cost of a recession in France and Italy than in the US and Germany. The suggestive reason is that employment protection is almost perfect for workers above 30 years of age in Italy and France, but much less so in the US and Germany. There may, of course, be good reasons for social policies to protect workers above the age of 30 more strongly

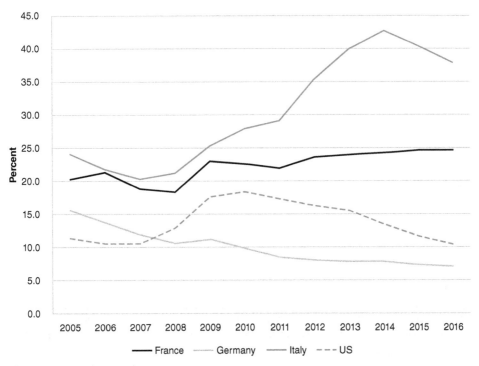

**Figure 1.19** Youth unemployment rates
*Source*: OECD, short-term labor market statistics.

than young people. The point here is that such policies are not without visible consequences.

### 1.7.4  Productivity

From the AS perspective, we can think about a nation's output as the product of the number of people employed, the average number of hours each person works, and the average amount of output generated per hour of employment. The latter is an indicator of the productivity of labor. It tells us how effective an hour of work is on average in the economy. As we shall see later, productivity is an important concept determining the wages employees receive but also the general wellbeing of a nation as a whole.

Figure 1.20 shows the average amount of real output per hour of work in the US business sector. You see that productivity grew by a factor of about 2.5 between 1970 and 2016. On average, an hour of work in the US in 2016 produces 2.5 times the value it produced in 1970. You can observe that productivity growth accelerated in the 1990s compared to the years before and slowed down after the turn of the century. How come? There are long-run factors like technological progress that we will discuss in Chapter 7. Some of these can be impacted by government policies we will discuss in Chapters 6 and 7.

**Figure 1.20** US labor productivity (business sector)

*Source*: US Bureau of Labor Statistics, Business Sector: Real Output Per Hour of All Persons [OPHPBS], retrieved from FRED, Federal Reserve Bank of St. Louis; https://fred.stlouisfed.org/series/OPHPBS, August 30, 2018.

## 1.8  SUMMARY

This chapter has introduced you to the main economic concepts and indicators you will encounter in reports and analyses of macroeconomic developments provided by the government, by institutions making economic policy such as the Fed, and discussed in the media and by policymakers. It has introduced much of the vocabulary used in such reports and discussions. You should have a firm understanding of the concepts of aggregate demand, aggregate supply, aggregate income, national accounting, and why aggregate demand, supply, and income must be the same at the macroeconomic level. The economic circuit is a fundamental concept to take away from this. You have seen how this concept forms the basis of national accounting.

You have also learned to distinguish between real and nominal magnitudes. Furthermore, you been introduced to several indicators relating to inflation and labor market performance.

In the following chapters, we go from measurement and accounting to analysis and prediction. Make sure that you have a firm understanding of the terms and concepts introduced in this chapter as a firm basis for what follows.

## 1.9  REVIEW QUESTIONS

1. What are the three ways in which we measure GDP?
2. Why do central banks look at core or median inflation?
3. How useful is real GDP as a measure of a country's wellbeing?
4. The government announced that the real GDP gap is (−4.0) percent. What does that tell you about the state of the economy?
5. What are the main accounting principles of national accounting?
6. Is there a difference between how male and female unemployment rates behave over the business cycle?
7. How have labor market reforms changed the behavior of unemployment in Germany since 2000?
8. What is the difference between a CPI and a producer price index?
9. You are interested in knowing whether a recession might be lurking around the corner. Which variables would you look at to see whether that is true?

## NOTES

1 Quoted from George R. Feiwel (ed.), *Issues in Contemporary Macroeconomics and Distribution* (New York: State University of New York Press, 1985), p. 421.

2 For more information about SHMOOs and how they almost destroyed humankind, see: www.deniskitchen.com/docs/new_shmoofacts.html. Thanks to former student Wayne Blankenbeckler for providing more information on this topic.

3 In the BEA's NIPA, households have production accounts, too. Household sector production consists mainly of the production of housing services and production for own use as well as the services produced by nonprofit organizations such as churches. To keep the exposition short, we subsume that production under the business sector's production.

4 See e.g. Stephanie H. McCulla, Vijay Khosa, and Kelly Ramey, *The 2017 Annual Update of the National Income and Production Accounts,* www.bea.gov/information-previous-updates-nipa-accounts

5 https://unstats.un.org/unsd/nationalaccount/sna.asp

6 http://ec.europa.eu/eurostat/web/products-manuals-and-guidelines/-/KS-02-13-269

7 www.bea.gov/methodologies

8 The June 2017 OECD Economic Outlook can be found at: www.oecd-ilibrary.org/economics/oecd-economic-outlook_16097408;jsessionid=1tx1q3vrnn7cj.x-oecd-live-03

9 You can find the Fall 2017 World Economic Outlook at: www.imf.org/en/Publications/WEO/Issues/2017/09/19/world-economic-outlook-october-2017

10 You can find the Commission's report at: ec.europa.eu/eurostat/documents/118025/118123/Fitoussi+Commission+report

11 http://rprogress.org/sustainability_indicators/genuine_progress_indicator.htm

12 happyplanetindex.org

13 You can find information on GNH at the Center for Bhutan Studies at: www.grossnationalhappiness.com

14 www.un.org/millenniumgoals

15 www.oecdbetterlifeindex.org

16 "Statisticians have a near-impossible task." September 13, 2006, p. 4 of the Special Report Global Economy.

17 These numbers are published in the monthly *Employment Situation* available at: www.bls.gov/news.release/empsit.a.htm

# 2 Aggregate Demand

Economics is all about supply and demand. If the demand for Jack Daniel's rises relative to supply, we predict that the price of Jack Daniel's will rise and its quantity sold in the market will increase. Supply and demand, therefore, are common tools in the economist's toolbox. This tool allows us to analyze why prices and quantities change and to think of both the reasons for these changes and what policies might be used to combat them if deemed necessary.

Supply and demand tools are used in macroeconomics, too. The basic approach is the same, but the actors are larger or, we say, more aggregated. Instead of a focus on single goods or services like JD, macroeconomics analyzes changes in the nation's output and the prices of all final goods and services. We use terms like aggregate demand and aggregate supply to communicate that the engine of the supply-and-demand model is being applied at the macroeconomic level. We started our examination of aggregate demand in Chapter 1 and the AD curve will be a star performer throughout this book.

The drama of aggregate demand is played out each quarter. Each quarter the government and the media announce the measured performance of real GDP and the GDP implicit price deflator. The emphasis in these reports is on how the components of aggregate demand changed in the most current quarter. That is, we read how consumption, investment, government spending, and net exports rose or fell to bring about changes in national output growth and inflation. In a given quarter, much of the output increase might have been the result of consumers buying more cars than usual. Another quarter the star AD performer might be business investment or housing.

If that is not enough motivation to read this chapter, the final *coup de grâce* is policy. As a planner and decision maker, you are interested in the future. The present influences the future and therefore you need to think about how national policymakers will react to the last reading of GDP and aggregate demand. If GDP had a weak quarter or two, Congress might decide to give consumers a tax break to motivate them to spend more. If inflation is beginning to rise too fast, perhaps policymakers will vote to raise interest rates so as to reduce your desire to buy a new home. To make this even more exciting, you have to deal with the fact that policy-makers can have very different opinions about using AD policy.

In Chapter 1 you learned about GDP, employment, prices, and unemployment. All that terminology and accounting might seem annoying, but they are useful because each term and concept you learned is used daily in the media and the business world. With that under our belts, we now turn from *ex post* measurement and identities to *ex ante* planning and equilibrium. Obviously, the future is always *ex ante* – so to predict we need a framework for analysis and forecasting. Some call it *modeling* or *theory* which sounds nerdy, but the main idea is that we move from definitions and accounting to a framework that helps us understand and predict macroeconomic developments and the consequences of macroeconomic policies. This is what makes macroeconomics interesting and useful for business leaders. Chapter 2 starts with a focus on aggregate demand. Recall that the word *aggregate* conveys the idea that we think in terms of the total demand for a nation's goods and services. The term *demand* implies that we are focusing on how much of a nation's goods and services consumers, companies, and the government want to buy and why they might buy more or less this year than they bought last year.

Chapter 2 takes a closer look at the developments over time of some of the components of GDP introduced in Chapter 1. First, we examine some data and then begin the discussion of the causes and consequences of changes in these economic indicators. We begin the development of a macroeconomic model with the AD curve, which represents all those factors that influence aggregate demand. This leads to a discussion about short-run economic policies aimed at increasing or decreasing aggregate demand and how and why we can hold very different opinions about the use of these policies. In Chapter 3 we will turn to aggregate supply.

## 2.1   Working with Data: AD Components

Figure 2.1 plots the annual growth rates of the main components of US real aggregate demand, namely real personal consumption expenditures (C), real gross private domestic investment (I), and real government consumption expenditures and investment (G) at quarterly frequencies. By looking at the chart in Figure 2.1, you can get a good feel for the dynamics of these components of aggregate demand. Notice that real personal consumption growth is relatively steady over time. It has its ups and downs, but these are quite small. In contrast, the growth of real gross private domestic investment shows some pretty wild swings. In fact, investment is generally much more volatile than consumption in all industrialized market economies. Investment decisions are more easily shifted across time –

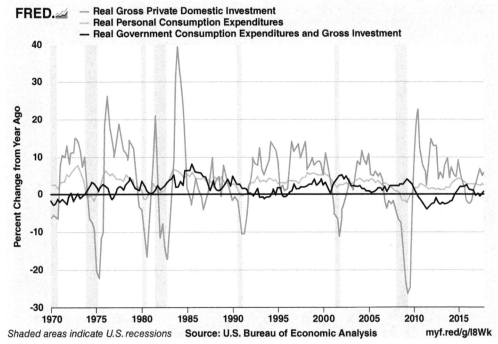

**Figure 2.1** Growth rates of components of aggregate demand (1970–2017)

*Source*: US Bureau of Economic Analysis, Real Gross Private Domestic Investment, Real Personal Consumption Expenditures, Real Government Consumption Expenditures and Gross Investment, retrieved from FRED, Federal Reserve Bank of St. Louis; https://fred.stlouisfed.org, September 10, 2018.

pulled forward or postponed according to what seems right in an ever-changing macroeconomic environment – than consumption. You can also see that recessions – the periods marked by shaded columns – are typically preceded by periods of falling investment growth. This suggests that business cycles have a lot to do with investment dynamics. The graph also shows that the volatility of real government spending is even smaller than the volatility of private consumption. By looking closely, you can see that government typically increased the growth rate of its real expenditures during recessions, the exception being the recession of 1991.

Figure 2.2 looks at the growth of real personal consumption expenditures in more detail. It plots the growth rates of real consumer spending on durables, nondurables, and consumer services individually. Consumption growth was generally positive except during recessions. The consumption of durables is much more volatile than the consumption of services and nondurables. This reflects the fact that purchasing durable goods involves decisions over time much like investment decisions – households purchase cars or appliances for use over relatively long periods of time and this involves the same kind of intertemporal decisions as

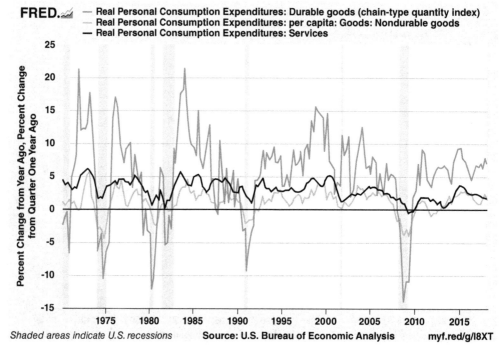

**Figure 2.2** Growth rates of consumption (1970–2017)

*Source*: US Bureau of Economic Analysis, Real Personal Consumption Expenditures: Durable goods (chain-type quantity index), Real Personal Consumption Expenditures per capita: Goods: Nondurable goods, Real Personal Consumption Expenditures: Services, retrieved from FRED, Federal Reserve Bank of St. Louis; https://fred.stlouisfed.org, September 10, 2018.

business investments. Such decisions are easily postponed or pulled forward and, therefore, more sensitive to changing macroeconomic circumstances than buying food or clothing.

Figure 2.3 shows the growth performance of the components of real gross domestic private investment. Residential investment exhibits the largest up- and downswings over time and large drops in residential investment can be observed to occur before all recessions except the one of 2001. Non-residential investment in structures shows more pronounced swings than non-residential investment in equipment and quarters of declining growth in investment in structures also tend to precede recessions. You can use the quarterly growth rates of residential investment and of non-residential investment in structures as *leading indicators* of recessions. Keep an eye on them to see whether a recession is around the corner.

Figure 2.4 shows the quarterly changes in inventories. Here we use levels rather than growth rates, because inventories are often small so that relative changes can be very large and growth rates become meaningless. Notice that inventories tend to

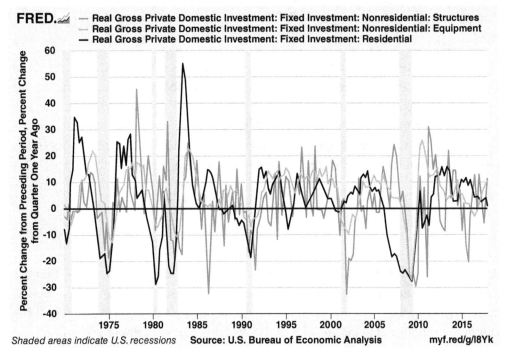

**Figure 2.3** Growth rates of gross domestic private investment (1970–2017)

*Source*: US Bureau of Economic Analysis, Real Gross Private Domestic Investment: Fixed Investment: Nonresidential: Structures, Fixed Investment: Nonresidential: Equipment, Fixed Investment: Residential, retrieved from FRED, Federal Reserve Bank of St. Louis; https://fred.stlouisfed.org, September 10, 2018.

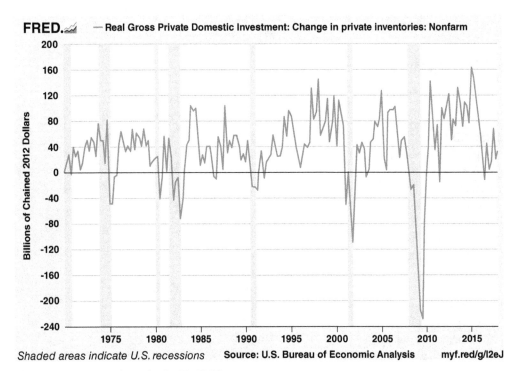

**Figure 2.4** Inventory dynamics (1970–2017)

*Source*: US Bureau of Economic Analysis, Real Gross Private Domestic Investment: Change in private inventories: Nonfarm, retrieved from FRED, Federal Reserve Bank of St. Louis; https://fred.stlouisfed.org, September 10, 2018.

fall before recessions start and tend to reverse and grow when recessions are about to end. For example, inventories fell dramatically before the beginning of the 2008–9 recession, and snapped back into positive change as the recession ended. Thus, changes in inventories are leading indicators of both upswings and down-swings over the business cycle. Observing them can help you predict a recession looming around the corner or the upcoming end of a recession.

## 2.2   BEA Announcements

Announcements of the BEA give you the most recent estimates for GDP that are available. They are your best source of information to know how the US economy is currently doing. For each quarter, the BEA publishes an *AD advance estimate* at the end of the month following the end of the quarter, a *second estimate* a month later and a *third estimate* another month later.

Here is an excerpt from a typical BEA announcement of GDP.[1] It is a good example of how people regularly write about a country's economic performance. Table 2.1 comes from the report for the third quarter of 2017, published in December 2017.

**Table 2.1** Contributions to real GDP growth (third quarter of 2017)

|  | Percent change at annual rate | Contribution to real GDP growth |
|---|---|---|
| Real GDP | 3.2 | 3.2 |
| PCE | 2.16 | 1.49 |
| Goods | 4.46 | 0.97 |
| Durable goods | 8.63 | 0.63 |
| Nondurable goods | 2.34 | 0.34 |
| Services | 1.11 | 0.52 |
| Gross domestic private investment | 7.27 | 1.19 |
| Fixed investment | 2.41 | 0.40 |
| Nonresidential | 4.65 | 0.58 |
| Residential | −4.70 | −0.18 |
| Change in private inventories | 24,000 | 0.79 |
| Net exports | 10.1 | 0.36 |
| Government consumption expenditures and gross investment | 0.66 | 0.12 |

*Source*: BEA tables 1.1.2 and 1.1.6. December 21, 2017.

## BOX 2.1 **National Income and Product Accounts GDP: Third Quarter 2017 (Third Estimate)**

Real GDP increased at an annual rate of 3.2 percent in the third quarter of 2017, according to the "third" estimate released by the BEA. In the second quarter, real GDP increased 3.1 percent. The GDP estimate released today is based on more complete source data than were available for the "second" estimate issued last month. In the second estimate, the increase in real GDP was 3.3 percent. With this third estimate for the third quarter, PCEs increased less than previously estimated, but the general picture of economic growth remains the same.

The increase in real GDP in the third quarter reflected positive contributions from PCEs, private inventory investment, nonresidential fixed investment, exports, federal government spending, and state and local government spending that were partly offset by a negative contribution from residential fixed investment. Imports, which are a subtraction in the calculation of GDP, decreased.

The slight acceleration in real GDP in the third quarter primarily reflected an acceleration in private inventory investment and an upturn in state and local government spending that were partly offset by decelerations in PCEs, nonresidential fixed investment, and exports.

### Updates to GDP

The downward revision to the percent change in real GDP primarily reflected a downward revision to PCE that was partly offset by an upward revision to state and local government spending.

|  | Advance estimate | Second estimate | Third estimate |
|---|---|---|---|
|  | (percent change from preceding quarter) | | |
| Real GDP | 3.0 | 3.3 | 3.2 |
| Current dollar GDP | 5.2 | 5.5 | 5.3 |

Real GDP increased at an annual rate of 3.0 percent in the third quarter of 2017 according to the "Advance" estimate released by the BEA.

Notice that announcements of recent GDP developments are framed in terms of growth rates rather than levels. This is because business leaders and analysts consider dynamics more informative of current developments than levels. For example, forecasters think a good year for US real GDP growth would be around 3 percent. Why? Because that seems to be a reasonable average growth rate based on the past. Third-quarter real GDP increased by 3.0 percent according to the AD advance estimate published in October. So, on that account, it was a good quarter in terms of macroeconomic performance. The second estimate revised this figure upward to 3.3 percent, while the third estimate was a downward revision to 3.2 percent. Note that these percentage changes are annualized, i.e., they are computed as if the increase between two quarters had been going on for four consecutive quarters.[2]

You may also have noticed that the BEA speaks of various *contributions* to real GDP growth. These contributions are calculated by taking the growth rate of an individual component of real GDP such as real personal consumption expenditures and multiplying it by the share of that component in real GDP. Table 2.1 has the details for the third quarter of 2017.

For example, the growth rate of real personal consumption expenditures was 2.16 percent in that quarter. The share of real personal consumption expenditures in real GDP is 68 percent. Multiplying 2.16 by 68 percent gives a contribution of real personal consumption expenditure growth to real GDP growth of 1.49. Table 2.1 is interesting for two points. First, it shows that the growth rates of different components of real GDP have very different short-term dynamics. Expenditures for durable goods increased by 8.63 percent, those for real gross domestic private investment by 7.27 percent. However, the contribution of durable goods to real GDP growth was much smaller than that of real gross domestic private investment because of the greater importance of the latter in real GDP.

Second, Table 2.1 provides you with a perspective for your business performance in a given quarter. For example, suppose that your sales corrected for price changes increased by an annualized rate of 5 percent in the third quarter of 2017. You would have done quite well compared to the US economy as a whole, even better if you were in the consumer services business, but quite badly, if your business is to sell durable goods!

## 2.3 Causes of AD Changes

The figures above show that the components of aggregate demand change all the time. The big challenge is to understand what causes all those ups and downs. When we talk about *why* aggregate demand has been growing or falling, and why it is doing so too fast or too slow, we frame our discussions around such things as:

- consumer confidence and its impact on purchases of autos – part of C;
- high interest rates and their negative effects on housing demand – part of I;
- the obsolescence of computers and how it might reinvigorate business investment – part of I;
- government deficits and how cutting them might reduce the spending stimulus from government – G;
- exchange rates, i.e., the value of the dollar in terms of other currencies and how it affects the demand for US goods from foreigners – NX;
- optimism about the future and how it might make companies increase inventory levels – ΔINV.

**Table 2.2** Causal factors for aggregate demand

| Private consumption expenditure | Gross domestic private investment | Government expenditures | Exports | Imports |
|---|---|---|---|---|
| Employment and hours worked | | Natural disasters | Incomes abroad | Employment and hours worked |
| Value of financial assets and real estate | | War | Domestic prices, foreign prices and exchange rates | Domestic prices, foreign prices, and exchange rates |
| Interest rates | Interest rates | Recessions | Foreign interest rates | Interest rates |
| Energy prices | | Energy prices | Energy prices | Energy prices |
| Income taxes | Corporate income taxes | | Tariffs, foreign income taxes | Tariffs |
| Consumer confidence | Business confidence | | Business and consumer confidence abroad | |

Here is where we need to think deeper about causality – the things that typically *cause* changes in aggregate demand. Without a lot of fanfare, we list some of these key causal factors that forecasters and analysts track because they are believed to impact the spending of households, firms, governments, and foreigners. Table 2.2 is not a complete list but it does contain the most important causal factors for aggregate demand.

We discuss how each of these affects aggregate demand, that is, the amount of final goods and services and newly produced fixed assets households, firms, and the government plan to buy and use. In each explanation we act like good scientists – we change one item while believing that all the rest are constant. Of course, we know that the world is never so still or well behaved. In the real world all these things are changing. But it helps a lot if we start the journey by studying one thing at a time![3] Below are some lines of reasoning involved in Table 2.2.

### Private Consumption Expenditure

- If a forecaster believes that positive momentum in the economy will lead to more jobs in the coming year, then her reasoning about aggregate demand might be as follows: More jobs create more income and more income causes households to spend more. This might cause aggregate demand to increase faster this year. In contrast, higher taxes and tax rates reduce a household's disposable income, inducing the household to both spend and save less.
- Similarly, when valuations on assets (like stocks, bonds, and real estate) rise, households may feel "richer" and want to spend more.

- In contrast, when interest rates rise, households may decide to postpone consumption and save instead, enjoying the higher returns on their savings. With rising interest rates, consumption loans become more expensive, making consumers cut back on borrowing and spending. Rising income taxes reduce disposable household incomes and, therefore, consumption.
- In a similar vein, rising energy prices act like a tax on disposable incomes, since households cannot easily cut back their energy consumption in the short run. Note that this argument assumes that a large part of the domestically consumed energy is produced with *imported* inputs such as crude oil from Arab countries, implying that the higher energy revenues do not generate domestic incomes.
- Rising consumer confidence means that households have more optimistic views about the future, which makes them save less and spend more.

### Gross Domestic Private Investment

- Rising interest rates cause businesses to cut back investment expenditures. Why? The trivial answer is that a rising real interest rate means higher costs of borrowing which makes any given investment project less lucrative. The more sophisticated answer is that firms invest only in projects that promise a higher rate of return than the representative real interest rate one can earn on average on other investment projects or on bonds, which, for simplicity, we consider as the main alternative investment opportunity. A rising real interest rate then implies that fewer projects will be selected for investment. The more sophisticated answer is more convincing, because in practice, borrowing costs are small compared to total investment outlays as most business investment is financed through cash flow.
- Rising stock prices reduce the cost of capital to the firm and this leads to more investment.
- Rising corporate income tax rates reduce the net profit businesses obtain from investment projects. This leads to a cut back in investment spending. The opposite happens when government subsidies on production increase.
- Rising business confidence means that firms have more optimistic views about future profits. This makes investment opportunities look more attractive and investment spending rises.

### Government Expenditures

- Natural disasters and wars lead to spending increases as the government provides disaster relief and steps up military spending.
- Recessions lead to increasing government spending on unemployment compensation and welfare payments. In addition, governments sometimes undertake *countercyclical* policies meaning that they increase spending as a recession begins in order to work against the drop in aggregate demand.
- Rising energy prices induce higher government spending through the government's own consumption of energy.

Exports of Goods and Services
- Foreign demand for domestically produced goods and services is part of foreign consumption and investment. Therefore, the same type of factors that impact domestic consumption and investment impact on export demand as well.
- In addition, foreign import and domestic export tariffs affect export demand negatively by making domestic goods more expensive abroad.
- The same argument holds for a rise in the foreign-currency value of the domestic currency.

Imports of Goods and Services
- Domestic imports are part of domestic consumption and investment. Therefore, the same factors impacting the latter also impact import demand.
- In addition, domestic import tariffs and foreign export tariffs affect imports negatively by making foreign goods more expensive at home.
- The same argument holds for a drop in the foreign-currency value of the domestic currency.

This discussion illustrates the key channels of how we get from AD-side demand change factors to things like GDP growth and inflation:

Aggregate Demand causal variable changes

One or more Aggregate Demand components  (G, C, I, X, Im)

change

Aggregate Demand changes

Real GDP and GDP deflator change

Remember from our discussion of the economic circuit that an increase in aggregate demand is likely to lead to an increase in aggregate income, because more aggregate demand means more revenues to firms, which means more income to households. What we need to find out next is how aggregate demand and aggregate income are compatible following a change in aggregate demand. Before we go there, we consider two applications of these arguments.

### 2.3.1    International Application: IMF Announcement

What does the following extract tell you that you should be looking at – what important economic data should you be focused on to try to decide how much to trust the baseline (optimistic) forecast?

---

**BOX 2.2  IMF *World Economic Outlook* (October 2017)**

The global upswing in economic activity is strengthening. Global growth, which in 2016 was the weakest since the global financial crisis at 3.2 percent, is projected to rise to 3.6 percent in 2017 and to 3.7 percent in 2018. The growth forecasts for both 2017 and 2018 are 0.1 percentage point stronger compared with the April 2017 *World Economic Outlook* (WEO) forecast. Broad-based upward revisions in the euro area, Japan, emerging Asia, emerging Europe, and Russia – where growth outcomes in the first half of 2017 were better than expected – more than offset downward revisions for the United States and the United Kingdom. But the recovery is not complete: while the baseline outlook is strengthening, growth remains weak in many countries, and inflation is below target in most advanced economies. Commodity exporters, especially of fuel, are particularly hard hit as their adjustment to a sharp stepdown in foreign earnings continues. And while short-term risks are broadly balanced, medium-term risks are still tilted to the downside. The welcome cyclical pickup in global activity thus provides an ideal window of opportunity to tackle the key policy challenges – namely to boost potential output while ensuring its benefits are broadly shared, and to build resilience against downside risks. A renewed multilateral effort is also needed to tackle the common challenges of an integrated global economy.

---

The IMF report is interesting because it reports a possible improvement in world growth, but is clearly not impressed with its staying power. The US is not among the leaders, and commodity-exporting countries continue to face challenges. The IMF sees this as a great time for countries to continue to work together to find ways to overcome common economic hurdles.

### 2.3.2    Working with Data: Consumer and Business Confidence

There are several measures of confidence. Two are included in Figure 2.5. Both have been produced by the OECD. The black line is the Indicator of Consumer Confidence; the blue line is the Business Tendency for the manufacturing industry, an indicator of business confidence for that industry. Both indicators are based on surveys, the first among consumers, the second among business managers. They have the advantage of being available much earlier than GDP statistics and, therefore, contain valuable early information about current macroeconomic developments. Notice how

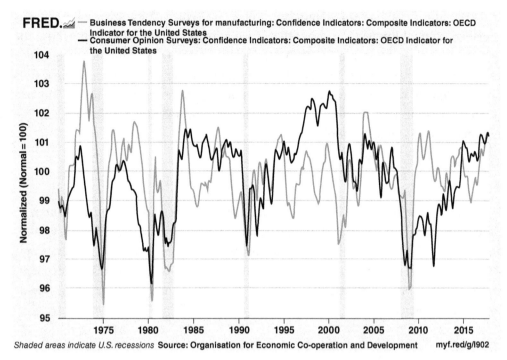

**Figure 2.5** Consumer and business confidence (1980–2017)

*Source*: Organisation for Economic Co-operation and Development, Business Tendency Surveys for Manufacturing: Confidence Indicators: Composite Indicators: OECD Indicator for the United States; Consumer Opinion Surveys: Confidence Indicators: Composite Indicators: OECD Indicator for the United States, retrieved from FRED, Federal Reserve Bank of St. Louis; https://fred.stlouisfed.org, 10 September 2018.

consumer sentiment typically falls during recessions and then recovers afterward. The same holds true for business confidence for the manufacturing industry. Thus, confidence indicators appear to be correlated to economic cycles. But one still cannot easily resolve an important question – does sentiment cause macroeconomic change or does macroeconomic change cause sentiment? Both could be true.

### 2.3.3 The Real Interest Rate

The real interest rate is thought to be an important factor impacting aggregate demand mostly through its impact on interest-sensitive components of aggregate demand like spending on autos, houses, business equipment and structures. Although there is a multitude of interest rates in the economy we talk about *the* interest rate as a representative one. But what is the *real* interest rate?

We previously distinguished between *nominal* GDP (GDP in dollar terms) and its components and *real* GDP (GDP corrected for changes in the price level) and its components. Nominal GDP measures the dollar value of GDP, while real GDP measures a quantity of aggregate output. We must now make a similar distinction between the *nominal* and the *real* interest rate.

Of course, we are all very familiar with nominal interest rates. Our saving account might offer us a 1 percent rate of return annually. That would mean that if we keep

USD 100 in it for a year, we obtain one dollar as a return. A car loan might cost us 5 percent annual interest, meaning that if we borrowed USD 5,000 to purchase the car, we pay USD 250 interest every year. These are dollar, or nominal, amounts. If the price level rises subsequently, the real value of these interest payments falls and the lender will be able to buy fewer goods and services for them. The real interest takes this into account by subtracting the expected rate of inflation from the nominal interest rate. In short:

The real interest rate is the difference between the nominal interest rate and the expected rate of inflation.

We call the rate of return in terms of purchasing power the *real rate of interest*. Since investors are interested in the future purchasing power of their wealth, economic decisions are guided by real interest rates, not nominal interest rates. An asset promising a nominal interest rate of 5 percent might be a great investment, if the expected rate of inflation is 1 percent, but a lousy one, if the expected rate of inflation is 5 percent.

## BOX 2.3  Formal Analysis: the Real Interest Rate

Consider an example. Take an asset like a US treasury security worth USD 100. Assume that the asset matures after one year. The asset promises a payment of USD 4, at the time of maturity. Therefore, the (nominal) interest rate, i, on this security is

$$i = 4\%$$

This means that at the time of maturity, the owner can buy goods and services worth USD 104 instead of USD 100, which he was able to spend when he bought the asset. But will he be able to buy the same amount of goods and services that USD 104 would buy him when he bought the asset? That depends!

Let P be the price level at the time when he purchases the asset and $P_{+1}$ the price level at the time of maturity. The purchasing power of USD 100 is USD 100/P when he buys the asset. The purchasing power of USD 104 will be USD 104/$P_{+1}$ at the time of maturity. Therefore, in terms of purchasing power, the return on the asset is

$$r = \frac{\frac{104}{P_{+1}} - \frac{100}{P}}{\frac{100}{P}} = \frac{104}{100}\frac{1}{\frac{P_{+1}}{P}} - 1$$

$$= \frac{104}{100}\frac{1}{1+\pi} - 1$$

$$\approx 4\% - \pi\%$$

where $\pi = (P_{+1} - P)/P$ is the expected relative change in the price level between the time of purchasing the asset and the time of maturity, or the expected rate of inflation. The sign "$\approx$" means approximately and refers to the approximation in the last step of the equation above, $1/(1+\pi) \approx (1-\pi)$, which is good, if the expected rate of inflation is a small number. The word "expected" refers to the fact that, at the time of purchasing the asset, the future price level may not be known. Therefore, the best we can do is to form an expectation about it.

The St. Louis Federal Reserve Bank publishes measures of inflation expectations which are derived from household surveys conducted by the University of Michigan.[4] Figure 2.6 shows one such measure. Inflation expectations refer to the one-year ahead expected rate of CPI inflation. The figure shows these expectations together with the actual realizations of core CPI inflation, which is based on the CPI with prices of food and energy removed. Since the expectations measured in January 1978 are for inflation in January 1979, we pull the core inflation data forward by a year. That is, the core CPI inflation rate shown for January 1978 is the actual rate in January 1979. In this way,

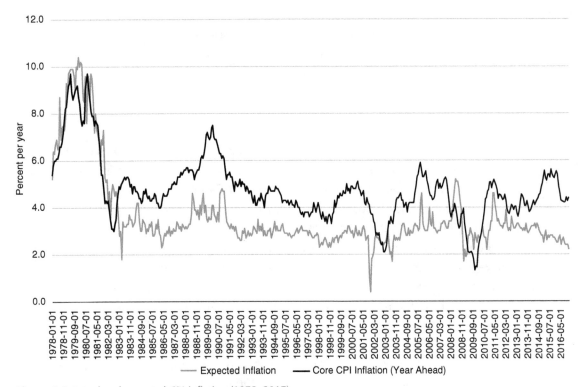

**Figure 2.6** Actual and expected CPI inflation (1978–2017)

*Source*: University of Michigan, University of Michigan: Inflation Expectation, US Bureau of Labor Statistics, Consumer Price Index for All Urban Consumers: All Items Less Food and Energy, retrieved from FRED, Federal Reserve Bank of St. Louis; https://fred.stlouisfed.org, September 10, 2018.

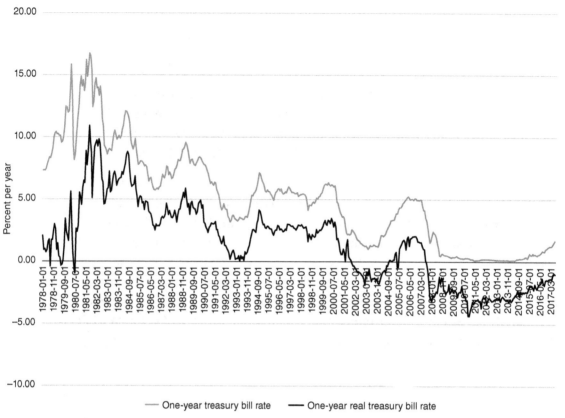

**Figure 2.7** Nominal and real interest rates (1978–2016)

*Source*: University of Michigan, University of Michigan: Inflation Expectation, Board of Governors of the Federal Reserve System (US), 1-Year Treasury Constant Maturity Rate [GS1], retrieved from FRED, Federal Reserve Bank of St. Louis; https://fred.stlouisfed.org/series/GS1, September 10, 2018.

the difference between the two lines is the expectation error households committed in January 1978 regarding inflation in January 1979. You can see that inflation expectations tracked actual inflation very well when inflation was high and variable in the later 1970s and early 1980s. Since inflation came down in the 1990s, expected inflation is typically less volatile and somewhat lower than core inflation.

Figure 2.7 illustrates the concept of the real interest rate. It takes the yield on a one-year US treasury bill as the nominal interest rate and subtracts from that the expected one-year ahead rate of inflation shown in Figure 2.6.

The result is the one-year-real interest rate shown in the figure. Since inflation expectations are generally positive, the real interest rate is below the nominal interest rate. One-year real interest rates became negative in 2003 and in the years following the Great Recession. The Treasury also issues securities which are inflation protected, so-called treasury inflation protected securities (TIPS). The difference in yields between TIPS and nominal treasury securities is a good indicator for market expectations of future inflation rates.

## 2.3.4    Aggregate Demand and the Real Interest Rate

Two important components of aggregate demand depend on the real rate of interest. One is investment demand. When the real rate of interest increases, we expect that investment demand weakens.

The other variable responding to real interest rate changes is consumption. When the real rate of interest increases, it becomes more attractive for households to reduce consumption and save a larger part of today's income for future consumption. As a corollary, household savings depend positively on the real interest rate.

Therefore, when the real interest rate rises, consumption is likely to fall. Thus, we have:

A rise in the real interest rate causes aggregate demand to fall.

A fall in the real interest rate causes aggregate demand to rise.

## 2.3.5    Aggregate Demand and Aggregate Income

We are now ready to consider the relationship between aggregate demand and aggregate income. Recall that the two are always equal *ex post*, in an accounting sense. But, in order to understand the economy and to make good plans for the future, we must understand how aggregate demand and aggregate income are made compatible *ex ante*, i.e. in the economic plans and behaviors of firms, households, the government, and the rest of the world. For now, we forget about the RoW and consider only the domestic economy as if it were isolated. We return to the international economy in Chapter 8.

In order to understand how aggregate demand and aggregate income are made compatible, we begin with a situation in which they are in fact equal: aggregate demand = aggregate income. Going from there, we ask: What happens, if some households or the government decide to increase spending? Or, what happens if firms decide to increase their purchases of new equipment? Whatever the cause, the initial rise in aggregate demand implies that aggregate demand is now larger than aggregate income. Something must happen to either bring aggregate demand down to the level of aggregate income again, or to raise aggregate income to the new level of aggregate demand, or a mixture of both so that aggregate income rises and aggregate demand falls until the two are equal again.

A first important point to consider is the *spending multiplier*. The multiplier is a direct consequence of the economic circuit and one of the most beautiful things in macroeconomics. Suppose that the rise in aggregate demand causes firms to produce and sell more goods and services. This is plausible in the short run, simply because greater aggregate demand means that people buy more stuff. As firms produce more, workers earn higher incomes and shareholders earn greater dividends. As a result, aggregate income increases. But as aggregate income increases, households have larger disposable incomes, which cause them to consume more. That is, aggregate demand rises again. Thus, the initial increase in aggregate demand causes an increase in aggregate income which causes a second increase in aggregate demand. But it is even more exciting than that. The second increase in aggregate demand causes a second increase in aggregate income which causes a third increase in aggregate demand, which causes a fourth increase in aggregate demand and so on:

Aggregate demand rises – aggregate income rises – aggregate demand rises (households consume more) aggregate income rises – aggregate demand rises (households consume more) – and on and on.

Eventually, this process ends, because in each round the additional amounts get smaller and smaller until they get close to zero. Why? Because in each round, the amount of additional consumption is smaller than the amount of additional disposable income, since households tend to save part of the additional income. The *marginal propensity to consume* (MPC) is the key to the size of the multiplier. The MPC is the increase in consumption due to an increase in disposable income by USD 1. The higher the MPC, the more a household will spend out of a given additional dollar of aggregate income. This makes the multiplier larger. In contrast, if a rise in aggregate income has a small impact on consumption, then the multiplier is smaller. The actual size of the MPC varies over time and depends on many factors including household indebtedness and confidence.

Note that the spending multiplier potentially increases the impact of changes in government on aggregate demand. We say *potentially* because the size of the multiplier is quite uncertain. Similarly, the multiplier increases the impact of an increase in investment caused by changes in business confidence or some other factor on aggregate demand. The general insight is that the initial change in aggregate demand caused by a change in one of the causal factors mentioned above is amplified by the interaction of aggregate income and consumer spending.

This brings us back to the question how, following an initial change in aggregate demand, aggregate demand and aggregate income are brought back into equilibrium. We think of the real rate of interest as being the variable that achieves this result. That is, the real interest rate assures that aggregate demand equals aggregate income, i.e., the economy does not spend more or less in a given period than it can afford out of its current income. It cannot spend more because, as the economic circuit tells us, the value of total output equals the value of total aggregate income. If the economy wanted to spend more than aggregate income, the value of aggregate spending would have to exceed the value of total output, which is impossible. If the economy wanted to spend less than aggregate income, some goods and services would be produced only to be thrown away. Furthermore, total revenue of the firms would not suffice to pay total household incomes. That is impossible, too.

Thus:

If aggregate demand > aggregate income, the real interest rate must rise to achieve equality.

If aggregate demand < aggregate income, the real interest rate must fall to achieve equality.

Taking our arguments so far together, we now have the following line of reasoning:

Aggregate Demand causal variable changes

Aggregate Demand changes

Aggregate Income changes

If Aggregate Demand > Aggregate Income, the real interest rate

rises

If Aggregate Demand < Aggregate Income, the real interest rate

falls

Aggregate Demand = Aggregate Income

Depending on the initial causal effect, aggregate demand and aggregate income will be larger or smaller in the end.

The spending multiplier implies that an increase in government spending by USD 1, keeping taxes constant, causes a rise in aggregate demand by more than USD 1. This gives the government *more bang for the buck*, i.e., it makes government spending more powerful to control aggregate demand. For example, if households consume 90 cents out of every additional dollar disposable income, the spending multiplier would be 10, and an increase in government spending by one dollar would raise aggregate demand by USD 10. But that is a big *if*. How large the spending multiplier actually is, is a much-disputed question in economic policy. People who call for more government spending in recessions typically believe that the spending multiplier is large. People who warn against too much government activism in such situations believe that the spending multiplier is small. In practice, the multiplier is difficult to forecast and creates considerable uncertainty about the effects of government spending on aggregate demand.

## BOX 2.4 DIFFERENCE OF OPINION: HOW LARGE IS THE GOVERNMENT SPENDING MULTIPLIER?

In *Explainer: Understanding Fiscal Multipliers* Mark Thoma writes:

It has been five years this month that President Obama signed an USD 816.3 billion fiscal stimulus package, known as the American Recovery and Reinvestment Act, into law. Has it worked? To answer this question, economists look at something known as the expenditure multiplier. It tells us how a change in consumption, investment, net exports or, in this case, government spending and tax changes, impacts GDP. For example, if the expenditure multiplier is 1.5, then every dollar of new government spending generates USD 1.50 of new GDP.

How is it possible for a USD 1 change in government spending to translate into more than USD 1 in economic growth? In traditional macroeconomic models, the key to understanding the multiplier is first to recognize that money spent purchasing goods and services translates into income for the store owner and the people who provided the raw materials used to produce the product. Second, income generated from that initial sale is used to purchase even more goods and services. For example, if the government spends USD 1,000 on a new desk – which increases GDP by USD 1,000 – the USD 1,000 covers the wages of the people who made the desk, the cost of the raw materials and the profit that goes to the owner of the furniture store. In other words, USD 1,000 of income is created from selling the desk. Part of that income will be saved and part will go to taxes – say, USD 400 for both, leaving USD 600 in income to be used to purchase new goods and services. When those goods and services are purchased, GDP goes up by another USD 600, and USD 600 in additional income is created at the same time. Notice that the total increase in GDP at this point – USD 1,000 plus USD 600 – is greater than the initial change in government spending of USD 1,000. This process then continues, part of the USD 600 will be saved, part will go to pay taxes, and the rest will be used to purchase goods and services, and so on. In this particular example, if we add up the total change in GDP arising from the initial USD 1,000 in GDP, it would amount to USD 2,500, implying a multiplier of 2.5. Actual multipliers are smaller than that, probably closer to 1.5 in severe recessions (when multipliers are the largest). That means a USD 1,000 increase in government spending leads to approximately a USD 1,500 change in GDP, which should also increase employment. Multipliers can also differ across countries depending on their individual propensities to save out of income and on where they are in the business cycle.

In modern *New Keynesian* models, the mechanism producing the multiplier is a bit different. It arises from how the change in spending alters expectations about the future course of the economy. But the bottom line is the same – the government spending multiplier in deep recessions is greater than one, and likely around 1.5 (there is a large range of estimates in the economics literature, but a value of 1.5 seems like a reasonable estimate of what most economists believe based upon this econometric work).

Returning to our initial question, it's important to note that the 2009 stimulus wasn't just government spending: 36 percent of the package – USD 290.7 billion dollars – came in the form of tax cuts, and the multiplier is smaller for tax cuts than for government spending. The reason is that while government spending impacts GDP one for one on the initial sale of goods and services, tax changes have a smaller impact. An increase in taxes, for example, will be paid partly by reducing consumption which has multiplier effects, and partly by reducing saving, which does not. Conversely, a tax cut will be used partly for consumption, and partly to increase saving. Thus, for example, if 25 percent of the tax cut is saved, the initial impact of a USD 1,000 tax cut will only be USD 750, and the subsequent multiplier effects described above will be smaller as well (the total effect would be 2.5 x USD 750 = USD 1,875, instead of 2.5 x USD 1,000 = USD 2,500).

Since there is evidence that in recovering from the financial crisis US households used tax cuts to rebuild the loss of retirement and education saving, and to offset losses of home equity, there is reason to believe that the tax cuts were not as effective as government spending at stimulating the economy.

It's clear in retrospect that the stimulus package was too small and ended too soon, and thus did not have as large of an impact as hoped. But it still mattered. As economist Paul Krugman says, everything we have seen since 2009 confirms that expansionary fiscal policy is expansionary . . . There is every reason to believe that the Recovery Act boosted GDP and employment while it was in effect relative to what would have happened without it.

To quantify precisely how much fiscal policy mattered, fiscal policy multipliers are an essential tool.

*Source*: Mark Thoma: "Explainer: Understanding Fiscal Multipliers," *Money Watch*, February 27, 2014, www.cbsnews.com/news/explainer-fiscal-policy-multipliers

## 2.3.6   Aggregate Demand and the Price Level

Everybody knows that the demand for apples falls when the apple price rises. Does aggregate demand fall when the price level rises? The answer is yes, but for completely different reasons. The demand for apples falls, because buying apples becomes less attractive to the consumer compared to buying oranges – a relative price effect. Since GDP includes all final goods and services, there can be no relative price effect, because there are no alternative goods to consider. Furthermore, the demand for apples goes down, because a higher apple price means that the consumer's income has less purchasing power – a negative income effect. But there can be no negative income effect for GDP, because, by virtue of the economic circuit, higher prices means higher incomes for some people in the economy and these people will step up their demand.

So, why does aggregate demand fall when the price level rises? Because a rise in the price level causes the real interest rate to rise and this causes aggregate demand to fall. The full explanation of this point is pretty complex and we leave it to the technical Appendix to this chapter for you to study. Here, we only sketch the argument. The answer comes again from the economic circuit. Call the price level P, and the number of units of money circulating in the economy the *quantity of money* or the *money stock*, M. Each unit of money can be used more than once in transactions during a given period, and the average number of times a unit of money changes hands each period is called the velocity of money, v. As we have seen above, there is a flow of payments in the economy which mirrors the flow of goods and services, and it must be true that

$$
\begin{aligned}
M * v \\
= &(\text{Number of units of money}) \\
&* (\text{velocity of money}) = \text{value of expenditures for final goods and services} \\
= &\, P * \text{aggregate income}
\end{aligned}
$$

For a given quantity of money and a given velocity of money, we see immediately that aggregate income must fall, if P rises. But how does this fall come about? For now, think about the quantity of money as being determined by the central bank. The velocity of money is determined by the payment habits and technology prevailing in the economy. Furthermore, the velocity of money rises, when the real interest rate rises, and the velocity of money falls when the real interest rate falls. This is because a higher real interest rate means that people wish to hold more of their financial wealth in bonds and other interest-bearing instruments rather than in cash or checkable deposits. In contrast, when the real interest rate is low people tend to hold more cash to enjoy the convenience of it.

Now we can see what happens when the price level rises. For a given level of aggregate income and given quantity of money, M, the rise in the price level means the flow of payments now falls short of the value of expenditures, so that

$M * v < P *$ (aggregate income). The velocity of money must rise to keep the flow of payments in balance with the value of expenditures. Again, it is the real interest rate which does the work. The real interest rate must rise so that the velocity of money increases. But, as we know by now, aggregate demand falls when the real interest rate rises. Thus, the left-hand side of the equation rises and the right-hand side falls until equilibrium has been restored. Similarly, when the price level falls, the velocity of money must fall. For this to happen, the real interest rate falls which brings up aggregate demand and real GDP. As a result, we can say: aggregate demand and the price level are negatively linked. Finally, following the same logic, when the central bank increases the stock of money, the real interest rate must go down to reestablish the relationship between the flow of payments, $M * v$, and the value of expenditures, $P * AD$, and AD rises in that process.

Sounds complicated? It is. After all, we are talking about a pretty complex machine called the US economy, which churns out stuff to the tune of USD 20 trillion every year and keeps millions of Americans in jobs. But then: Don't worry! Remember, first, that aggregate demand depends negatively both on the price level and the real interest rate. That's the important point. Afterwards, when you hear that little voice nagging inside you: "But why, why?" you can go through the Appendix to this chapter and get more and deeper insights into the arguments.

### 2.3.7 Graphical Analysis

With the above we have highlighted a number of key factors that impact aggregate demand. Now we want to build an analytical tool that we can easily use to apply all this information. This tool is called the AD curve. It is a representation of the relationship between aggregate demand and the price level.

Figure 2.8 is a graph showing an AD curve. In this figure, the price level, P, is on the vertical axis. The level of aggregate demand (AD) is on the horizontal axis. The

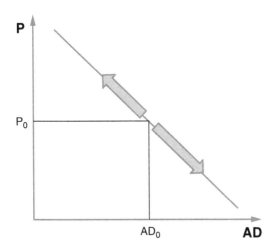

**Figure 2.8** The AD curve

AD curve represents the negative relationship between the price level and aggregate demand we have developed above. The negative slope of the AD curve indicates that, as the price level rises, aggregate demand falls, while, as the price level falls, aggregate demand rises.

Let's make sure we understand this graph properly. There are many more graphs to follow in this book and it is important to interpret them properly. The AD curve shows the relationship between the price level and aggregate demand assuming that all other causal factors that could change aggregate demand are fixed. If the price level is actually $P_0$, AD will be $AD_0$. Movements of the price level up and down lead to movements along the AD curve as indicated by the arrows, inducing lower or higher aggregate demand.

But, what if the other causal factors are not fixed? Consider an increase in government spending on goods and services. It implies that the same price level as before is now associated with a higher level of aggregate demand. Graphically, this means that the AD curve shifts to the right as shown by the blue arrow pointing rightward in Figure 2.9. The new AD curve is represented by the dotted line and the new level of aggregate demand is $AD_1$.

Conversely, if the government reduces government spending, the AD curve shifts to the left as indicated by the blue arrow pointing leftward. For a given price level, aggregate demand falls. The same arguments apply for the other causal factors affecting aggregate demand listed above. Other factors that shift the AD curve include, real interest rates, government spending, taxes, consumer and business confidence, and more.

We use diagrams like this to illustrate and analyze macroeconomic developments and policies. Of course, such an explanation is only qualitative. It shows tendencies, not exact results. But it is useful. Always be sure to know which variables are on the

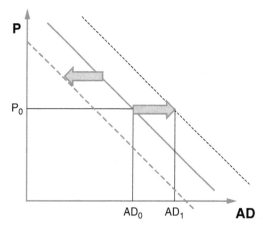

**Figure 2.9** Shifts in the AD curve

vertical and horizontal axes and to understand what constitutes a movement along a curve and a shift of the curve!

## 2.4   AD Policy

One hundred years ago business leaders and policymakers didn't think much about AD policy. It is a long story, but they pretty much believed that unusual AD changes would be temporary and self-correcting. After the Great Depression of the 1930s many economists began to rethink aggregate demand. One economist, John Maynard Keynes, promoted the idea that AD changes were not self-correcting and that, especially when aggregate demand got very low, it might need some help from the government. People who call themselves Keynesians today generally believe that when aggregate demand is too low, the government ought to do something to resuscitate it. Of course, aggregate demand can also be too large. In that case, policymakers should engage in policies to reduce aggregate demand.

But why should you care about all this? Because when policymakers do something to increase or reduce aggregate demand, their actions will affect the environment you do business in. Businesspeople watch the Fed and government policies, because they realize that their policy actions impact aggregate demand, real GDP growth, and inflation. So, business plans are often as much impacted by the government's AD policies as they are by changes in oil prices or business confidence.

Generally, we think of AD policy in the following terms:

If aggregate demand appears *too weak* (as evidenced by a negative output gap), then aggregate demand can be increased by any of the following policies:
- The central bank increases the money supply and reduces interest rates.
- The government reduces income or other taxes.
- The government spends more on goods and services.
- The government increases entitlement programs.

Each of these shifts the AD curve to the right.

If aggregate demand appears *too strong* (as evidenced by a positive output gap), then aggregate demand can be decreased by policy:
- The central bank reduces the money supply and raises interest rates.
- The government increases income tax rates or other taxes.
- The government spends less on goods and services.
- The government decreases entitlement programs.

Each of these shifts the AD curve to the left.

While the policy idea is pretty straightforward, the real world is a very challenging place for business planners and macro forecasters, because AD policies create their own sources of uncertainty. For example, when the Fed began reducing interest rates right after the onset of the 2001 recession, at least three kinds of uncertainties emerged:

1. *How low will the Fed go? How low will they push interest rates?*
2. *How long will it take the lower interest rates to impact aggregate demand?*
3. *How much will aggregate demand be impacted? Will aggregate demand come roaring back?*

There was a similar set of questions with respect to what the US government along with the Canadian, European, and Japanese governments would do to respond to the incipient recession in 2008. You can see why business managers were and continue to be very interested in these policy questions.

Unsurprisingly, analysts and commentators have very differing views about AD policy. *Conservative* analysts and commentators believe that the market system generally responds to changes in the economic environment in a way that the system returns to *normal* – we will see what that means more precisely later – and that activist government policies trying to control aggregate demand result in too much uncertainty about economic outcomes. *Liberal* analysts and commentators don't think the economic problems will disappear on their own and they are more likely to advocate more government intervention in the economy.

The importance of these differences of opinion is that governments at most times are exposed to a wide range of statements about what they *should be doing*. It is, therefore, not always easy for a business planner to predict exactly when and by how much a given government or central bank will change its AD policies. Here is where knowledge about these issues is helpful to business executives. Keeping up with good analysis provides the clues to anticipate correctly what policymakers will do.

## BOX 2.5 DIFFERENCE OF OPINION: WE ARE ALL CONSERVATIVES NOW

I knew that headline would get your attention. No, I am not into my third JD of the evening. But something is going on out there – or not going on out there – that supports my wild contention.

First, I am focused on financial conservatism – not the social variety. Second, I am speculating about conservatism as it plays out in macroeconomics policy. This idea has been ruminating in the dark recesses of my brain and jumped to the surface this week after I read one brief article online worrying over the uncertainty about US policy under Trump and then read another lengthier piece about the global economy by the IMF.

The shorter Bloomberg article thought that stalling new policies for infrastructure spending and tax reform would injure corporate profits and lead to a slower economy. The IMF piece – a magnum opus on the world's future output growth published this month – was more sanguine and predicted that the world and US economies would grow faster in 2017 and 2018.[5]

These two recent pieces see different futures but agree on one thing – it is the lack of traditional policy that underlies our economic futures. In macro, we learn two opposing schools of thought. The conservative macros believe good macro outcomes are the result of less government intervention. The liberal macros believe the opposite. The liberal macros believe that activism known as monetary and fiscal policy is necessary to rev up spending and will lead to full employment and strong economic growth. This liberal belief has become traditional.

While the IMF often shows, in my view, a liberal tilt in their outlook reports, much of what they say in the April installment is lacking in liberal spirit. From this I conclude that we are in a new economic policy conservative era – at least for a while.

While the IMF is forecasting marginal improvements in economic growth around the world, they mostly see an economy stuck in neutral and not ready for the next drag race. Summarizing from a long and technical report, the IMF describes an economy hampered by dismal expectations. The usual monetary and fiscal policies are having little effect on spending, and the more they fail to work, the more pessimistic we become. And therefore the policies have even less impact and we become even more dismal.

Low and negative interest rates spurred some activity in housing and autos, but firms are sitting on their hands when it comes to expansions and modernization. Despite record amounts of fiscal stimulus, there is little bump to spending in the economy. The more the government lingers with these policies, the more dismal people become. The IMF wishes that governments could magically raise optimism. But how do you do that when the usual policies are not working?

What is refreshing is that the IMF is recommending some very conservative policies – policies that could be called supply-side. Imagine that. They admit that government is out of bullets. In fact they admit that there is already too much money outstanding and too little fiscal space (too much high debt) for most countries to resort to the usual policy practices.

The IMF names two major trends that are holding back the advanced countries. The first is a decline in the labor force participation rate. Fewer people want to work than in the past. Various reforms could help on that score, but these reforms have nothing to do with the usual macro policies. They focus on the reward to work and on labor market mismatches. The second major challenge is in firms' willingness to buy new capital and to innovate. Firms are reluctant because of a dismal outlook but there are many ways that government can try to raise the return to capital without resorting to demand management. Reforms with respect to regulations and tax rates could go a long way to creating a more sanguine future for business firms. Raising the reward to work and to buying new capital will make firms more productive and profitable and should improve the growth rate of the economy.

In addition to these trends are two global factors that dent our ability to grow faster. The first is recovery and reform in China. As these reforms start to work, China will resume its role as a locomotive pulling the rest of us along with them. Finally, there are the lingering impacts of commodity and energy prices. While we all love a low price of gasoline, the low prices of energy have stunted exploration and development of oil and gas. Emerging markets prospered with high energy and commodity prices. They tanked with low ones, and the contagion was global.

None of the above supports a role for the usual liberal macro policies of monetary accommodation or fiscal expansion. In fact, making people more optimistic might involve admitting the ineffectiveness of these old tools – and thus we come away thinking that monetary normalcy and budgetary restraints are the key to optimism and spending. But better than that is the simple idea that policy should fit the nature of our problems. Right now our problems are from the supply side. Demand is low *because* supply is low and because global challenges add to an uncertain outlook. Policies that directly target supply issues are what the IMF is recommending. What a refreshing change of message!

*Source*: https://larrydavidsonspoutsoff.blogspot.com/2017/04/we-are-all-conservatives-now.html

## 2.5   SUMMARY

This ends our initial excursion into aggregate demand. You might ask, aggregate demand for what? It is traditional these days to focus our macro-intentions and analysis on what happens to national output, or real GDP. It turns out that we can apply the same simple supply-and-demand concepts one learns in microeconomics to the analysis of a whole nation's output and its price level. We saw in this chapter that aggregate demand is the demand for all the final goods and services and fixed assets the nation produces. It comprises the demands of households, firms, governments, and foreigners. Depending on factors like interest rates, confidence, and exchange rates, aggregate demand can swing or change from time to time and it can be too little demand to keep everyone employed or too much spending so as to create problems of inflation. Since aggregate demand can swing in undesirable directions, we showed that government policy can be designed to moderate or ameliorate those changes. Of course, such policies are always controversial. We developed the AD curve to model or embody all the above causes and consequences of changes in aggregate demand. Next we develop our understanding of aggregate supply. While aggregate demand often drives changes in the economy there are times when aggregate supply gets behind the steering wheel. A complete understanding of output and prices, therefore, brings together everything impacting aggregate demand and aggregate supply. With this more complete model mastered we can then move on to investigating monetary and fiscal policies in the next chapters.

## 2.6   REVIEW QUESTIONS

1. Which component of GDP contains sales of new automobiles? Which component includes purchases of new equipment for business firms. Compare and contrast the behaviors of these two components of GDP.
2. Why are changes in inventories included in GDP?
3. Are rising inventories a positive sign for the economic growth of an economy?
4. What is the real interest rate and why is it important to aggregate demand?
5. A rise in the price level is shown as a movement along the AD curve. Why would a rise in the price level reduce aggregate demand?
6. Why should business executives care about monetary policy?
7. Why are governments exposed to very strong opinions about what they should and shouldn't be doing with AD policy?

# 2.7

# Appendix: IS–LM Analysis

In this appendix, we explain the ideas of sections 2.3.5–2.3.7 further and more precisely. Recall that aggregate demand and its components and aggregate income are defined in real terms, i.e., corrected for price level changes or measured in units of output. Call aggregate income Y, private household consumption expenditures C, private household savings S, government revenues from taxes T, government spending on government consumption and investment G, and gross domestic private investment I. Consider again the equality of aggregate demand and aggregate income. Aggregate demand equals C + G + I. Thus the equality of aggregate demand and aggregate income is

$$C + G + I = Y$$

Remember that private households have a budget constraint saying that their consumption plus savings equals their disposable income, which is the difference between aggregate income and taxes, Y − T. Thus, C+S = Y − T. The government's savings are tax revenues less government spending, T − G. Using this, we can rewrite the above equality as

$$S + T - G = I$$

This says that aggregate demand equals aggregate income when the sum of private household savings, S, plus government savings, T − G, is equal to gross domestic private investment. If the government increases its spending while tax revenues remain unchanged, the government absorbs a greater part of private household savings to finance its deficits and fewer resources are left for domestic investment. Something must happen to restore the equality.

Generally, household consumption and savings depend on household disposable income, Y − T, and the real interest rate. When household income goes up, so do consumption and savings. When the real interest rate rises, consumption declines and savings rise. The reason is that, with a higher real interest rate, it becomes more attractive to consume less today and consume more in the future. In contrast, gross domestic private investment demand depends negatively on the real interest rate as argued above.

Consider a rise in household disposable income. Savings go up and, therefore, the left-hand side exceeds the right-hand side. Aggregate demand is too small for

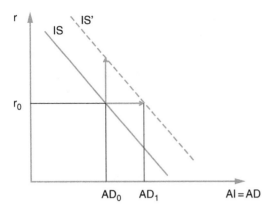

**Figure A1** The IS curve

aggregate income. Therefore, the real interest rate must fall to push up investment and reduce household savings until the equality is restored. Conversely, if household disposable income falls, savings decrease and the real interest rate must rise to push down investment and restore equilibrium. *The condition that aggregate demand equals aggregate income thus implies a negative relationship between the real interest rate and aggregate income.*

This negative relationship is indicated by the negatively sloped, solid curve IS in Figure A1. The figure has the real interest rate on the vertical axis and aggregate demand and aggregate income on the horizontal axis. We call this curve the IS curve. Movements along the curve describe the relationship between the real interest rate and aggregate income for given levels of taxes, government spending, and all other determinants of investment demand such as business confidence and of savings such as consumer confidence. At a given level of the real interest rate such as $r_0$, the corresponding level of aggregate demand that equals aggregate income is $AD_0$.

What happens if the level of government spending rises or the level of taxes falls? The arrows in Figure A1 give the answer: For a given level of aggregate income, the interest rate must rise to restore equality of aggregate demand and aggregate income (vertical arrow). Alternatively, for a given real interest rate, aggregate income must rise to restore that equality (horizontal arrow). Generally, therefore, a new combination of aggregate income and the real interest rate must be found which lies to the north-east of the initial one. The curve shifts to the right as shown by the broken line IS'. The level of aggregate demand corresponding to the real interest rate $r_0$ is now $AD_1$. By analogous reasoning, a decline in government spending or a rise in taxes shifts the curve to the left. Similarly, increases in business confidence increasing investment demand and increases in consumer confidence increasing consumption (and lowering savings) shift the curve to the right.

So far, we have considered the condition that aggregate demand equal aggregate income. From the economic circuit, we know that there is another condition, one that arises from the flow of money through the economy. Call the price level P and the number of units of money circulating in the economy the *quantity of money* or the *money stock*, M. The *velocity of money* is the average number of times a unit of money is used in a transaction during each period. As we have seen above, there is a flow of payments in the economy which mirrors the flow of goods and services, and it must be true that

$$M * v = P * Y$$

In words: The number of units of money multiplied by the velocity of money must equal the volume of monetary expenditures for final goods and services, which is aggregate income multiplied by the price level.

For a given quantity of money and a given velocity of money, we see immediately that aggregate income and, therefore, aggregate demand, must fall, if P rises. But how does this fall come about? At any point in time, the quantity of money is determined by the central bank. The velocity of money reflects the payment habits of the economy. The velocity of money is determined by how much money households and firms wish to hold and by the payments technology prevailing in the economy. Furthermore, the velocity of money rises when the real interest rate rises, and the velocity of money falls when the real interest rate falls. This is because a higher real interest rate means that people wish to hold more of their financial wealth in bonds and other interest-bearing instruments rather than in cash or checkable deposits. In contrast, when the real interest rate is low people tend to hold more cash to enjoy the convenience of it.

Now consider what happens if the price level rises. The right-hand side of the equation above is now larger than before. For a given stock of money, the velocity of money must also rise to restore equality. This requires an increase in the real interest rate. But when the real interest rate rises, aggregate demand falls and, as firms sell and produce fewer final goods and services, aggregate income falls. Thus, the right-hand side of the equation declines and the left-hand side rises until equality is restored. Conversely, when the price level falls, the real interest rate must fall to restore equality. When that happens, the velocity of money decreases and aggregate demand and aggregate income increase until equality is restored. *The condition that $M * v = P * Y$ induces a negative relationship between aggregate income and the price level.*

Note that this negative relationship between aggregate income and the price level works through the changes in the real interest rate. We can illustrate this mechanism graphically. Assume for a moment that aggregate income rises with the money stock M and the price level P unchanged. The equality of relationship $M * v = P * Y$ demands a rise in the real interest rate. Consider Figure A2. Here again we plot the real interest rate on the vertical axis and aggregate income on the horizontal axis. The positive relationship between the two we just discovered is shown by the solid,

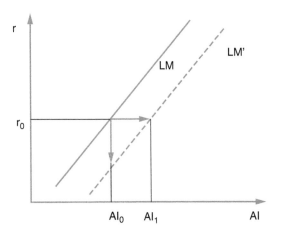

**Figure A2** The LM curve

upward sloping curve. We call this the LM curve. It shows that, when aggregate income rises, the real interest rate must also rise to make the velocity of money rise and maintain the equality of $M * v = P * Y$. Conversely, when aggregate income falls, the real interest rate falls so that the velocity of money decreases. For a given real interest rate $r_0$, the level of aggregate demand must be $AI_0$.

What happens if the money stock rises? For a given level of aggregate income, $M * v$ is now larger than $P * Y$. The real interest rate must fall in order to reduce the velocity of money. This is shown by the arrow pointing downward. Alternatively, for a given real interest rate, aggregate income must rise to restore equality. This is indicated by the arrow pointing to the right. Generally, the LM curve shifts to the right as indicated by the broken line LM'. The level of aggregate income corresponding to the same real interest rate as before is $AI_1$. Applying the same logic, a rise in the price level shifts the LM curve to the left leading to a rise in the real interest rate and/or a decline in aggregate income, while a decline in the price level shifts the LM curve to the right leading to a decline in the real interest rate and/or a rise in aggregate income.

Now let's put these points together: The IS curve shows how the real interest rate adjusts to make aggregate demand equal aggregate income. The LM curve shows how the real interest rate adjusts to make $M * v$ equal to $P * Y$. Put the two curves together into one diagram; see Figure A3. The point where they intersect is a combination of aggregate income and the real interest rate such that both conditions hold: aggregate demand equals aggregate income and $M * v$ equals $P * Y$. In Figure A3, we indicate such a point by $r^*$ and $AI^*$.

Note that this is the only point in the diagram which is consistent with the economic circuit in the sense that it fulfills the two fundamental equalities we started with *ex ante*, in the planning of households, the government, and firms. Points to the right of the IS curve have too little aggregate demand for a given level

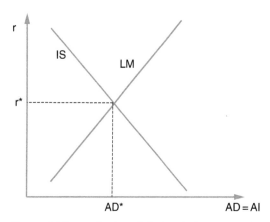

**Figure A3** Determination of the level of aggregate income

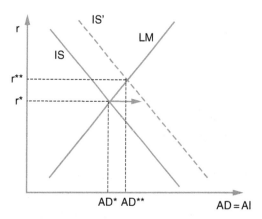

**Figure A4** An increase in government spending

of aggregate income. Points to the right of the LM curve have too low a velocity of money for a given aggregate income, money stock, and price level.

We are now ready to apply these concepts to changes in causal factors of aggregate demand. Consider Figure A4. Start from the point (r*, AI*) and assume that government spending increases. This, as we already know, shifts the IS curve to the right as indicated by the broken line IS'. At the same level of the interest rate, aggregate demand is now too large to fulfill the condition $M * v = P * Y$. As the LM curve does not change when government spending changes, the adjustment process requires the real interest rate to rise. In the process, we move up the LM curve until we reach the new intersection point (r**, AI**). At this point, aggregate income and aggregate demand are larger than before and so is the real interest rate. A cut in taxes, and improvements in business and consumer confidence, would have the same effects.

A rise in taxes, a cut in government expenditures, and declining business and household confidence would shift the IS curve to the left and result in lower aggregate income, aggregate demand, and a lower real interest rate.

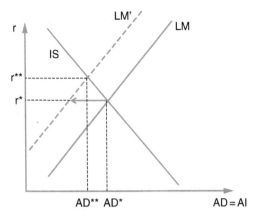

**Figure A5** A reduction in the money stock

Next, consider what happens when the price level rises. Consider Figure A5. As before, we start in the point (r*, AI*). As we know already, when the price level rises, the LM curve shifts to the left. At the initial interest rate, aggregate income is too large to fulfill $M*v = P*Y$. The real interest rate begins to rise to push up the velocity of money. In the adjustment process, we move up the IS curve until we hit the new intersection point of the two curves (r**, AI**). In this new point, aggregate income and aggregate demand are lower and the real interest rate is higher than before. A similar effect would result from a decline in the money stock. A decline in the price level or an increase in the money stock results in an increase in aggregate income and aggregate demand and a fall in the real interest rate.

Importantly, this analysis irmplies that there is a negative relationship between the price level and aggregate demand. This relationship works through the effect of a rise in the price level on the real interest rate (positive) and the effect of a rise in the real interest rate on the level of aggregate demand (negative).

## NOTES

1  www.bea.gov/newsreleases/national/gdp/gdpnewsrelease.htm
2  For example, the actual increase in real GDP between the second and the third quarter of 2017 was 0.79 percent. Taking 1.0079 to the power of four yields 1.032, the annualized growth rate is $100*(1.032-1)$.
3  Your professor might use the words *ceteris paribus* to describe a thought experiment that holds everything else constant.
4  https://fred.stlouisfed.org/series/MICH
5  www.imf.org/en/Publications/WEO/Issues/2017/04/04/world-economic-outlook-april-2017

# Aggregate Supply and Short-Run Equilibrium

Macroeconomic policy debates tend to focus on aggregate demand. When output is considered too low or unemployment is rising, policymakers, the media, and the public call on the Fed to cut interest rates or on the federal government to provide stimulus. When inflation is going up, the Fed is told to put it under control. We want fast solutions and the way to get them is by managing aggregate demand. Therefore, most of this book is devoted to aggregate demand.

But aggregate demand is not the whole story. Sometimes, households and businesses do not respond to low interest rates or fiscal stimulus in the way the Fed or the government would like, or their response is weak and slow. Furthermore, focusing on aggregate demand does not help when the economy is faced with changes in cost conditions such as energy or raw materials prices. And, finally, the government may try to increase aggregate demand and GDP by increasing government spending. But if this spending is financed by a rise in, say, income taxes, the government may see that people work less, because they get to keep less of an hour's wage. Real GDP may then rise less than hoped for and the fiscal stimulus primarily results in higher prices. Focusing on aggregate demand is also not helpful if we want to explain a country's level and growth of potential output, or its longer-term economic trend and standard of living. Adding aggregate supply to our understanding of aggregate demand allows for a complete approach to macroeconomic change and policy.

Now we turn to the supply side of the economy. This chapter introduces you to the determinants of aggregate supply. It is all about the quantity of goods and services the economy produces given its stock of productive capital, its stock of technological knowledge, and its labor force. In this chapter, we focus on short-run aggregate supply. Long-term developments of aggregate supply will be discussed in Chapters 6 and 7. We begin this chapter by reviewing the microeconomics of the firm that provides the building blocks for understanding aggregate supply. Then we move on to a full analysis of AS shocks and policies. This leads to a relationship between the price level and aggregate supply, which we call the *AS curve*. A discussion of short-term AS issues and policies will follow.

Once we understand aggregate supply and aggregate demand, we can put the two together and consider the macroeconomic equilibrium of aggregate supply and aggregate demand. This integrated AS–AD framework is designed to focus on changes in real output and prices and on the analysis and prediction of how the two react to changes in AS and AD policies as well as to changes in important variables such as energy prices, business and consumer confidence, and other factors.

A cousin of this framework is called the *Phillips curve* and highlights changes in the inflation rate and the unemployment rate instead of the levels of output and prices. We use the word "cousin" because the two frameworks are closely related. They are based on the same principles integrating aggregate supply and aggregate demand and they both focus on short-run changes and policies, but they look at the economy from different angles. The advantage of knowing both frameworks is that they expand our understanding to four key macroeconomic indicators: output, the price level, the unemployment rate, and the rate of inflation.

## 3.1  Macro Concepts and Analysis

Microeconomics generally aims its attention at a typical firm. By analyzing the constraints and motivations of a typical firm we can build the AS curve. We assume that firms attempt to maximize profits. But they have constraints between them and that million-dollar yacht. Constraints include such things as the price the market will bear, the wages paid to employees, taxes paid to the government, the size of their plant, the existing nature of technology, and the knowledge and training of their employees. In this chapter, we develop a framework explaining how aggregate supply changes in response to changes in these constraints in the short run. The short run is not a fixed time. Short run means that the firms find themselves with some fixed inputs and fixed costs. They can vary their production in the short run only by changing their use of variable inputs. Often labor is used as an example of a variable input, while capital is considered as fixed.

Mature firms generally face *short-run diminishing marginal productivity* of their variable inputs. This means that output increases when the amount of a variable input is increased, but the *additional* or *marginal* amounts of output become smaller and smaller with every *additional* or *marginal* unit of this variable input. For example, as more and more labor is applied to a fixed stock of capital, you should expect output to rise, but the increases diminish as more and more labor is used. You can turn this statement around and say: As more and more output is produced with a given capital stock, each additional unit of output needs a little more labor than the one produced before. Similarly, as more and more energy is used by a given labor force and applied to a given capital stock, output rises, but with decreasing increments. Or: As more and more output is produced with a given capital stock and labor force, each additional unit of output needs a little more energy input than the one produced before. And so on for all other variable inputs. Firms can produce more output, but, in the short run, diminishing marginal productivity implies that each extra unit they produce costs a little more than the one before it, because each one has a little more labor or energy or other variable input in it. Thus, we can go from talking about diminishing marginal productivity to *increasing marginal costs*. In the short run, the *additional* or *marginal* cost of an *additional* or *marginal* unit of output increases as output gets larger and larger. Firms can't simply produce all they want right away without incurring rising costs per unit.

If markets are sufficiently competitive, firms take the market prices of their products as given. In the short run, a profit-maximizing firm chooses the levels of production such that the marginal cost of production equals the market price of its product. This is easy to see: The output price is the firm's *marginal revenue*, the revenue earned by selling an additional unit of output. If the marginal revenue exceeded marginal cost, the firm could increase profit producing and selling an additional unit of output. If the marginal revenue was below marginal cost, the firm could increase profit by producing and selling one unit less. A profit maximum requires that marginal cost and marginal revenue are the same.

Now we can ask, how would the firm's output decision change, if the market set a higher price for its product, if all other key variables are constant? The answer is, it would produce more. Why? Starting from a profit maximum, if the output price rises, *marginal revenue* would be greater than marginal cost. The firm would see an opportunity to make higher profits. The firm would hire more labor and produce more output. If the new marginal cost is still below marginal revenue, the firm would increase its output further. This will continue until the marginal cost of producing an extra unit of output reaches the new marginal revenue. Going beyond that point would mean that marginal cost exceeds marginal revenue and profit falls. Thus, the process stops there. A reduction in price would have the opposite impact – it would lead to a decline in production. Thus, we can see that there is a positive relationship between the firm's level of output and the output price the firm can earn in the market. We call this relationship the short-run supply curve. It is upward sloping, meaning that output rises when the price rises.

Second, what would a firm do if its wages or cost of labor increased? Often, we just speak about wages, but we know that the firm's total cost of labor includes other things such as recruiting expenses, travel expenses, cost of training, the value of benefits and perquisites, and payroll taxes paid. In European countries, firms pay a part of their workers' social security and health insurance contributions, which make up another important part of the cost of labor there. Imagine a situation where nothing else but the cost of labor has changed. Workers are not more productive – they just cost more. The firm feels it cannot change its price without losing business to its competitors, but it can alter its output in response to the rise in wages. What would it do? We follow the same profit analysis. The rise in wages would cause marginal cost to exceed marginal revenue. Profits have decreased and are now suboptimal. Hiring less labor and producing less output would reduce marginal costs back to their lower level in equality with marginal revenue. The firm has lower revenues, but the profits are the maximum given the new situation with the higher wages.

Third, assume that oil prices increase. Oil has many uses in production. For one thing, oil is an important source of energy. Oil is an important component of a firm's transportation and travel expenses. Whether sending goods on highways or sales personnel on airlines, many companies' transportation costs are affected by changes in oil prices. Finally, many products use oil as a raw material. When oil prices increase, they can impact many firms in many ways by raising their marginal costs. A rise in oil prices, like an increase in wages, increases the cost of production and raises a firm's marginal cost. The optimal response is to bring marginal costs back down by using less oil and reducing output. This analysis equally relates to the costs of other primary resources or intermediate goods purchased by firms to produce.

More generally:

Anything that leads to an increase (a reduction) in marginal cost leads to a reduction (an increase) in supply. Anything that leads to an increase (a reduction) in marginal revenue leads to an increase (a reduction) in supply.

While increasing marginal costs are to be expected in the short run, we also know that the firm is always trying to avoid this constraint in the longer term. If it is to be competitive, it must find ways to reduce cost per unit. How could the firm increase output without incurring those rising costs per unit? By finding ways to improve its fixed inputs, the firm can raise the productivity of their variable inputs. For example, the firm can:

* do more research and development (R&D) internally or adopt better technologies developed by other firms;
* buy newer and better machinery and equipment;
* train its workers better.

Furthermore, the firm can also make efforts to reduce the cost of its inputs. For example, it may relocate parts of its production to places or countries where wages for workers with the same skills and training are lower than at home, or it may find better and cheaper supplies of energy or raw materials. These, however, are long-run considerations and we will discuss more of that in Chapter 7.

### 3.1.1  The Short-Run AS Sector

We now apply these basic microeconomic ideas to macro. Recall that in macroeconomics, we do not focus on individual consumers or firms. Aggregate demand represents the combined demand for newly produced final goods and services and fixed assets from all households, firms, and the government. (Remember that we treat changes in inventories as part of firms' investment demand.) Aggregate supply is its supply counterpart. It is the combined supply of newly produced final goods and services and fixed assets by all firms and the government – recall that the government produces government services such as the internal and external security it demands. The idea of how the nation's aggregate output responds to changes in the price level, taxes, and other factors is simply the "adding up" of how all the individual firms respond. If the typical firm responds in the ways described above, then we expect that the nation's aggregate output responds similarly. It is unnecessary and oversimplistic to think that every single firm responds in exactly the same way – but it is okay to believe that many firms behave like the average firm and that the others tend to cancel out each other's deviations from the average.

From the discussion above, there are three categories of variables affecting aggregate supply:

- factors impacting business marginal revenues: prices, sales taxes, profit taxes;
- factors impacting marginal production cost: wages, energy prices, raw materials prices, interest rates, taxes on labor, government subsidies;
- factors impacting productivity: R&D, education, physical infrastructure, IT.

We have already considered the most important of these factors in our microeconomic discussion. Government policies might impact AS decisions, too. An increase in payroll tax rates directly affects the cost of labor and has the effects discussed above. Legislated minimum wages have the same effect if they are binding, i.e., above-market wages. Government regulations of the labor market may increase the cost of hiring and dismissing workers adds to the cost of labor. Government taxes or subsidies and import tariffs on other variable inputs such as raw materials also directly affect the marginal cost of production with the effects explained above. In contrast, taxes and subsidies on the use of capital or subsidies on R&D activities do not affect aggregate output in the short run because the firm cannot change its capital stock nor its technology in the short run. This does not mean that such taxes and subsidies are unimportant, only that they take more time until their effects on aggregate supply are realized. We will come back to that in a later chapter.

## 3.1.2  The AS Curve

We express the preceding thoughts about the supply side of the economy by constructing a relationship between the price level and real GDP from the supply side. Assuming all other factors remain the same, what happens to aggregate supply when the price level goes up? All other factors remaining the same includes that marginal cost remains the same. If the price level increases, marginal revenues increase, and it is profitable for firms to increase output. They will ask their workers to work overtime, hire additional workers, and buy additional amounts of raw materials and energy, all to increase production. Aggregate supply increases, but the extra output is produced at higher marginal cost. Firms will increase production up to the point where marginal cost equals marginal revenue again.

What happens to aggregate supply, if the price level falls? By the same argument and assuming again that all other factors remain the same, firms will reduce output. Marginal cost will fall until it is equal to marginal revenue again.

Thus, from the supply side of the economy, there is a positive relationship between real GDP and the price level. We call this relationship the AS curve. Figure 3.1 shows an AS curve. For a given price level $P_0$, the AS curve indicates which level of output equates marginal revenues with marginal costs. The economy will produce a real GDP of $AS_0$. The positive slope indicates that aggregate supply rises as the price level increases and aggregate supply falls as the price level falls. This corresponds to movements along the curve as indicated by the blue arrows.

As in the case of the AD curve, we distinguish between movements along the AS curve and shifts of the AS curve. Consider a rise in wages. As we saw above, firms will respond to the resulting rise in marginal cost by cutting output. Thus, the level of output corresponding to the price level $P_0$ is now lower than $AS_0$. We have a leftward shift of the AS curve as shown by the broken line AS' in Figure 3.2. At the price level $P_0$, real GDP falls to $AS_1$.

Conversely, a decline in wages leads to a rightward shift in the AS curve (the dotted line AS"), meaning that the same price level will be compatible with a larger level of real GDP. In the same vein, an increase in government taxes on production reduces firms' marginal revenues at a given output price. The firms react by cutting output and the AS curve shifts to the left.

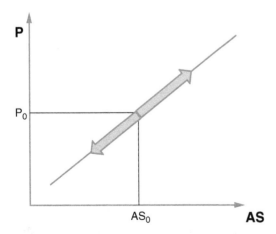

**Figure 3.1** The AS curve

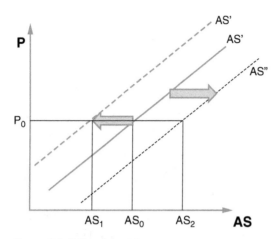

**Figure 3.2** Shifts of the AS curve

A common way to refer to shifts in aggregate supply is through changes in unit labor costs (ULCs). ULCs are defined as total wages times employment divided by output, or, equivalently, the average wage rate divided by average labor productivity (output per worker). ULCs can change because wages change or because labor productivity changes. A rise in labor productivity means that workers are able to produce more output for any given amount of labor and capital. Productivity changes are usually thought of as long-run factors, but they can occur in the short run. Imagine a new government regulation or an energy shortage that makes workers less productive. With wages unchanged, this decline in productivity means an increase in ULCs and in marginal cost. Additional units of output now cost more to produce, and firms will want to cut output as a result. The AS curve shifts leftward.

Finally, the AS curve also shifts with factors impacting marginal revenues at a given price level. For example, the imposition of a sales tax or the cutting of business subsidies reduces marginal revenues with the result that businesses cut back production. The AS curve shifts to the left.

Generally:

Anything that lowers marginal cost at a given price level leads to a rightward shift of the AS curve; anything that increases marginal cost at a given price level leads to a leftward shift of the AS curve.

Anything that lowers marginal revenue at a given price level leads to a leftward shift of the AS curve; anything that raises marginal revenue at a given price level leads to a rightward shift of the AS curve.

### 3.1.3   Working with the Data: IMF *World Economic Outlook* October 2017

Table 3.1 is an excerpt from table B3 from Appendix B of the October 2017 IMF *World Economic Outlook* (WEO).[1] It reports the IMF's analysis of changes in ULCs

**Table 3.1** Hourly earnings, productivity, and ULCs (annual % change)

|  | 2014 | 2015 | 2016 |
|---|---|---|---|
| **Hourly earnings** | | | |
| United States | 2.8 | 2.5 | 0.7 |
| Euro area | 1.2 | 1.2 | 1.6 |
| Japan | 1.3 | −0.2 | 2.6 |
| United Kingdom | 2.0 | 1.3 | 2.1 |
| **Productivity** | | | |
| United States | 0.1 | −0.6 | 0.2 |
| Euro area | 2.2 | 1.3 | 1.3 |
| Japan | 2.1 | −3.1 | 1.5 |
| United Kingdom | 3.5 | −2.1 | −1.0 |
| **ULCs** | | | |
| United States | 2.7 | 3.1 | 0.6 |
| Euro area | −0.9 | −0.1 | 0.2 |
| Japan | −0.8 | 3.0 | 1.1 |
| United Kingdom | −1.4 | 3.5 | 3.2 |

*Source*: IMF, *World Economic Outlook* October 2017.

and their causes – changes in hourly earnings and in productivity – in some of the major advanced countries around the world.

The table shows that unit labor increased significantly in the US in 2014 and 2015, driven by increases in wages that were not offset by increases in productivity. In contrast, the euro area saw a small decline in the same period. Japan and the UK also experienced declining ULCs in 2014 but rising ULCs in 2015.

At the international level, a country's manufacturing firms lose competitiveness against the manufacturing firms of another country, if their ULCs increase relative to those of the other country. For example, US ULCs increased by 4.1 percent relative to the UK in 2014, indicating a sizeable loss in competitiveness. This loss was driven by a strong increase in US hourly earnings and a strong increase in productivity in the UK.

## 3.2   AS Policy

AS policy is defined as a government policy designed to impact the aggregate supply sector. This means that the target of an aggregate supply policy is to change business costs or productivity. AS policies can increase real GDP and reduce the price level. Here is a caveat: Government policies targeting some other goal can have unintended negative side effects on aggregate supply. For example, the government may decide to introduce general health insurance to give people better protection against the calamities of falling ill. But compulsory health insurance will affect wage costs, if the insurance premiums are tied to the labor incomes of the newly insured persons. Wage costs rise, and this will have negative AS effects. As a result, policy debates often turn into debates about the unintended AS effects of what governments intend to do. Of course, when such negative AS effects do occur, it does not follow that the government should not undertake such a policy. Governments, however, are well advised to take such effects into consideration and business managers are well advised to watch out for them.

Naturally, the opposite can happen as well. In Europe, governments have been under pressure for many years to lift tight and complicated labor market regulations to reduce labor costs and improve aggregate supply. Such policies often meet the criticism that they leave workers, especially young and low-skilled members of the workforce, unprotected against the profit-maximizing actions of powerful corporations. More generally, AS policies often interfere with other spheres of public policy and can be politically controversial as a result.

AS policies to boost output sometimes have advantages over AD policies. Consider the following examples:

- *Situation 1:* Wage increases have pushed up marginal cost relative to marginal revenue. An appropriate antidote would be a policy designed to reduce marginal cost, such as a cut in payroll taxes.
- *Situation 2:* The country is in a *stagflation* situation – with high inflation and a negative output gap. AD policy could lead to higher output, but only at the cost of even higher inflation. AS policy involves no such trade-off because it improves both output and high inflation.
- *Situation 3:* A persistent negative output gap. AD policy could help but only at the cost of severe price level increases. Combining an expansionary AD policy with an appropriate AS policy would have a double whammy on increasing output while the AS policy offset any increases in prices.

In each of these situations, a policy designed to reduce business costs and increase business productivity would have the desired impact of increasing real GDP while simultaneously lowering prices. In the next section we discuss the policy tools required for this purpose.

## 3.2.1 AS Policy Tools

Until the 1980 US presidential election, the idea of AS policy was widely unknown. While many of its elements had clearly been used many times before, the notion of AS policy had hardly ever been explained to the public, and, therefore, was not well understood. This changed with the election of Ronald Reagan in the US and Margaret Thatcher as prime minister in the UK around the same time. Reagan and Thatcher inherited a recessionary world with very high inflation. Therefore, the setting was just right to try this novel approach. Because aggregate supply was not well known, it was very controversial. Competing against Reagan for the Republican presidential nomination in 1979, George Bush called it *voodoo economics*. Others called AS policy a *Trojan horse*. Some critics simply saw it as a way for Reagan to reward his rich friends. *Trickle-down* were words suggesting that the rich would get most of the rewards and the rest of the population would get some of the crumbs.

Despite these criticisms, both Reagan and Thatcher were able to push through programs based on AS policies. Below we describe some examples of AS policies recalling that the unifying concept is to reduce cost relative to productivity. Some of these policies can be expected to show results relatively quickly, while others require longer periods of time before their effects appear, because they operate through changes in market structures and institutions and adjustments in capital investment.

*Deregulation of business and privatization of government-owned enterprises:* By deregulating such major industries as transportation, communications, or banking the government hopes to break up monopolistic market structure and create more competition that would lead to more entrepreneurship, higher innovation, and reductions in costs and prices. Similarly, government-owned enterprises often enjoy monopoly positions in their markets and act more like public administrations than like private businesses. Privatization aims at creating more competition.

*Deregulation of labor markets:* By reducing administrative obstacles and costs of hiring and dismissing workers, governments seek to increase firms' willingness to hire more labor when demand increases and to react more flexibly to changing market conditions. This may also include attempts at curbing labor union power. For example, in 1981, President Reagan threatened to fire thousands of air traffic controllers unless they ended an illegal strike. This highly visible action against a union of federal government employees marked the beginning of a significant decline in union power in the US. In the UK, the Thatcher government refused to give in to the demands of the coal miners' union in a very long and violent strike in winter 1984–5, thus setting the stage for a decline in union power in the UK, too. Curbing union power gave businesses more flexibility in hiring and led to more modest wage increases in subsequent years.

*Lower tax rates on high incomes:* In most countries the majority of national savings come either from businesses or from individuals earning high incomes. Lowering tax rates on the highest incomes is expected to reduce the penalty on saving and create incentives for more saving. Why is that an AS policy? Because increased saving should lead to lower interest rates and more investment spending which would lead to gains in business productivity, output, and employment.

*Reduced capital gains taxes:* By reducing the penalty on capital gains, more investors would be willing to take more risk. This might also induce more saving.

*Accelerated depreciation and various subsidies aimed at capital spending:* By allowing firms to accelerate their capital depreciation they could gain faster benefits from new capital. By giving subsidies for direct purchases of capital, firms would be rewarded for buying more capital. The new and better capital should translate into higher business productivity.

*Lower income tax rates:* While this appears on the surface to be an AD policy, President Reagan argued that the emphasis on tax *rates* illustrated that households have choices about how much they want to work. Entrepreneurs have choices about how much risk to take. Lowering tax rates raises the reward to work and effort and risk relative to leisure. In 1979 the highest marginal tax rates in the US were at about 70 percent. Reagan believed that lowering them to less than 30 percent would greatly enhance the reward for risk-taking and work.

*Business credits and special write-offs for hiring or training:* By reducing the cost of hiring, the cost effects of government regulations were partially offset. Subsidies for training workers were meant to raise productivity.

## 3.2.2    International Application: US Competitiveness

An article by William Poole and Howard J. Wall argues that the US has much more entrepreneurship than other countries for a variety of reasons. The implication is that supply responses are quicker and involve a greater number of companies.[2] Why does the US have a much higher percentage of people who want to be entrepreneurs? The authors focus on four factors:

1. The US makes it very easy to start a business – it can take as little as four days and USD 210. In contrast, it takes thirty-one days and USD 3,500 in Japan. Whereas there is no stipulation that US entrepreneurs have any capital, Belgium requires a minimum equivalent to 75 percent of the country's per-capita income. In Germany and Greece, the amount of capital necessary exceeds each nation's average per-capita income.
2. US financial markets are competitive and allow banks and investors to take risk.
3. The World Bank believes that US firms have great flexibility in hiring and firing workers. They face fewer regulations that relate to conditions of employment. In contrast, the article singles out several country practices that promote labor market rigidity: Belgium for prohibiting fixed-term employment contracts, France for the 35-hourwork week regulation, Germany for mandatory closing times for shops, and various European countries for constraining allowable grounds for employee dismissal, third-party approval for layoffs, and high mandated severance pay.
4. The authors believe that high tax rates place high financial burdens on entrepreneurial firms. They cite OECD evidence for total tax rates showing that, in 2002, Japan (27.1%) was the only country with a lower tax burden (total taxes

as a percentage of GDP) than the US (29.6%). Sweden (54.2%) had the highest burden, followed by Denmark (48.8%), Belgium (45.5%), France (45.3%), Italy (42%), the Netherlands (41.4%), and Germany (37.9%).

Despite the much higher incidence of entrepreneurship in the US the authors believe the US could do even better. They cite several suggestions to improve supply responses and economic dynamism including reducing the burden of some environmental regulations, reductions in healthcare expenses, and tort law reform.

*If you are so smart, then why aren't you rich?* The question is, if AS policy is so good, then why doesn't it have a better reputation? There are several parts to this answer. For one thing, Reagan's AS policy was watered down. For another, only a partial program was legislated. In Reagan's case, within a year or two some of the key provisions were changed. Like all history, this record is subject to several interpretations and differences of opinion. Since Reagan, we have seen piecemeal aspects of AS policy incorporated into larger more diverse fiscal programs. In short, it is hard to find clear evidence of the effects of any AS policies and even harder to find unambiguous opinions about their effectiveness.

Furthermore, as pointed out above, the politics of aggregate supply policies can be terrible. As the terms *Trojan horse* and *trickle-down* suggest, the most salient aspect of AS policy is its direct impact on wealthy individuals and companies. Even if the deregulation of industries like telecommunications in the US and railroads in Britain and privatization of government-owned enterprises often involves the slaughtering of some fat cows, it is true that many policies designed to raise productivity relative to business costs will indeed make wealthy individuals and companies better off. The unhappy political fact is that it is easier to discredit AS policies as benefitting the rich alone than it is to explain their advantages for the general population. One must have an economics course under one's belt to understand and explain why AS policy might be best for the country. But all it takes is the shortest sound bite to show quite vividly that only a very tiny percent of the direct benefits will go to poor people. It is a tough row to hoe.

### 3.2.3 International Application: Germany's Hartz Reforms

In the second half of the 1990s, Germany was generally considered the *sick man of Europe* meaning that its economy suffered from persistent low growth and high unemployment. Real GDP growth had been trailing at an average of 1.47 percent in the decade from 1993 to 2002. The rate of unemployment increased from 6.6 percent in 1992 to 8.6 percent in 2002, meaning that over five million people were unemployed, and the rate was expected to increase further. A large part of that was permanent unemployment, i.e., people being out of work for more than a year. Since the country had surrendered its monetary policy to the European Central Bank (ECB) by adopting the euro, monetary policy could not help. Fiscal policy was constrained by already large deficits of 3.1 percent of GDP in 2001 and almost 4 percent of GDP in 2002. Public debt had increased from 41.6 percent of GDP in 1992 to almost 60 percent in 2002. Thus, fiscal policy was not free to create more aggregate demand to bring unemployment down.

Before this dire background, then German Chancellor Gerhard Schröder, a social democrat, proposed his *Agenda 2010* featuring far-reaching reforms of the German labor market and social transfer system. The reforms aimed at increasing the incentive of unemployed people to find jobs by reducing unemployment benefits and their duration, by forcing unemployed persons to actively seek jobs and accept job offers even if they were less attractive than previously held jobs, and by modernizing Germany's labor market administration.

Agenda 2010 was a stunning success. Unemployment began to turn around in 2005 and came down from 11 percent to 5.4 percent in 2012. During the Great Recession of 2008–9, Germany stood out as the country seeing almost no increase in unemployment (from 7.4 percent in 2008 to 7.7 percent in 2009) and further declines soon after. Germany's real GDP growth rate had recovered to 3.9 percent in 2006 and 3.4 percent in 2007. It took a steep dive in 2008 and 2009 (0.8 percent and −5.6 percent, respectively) but recovered to almost 4 percent in 2010 and 2011.

Nevertheless, Agenda 2010 turned out to be politically fatal for the Schröder government. Increasing dissatisfaction with supply-side policies among its traditional social democrat voters caused Schröder's party to consistently lose regional elections in 2004 and 2005. In view of that, Schröder stepped down in 2005 and a new government led by the conservative party under Angela Merkel came into power. That Merkel reaped the benefits of her opponent's policies is an irony of history. It underscores the political difficulties of adopting policies that take a long time to bear fruit.

## 3.3  Macroeconomic Equilibrium: Putting Aggregate Demand and Aggregate Supply Together

In this section, we bring together the ideas we have developed about aggregate demand and aggregate supply. What we do now could be called *macroeconomic equilibrium analysis*. The purpose is to better understand all the things that impact the two key macroeconomic variables: real GDP and the price level. *Changes in real GDP and the price level are best understood as the result of changes in aggregate demand and aggregate supply and their interaction.*

A *macroeconomic equilibrium* is a situation in which there is no tendency for the price level or for real GDP to change, meaning that any past changes have had plenty of time to impact real GDP and the price level and all their consequences have worked

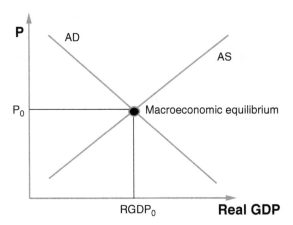

**Figure 3.3** Macroeconomic equilibrium

themselves through the economy. At this equilibrium, aggregate supply equals aggregate demand. That is, the price level is such that the level of aggregate demand equals the level of aggregate supply. The quantity of output demanded by households, businesses, the government and foreigners together equals the quantity of output firms are willing to produce in all markets. We have already discussed briefly why a situation where aggregate demand does not equal aggregate supply cannot prevail for long in an economy – either output is produced to be thrown away or the economy spends more than it can afford. Without going into any detail, note that the macroeconomic equilibrium implies that all the identities noted in the economic circuit hold *ex ante*. The equilibrium makes the decisions and plans of thousands of different households and businesses compatible with one another.

In Figure 3.3, the macroeconomic equilibrium is shown to be the intersection of the AD curve with the AS curve and marked by a black dot. Note that we now have real GDP on the horizontal axis, because at the intersection of the two curves aggregate supply, aggregate demand, and aggregate income all coincide in one level of real GDP.

Is there any hope that such an equilibrium exists in the real world? Or, to ask the same question in a slightly different way: Starting from a macroeconomic equilibrium and assuming that some causal factor shifts the AD or AS curve, is there any hope that the economy would find a new macroeconomic equilibrium? The honest answer to this question relies partly on science, while partly it depends on your worldview. Science can identify the conditions under which a macroeconomic equilibrium can prevail, but it can neither prove nor disprove that the US economy is in a macroeconomic equilibrium at a given point in time. Worldviews involve beliefs about whether a market system will find and settle on an equilibrium. Such beliefs are part of our political convictions and are the object of public debates and political elections. *Conservative* analysts, commentators and policymakers typically assume that the market system is robust in the sense that, after some shock or disturbance, it will return to a macroeconomic equilibrium all by itself. *Liberal* and *left-leaning* analysts, commentators and policymakers typically think that the market system is not robust in that sense and needs the assistance of government policies to return to an equilibrium. *Eclectic* analysts, commentators, and policymakers think that conservatives and liberals are both sometimes right and sometimes wrong, and that all depends on the situation.

What's so special about macroeconomic equilibrium? The answer is that it gives us a tool to analyze and a framework to predict co-movements of real GDP and the price level in response to changes in other macroeconomic factors. Starting from an equilibrium position, we first determine whether such changes in other factors would lead to a shift in the AD curve or a shift in the AS curve. Then we apply the relevant shift to see how real GDP and the price level respond. The only justification for using the concept of macroeconomic equilibrium is its usefulness for understanding and predicting economic developments. But is it really that useful? The answer to that question has two dimensions. One is practical experience. Try it out and you will see. The other is competition. Check to see if there are alternative frameworks not relying on macroeconomic equilibrium that work better.

Now let's see how we can use macroeconomic equilibrium. In the next section, we analyze the impact of two kinds of *shocks* on aggregate supply and aggregate demand and their effects on real GDP and the price level. A *shock* is a change in one of the causal factors on the AD and the AS side of the economy which is not itself a reaction to a macroeconomic development. For example, an oil price hike caused by military conflicts in the Middle East would be an oil price shock. In contrast, an oil price hike caused by an increase in firms' demand for oil following an increase in aggregate demand would not be considered to be a shock.

### 3.3.1  Short-Run Supply Shocks

Consider a sudden increase in crude oil prices as an example of an oil price shock:

- Above we argued that this should cause a reduction in aggregate supply – that is, the increase in business costs would lead to lower employment and output at the initial price level. In Figure 3.4, the AS curve shifts to the left as indicated by the blue arrow and the curve labeled AS'. At the initial price level $P_0$, aggregate supply is now less than aggregate demand. Find the level of output firms would produce at the initial price level, $P_0$.
- As firms begin to reduce output, the markets for goods and services are disrupted.
- This aggregate shortage leads to pressure for the price level to rise.
- A rise in the price level reduces aggregate demand toward the lower level of aggregate supply. At the same time, the rise in the price level makes firms willing to produce more than at the price level $P_0$. We move along the AD curve until the

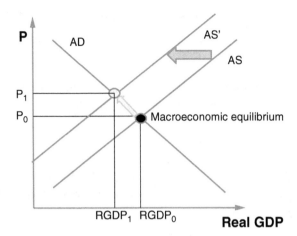

**Figure 3.4** A negative supply shock

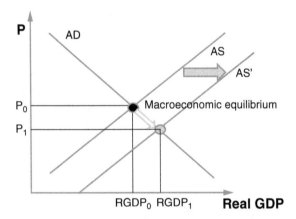

**Figure 3.5** A positive supply shock

new intersection with the AS curve is reached. This is indicated by the light-blue arrow.

- The result is a new macroeconomic equilibrium indicated by the light-blue dot. It comes with a higher price level, $P_1$, and a lower real GDP, $Y_1$.

Next, consider a reduction in the cost of labor due to a cut in payroll taxes:

- The tax cut is tantamount to a reduction in marginal cost and leads to an increase in employment and output. In Figure 3.5, the AS curve shifts to the right as indicated by the blue arrow and the line labeled AS'.
- At the initial price level $P_0$, aggregate supply becomes larger than aggregate demand.
- This excess of supply over demand leads to a decreasing price level.
- The lower price level increases aggregate demand as we move along the AD curve. This is indicated by the light-blue arrow.

- The result is a new macroeconomic equilibrium with a lower price level, $P_1$, and higher real GDP, $Y_1$, in the intersection of the AD curve with the AS' curve and the light-blue dot.

Studying the interactions of aggregate demand and aggregate supply following a supply shock, we can determine their effects on real GDP and the price level.

### 3.3.2    Short-Run Demand Shocks

Now we turn to factors impacting aggregate demand. One example of a demand shock would be an increase in consumer confidence that makes consumers increase their spending on consumption goods.

Consider the effects of such an increase as shown in Figure 3.6.

- The increase in consumer confidence increases aggregate demand at the initial price level $P_0$. In Figure 3.6 this is a shift of the AD curve to the right as shown by the blue arrow and the AD' curve.
- As a result, aggregate demand now exceeds aggregate supply at the initial price level. The price level begins to rise to restore equilibrium.
- The rise in the price level increases marginal revenue relative to marginal costs and creates a profit incentive for firms to hire more labor and increase output. Aggregate supply rises in a move along the AS curve shown by the light-blue arrow.
- The end result is that consumer confidence is higher, the new price level, $P_1$, is higher, and real GDP is higher. The new equilibrium is shown by the light-blue dot at the intersection of the AS and the AD' curves.

Note that we have just seen a wonderful story of self-fulfilling expectations. We started by saying that consumer confidence increased, i.e., consumers feel better and more optimistic about the future. We ended by saying that real GDP was higher, which means that households have higher incomes to spend on consumer goods,

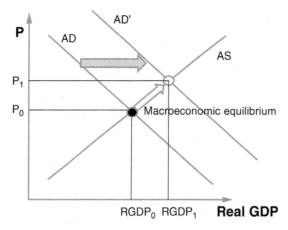

Figure 3.6 A positive demand shock

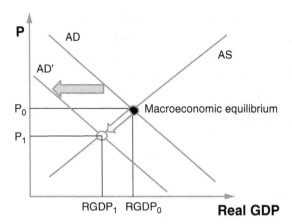

**Figure 3.7** A negative demand shock

employment has increased, and people are generally better off. Wow! Expecting a better economy makes the economy improve. Improving business confidence could do the same trick by inducing a rise in business investment. It will not always be so easy, but expectations can have powerful effects in an economy. But here is a catch: Pessimistic consumers or businesspeople can drag down the economy. It is better to be happy than to feel down.

Next, let us look at the impact of a cut in government expenditures. Consider Figure 3.7.

- Due to reduced government spending aggregate demand is now lower at the initial price level $P_0$ than before. This is a shift of the AD curve to the left, indicated by the blue arrow and the AD' curve.
- At the initial price level, aggregate supply is now larger than aggregate demand.
- The excess of supply over demand creates pressure on prices. The price level begins to fall.
- The decline in the price level means that marginal revenues fall, causing businesses to cut back production. We move along the AS curve until the new intersection with the AD' curve. This is shown by the light-blue arrow and the light-blue dot is the new equilibrium.
- At the new equilibrium, the price level, $P_1$, is lower, and output, real GDP$_1$, is lower than before.

Once again, we have used the interaction of aggregate demand and aggregate supply to figure out the impact of these shocks on real GDP and the price level.

### 3.3.3   Wages and the Price Level

So far, we have analyzed the reaction of aggregate supply and aggregate demand to supply-and-demand shocks assuming all other relevant variables remain the same. That includes wages. The upward-sloping AS curve says that firms will increase output as the price level increases assuming wages will remain the same. But, is it reasonable to assume that wages will remain unchanged when the price level increases? Probably not! The reason is that, when the price level rises and wages remain the same, *real* wages fall. The real wage is the ratio of the wage rate in dollars and the price level. From the point of view of a firm, a falling real wage is just another way of saying that marginal cost falls below marginal revenue. But from the workers' point of view, the real wage represents the purchasing power of an hour of work, and a falling real wage means that workers receive less in terms of final goods and services per hour of work than before. It seems obvious, then, that workers are not interested in high dollar wages *per se*. They are interested in how much they can buy with their wages, i.e. in high *real* wages.

Most employment arrangements are covered by contracts which fix a dollar wage rate for a certain period of time. This means that, at the time of signing the contract, workers do not know what the price level and, therefore, the purchasing power of their dollar wages will be during the period when they work. However, they will be locked into a set dollar wage rate for that period. Once that period is over, however, and there is a new round of wage negotiations, workers will demand compensation for any changes in the price level during the previous period. Furthermore, it is plausible that workers form expectations about future changes in the price level at the time when they negotiate their wages. For example, if the price level was 100 in 2018 and workers expect a rate of inflation of 4 percent, they would expect the price level to move to 104 during 2019. They would then face a decline in their real wages during 2019, if they accept the same dollar wage rate for 2019 as for 2018. To maintain a stable real wage, they would have to ask for a 4 percent wage increase.

Now consider the case of a positive AD shock. Suppose that workers did not expect an increase in the price level during the period under consideration. We already know what happens. The price level rises as the AD curve shifts out. Firms see their profits increase and hire additional workers to benefit from the situation, producing more output until their marginal costs equal prices again.

Now suppose that, in the next round of wage negotiations, workers demand a wage increase compensating them for the unexpected loss in purchasing power of their wages and that they obtain it. This means that marginal costs increase. The AS curve shifts to the left. As that happens, the price level rises again and real GDP declines relative to the equilibrium before wages reacted.

We can illustrate this argument graphically using our AS and AD diagrams (see Figure 3.8). Initially, aggregate demand and aggregate supply correspond to the curves $AD_0$ and $AS_0$, respectively. The economy is at an equilibrium price level $P_0$. Suppose that the AD curve shifts outward to $AD_1$ (gray arrow). Since wages remain unchanged initially, the AS curve remains the same and the economy moves to the intersection of $AS_0$ and $AD_1$. The price level rises to $P_1$. Output increases to real $GDP_1$.

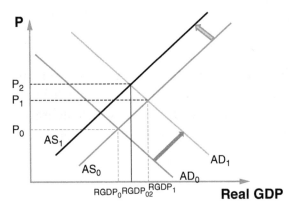

**Figure 3.8** Wage reactions to an AD shock

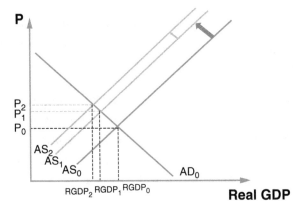

**Figure 3.9** Wage reactions to an AS shock

Since dollar wages do not change, real wages are lower than before. If workers demand compensation for that, the AS curve shifts to $AS_1$ after the next round of wage negotiations. This shift is indicated by the blue arrow. Real GDP declines to real $GDP_2$ and the price level rises to $P_2$.

Now consider what happens after a negative AS shock. Initially, the AS curve shifts to the left, from $AS_0$ to $AS_1$ in Figure 3.9. The price level rises to $P_1$ and real GDP falls. In the next round of wage negotiations, workers will demand compensation for the reduced purchasing power of their wages, leading to another leftward shift of the AS curve, to $AS_2$. The price level rises again, to $P_2$ and real GDP falls further.

We learn from this discussion that the reaction of wages to changes in the price level modifies the effects of AD and AS shocks over time.

When wages react to changes in the price level, the output effects of AD shocks become smaller and their price level effects are amplified.

When wages react to changes in the price level, the output effects and the price level effects of AS shocks are amplified.

We return to this argument later when we discuss the long-run effects of AD policies in Chapter 6.

Note, finally, that, if workers expect a future expansion of aggregate demand and an increase in the price level with it, the short-run AS curve will shift to the left already today. If the expansion of aggregate demand does not happen, output will fall and the price level will rise. Inasmuch as that is undesirable, governments should be careful not to create false expectations about future policies.

## BOX 3.1 DIFFERENCE OF OPINION: INFLATION EXPECTATIONS AND SHORT-RUN AD POLICIES

At the center of many controversies in macroeconomics is how workers and other suppliers form expectations of future inflation. The results of short-run stabilization policies depend very much on how these expectations are formed.

Early models assumed that workers had fixed expectations. One can rationalize such expectations in more than one way. It could mean that workers are fixed into contracts that prevent them from asking for higher wages when prices are rising. It could also mean that workers, having lived through recent periods of very low inflation, simply do not invest in learning about inflation. In either case, the result is that an expansionary aggregate demand that raises prices will reduce actual real wages and raise employment and output.

We used to use words like: If policymakers can "fool" the workers, then they can use monetary and fiscal policy to expand the economy. Of course, workers will eventually learn that they have been fooled and react in subsequent periods. This explains why economic expansions are often followed by contractions as workers demand higher wages and the AS curve shifts leftward. In terms of the Phillips curve (see section 3.4) this explains how policymakers can drive the unemployment rate below the natural rate – and why the Phillips curve would subsequently shift leftward.

At the other extreme are rational expectations models. John F. Muth believed that subjective expectations would not waste valuable information and would be formed according to the same ideas that generate actual outcomes.[3] Thus, workers could not be fooled systematically. While suppliers' expectations of future inflation might not always be perfect, they would not allow for systematic exploitation. The upshot for macroeconomic policy is that policymakers could not systematically fool the workers and their inflation expectations and wage demands would not lag price increases. In rational expectations models the AS curve shifts (leftward) at the same time as the AD curve shifts rightward. The Phillips curve would essentially be vertical.

Between these extremes are adaptive expectations in which suppliers attempt to keep up with future inflation but are always a bit behind. Thus, wage demands today reflect current and future expected changes in prices, but not fully. Wage demands catch up more quickly than in fixed expectations models though more slowly than in rational expectations models. With adaptive expectations, policymakers can impact short-run changes in aggregate demand but the effectiveness is less and more fleeting.

As important as expectations formation is to macroeconomic results, it is not surprising that the concept has been tested numerous times, with different approaches, and with different applications. Do workers explicitly invest resources in price expectations? Are their expectations rational or adaptive? Can policymakers systematically impact the economy with AD policies? We know of no definitive answers to these critical questions that hold over time and geography. Nevertheless, these expectations are fundamental to policy impacts and we try to accommodate them as we discuss policy. Difference of opinion about the use of monetary and fiscal policy will always at least in part be driven by these different assumptions about inflation expectations.

### 3.3.4  Working with the Data: Oil Price Increases in 2004 and Beyond

The cover page of the July 2004 edition of the *Annual International Economic Trends* (of the St. Louis Fed) had this title "Will Oil Prices Choke Growth?" The author, Christopher J. Neely, concluded by answering his question with a big *no!* [4]

First, note that Neely certainly did view oil price increases as adverse shocks that have large negative impacts on aggregate supply and real GDP. Nevertheless, for several reasons he did not believe that the 2004 increase in oil prices would have a large negative impact. He compared several factors in 2004 to time periods in the past when oil shocks did have large impacts.

- First, he noted that these increases in oil prices came as a result of a strong economy and large increases in oil demand. It is harder to damage a strong economy.
- Second, while oil prices reached into the range above USD 40, the increase was small in relative terms. It was nothing like the tripling or quadrupling of oil prices in 1973 and 1979.
- Third, he found that the US now uses much less oil per dollar of GDP. That is another way of saying that oil is a smaller part of the economy – and thus oil price changes impact aggregate supply much less than in the past.
- Finally, he concluded that policymakers learned from past experiences how not to react to oil prices.

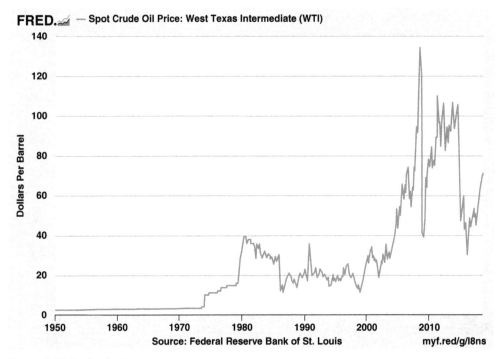

Figure 3.10 Crude oil prices

*Source*: Federal Reserve Bank of St. Louis, Spot Crude Oil Price: West Texas Intermediate (WTI), retrieved from FRED, Federal Reserve Bank of St. Louis; https://fred.stlouisfed.org/series/WTISPLC, September 9, 2018.

Gerald Ford, president in 1974, imposed his *WIN* program – *Whip Inflation Now* – in reaction to rising US inflation. That policy more than assured a recession in 1974 and 1975. Neely cautioned that if tensions in the Middle East worsened, there would be room for further disruptions in energy supply that could increase the negative impacts of rising oil prices.

Figure 3.10 shows oil prices since the 1950s. You can clearly see the abrupt rise from around USD 3 per barrel to USD 12 per barrel in 1973. That fourfold increase did not last very long, but it nevertheless had some large macroeconomic impacts. Oil prices increased again to almost USD 40 in 1979, but this spike was followed by a very long period of declining and low oil prices through most of the 1980s and 1990s. During Desert Storm (1990–1) and then again in the War on Iraq (2003) oil prices were highly volatile. The mid 2000s saw a large increase in oil prices reaching almost USD 140 per barrel right before the beginning of the Great Recession. Starting USD 50 in 2014 oil prices tumbled from around USD 120 a barrel to below USD 50. At the end of 2017 the price had returned to around USD 50 per barrel. We can only wonder what will happen in the future but we can be sure of one thing – oil prices will continue to be one of those supply-side factors causing the AS curve to shift around like an NFL running-back.

## BOX 3.2 DIFFERENCE OF OPINION: MACROECONOMIC POLICY OUT OF BULLETS?

Yesterday: General Sir – the enemy keeps coming should we keep firing at them? Yes, Private keep firing. But Sir, I am running low on ammo and most of the enemy intruders are the weak ones carrying no weapons. Private – I said keep firing. You never know when one of those weaklings might hit you on the head with a broom stick.

Today: General Sir, I am now out of ammo and a whole new army is coming at me. What should I do? General? Are you there General? What should I do General? Click. Buzz.

When the stock market fell in late August 2015, it became more and more obvious that our policymakers were out of bullets. Which brings up the topic of what we mean by macroeconomic policy.

My parents never tired of warning me about jeopardy – meaning that today's decisions can put you in a vulnerable place. My mother would shout: "Larry, if you don't do your math homework you will someday be a horrible guitar player with no source of financial stability." So I learned the concept of jeopardy at a young age. And that explains why I have been writing for at least five years about how the US government and the Fed have put the nation in jeopardy.

Liberal or conservative, there is room to believe in the efficacy of national macroeconomic policy. But let's start at the beginning using some questions. What is macro policy? Macro policy is aimed at making national policy variables approach desired ends. It is not about specific industries or specific companies or specific regions. National policy ends are economic growth, low inflation, and unemployment, and so on.

What are the options for macro policy? They boil down to four policy areas: monetary policy, demand-side fiscal policy, supply-side fiscal policy, and international trade policy.

Monetary policy consists of the Fed managing interest rates and money. Demand-side fiscal policy involves the government (Congress and President) implementing policies designed to impact spending in the economy. Supply-side fiscal policy is about the government legislating policies that improve incentives to produce goods and services – more efficiently and in greater volumes. International trade policies are not popular in the US but generally involve countries trying to improve their competitiveness so they can sell more goods abroad. These policies include exchange rate manipulation as well as policies like free trade agreements (FTAs) that would make US goods more desired by the rest of the world.

So are we out of policy bullets? Fed policy is easy to start with. After the Great Recession that began in 2008, the Fed spewed a lot of money into the system and lowered interest rates to zero. None of that inspired a strong recovery. The Fed admits to economic weakness every time they explain the economy is too anemic to return to normal policies. So if a future shock weakens the US economy the Fed has little left that it can do.

How about demand-side fiscal policy? The story is similar. The US government reacted to the past world economic crisis with huge increases in spending accompanied by policies to reduce tax rates. This was meant to prevent the economy from tanking, but it took us into new territory when it comes to national debt. Without throwing around big numbers let's just say that the relative size of our nation's debt more than doubled and so far the debt burden is planned to get even higher in the future. When times improve we are supposed to reduce debt. But that never happened. Now as we approach a possible new economic contraction the government has no room to increase spending and/or reduce taxes.

How about international trade policy? I think we are out of bullets there since problems abroad mean that other countries are not buying much from the rest of the world and definitely are not buying from us. The value of the dollar is rising – not falling. FTAs won't do much to solve a crisis since the fundamentals mean that foreigners will not be buying more goods from us. They can barely buy goods from themselves.

What a pessimistic picture. Or is it? I left out one type of macro policy – supply-side fiscal policy. Supply-side policy is interesting, but it is saddled with cuss words like Reaganomics, Trojan horse, trickle-down, and more. Liberals light up and glow when they use these terms. But SSFP – let's call it that since it is less provocative – is simple and straightforward economics. It does wonders when suppliers of goods and services are reluctant to produce. SSFP attacks disincentives to produce. SSFP looks at things that unnecessarily add to business costs. SSFP is *not* about getting consumers to buy more. But it ends up increasing demand if it promotes firms to compete better and harder.

SSFP tools are many. The best tool for today comes from examining what is constraining businesses right now. Why aren't firms hiring more workers? Why are firms reluctant to purchase new capital equipment and software? Why are some firms moving their assets abroad? Answer those questions and then use SSFP to remove the impediments. I won't prioritize the answers but clearly there are many areas of policy we can examine including minimum wage increases, environmental regulation, Dodd–Frank banking regulation, Obamacare impacts on employment, and corporate taxation. My liberal friends will scream that we need all those taxes and regulations. Don't interpret me as saying we need to get rid of them. But just acknowledge that if we are truly out of policy bullets, then some small backtracking on these priorities could be very useful in getting this train wreck of an economy back on its rails. As J. Cash would sing – Look Yonder Coming – Coming down that railroad track. It's the SSFP Special bringing my baby back! Humming is permitted.

*Source*: https://larrydavidsonspoutsoff.blogspot.com/2015/09/lesson-8-macroeconomic-policy-out-of .html

## 3.4    Short-Run Equilibrium: the Phillips Curve

The Phillips curve is a framework for organizing our thinking about inflation and unemployment. It focuses on some key aspects of inflation and unemployment that we already learned from the AS and AD analysis. It is called the Phillips curve after the New Zealand statistician A. B. H. Phillips (1914–75) who first detected a version of this curve in the 1950s. Recently we heard exclamations that the Phillips curve was dead as US unemployment fell to very low levels while inflation seemed to lie dormant. We do not believe the curve is even ill much less dead, and the following sections explain why.

### 3.4.1    The Unemployment–Inflation Trade-off

The Phillips curve describes a negative trade-off between unemployment and inflation. If inflation goes up, the rate of unemployment falls. If inflation comes down, unemployment rises. How come? We know from our previous discussion that any increase in aggregate demand makes firms want to produce more. To do that they hire more labor, and this is likely to bring unemployment down. Reversing the argument suggests that a decrease in aggregate demand brings lower prices, lower employment, and higher unemployment. This is a quick recapitulation of the argument behind the downward slope of the Phillips curve. Recall also from the previous discussion that an increase in workers' price level expectations with no subsequent increase in aggregate demand leads to a leftward shift in the AS curve, rising prices, falling employment, and, therefore, rising unemployment.

Taking last period's price level as given, an increase in the price level amounts to a positive rate of inflation and an expected increase in the price level amounts to an expected positive rate of inflation. If the price level rises more than expected, actual inflation exceeds expected inflation; if the price level rises by less than expected, actual inflation falls short of expected inflation. We can now rephrase the preceding argument in terms of actual and expected inflation rates. If actual inflation equals expected inflation, output, employment, and unemployment remain unchanged. If actual inflation exceeds expected inflation, output and employment rise, unemployment falls. If actual inflation falls short of expected inflation, output and employment fall, unemployment rises.

The Phillips curve represents the negative relationship between unexpected inflation and the unemployment rate following from this argument (consider Figure 3.11).

The blue line is a Phillips curve for a given expected inflation rate. If actual inflation is equal to expected inflation, the unemployment rate is at the *natural* rate. This is merely the definition of the *natural rate of unemployment*: It is the rate that comes about when actual and expected inflation are the same. This natural rate

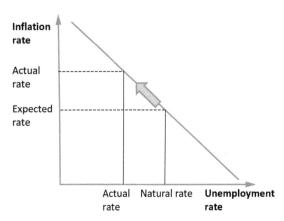

Figure 3.11 The Phillips curve

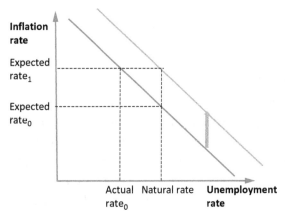

Figure 3.12 The Phillips curve and rising inflation expectations

cannot be changed by AD policies, hence the name *natural*. Governments must use appropriate AS policies to influence it. If actual inflation is higher than expected, we move upward along the blue Phillips curve, indicating that unemployment falls. If inflation is lower than expected, unemployment will be higher than the natural rate.

What happens if expected inflation rises? Note that a change in *expected* inflation is different from a change in *actual* inflation. A rise in expected inflation could be the result of wage earners experiencing higher-inflation rates in the past. It could also be the result of a government coming into power that has a reputation of not caring about low inflation, or simply the result of rumors flying through the air.

Whatever the reason for the increase in expected inflation, it now takes a higher *actual* rate of inflation to reach the natural rate of unemployment. As shown by the gray arrow in Figure 3.12 and the gray Phillips curve, this means that the Phillips curve shifts upward. The situation becomes worse in the sense that the same unemployment rate now goes together with a higher rate of inflation as before. Reversing the argument you can see in what sense it is desirable to have a central bank whose commitment to low inflation policies is credible. It allows the economy to achieve its natural rate of unemployment at a low rate of inflation. An increase in the natural rate of unemployment would shift the Phillips curve to the right.

The Phillips curve communicates several important ideas about economic policy. First, workers react to expected future events today. An expected future increase in inflation will create pressure for higher wages today. Depending on how these inflation expectations change relative to current inflation will determine whether the Phillips curve remains constant or shifts.

Second, governments can use AD policy, monetary or fiscal, to increase output and employment and to decrease the unemployment rate. They do so by bringing about an increase in the price level. However, the desired increase in output or decline in unemployment will be achieved only to the extent that inflation is unexpected. Perfectly expected inflation is *neutral* in the sense that it has no effects on output, employment, and unemployment.

The Phillips curve thus says something important about AD policy: It works to increase output, but only if it is not expected by those working for wages in the economy. According to a famous adage, you can fool everybody sometimes, but you cannot fool everybody all the time. Once workers have figured out what governments try to do, they adjust expectations and neutralize AD policies.

### 3.4.2   Working with Data: the Phillips Curve in the US

The Phillips curve is a bold statement! But is it real? Finding it in the data is a tricky exercise because, in any given period, we can have movements along the Phillips curve and shifts of the Phillips curve. Nevertheless, if the Phillips curve is to be useful, movements along the curve should be dominant in the data for some periods at least.

A first way to look at this issue is to plot the two variables – inflation and unemployment – on a graph for the US from the early 1960s to 2017 (see Figure 3.13). We use this graph to illustrate historical time periods when we moved along a given Phillips curve and other times when the curve shifted. Inflation is measured as the annual percentage change in the CPI. The unemployment rate is the civilian unemployment rate.

Movement along a Phillips curve occurs when the rate of inflation and the rate of unemployment move in opposite directions during a period of time. In Figure 3.13, we see that this was generally the case from 1961 to the early 1970s, from 1979 to 1982.

Movement along a Phillips curve: From 1979 to 1982 the unemployment rate is rising as the inflation rate decreases.

Downward shift in the Phillips curve: From 1993 to 2000 we see inflation and unemployment rates both generally declining.

Upward shift in the Phillips curve: From 1973 to 1976 we observe both inflation and unemployment generally rising.

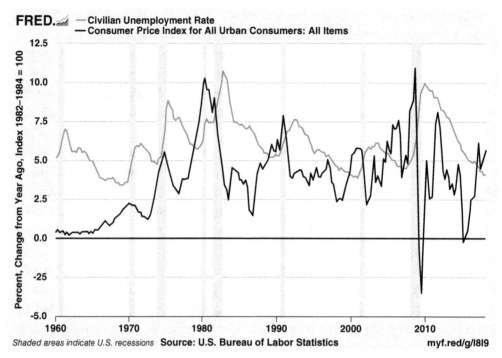

**Figure 3.13** Inflation and unemployment in the US (1960–2017)

*Source*: US Bureau of Labor Statistics, Civilian Unemployment Rate and Consumer Price Index for All Urban Consumers: All Items, both retrieved from FRED, Federal Reserve Bank of St. Louis; September 8, 2018.

In the early 1960s, the US economy was a low-inflation economy. Therefore, inflation expectations were low, too. AD policies were tried and pursued by the US government but they were relatively modest. This changed after the oil price shocks of the early 1970s. As the US economy tanked, the US government tried to use inflation to push up aggregate demand and output and push unemployment down. As a result, inflation rates shot up. The US became a high-inflation economy and workers expectations adjusted. This is shown in Figure 3.13. The Phillips curve of the early 1970s was a benign one. The US could achieve an unemployment rate of 2 percent with a rate of inflation of about 6 percent. The Phillips curve of the early 1980s, after expectations had changed, was a lot more vicious: 6 percent inflation came with an unemployment rate of more than 10 percent.

The picture changed from the early 1980s to the mid and late 1990s. The Phillips curve shifted down and left again and became more benign than before. By the late 1990s, the US could achieve 4 percent unemployment with an inflation rate of 2 percent. What had happened? Following Paul Volcker's chairmanship of the Fed, monetary policy had given up trying to keep unemployment low at the cost of high inflation. Instead, the Fed had committed to low inflation policies. Workers adjusted their expectations accordingly. As economists like to say, low-inflation monetary policy had gained credibility. But remember: Like all credibility in life, this one is a

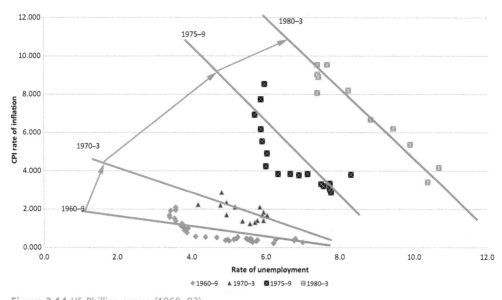

**Figure 3.14** US Phillips curves (1960–83)
*Source*: own calculations based on the data in Figure 3.13.

precious good. As the experience of the 1970s and 1980s shows, it is easily wasted and painfully gained. Most monetary policymakers around the world today agree that it is better not to exploit the Phillips curve systematically to keep unemployment below the natural rate.

A second way to look at this issue is to plot inflation rates against unemployment rates. Knowing by now that the US Phillips curve shifted several times, we do this in two steps. Figure 3.14 shows a plot of CPI inflation rates against unemployment rates for the period from 1960 to 1983. We use quarterly rates for this purpose. The straight lines in Figure 3.14 are simply fitted by eye-balling to indicate the unemployment–inflation trade-off and its changes during this period. On this basis, we identify four different Phillips curves: One for 1960 to 1969, one for 1970 to 1973, one for 1975 to 1979, and one for 1980 to 1983. In the intermittent periods, shift in the curve dominated and no clear trade-off is detectable.

Simple as it is, the figure conveys two clear messages. First, the Phillips curve seems to have shifted outward over this period, indicating the rise in inflation expectations. Second, the trade-off seems to have become steeper. This means that, for a given reduction in unemployment, a greater increase in inflation was necessary in the early 1980s than in the early 1960s. Reducing unemployment in this way became more *costly* in terms of inflation.

Figure 3.15 presents a similar exercise for the period from 1987 to 2017. During this period, more pronounced shifts of the Phillips curve occurred, and, therefore, the evidence is less clear as in the earlier period. This is probably due to a number of developments, some of which we will discuss later in this book. From the early

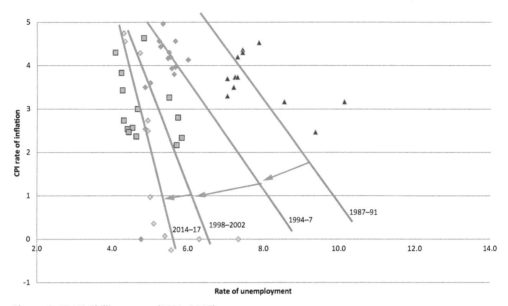

**Figure 3.15** US Phillips curves (1983–2017)
*Source*: own calculations based on the data from Figure 3.13.

1990s onward, the Fed managed to achieve a relatively high and consistent degree of price stability in what became known as the period of the *great moderation*. The *dot.com* economy of the turn of the century contributed to low unemployment from the supply side of the economy. From 2007 on, financial markets turmoil created new shocks to the economy. We can see that the US Phillips curve gradually shifted to the left again, but it also seems to have become steeper over time. The leftward shift indicates the growing credibility of the Fed's commitment to low inflation since the early 1980s. Other factors may have contributed to that, such as the increasing global competition that created downward price pressures and periods of declining oil prices.

Economics Nobel laureates Paul Samuelson and Robert M. Solow wrote in the early 1960s that the US government could use the Phillips curve as a technical menu of choices.[5] Their argument boils down to this: Give me an unemployment rate you like, and I tell you what inflation rate you need. For a little over ten years, this became the guide to macroeconomic policy. Overall, the experience since then has shown that the Phillips curve is real but that it is an elusive concept for policy. It is not stable enough to be exploited systematically.

Note that the natural rate of unemployment also seems to have increased over the 1970s, leading to a shift of the Phillips curve to the right as well. The shifts of the US Phillips curve in the 1970s can be explained by a combination of factors that ultimately impact the AS curve, such as too much government spending in the late 1960s (wars on poverty and Vietnam), increases in government regulations of goods, and labor markets.

### 3.4.3 NAIRU

Janet Yellen writing in the *FRBSF Economic Letter* ("Monetary Policy in a Global Environment," June 2, 2006) concedes that globalization might have impacted the non-accelerating inflation rate of unemployment (NAIRU), but she concluded that there is no real evidence to support this conjecture. This is an important issue for the Fed, as if lower import prices, lower wages, or other aspects of globalization have caused US NAIRU to decline, then the Fed could administer a looser monetary policy without fear of higher inflation. But if NAIRU is not lower, such a policy could have very undesirable consequences. What's NAIRU?

For example, if NAIRU is 6 percent, then as long as the actual unemployment rate stays above 6 percent then the inflation rate will not rise (and it probably will fall). If the actual unemployment rate is less than 6 percent, then inflation will probably rise. In general terms, the difference between the actual unemployment rate and the NAIRU is a predictor of the future change in the inflation rate.

- actual unemployment rate > NAIRU . . . . . . . . . inflation rate falls
- actual unemployment rate < NAIRU . . . . . . . . . inflation rate rises
- actual unemployment rate = NAIRU . . . . . . . . . inflation rate is unchanged

How do we get from the Phillips curve to the NAIRU? Simply assume that the expected rate of inflation generally equals the last period's rate of inflation. That is plausible: People learn from experience. Higher than expected inflation then means accelerating inflation.

Consider Figure 3.16. Expected inflation is now the rate from the previous year. If we subtract the previous year's rate from the current rate, we obtain the change in the rate of inflation. We now plot the change in the rate of inflation on the vertical axis. Points above the horizontal axis mean that inflation accelerates unexpectedly, points below mean that inflation slows down unexpectedly. The Phillips curve now says that if the rate of unemployment is below the natural rate, inflation will accelerate.

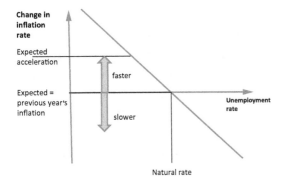

**Figure 3.16** The NAIRU

Some people use this simple NAIRU theory as a basis for inflation forecasting. It sounds pretty straightforward but several things make this challenging.

- First, you have to know the exact value of NAIRU. As it turns out, NAIRU is one of those economic ideas that is hard to nail down. It has the annoying habit of being both complex and changing.
- Second, there is no published data on NAIRU. It is something that economists try to estimate using other figures but there is no direct measure of it.
- Third, inflation forecasts and NAIRU depend very much on the public's inflation expectations. As we noted above, forecasting measures of inflation expectations is not easy either.

Other people claim that the Phillips curve has broken down and NAIRU cannot be used for forecasting anymore.[6] But don't fret. Economists are a contentious lot and you have to know how to read between the lines. What these economists are saying really is that you can't just use the slope of the Phillips curve to predict inflation. They underscore how things like changes in NAIRU, or AS shocks, or inflationary expectations need to be added to any inflation forecast. The upshot of this is that we may never forecast inflation and unemployment perfectly, but hopefully by knowing as much as possible about short-term and long-term AD and AS shocks and trends, we may do a little better at this process.

### 3.4.4    Unemployment and Inflation Policy

Most countries want to have low unemployment rates, probably for two reasons. First, there is personal loss of income and self-esteem when a person is unemployed for too long. Second, from a macroeconomic standpoint, it is wasteful to have people not producing when they could be. As a result, most countries have policies designed to reach a good unemployment rate. We can think of this policy issue as having two dimensions:

1. eliminating the output gap so as to bring the actual unemployment rate down to the natural rate; and
2. reducing the natural rate.

Most unemployment policies we see in the real world are attempts to reduce the output gap – that is, they are expansionary monetary or fiscal policies designed to increase aggregate demand, output, and employment. History is full of examples. Pick up today's business paper and there should be at least one story about one country that is trying to reduce its output gap so as to reduce the unemployment rate. If not, today was a bad day. Try again tomorrow!

Common sense tells us that if the output gap is large enough, these policies have a good chance of working without causing much higher inflation. It is only when the output gap starts to get smaller (real GDP gets closer to potential GDP) that these policies raise the possibility of higher inflation. When they do, the Phillips curve trade-off becomes a real policy dilemma – should we reduce the unemployment rate at the risk of higher inflation? Inflation worry, therefore, becomes a constraint on unemployment policy.

But, of course, the reverse is true as well. If a government attacks a problem of high inflation by using monetary and fiscal policies to contract aggregate demand, then we find ourselves on the trade-off curve. An AD policy to lower inflation would mean lower output and employment – a higher unemployment rate. People sometimes use the term *sacrifice ratio* to describe this trade-off. The ratio calculates the number of unemployment points you have to give up in order to gain an inflation point. So, if you want to reduce the inflation rate from 3 to 2 percent and you expect the unemployment rate to go from 4 to 6 percent in the process, then the sacrifice ratio would be 2. The policymaker at this point needs to evaluate if the benefit in inflation reduction is worth the cost of the higher unemployment. The unemployment rate in this case becomes the constraint on attempts to reduce inflation.

There is a way out of this dilemma! That is to attack both inflation and unemployment together – that is, use a policy whose impact is to shift the Phillips curve inward so that both the inflation and the unemployment rates are lowered. This can be done by reducing inflation expectations and by appropriate AS policies reducing business cost relative to productivity. These policies shift the Phillips curve inward – avoiding the trade-offs discussed above.

Consider again Figure 3.13. It shows the complicated relationships between inflation and unemployment in the USA since the 1970s. In most recessions (gray bars) when aggregate demand is diving you see inflation falling and unemployment rising. The unemployment rate generally fell during the 1990s, but notice that inflation first decreased but then it increased. Unemployment fell after the 2001 recession as the inflation rate climbed. Unemployment fell after the 2008 recession accompanied by a falling inflation rate. In 2016 inflation started rising and there was concern that it might rise a lot more if the unemployment rate stayed low or fell further.

Page 11 of the *Financial Times* on June 8, 2006 offered several articles about inflation and central bank policy. The lead article was titled, "Is It Back to the 1970s? Why Inflation Is Again a Spectre." With headline inflation rising in the US and Europe, many people were betting that the Fed and the ECB would raise interest rates as a clear signal to defeat rising inflation expectations. In 2001 and thereafter, much of the world had been focused on exiting a recession. The policies worked and the world economy had come out of the recession and started to grow again. By 2006, output was near or above potential, oil and other commodity prices were rising, and it was clear that inflation was again public enemy #1. But was it? The answer was uncertain and the uncertainty differed by region. With respect to the US, most people were willing to declare inflation as the main evil. But not everyone agreed. While inflation was rising, many private forecasters expected it to fall toward the end of 2006 and in 2007. Should the Fed fight inflation and risk a trade-off? But in Europe and Japan, where the economy was not quite so strong, the consensus seemed to be that the sacrifice ratio was too high. Fighting inflation too hard could mean a central bank-induced recession.

In this difficult situation, former IMF chief economist Kenneth Rogoff argued that supply-side policies offered a way to increase output growth while reducing inflation.[7] He acknowledged that central bankers deserved some credit for bringing inflation down but they could not take credit for avoiding the Phillips curve trade-off. Rogoff wrote: "Instead one should think of the modern era of rapidly expanding trade and technological progress as providing a spectacularly favorable milieu for monetary policy . . . Rather than face the usual historical trade-off, central banks have let citizens have their cake and eat it." However, Rogoff worried that globalization might reverse itself. Failing to understand that, without globalization, central bankers have no way to deliver lower inflation without sacrificing economic growth, people might underestimate the benefits of globalization. Opposing globalization could, therefore, have significant macroeconomic consequences in terms of either higher unemployment or higher inflation or both.

Inflation and unemployment are at the core of many important macro variables – like interest rates, wages, investment spending, and many others. They are also part and parcel of forecasts about the overall wellbeing of the economy. Your own personal and company forecasts will depend on many things. What AD and AS shocks have been impacting and threaten to continue to impact the economy? Will these shocks lead to trade-offs of inflation versus unemployment? What problems would be associated with the change in inflation? What problems would be associated with the change in unemployment? How will households and business firms be impacted by these changes? Will the national policymakers perceive the new inflation or unemployment to be a big enough problem to require addressing with policy? Which problem is public enemy #1? Will policymakers trade off one problem for the other? Will policymakers find means to avoid a trade-off? How will these policies impact your own decisions? These questions illustrate the kinds of things business planners should understand as they make their decisions in a world of uncertainty.

## BOX 3.3 DIFFERENCE OF OPINION: POP-UP INFLATION

In a post on May 21, 2013, I worried that inflation was coming back and likened Fed policy to – frying pan, fire, frying pan. In writing that I admit that trends showed there was some room for the inflation rate to fall further and I don't have a good prediction for when inflation will rise again. The importance of this is that important people keep putting pressure on the Fed to keep the pedal to the metal.

Any deviation from this monetary flooding is met with fear. Last week Bernanke happened to mention that the Fed was thinking about reversing policy – and the markets immediately went into the tank.

It is interesting that the markets are testing the Fed. The markets seem to love all that money. But that doesn't mean it is good for Main Street or for employment. A recent article by Andy Kessler (*Wall Street Journal*, "The Fed Squeezes the Shadow Banking System," May 23, 2013, p. A17) explains that the Fed has robbed the private sectors of a lot of government bonds and mortgage-backed securities. All this stuff is sitting in the Fed's vaults and is not being used as collateral for the private sector's loans. I love Kessler's line, "In other words the Fed's policy – to stimulate lending and the economy by buying Treasuries . . . is creating a shortage of safe collateral, the very thing needed to create credit."

James Bullard of the St. Louis Fed is worried that inflation is too low and he wants the Fed to keep stimulating the economy. As Kessler says, that is strangling the economy. Worse yet, the risk of a giant pop gets larger and larger the more money is out there. Bernanke is afraid to remove even a dime of it because of the market's reactions. It is like promising to go on a diet tomorrow. Really, I have a headache today, but I will start it tomorrow. Sure, you will! Imagine how the financial markets are going to react when he finally has to remove some money from the system.

Back to disinflation. It is easy to see why the US inflation rate is not going to increase in the next few months. The most obvious factor is slower expected growth in Europe, China, Japan, and most of the world outside of the US. World economic growth spills over into US markets for good reasons. First, when those countries stagnate they buy fewer of our goods. Thus, US export sales decrease. Second, as money moves out of those countries and into ours, this has the effect of raising the value of the dollar. The higher value of the dollar dents exports further but it also makes imports cost less. Both factors push US inflation and inflationary expectations downward. In my last posting I showed a strong medium-term downward trend in inflation. Clearly both medium- and short-term trends are pushing inflation expectations downward. That means less upward pressure on wages and the prices of various other inputs to the production process.

So long as world economic growth is restrained, it is hard to imagine the US inflation rate soaring back this summer. But damaging risk remains. Many people who worry about global warming admit that temperatures have not been rising in the last decade. But they look beyond all that and focus on what happens if you don't combat warming immediately. They are alarmed. Well I am alarmed about inflation coming back and putting us back into another deep recession. Europe will not be in a recession forever. China will find a way to grow faster. Japan may figure out its problems. The US is seeing wealth rise as stock and housing prices return to stable values. Many emerging nations are devaluing and restructuring.

No, these problems do not have to be solved soon or at one time. The way our financial markets work is through bits and pieces of information that begin to form a mosaic. When the image of a stronger world economy starts to emerge, it won't take long for inflationary expectations to rise. It is like the jack-in-the-box – you turn and turn and turn the crank but Jack stays in the box – at least until that critical moment. Jack-in-the-box is fun but not when the Fed is at the crank. If the Fed has not done a thing to impede rising inflationary expectations, we can expect a quick return trip from the frying pan to the fire. And it won't be pleasant. They can take some of the sting out by starting the process now.

*Source*: https://larrydavidsonspoutsoff.blogspot.com/2013/05/pop-up-inflation.html

## 3.5  SUMMARY

After the initial emphasis on aggregate demand, this chapter builds on the concepts of aggregate supply. Aggregate supply models the behavior of the firms that produce the output. Based on managerial economics foundations, these firms set output and price in accordance with profit-maximization goals. We develop short-run models of aggregate supply. Once developed, we look at the numerous determinants of aggregate supply to see how cost and productivity developments are equally important to aggregate supply in determining the resulting changes in changes in market output and prices. Then we bring the AD and AS curves together to complete a full analysis of the economy. We find that while AD shocks cause output and prices to always move in the same direction, AS shocks help us to understand why at times, output and prices move in opposite directions. Aggregate supply theory points to very different policy tools to influence the economy and explains why it is possible through AS policy to increase output without a corresponding increase in prices.

Aggregate demand and aggregate supply work together to determine the performance of the macroeconomy. We call the situation where the two are equal macroeconomic equilibrium. We can use macroeconomic equilibrium as a framework to analyze how aggregate supply and AD short-run shocks can impact the two key macroeconomic variables, real GDP and the price level. This technical apparatus probably seems somewhat stiff and artificial. The world is a very complex entity and what really happens is clearly a lot more dynamic and interesting. But if we back away from all the noise and chaos and we let all the dust settle, this analysis does a pretty good job of explaining what causes what. If you pay close attention to what journalists and economists write about the macroeconomy, you will see the above stories unfold time and time again.

We have seen that there is a great contrast between the effects of AS and AD shocks on the price level and real GDP.

- Aggregate supply shocks always cause inverse or opposite movements in prices and real GDP.
- AD shocks always cause parallel movements in prices and real GDP.

Therefore, looking at price level and output co-movements during a given period allows us to determine whether AD shocks or AS shocks were more important.

Here is a final caveat: Ever since the 1950s, the US economy, like most advanced countries around the world, has experienced positive inflation every year, i.e., the price level was on an upward trend. From year to year, businesses and households were expecting prices to rise, and wages and other cost factors were following the same trend. In such a world:

- A positive AD shock will cause prices to rise faster than trend and output to increase.
- A negative AD shock will cause prices to rise slower than trend and output to fall.
- A positive AS shock will cause prices to rise slower than trend and output to increase.
- A negative AS shock will cause prices to rise faster than trend and output to fall.

Thus, in an economy accustomed to positive inflation:

- AS shocks cause inverse movements of the rate of inflation and the level of real GDP.
- AD shocks cause parallel movements of the rate of inflation and the level of real GDP.

In this chapter we also looked more deeply into issues related to inflation and unemployment. We showed that AD shocks and policies create trade-offs with respect to inflation and unemployment. The negative slope of the Phillips curve vividly depicts these trade-offs and explains why one cannot eliminate one of these problems without exacerbating the other. Yet, AS shocks and policies offer an escape from these onerous trade-offs. Aggregate supply shocks and/or policies can move the Phillips curve in an inward (left) direction, causing improvements in both inflation and unemployment. A checkered past, uncertain outcomes, and sensitive political problems, however, make it difficult for leaders to forcefully advocate these policies.

An interesting short article in the *Financial Times* appeared on February 4, 2005 (p. 3), "Figures Point to Pressure for New US Jobs," by Christopher Swann and

Andrew Balls. The column was written because US productivity data for the fourth quarter of 2004 was announced and revealed a slowdown in that quarter – with productivity rising at a 0.8 percent annualized rate in that quarter. Productivity for the whole year had increased by 4.1 percent. Thus, the authors felt this would create some uncertainty for the Fed. If productivity in 2005 would grow at 4.1 percent, the Fed could easily forget about inflation problems and would not need to increase interest rates. The authors also noted that there remained in the fourth quarter plenty of slack in labor markets (the unemployment rate above NAIRU), and this boded well for inflation. But if the fourth quarter was a good indication of a significant slowdown in productivity in 2005, then costs might continue rising faster than productivity (implying an undesirable shift in the Phillips curve) and the Fed would need to be more concerned about future inflation and unemployment.

The year 2017 was not much different than 2005. Productivity and inflation were growing at a snail's pace and the Fed could not decide between further stimulation of the economy and the opposite. Those who believed inflation would remain subdued encouraged the Fed to keep interest rates low. An equally vocal group of economists believed that the Phillips trade-off was back in play and that a further reduction in the unemployment rate would cause inflation to rise. They advised the Fed to begin the process of raising interest rates to more normal levels. Without perfect knowledge of the future we are destined to continue these kinds of arguments into the future. But that's no excuse for business executives who must buy and sell daily. With a better knowledge of aggregate supply and aggregate demand they can try to make decisions regardless of the uncertainty of the real world.

## 3.6   REVIEW QUESTIONS

1. What does it mean when we say the AS curve is upward sloped?
2. Other than the price level, what else causes an increase in AS? How would that change be shown with the AS curve?
3. What is the main difference between AS policy and AD policy?
4. Using an AS and AD model explain the impacts of a reduction in energy prices on output and prices.
5. Now assume that energy prices rise. How might that impact the economy and what AD or AS policy would you recommend for that situation?
6. Why are policymakers often reluctant to use AS policy?
7. What does it mean that the Phillips curve is a close cousin to the AS and AD analysis? Why is there a trade-off?
8. What causes the Phillips curve to shift inward? What implication does that have for NAIRU?

## NOTES

1 www.imf.org/en/Publications/WEO/Issues/2017/09/19/world-economic-outlook-october-2017

2 See "Entrepreneurs in the US Face Less Red Tape," *Regional Economist*, October 2004, Federal Reserve Bank of St. Louis, pp. 5–9.

3 For more background on AS policy, the following article is excellent, keeping in mind that it was written by an advocate of AS policy. "A Walk on the Supply Side," Raymond Keating, at: https://fee.org/articles/a-walk-on-the-supply-side/

4 http://research.stlouisfed.org/publications/aiet/20040701/cover.pdf

5 Paul A. Samuelson and Robert M. Solow, "Analytical Aspects of Anti-Inflation Policy," *American Economic Review* 50 (1960): 177–94.

6 See Kevin Kliesen, "The NAIRU: Tailor-Made for the Fed," *Regional Economist* (Federal Reserve Bank of St. Louis) October 1999, at: www.stlouisfed.org/publications/regional-economist/october-1999/the-nairu-tailormade-for-the-fed; Kevin J. Lansing, "Can the Phillips Curve Help Forecast Inflation?," FRBSF Economic Letter, October 4, 2002, at: www.frbsf.org/economic-research/publications/economic-letter/2002/october/can-the-phillips-curve-help-forecast-inflation

7 Ken Rogoff, "The Myth of How Central Banks Slayed the Hydra of Inflation," *Financial Times*, August 30, 2006, p. 11.

# 4 Monetary Policy and Aggregate Demand

A country's economy is continually buffeted by shocks to aggregate demand and aggregate supply. AD shocks come from households, firms, governments, and foreign buyers. They change their spending patterns because the causal variables discussed in Chapter 3 change and impact them. These changes in aggregate demand are often large and persistent enough to become the subject of economic policy. Should governments intervene in the economy and attempt to bring aggregate demand back to a normal and sustainable level, or one that the government deems more appropriate? If so, monetary and fiscal policies are often used to stabilize AD changes.

Today, monetary policy is the most active and most written about type of AD policy for almost any country. Monetary policy is both very simple and very complex at the same time. It is sometimes considered to be mysterious since deliberations concerning monetary policies are not always perfectly transparent and information is often slow to be announced or published. Monetary policy has its own jargon and therefore requires its own study of terminology.

You can run away but most businesspeople cannot hide from the constant barrage of information published about money, interest rates, inflation, the Federal Reserve (the Fed), and monetary policy. Like other aspects of macroeconomics, monetary policy is typified by differences of opinion. These differences filter through to most of us through uncertainty about when and by how much the central bank should or will act. In every country we have a pretty active group of central-bank watchers. Whether we call them ECB watchers, or Fed watchers, or Bank of Japan watchers – the game is always the same: To try to predict when the central bank is going to announce its next policy change, so that we can predict changes in interest rates, aggregate demand, real GDP, inflation, and the rest.

One thing to stress from the outset: This chapter is all about aggregate demand. No matter how many concepts, theories, differences of opinion, or histories we discuss, everything here is about how and to what extent a central bank can impact aggregate demand so as to influence output, employment, unemployment, and inflation in the short run and the long run. We will see below that while there is plenty of controversy and uncertainty about the impacts of monetary policy, there is much agreement that monetary policy consists of one basic tool and the direct goal of that tool is to have a desired impact on aggregate demand.

## BOX 4.1 DIFFERENCE OF OPINION: CAN MONETARY POLICY HAVE *REAL* EFFECTS?

We will discuss several different opinions about monetary policy but central to the debate is that supply-side economists tend to believe that monetary policy can influence nominal aggregate demand and output, but that it has only short-lived effects on real aggregate demand and output. In other words, central banks can get us to want to buy more goods and services but they cannot affect a country's long-run capacity to produce (potential real GDP). If central banks can influence demand but not supply, then we predict they will mostly impact the price level and the inflation rate. The famous *monetarist* Milton Friedman of the University of Chicago said that inflation is the result of too many dollars chasing too few goods.

Demand-side (so-called *Keynesian*) economists disagree and are more optimistic that central banks can influence real output as well as inflation in the long run. There is some middle ground here when it comes to the short run, however. Most macroeconomists will admit that monetary policy can impact aggregate demand and real GDP in the short run. So when the US Fed aggressively lowered interest rates in 2001 and 2002, and again in the incipient Great Recession in 2008, most economists were willing to admit that at least for the following year or two this policy would prevent output in the US from falling too much.

The more interesting questions and more controversial debate centered on what would happen after the economy recovered from the recession. Supply-side economists worried that the Fed might stimulate aggregate demand too much and for too long. In that case, inflation would become a real concern. Demand-side economists, in contrast, worried that the Fed did not exert enough stimulus and that unemployment would remain too high and employment too low for too long.

Since monetary policy is conducted by the Fed and other central banks, Chapter 4 begins with central banks – their motivations, goals, rules, and organization. We then examine their tools, including some new ones developed and used during and after the Great Recession. We then turn to the theoretical side – detailing exactly how and why monetary policy comes to impact the economy. Our focus in Chapter 4 is on how money impacts the economy in the short run. We end the chapter with applications relating to the 2008–9 financial crisis and the Fed's reaction to it during the following years.

## 4.1   Macro Concepts and Analysis

Money is generally defined as a highly liquid asset serving as the medium of exchange in an economy. That is, people use this asset to make final payments for the goods and services they purchase and to settle their debts, and firms use it to pay their workers, capital owners, and suppliers. In modern, developed economies, the government defines a specific asset as *legal tender*, i.e., as valid for meeting financial obligations. In the US, dollar bills and coins are legal tender, in the euro area, euro bills and coins, in the UK, sterling bills and coins.

---

### BOX 4.2 **Are Credit Cards *Money*?**

Many people think that, because they can pay with credit cards, credit cards or the balances on them should be regarded as money. This brings up the difference between money and credit. Money is an asset that you use primarily for the purpose of buying things. Credit may be used to obtain goods, but notice that when you use credit you are chalking up a liability that has to be repaid using money.

Credit cards and money are two very different things. For one thing, you will need money to pay off at least part of your balance each month. The part you don't pay off is credit, or a debt that you will have to pay off with money in the future. Money is not the only thing that impacts spending, but it is believed to have a regular impact on it. Credit also affects spending, but its impact is generally kept separate from the impact of money.

---

In practice, most payments are not made in legal tender, because people do not want to carry around large amounts of cash. Instead, they use close substitutes to cash, i.e., certain types of bank deposits. Since checks drawn on demand deposits are widely accepted as payments, it is plausible to include demand deposits issued by domestic banks in a definition of money. So is the inclusion of traveler's checks and other checkable deposits at banks and depository institutions such as credit unions. This gives us a first (narrow) definition of money:

*Narrow money* (M1) is the sum of currency circulating in the economy plus the stock of demand deposits at domestic banks and other checkable deposits at domestic depository institutions plus traveler's checks issued by domestic banks held by non-banks in the economy.

One criticism is that M1 may be too narrow to include everything used as money. You may have some very liquid financial assets that you could sell quickly to purchase something. This may include your savings account or a short-term asset like a ninety-day time deposit (a deposit which cannot be liquidated at no cost before maturity), or claims on money market mutual funds. Because people do seem to regularly liquidate these assets and use the proceeds for payments, we include them in broader measures of money like M2. Thus, we have:

*Broad money* (M2) is the sum of M1 plus savings deposits including money market deposit accounts, small-denomination time deposits (in amounts of less than USD 100,000); and balances in retail money market mutual funds.

There are even broader definitions of money, but we neglect those here. Note that the precise definition of narrow and broad money differs from country to country because of differences in payment habits and the kinds of product offered by the financial sector. This discussion may seem to become too technical for us, but it is necessary to understand one source of differences of opinion about policy. Most central banks publish data on these various definitions of money.

Figure 4.1 plots the monetary aggregates M1 and M2 for the US during the period from 1960 to 2016. During this period, M2 has grown much faster than M1 and it is now much larger than the narrow aggregate.

Since money stocks are very persistent, it is generally more informative to look at rates of change of money stocks. This we do in Figure 4.2. Notice that in the time period from 1960 to 2014, M1 growth is much more volatile than M2 growth.

One important reason why we are interested in data on money stocks is that they might tell us something about the current stance of monetary policy. For example, if money growth is very fast, we might think that monetary policy is rather easy or expansionary; while, if money growth is low or even negative, we might think of

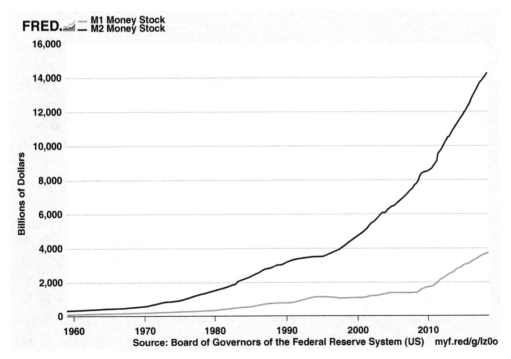

**Figure 4.1** US money stocks (1960–2016)

*Source:* Board of Governors of the Federal Reserve System (US), M1 Money Stock and M2 Money Stock, retrieved from FRED, Federal Reserve Bank of St. Louis; October 12, 2018.

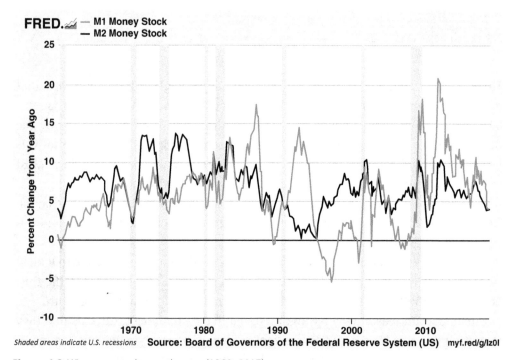

Figure 4.2 US money stock growth rates (1960–2017)

*Source*: Board of Governors of the Federal Reserve System (US), M1 Money Stock and M2 Money Stock, retrieved from FRED, Federal Reserve Bank of St. Louis; https://fred.stlouisfed.org/series/M1SL, October 12, 2018.

monetary policy being restrictive or tight. Consider the money growth rates during the 1960s. We see both M1 and M2 growing at moderate rates over the first six years of that decade, then falling, increasing again, and falling at the end of the decade. This indicates that the recession of 1970 had something to do with overly tight monetary policy. Once in the recession, both money stocks started growing more strongly again, suggesting that easier monetary policy had something to do with the recovery.

But things are not always that clear. Notice, for example, that in the years from 1990 to 1992 M1 growth was accelerating, while M2 growth was slowing down. For this particular period, narrow money suggests a policy of monetary expansion while broad money indicates a tight policy. After 1995, the reverse happened, as M1 growth became negative while M2 growth was rising. More generally, different measures of money growth do not always convey the same information about the current stance of monetary policy. When this happens, it is hard to tell whether the central bank will judge its own policy as too easy and too tight, and, therefore, it is difficult to predict its future policy actions. Since central banks typically do not tell the public which definition of money they look at, this adds uncertainty to our business lives. In fact, the question which one is the better indicator of monetary policy is an issue of debate. Many economists have concluded from this debate that money growth is not a good indicator of the stance of monetary policy at all, nor a good predictor of future economic activity and propose to use interest rates instead. However, as we shall see below, there are similar ambiguities connected to the use of interest rates as indicators of monetary policy.

## 4.1.1    Central Banks and Their Goals

A central bank is the monopoly provider of the currency of a country and conducts its monetary policy. Unlike you and me, who would be convicted of counterfeiting, the central bank has the legal right to create or produce paper money and coins. In the US, the Fed does not actually do the printing of the money (the US Treasury has the plates), but it does make the decision as to how much currency gets printed and minted and how much is injected into the economy. Central banks also act as lenders of last resort for the banking system (more about this below) and supervise banks and other financial institutions. The first official central bank in history was the Bank of England, which rose to this position in 1844.

Conducting monetary policy essentially means making sure the country has just the right amount of money. What does it mean when we say that the central bank should provide just the right amount of money? One way to look at this is to say that the right amount is just enough money so that aggregate demand grows at a rate that will let the economy expand at an acceptable rate with an acceptable rate of inflation. Recall that potential real GDP is the level of output that is compatible with fully employed resources. US history tells us that potential real GDP growth averages around 3 percent per year, although, nowadays, it might be closer to 2 percent. Not every country will have the same growth rate of potential real GDP. Nor does the growth rate of potential real GDP necessarily stay the same over time. Germany, for example, grew by less than 1 percent on average between 1994 and 2007, and by 1.7 percent on average in 2013 to 2017. Developing countries often can grow at rates much faster than that without generating inflation.

If US aggregate demand grew by about 2 to 3 percent, that would be compatible with normal economic growth without inflation. It turns out that most countries, including the US, do not necessarily want to have zero inflation – more on that below. Most central banks would be more than pleased to have an inflation rate in the range of 2 to 3 percent per year. If a central bank desires output to grow by 3 percent per year and the prices of that output are allowed to rise by 2 to 3 percent, then we are talking about a target of nominal aggregate demand growth of 5 to 6 percent per year.

Recall from Chapter 2, section 2.3.6, that the *velocity of money* is the average number of times a unit of money is used in transactions during a given period of time, and that nominal aggregate demand equals the money stock, M, times the velocity of money. In growth rates, this means that the growth rate of nominal aggregate demand equals the growth rate of money plus the growth rate of the velocity of money, or that the growth rate of money equals the growth rate of nominal aggregate demand less the growth rate of the velocity of money. Therefore, if the velocity of money is constant, a target of nominal aggregate demand growth of 5 to 6 percent per year would call for a growth rate of money of 5 to 6 percent per year. In practice, however, the velocity of money is not necessarily constant. Therefore, a more appropriate version of this statement is: If the central bank aims at a growth rate of nominal aggregate demand of x percent per year, it should let the money stock grow by x percent less the projected rate of change of the velocity of money.

In practice, central banks are not concerned about inflation alone. They also pay attention to the level or growth of real output, trying to *stabilize* output or keeping it close to potential. They are also concerned about unemployment, trying to keep the rate of unemployment close to the natural rate. Thus, if output falls too much below potential and/or the rate of unemployment rises too much above the natural rate, central banks will typically ease monetary policy, i.e., they will let money grow faster and allow for some more inflation. Conversely, if real output rises too far above potential and/or the unemployment rate falls too much below the natural rate, central banks will typically tighten monetary policy, letting money grow less and allowing for lower inflation. In practice, therefore, central banks conduct monetary policy facing trade-offs between inflation, real output growth, and unemployment.

### 4.1.2   Why Do Central Banks Care about Inflation?

Perhaps it seems obvious that high inflation would not be good for a country. But if it were so obvious, more countries would have low inflation. If inflation is so bad, then why don't we eliminate it altogether? The answer is that there is a cost to eliminating inflation just like there is a cost of eliminating the incidence of accidents and disease. Accidents, disease, and inflation are not good things, but the cost of getting rid of them completely does not seem to be worth the effort.

Before we discuss the costs of getting rid of inflation, let's look at the problems it causes. High inflation is typically unstable in the sense that monthly and quarterly inflation rates fluctuate a lot. High and unstable inflation undermines the economy's ability to generate long-lasting growth and job creation. Recall from Chapter 3 that much of the long-term growth of an economy is owed to business investment in plant, equipment, knowledge, and technology. High and unstable inflation can detract from the confidence that is needed for planners to risk their capital. This amounts to inflation adding a permanent uncertainty margin to real interest rates – making them higher than necessary for long periods of time.

Hyperinflation is even worse for a country, as it destroys the use of money as a medium of exchange. There were jokes in Germany during the hyperinflation of 1922–3 that, if one left a basket of money on their doorstep for a minute, the money would still be there, but the basket would be gone, when he returned. Money was losing value so rapidly that people would try to turn it into goods as quickly as possible. People began to trade by exchanging goods for goods instead of money. This kind of barter world is very wasteful and time-consuming. People spend too much of their time figuring out how to "beat the inflation" and not enough time doing their ordinary work and production.

Inflation creates uncertainty for consumers and investors and can lead to painful cycles of economic boom and bust. If inflation rises faster than expected, real interest rates tend to fall and cause too much investment and spending and too little saving. This leads to a boom. If inflation is falling relative to expectations, the opposite happens and a bust occurs.

High inflation erodes the value of money wages and savings held in monetary assets such as bank deposits or bonds. Wage earners can protect themselves against that by insisting on frequent renegotiation of their wages, but this increases the cost of bargaining. Alternatively, they can insist on *indexing* their wages, i.e., tying them automatically to the development of a price index such as the CPI. Indexing, however, means that the economy can no longer react to shocks emanating from the supply side by lowering wages. Furthermore, there are many people who receive money incomes for whom indexing is not an option, e.g., people on social security. Savers can protect the value of their assets by demanding higher interest rates or by acquiring real assets such as real estate. This, however, distorts asset prices with negative consequences for business investment.

On the positive side, a little bit of inflation may not be a bad thing. So long as people do not think it is going to get out of control, a little bit of inflation is often considered to be a good sign about the future. To the firm, a little bit of inflation implies the possibility of higher prices and profits in the future. To the worker, a little bit of inflation may promise rising wages in the future. A close reading of these last points suggests that they are based more on psychology than economics. If the firm expects higher prices in the future, it probably ought to expect higher costs as well. If the worker expects higher wages, then he or she probably knows this means higher future prices as well. So this story is not based on good economics – but it is one often told and deserves to be listed here. One plausible version of it is that a little bit of inflation allows firms to reduce real wages when business conditions call for that without reducing nominal wages, which would be considered unfair by their employees.

Also on the positive side is the idea that zero inflation is too close to deflation. That is, once you get to zero, you are very close to a negative number. Additionally, deflation increases the real value of nominal debt, driving households and businesses into default. In a world of non-negative nominal interest rates, deflation raises the real interest rate. This would have a negative impact on investment and consumption. The prospect of falling prices may keep households from spending their incomes and this may weaken aggregate demand. Such fears of deflation explain why some people would rather see inflation above the zero mark. Tao

Wu, economist at the San Francisco Federal Reserve Bank, explains some issues about deflation.[1,2] Of interest is that deflation may be good or bad for a country – and much depends on the cause of the deflation. Deflation worries, such as in the US in 2003 and again in 2009, usually arise when aggregate demand is very low and leads to declining prices. Japan experienced deflation during the 1990s resulting from a loss of confidence that kept both business firms and households from buying. It was associated with weak real GDP growth. However, deflation can also be the result of very positive supply-side developments like rising productivity. If that is the case, falling prices may reflect a very positive trend. The very low inflation in the US after 2000 probably also had something to do with positive supply-side shocks.

What, then, is a little bit of inflation? Is there an ideal inflation rate? Alan Greenspan, former chairman of the Fed's most important decision-making body, the Federal Open Market Committee (FOMC) is quoted as saying that "price stability is best thought of as an environment in which inflation is so low and stable over time that it does not materially enter into the decisions of households and firms."[3] It varies from country to country and from time to time. Economists generally agree that a lower inflation rate is better than a higher one. Central banks of most developed economies, including the US, the euro area, the UK, and Japan, today define an implicit inflation target rate of around 2 percent. Emerging economies exposed to rapid structural changes of the economy might target slightly higher annual price increases.

### 4.1.3   Central Bank Policy Targets, Rules, and Discretion

Central bank charters determine the monetary policy goals as well as the structure and organization of central banks. The US Fed and the ECB are interesting examples, as they adhere to similar policy approaches, but have very different explicit goal statements.

The following quotes come from the ECB website and explains its goal. Here, the term *Eurosystem* refers jointly to the national central banks of the member states of the European Monetary Union and the ECB:

> To maintain price stability is the primary objective of the Eurosystem and of the single monetary policy for which it is responsible. This is laid down in the Treaty establishing the European Community, Article 105(1).

> "Without prejudice to the objective of price stability," the Eurosystem will also "support the general economic policies in the Community with a view to contributing to the achievement of the objectives of the Union." These include a "high level of employment" and "sustainable and non-inflationary growth."

> The Treaty establishes a clear hierarchy of objectives for the Eurosystem. It assigns overriding importance to price stability. The Treaty makes clear that ensuring price stability

is the most important contribution that monetary policy can make to achieve a favorable economic environment and a high level of employment.

The primary objective of the ECB's monetary policy is to maintain price stability. The ECB aims at inflation rates of below, but close to, 2% over the medium term.

The Fed's charter is not so specific and leaves room for it to consider a wider set of economic problems. Nevertheless, the Fed is quite clear that its principal goal is to keep inflation low and stable. The implicit target for inflation is around 2 percent, too, which is what Fed representatives call "the comfort zone of inflation."[4] If inflation is under control, however, and a short-run shock causes slow growth, high unemployment, or otherwise low aggregate demand, then the Fed's official goals are broad enough to allow it to try to stabilize the economy. Sometimes people use the word *eclectic* to describe the Fed's mandate of controlling inflation and trying to keep economic growth close to potential output growth. Eclectic means that it is derived from various strands of economic thinking and is not dogmatic.

The following quote about the Fed's goal is from the website of the Federal Reserve Bank of San Francisco:[5]

> The Federal Reserve has seen its legislative mandate for monetary policy change several times since its founding in 1913, when macroeconomic policy as such was not clearly understood. The most recent revisions were in 1977 and 1978, and they require the Fed to promote both price stability and full employment. The past changes in the mandate appear to reflect both economic events in the US and advances in understanding how the economy functions. In the twenty years since the Fed's mandate was last changed, there have been further important economic developments as well as refinements in economic thought, and these raise the issue of whether to modify the goals for US monetary policy once again. Indeed, a number of other countries – notably those that adopted the Euro as a common currency at the start of this year – have accepted price stability as the new primary goal for their monetary policies.

In an editorial "Resist the Siren Song," the *Financial Times* (October 12, 2004) argued that monetary (and fiscal) policymakers should learn from the legend of Ulysses – and from recent Nobel laureates in economics. Ulysses asked his fellow sailors to tie him to his boat's mast so he wouldn't be tempted by the beautiful but deadly sirens. Nobel laureates Finn Kydland and Edward Prescott emphasized that policymakers should be *time consistent*, i.e., stick to their good long-run policy goals and not have their attention diverted to short-term exigencies. Sticking to what is good in the long run tends to keep inflationary expectations stable and the economy growing despite what appear to be short-run disturbances. In the context of monetary policy, the temptation is primarily to create unexpected inflation in order to reduce unemployment. The editorial credits the euro system, the US, and the UK with having resisted the sirens' song and keeping their policy focused on low and stable inflation.

The general idea here is that, if a central bank frequently uses monetary policy to address short-term goals other than low inflation, its efforts to keep inflation low and stable will lose credibility in the eyes of the public. Inflation expectations will embed likely deviations from the long-term goal and, therefore, exceed the central bank's long-run inflation target. Once that happens, the central bank is trapped in its own policy in the sense that it cannot deliver low inflation except at relatively high rates of unemployment. Refraining from the use of monetary policy to pursue short-term gain on the unemployment front has the advantage of keeping inflation expectations low and enabling the central bank to pursue low inflation without the cost of higher unemployment.

The question then is: How can the central bank make its low-inflation policy credible? This leads to the contrast between explicit policy rules and policy discretion. A monetary policy rule is like an equation – once it is put into force, the decision makers at the central bank do not deviate from it. For example, Milton Friedman, the famous monetarist, once proposed that the Fed should increase the money supply by a constant rate, say 5 percent, every year, regardless of any macroeconomic developments. Other economists have proposed tying the central bank interest rate to the difference between the current and the target rate of inflation and the output gap, an approach known as the *Taylor rule*. Under a discretionary approach, in contrast, the central bank is free to react to current circumstances as it sees fit.

People who favor rules are usually people who mistrust central bankers. Supply-side economists worry that the potential for harm is great when central bankers are too free to make too many decisions. These economists prefer rules, and they point to episodes of high inflation like the 1970s to support their arguments. Of course, the history of central banking has plenty of examples of good decisions. More liberal economists often like to see more discretion used in policy and argue that the central bank should not waste its ability to stabilize output and employment in the short run.

The Greenspan Fed (1987–2006) was often given high marks by economists who believe the discretionary policy of the 1990s was pretty good. Janet Yellen, who was then president of the San Francisco Federal Reserve Bank and, from 2014 to 2018, chair of the FOMC, wrote about it in the Federal Reserve Bank of San Francisco *Economic Letter* on January 27, 2006, evaluating the record.[6] "While the Fed does not follow a policy rule, it has been consistent in its approach to achieving its dual mandate – keeping inflation low and stable and promoting maximum sustainable employment." She also noted that the Fed showed flexibility, citing how it seemed to worry less about future inflation when it knew that productivity growth was very strong. She then went on to say that another Greenspan achievement was in the area of communications. The Fed made monetary policy more understandable and transparent. "The [Fed] press release has come to include a statement about the balance of risks to the attainment of its dual mandate, and at least some indication of where policy was going in the future."

In a follow-up article "Enhancing Fed Credibility," Yellen went on to conclude that the improvements in consistency and transparency have led to greater credibility.[7] Here is what Yellen says about credibility: "But credibility is not only virtuous; it is also useful. I will argue that one of the most important benefits is shaping public expectations about inflation, and in particular, 'anchoring' those expectations to price stability. As a consequence, credibility enhances the effectiveness of monetary policy."

But just how much credibility the Fed has gained remains controversial. Eric Swanson, also from the San Francisco Fed, argued that, if the Fed had had an explicit inflation target, US inflation expectations would have been better anchored in the past.[8] Having an inflation target would mean that the Fed announces the rate it wants to achieve every year, conducts its policy in order to reach that target, and makes the inflation target a yardstick of the success of its monetary policy.[9] In direct contrast to Swanson's argument, Bharat Trehan and Jason Tjosvold found that, after recent oil price shocks in the US, inflation expectations had performed no differently than those in countries where the central bank did have explicit inflation targets (Canada and the UK).[10] This suggests that the Fed did not need inflation targets to be credible.

### 4.1.4   Central Bank Structure and Organization

The Fed and the ECB have similar decision-making bodies. We purposely do not go into too much detail on this topic and advise that interested students find other sources.[11] There is a centralized governing body in both central banks. The Fed has the *Board of Governors* in Washington, DC. The ECB has the *Executive Board* in Frankfurt, Germany. These are relatively small bodies composed of individuals who serve long terms and who are appointed with staggered terms by national governmental officials. They are considered to be monetary *technocrats* – economists or bankers or otherwise experts in money and banking.

In both of these central banks there is a main monetary policy decision-making body. The *FOMC* is the Fed's main decision-making body. The ECB counterpart is called the *Governing Council.* The FOMC and the Governing Council have centralized representation since they contain the members of the Board. They also have decentralized representation, because their memberships include the heads of the central banks from twelve US Federal Reserve Districts and the presidents of the national central banks of the countries that have adopted the euro, respectively. Among the regional Fed presidents, only five have voting rights on the FOMC at any point in time, so that the Board of Governors, with seven out of twelve votes, always holds the majority. In contrast, the Governing Council of the ECB is dominated by the presidents of national central banks.

The FOMC and the ECB Governing Council each meet regularly and make monetary policy decisions. The central/regional composition and the independence of the central bank (see section 6.2.2) should work together to guarantee that monetary policy represents the needs of the aggregate US economy and the European Monetary Union, respectively. This is important, because different regions (in the US) or countries (in the European Monetary Union) may experience different economic trends and business cycles at a given moment. Thus, when the Fed meets in Washington the specific needs of cattle farmers in Texas and the issues of aircraft workers in Seattle can, in principle, be brought up in the discussion. Likewise, when the ECB Governing Council convenes, the German Central Bank president can, in principle, discuss the economy in his country and the president of the Bank of Finland can talk about the latest fortunes of Nokia. In practice, however, this rarely happens and would be frowned upon by the other members of the Governing Council. The reason is that monetary policy controls only the money supply or the interest rate for the entire area. Therefore, it cannot and should not cater to the demands of individual regions.

The FOMC meets eight times a year, while the ECB governing council meets every two weeks. At the end of these meetings, both issue official statements and explain them in press conferences. You can find these statements on their websites. Explicit transcripts of their meetings are published with considerable time lags – five years in the case of the FOMC.

## 4.2   Monetary Policy Tools and Implementation

Central banks have the monopoly right to issue currency. *Money,* as defined above, consists of currency and various types of bank liabilities. This means that central banks do not control the money stock directly. Instead, monetary policy operates through their influence on the business conditions of commercial banks and other financial institutions.

Currency is not the only type of money created by central banks. Commercial banks and other financial institutions hold overnight deposits at their central bank. They acquire such deposits by borrowing from the central bank or by selling financial assets to the central bank, the value of which is credited to their deposit accounts. They reduce their holdings of such deposits by buying financial assets from the central bank, with the respective value charged to their deposit accounts. They need such deposits in order to make payments to other financial institutions or to non-banks.

The sum of the currency and overnight deposits issued by the central bank is called the *monetary base* or *base money.* Base money is held in part by non-banks (e.g., the cash in your and my pockets or under your mattress), and in part by commercial banks and other financial institutions. The part held by the latter is called *central bank reserves*. Commercial banks and other financial institutions trade central bank reserves, called *federal funds* in the US, among each other in the interbank market for overnight central bank money deposits. In the US, this is called the *federal funds market*. Banks facing a surplus of reserve holdings relative to their needs lend federal funds to banks facing a deficit. In the US, the interest rate paid on such overnight loans is called the *federal funds rate* (FFR), in the euro area it is the *Eonia*. This interest rate is an indicator of the scarcity of base money in the economy. It is also the only interest over which the central bank can exert immediate control. The more base money the central bank creates, the lower will be this interest rate; the less base money the central bank creates, the higher this rate will be.

The primary way in which the amount of base money is changed in the US is by *open market operations*, in which the Fed buys or sells short-term treasury bills from the banks. When the Fed buys treasury bills, it pays with newly created base money and, therefore, the amount of base money held by the banking sector increases. As a result, the fed funds rate will fall. If the Fed sells treasury bills to the banks, the opposite happens. The banks pay with base money from their Fed accounts and the amount of base money falls. As base money becomes more scarce, the fed funds rate increases.

Many central banks of emerging economies buy and sell foreign currency, usually USD or euros. When a central bank outside the US buys USD reserves from the banks in its own country, the domestic base money supply increases. In addition to affecting the interest rate, this will also impact the USD exchange rate of the domestic currency. Thus, foreign currency operations have two effects. We will discuss more of this in Chapter 8.

In the US, banks can borrow base money from the Fed at the *discount window* – the name comes from the fact that such loans must be collateralized by submitting high-quality commercial bills of exchange to the Fed. The interest charged on such loans is called the *discount rate*. When the Fed raises the discount rate, borrowing from it becomes more expensive and, therefore, base money becomes more scarce. The FFR will rise as a result. Banks will normally pass on the higher cost of borrowing to their customers by increasing loan rates. When the Fed lowers the discount rate, borrowing from it becomes cheaper, the FFR will fall, and banks will pass on the lower cost of borrowing to their customers.

Commercial banks cannot loan out all their deposits. They need cash or base money reserves to pay customers who wish to withdraw their deposits. In addition, most central banks require commercial banks to hold a minimum amount of base money reserves, called *minimum required reserves*. Minimum required reserves are defined as a fraction of the deposits a bank has issued. This fraction is called the *minimum required reserves ratio* and it serves the central bank as an instrument to control the banks' demand for base money.[12] By increasing the minimum required reserves ratio, the central bank can effectively make base money more scarce and push up the overnight interbank rate. Given an amount of base money issued by the central bank, an increase in the minimum required reserves ratio will effectively limit the amount of deposits banks can issue and, therefore, the amount of loans they can make. If the central bank reduces the minimum required reserve ratio, banks will normally quickly move to loan out the freed base money. To loan out these extra funds, commercial banks often need to lower their own interest rates on loans for cars, homes, etc. Thus, we see the connection between the interest rates that impact aggregate demand and one of the tools of the central bank.

The practical implementation of monetary policy evolves around the discussion and the setting of the interest rate on overnight loans of federal funds. Since the early 1990s, the Fed has used the FFR as a target for its short-term operations. The FOMC decides on a target value for the FFR and the New York Federal Reserve Bank implements this target through open market operations. If the FFR is above target, the NY Fed will buy government securities; if the FFR is below target, the NY Fed will sell government securities. In the fall of 2008, the Fed changed its practice and announced a minimum and a maximum FFR, instead. Figure 4.3 shows the FFR rate

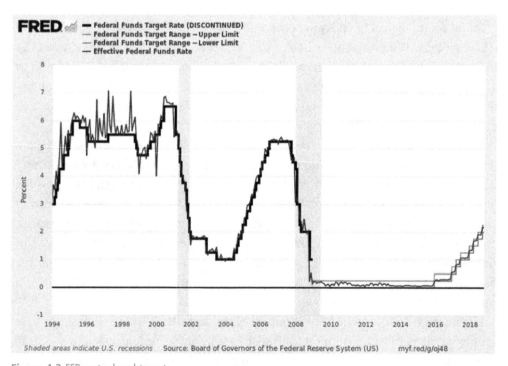

**Figure 4.3** FFR: actual and target

*Source*: Board of Governors of the Federal Reserve System (US), Effective Federal Funds Rate, Federal Funds Target Upper and Lower Limits, retrieved from FRED, Federal Reserve Bank of St. Louis; https://fred.stlouisfed.org/series/FF, October 12, 2018.

together with the Fed's FFR target rate from January 1994 to December 2008. After December 2008, it shows the target range and the actual rate. Figure 4.3 shows that during the 1990s, the Fed allowed deviations from the target rate which could at times be substantial. Since 2001, in contrast, the New York Fed, through its open market operations, has kept the actual rate very close to the target rate or within the target range.

Between January 2005 and July 2006, the Fed pushed the FFR up in an effort to tighten monetary policy. After about a year of a stable rate, the Fed lowered its target rate again. When the financial crisis hit with full force in mid-October 2008, the Fed managed to push the rate down to almost zero.

To explain the implementation of monetary policy more fully, we expand the case of open market purchases to increase the money supply. Suppose that the Fed has decided to reduce interest rates and to increase the money supply by buying treasury bills from the banking sector.

**Step 1    Open Market Purchase**  In practice, the Fed buys treasury bills from a very small number of banks, so-called primary dealer banks. To do that, the Fed participates in an auction with these banks. When the Fed buys bonds, the banks quote the price they are willing to sell and the offered quantity. By buying bonds from banks, the Fed increases the price for treasury bills and because prices and yields on treasury bills are inversely related, the purchase of treasury bills by the Fed decreases interest rates for government bonds. The reduction of yields on treasury bills affects the interest rates on corporate bonds as well; they will decrease.

**Step 2    Increase in Bank Reserves**  The Fed pays by crediting the banks' accounts with the Fed, thus increasing reserves or Fed funds by the respective amount.

**Step 3    The Fed Funds Market and the FFR**  As a result of the increase in the amount of Fed funds, the FFR falls and other money market rates will fall with it.

**Step 4    The Term Structure of Interest Rates**  The Fed will usually only use the treasury bill market, securities with a maturity of max one year for its open market operations. All other yields for treasury securities with a maturity longer than one year will be entirely determined by demand and supply. Market competition generally keeps rates for securities with different maturities close to one another. For example, movements over time of the interest rate on a one-year note and a ten-year note are usually fairly similar. But, during normal times, a ten-year note usually has a higher interest rate. This is due to the higher risk associated with longer holding periods, differences in inflation expectations over different time horizons, and various special factors. If you expect less financial uncertainty over the coming year than over the next ten years, then you would expect a lower market

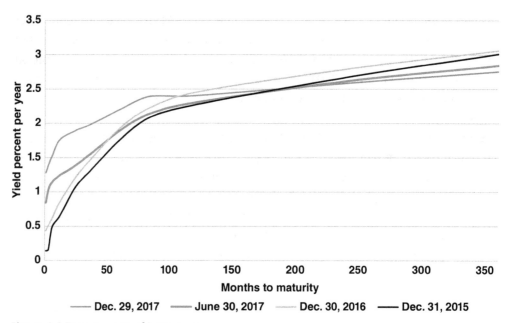

**Figure 4.4** Term structure of interest rates
*Source*: own calculations based on US Treasury Data, downloaded October 12, 2018.

yield on the one-year note. If you expect a lower inflation rate over the coming year than over the coming ten years, you would expect a lower market yield on the one-year note. If special supply-and-demand conditions imply an insufficiency of demand for ten-year notes, then you would expect a lower market yield on the one-year note (assuming the ten-year and one-year notes are imperfect substitutes).

Figure 4.4 has a graph of the *term structure of interest rates* which plots the yields to maturity for treasury securities with maturities from one month up to thirty years or 360 months. The light-blue line is based on data as of December 29, 2017; the dark-blue line uses data from June 30, 2017; the gray line uses data from December 30, 2016, and the black line data from December 31, 2015. The graph shows that short-term rates are usually lower than longer-term yields. Over the course of the two years between the end of 2015 and 2017, yields with maturities of a little more than seven years increased, and the shorter the maturity, the larger the increase. In contrast, yields of maturities longer than seven years decreased a little bit. As a result, the December 2015 yield curve was flatter than the December 2017 curve. A steeper yield curve indicates market expectations of higher interest rates in the future than at present.

Step 5   Real Interest Rates, the Term Structure, and the Success of Fed Policy  Monetary policy may be aimed at reducing the whole term structure of real interest rates, but it doesn't always work that way. Any given Fed policy or other AD shock might affect inflation expectations and risk. Other shocks might also impact markets as when the government decided to stop issuing thirty-year government securities and that expected scarcity drove down rates on longer-term bonds relative to short-term bonds.

The point is that the Fed's policy isn't fully successful unless it moves most interest rates in the desired direction. Otherwise, the full impact of the policy will not materialize. One important condition to achieve that is that the Fed keeps inflation expectations stable at 2 percent over all time horizons.

**Step 6   The End of the Story – Interest Rates Fall and Aggregate Demand Rises – Or Do They?** That is just about the whole story. If the stimulus was too little, then interest rates might not fall enough: aggregate demand and the economy would not be much impacted. Various types of uncertainty may come into play at this point. People may feel uncertain about the stability of the banking system and be unwilling to put their money into banks. Banks may feel uncertain about the creditworthiness of potential borrowers and be unwilling to use the money in their accounts to make loans. Businesses may feel uncertain about future market conditions and be unwilling to borrow money. Under all these circumstances, the Fed's policy would neither affect interest rates nor aggregate demand, and the policy would not reach its goal. If the stimulus raised inflation expectations or increased inflation risk across the whole maturity spectrum, the policy would not affect the term structure of real interest rates, and aggregate demand and the economy would not be impacted.

## 4.3   Short-Run Impacts of Monetary Policy

When the central bank injects money into the system at a faster pace than what corresponds to the growth of the economy, or reduces short-term interest rates, we speak of an *expansionary monetary policy*. Such a policy aims to reduce real interest rates, and increase interest-sensitive spending and aggregate demand. The rise in aggregate demand then causes firms to want to produce more and raise prices. The macro impact is a rise in real GDP and an increase in the price level. Graphically, a monetary expansion would shift the AD curve to the right (thick blue arrow in Figure 4.5). Aggregate demand increases and the price level rises in a movement along the AS curve to the new equilibrium. This is shown in Figure 4.5, where we assume that actual output was below potential output initially. The monetary expansion serves to move output close to potential and, thus, close to the output gap.

Having achieved that, the central bank should return to normal monetary policy when aggregate demand equals aggregate supply at the level of potential output. This means that the central bank should stop injecting more liquidity into the economy and let short-term interest rates return to their initial levels. Otherwise

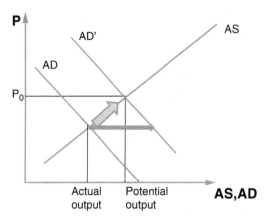

Figure 4.5 A monetary expansion

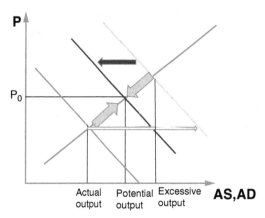

Figure 4.6 Overshooting monetary expansion

the central bank risks increasing aggregate demand and real GDP too much. There would be overheating and too much inflation in the economy. To avoid that, central banks must be cautious in the use of monetary policy. A prudent central bank would engage in such an expansionary AD policy only if real GDP were significantly lower than potential real GDP, that is, if there was a quite large negative output gap.

Figure 4.6 illustrates what happens if a central bank expands aggregate demand too much with its monetary policy. To avoid too much overheating, it would have to quickly counteract that with a contractionary monetary policy, i.e., reduce the supply of money and push up interest rates. This is shown by the black arrow. Output would first rise above potential, and then fall back again. The price level would first increase too much and then fall. Thus, the central bank would destabilize the economy and output and prices or inflation would fluctuate because of a *stop-and-go* monetary policy. Interest rates would be too volatile as well, making it harder for business managers to predict future developments. Too much *fine-tuning* of the economy or too much AD management may worsen macroeconomic performance.

## 4.4    International Application

There was much pressure on the ECB to reconsider how it employed monetary policy in the years 2001–5. Policymakers in Germany and France were among the loudest critics of ECB policy. Growth in those countries was quite slow – and negative GDP gaps were large. Yet, these countries had given up their currencies in 1999 to be part of the euro area. While France and Germany had negative GDP gaps, the condition of the whole euro area was more balanced and there was no clear need for a euro-wide expansionary monetary policy. Furthermore, the charter of the ECB required a very narrow focus on inflation. The ECB may not employ an expansionary monetary policy if inflation is around 2 percent or higher. Inflation was above 2 percent in most of the euro area and therefore there was little that the ECB could do to help Germany and France with their deficiency of aggregate demand and their sluggish economies.

This European story is interesting for all of us. It shows how strongly some countries feel about inflation. Germany and France felt so strongly about never letting inflation get out of control that they were willing to join a monetary union whose main focus seems to be to keep inflation low. In creating the bank charter for the ECB, the founders were convinced that it is very important to keep inflation low and stable. Germany and France believed that in 1999. But later in 2002 they wished that their central bank could be more responsive. They wished that their central bank was not so rule based. They wished they had a central bank that was more short-run aggregate-demand oriented.

Only with more time will we know whether Germany and France were made better off by not having a choice of a more aggressive counter-cyclical policy. Another interesting by-product of this less active monetary policy is that it has caused countries to think about non-monetary solutions to their economic problems. In the case of Germany and France much has been written about the overall inflexibility of their labor and product markets. Some economists believe that their real problems are not monetary in origin and that the real long-run solutions do not involve monetary policy.

## 4.5    Working with Data: the 2008–9 Financial Crisis

"Money" is an aggregate of cash and various types of deposits offered by commercial banks. As we learned earlier, banks create deposits in the process of supplying credit. The Fed creates cash and the reserves held by the banking sector by purchasing assets (open market operations) or lending to banks through the discount window. The money supply thus results from the interaction of the Fed, the banks, and their customers, the non-bank sector. This interaction works through the balance sheets of these three. The Fed's balance sheet can be summarized as

$$NFA + S + REF + OA = B = CP + R$$

Here, NFA stands for the Fed's net foreign assets, i.e., gold reserves and international assets less international liabilities, S for the central bank's portfolio of domestic financial assets acquired in open-market operations, and REF denotes the Fed's total discount window loans to banks, and OA stands for all other Fed assets (net). CP is the amount of cash held by the non-banks – the dollars in your pocket – and R the amount of reserves held by the banks. The sum of these two, B, is called the monetary base. The left-hand side shows how the Fed changes the monetary base, namely by buying and selling foreign assets (NFA) or domestic assets (S) and by lending to domestic banks. The right-hand side shows how the banks and non-banks make use of it, either as cash holdings or reserves.

The balance sheet of the banking sector can be summarized as

$$L + R + S^B + OAB = D + T + REF$$

Here, L is the amount of bank credit supplied to non-banks, $S^B$ the banks' holdings of government and other securities, OAB, are other assets of the banking sector (net), while D stands for checkable deposits and T for all other types of deposits, which we dub time deposits for short. Finally, we have the balance sheet of the non-banks, which we simplify to

$$CP + S^P + D + T = L + NW$$

Here, $S^P$ stands for the non-banks' portfolio of securities, and NW is the non-banking sector's net worth.

The narrow money supply, M1 = CP + D, is the sum of cash and checkable deposits held by non-banks, while the broad money supply (M2 = CP + D + T) adds other types of bank deposits such as time and savings deposits to that.

The money multiplier separates the money supply into the monetary base, B, and the money multiplier, m1 or m2. The idea is that the monetary base indicates the Fed's behavior and the multiplier summarizes the banks' and non-banks' behavior. That separation is only an approximate one, because all three sectors interact in equilibrium and, therefore, all magnitudes in the process are interdependent.

The money supply M1 is

$$M1 = \frac{1+k}{k+r}(NFA + S + REF + OA) = m_1 B$$

where the *cash coefficient*, k = CP/D, indicates how much cash non-banks hold relative to checkable bank deposits, and the *reserves coefficient*, r = R/D, indicates how much central bank reserves banks hold relative to checkable deposits, and $m_1$ is called the M1 money multiplier. Similarly, the money supply M2 is

$$M2 = \frac{1+k+t}{k+r}(NFA + S + REF) = m_2 B$$

where the *time deposit coefficient*, t = T/D, indicates the ratio in which non-banks hold other time deposits to checkable deposits, and $m_2$ is the M2 money multiplier. Since the reserves ratio, r, is typically very small, the money multiplier is normally larger than 1, indicating that the banks and the non-banks together create more than a dollar of "money" out of each dollar of monetary base created by the Fed. Both multipliers fall, when the cash or the reserves coefficient increases.

Figure 4.7 shows the evolution of the monetary base and the monetary aggregates M1 and M2 from 2005 to 2012. To simplify the graph and its understanding, all three are normalized to their levels in September 2008, which we set equal to 100. The figure shows that, before the crisis, both monetary aggregates and the base moved in a very parallel fashion, implying that the money multipliers were quite stable over time. This is confirmed by Figure 4.8 which shows the money multipliers, also normalized to 2008 levels.

When the financial crisis hit with full force in October 2008, the money multipliers immediately dropped by 40 percent.

To understand this dramatic decline, consider Figure 4.9, which shows the components of the money multipliers.

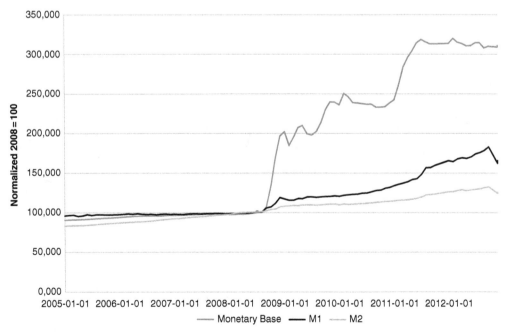

**Figure 4.7** US monetary base and money stocks (2005–12)

*Source*: own calculations based on data from the Federal Reserve Board of Governors.

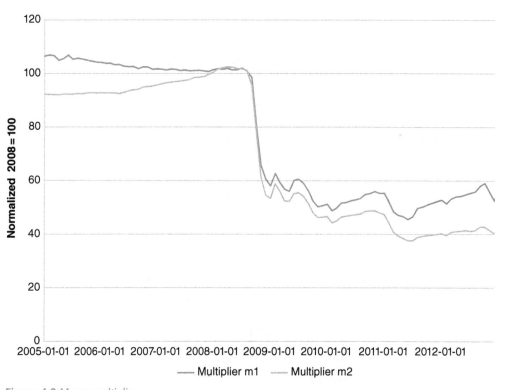

**Figure 4.8** Money multipliers
*Source*: own calculations based on data from the Federal Reserve Board of Governors.

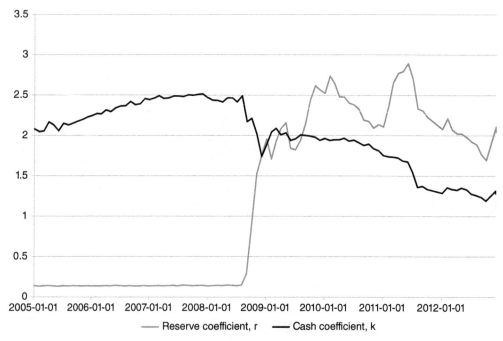

**Figure 4.9** Reserves and cash coefficients (2005–12)
*Source*: own calculations based on Federal Reserve Board data.

The most dramatic change is the increase in the reserves ratio from about 2 percent to almost 200 percent. Before the crisis, banks held an average of 1.4 cents reserves against every dollar of checkable deposits. As the crisis hit, the banks' preference for reserves increased dramatically to almost USD 2 for every dollar of checkable deposits. As the crisis unfolded, this preference rose to more than USD 2.50 reserves for every dollar of checkable deposits.

The huge increase in the banks' preference for reserves reflects the sudden unwillingness of banks to lend reserves to other banks in the interbank market. The crisis was triggered by the collapse of Lehman Brothers, one of the oldest and largest financial institutions globally. That such a venerable institution could default triggered fears within the banking industry that other banks might collapse, too. As a result, banks became extremely reluctant to lend to other banks even overnight without collateral. The extreme ups and downs of the FFR immediately after the collapse of Lehman Brothers shown in the first figure reflect the huge tensions in the market during that period. Figure 4.10 shows the counterpart to that by plotting the ratio of total interbank loans to reserves in the banking sector. This ratio increased from 6 to about 10 between 2005 and early 2008, indicating that each dollar of reserves was traded ten times on average in the interbank market right before the crisis. As the crisis hit, this ratio dropped like a rock and remained

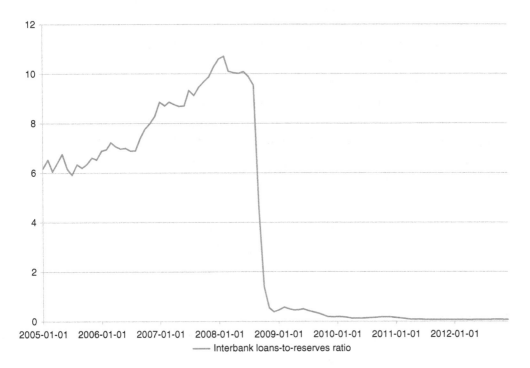

**Figure 4.10** Interbank loans
*Source*: Federal Reserve Board.

flat at values of 0.30 and below afterwards. That is, the interbank market largely dried out as a result of banks losing confidence in each other's creditworthiness.

The increase in the banks' preference for reserves caused the money multipliers to contract by about 40 percent. In fact, the multiplier $m_1$ fell to below 1. The chart shows that the cash coefficient also declined.

The decline in the money multiplier implies that the money supplies M1 and M2 would have contracted by about 40 percent due to the crisis without a reaction by the Fed. This reaction came almost immediately, as the Fed embarked on a huge expansion of the monetary base (see Figure 4.7). By first doubling and then further expanding the base, the Fed managed to shield the money supply from any effect of the financial crisis; in fact, both monetary aggregates continued on their growth paths almost as before. But, as the Fed's FFR target hit zero, the Fed's normal way of implementing monetary policy through FFR targets was no longer feasible, since the FFR cannot turn negative.

Therefore, the Fed invented a new procedure, called *quantitative easing* (QE). It amounts to setting quantitative targets for the monetary base instead. This in itself was not much more than a technicality. The new thing about QE is that the Fed started expanding the monetary base by buying financial assets which it had never bought before, such as commercial paper, securities issued by private institutions, and mortgage-backed securities. As a result, the Fed has assumed considerable credit risk in its balance sheet, and it has been blamed for crossing the line between monetary and fiscal policy, for which it has no congressional authority, in doing so. In late 2010, the Fed embarked on another expansion of the monetary base that became known as QE2. The expansion is clearly noticeable in Figure 4.7, where the base jumps upward again starting in October 2010.

Was QE effective? Our graphs suggest that the Fed mainly managed to absorb the bank's huge increase in the preference for reserves. In doing so, it has pretty much replaced the pre-crisis function of the interbank market. What it failed to achieve is to create any sizeable monetary stimulus beyond that which might have helped to pull the US economy out of the post-crisis recession.

## 4.6  SUMMARY

Monetary policy can be aimed at price stability alone or more. Central banks' control of money has the potential to impact and stabilize aggregate demand. By setting the right level or growth rate of aggregate demand, monetary policy should achieve an appropriate amount of output together with low and stable inflation. Central banks use a number of different tools but they all boil down to injecting just the right amount of money into the economy so that interest rates and loans are just right for the economy. Because monetary policy can have important impacts on the economy, most business planners keep a constant eye on central banks and their actions. Many of us try to predict what these central banks will do next. Once central banks act, we then try to understand and predict just how much and how fast their policies will affect interest rates, aggregate demand, output, and inflation. Predicting central bank actions and impacts is never easy because these predictions are impacted by so many things. So we try but we realize that all of our own planning relies on our best educated guesses about money and monetary policy.

## 4.7   REVIEW QUESTIONS

1. What would the Fed do in order to stimulate aggregate demand?
2. Why did the huge expansion of the US monetary base after 2008 not lead to high inflation?
3. What is the difference between the money stock M1 and the central bank money stock?
4. What is the connection between the money stock M1 and the central bank money stock?
5. Suppose that the central bank buys large amounts of foreign currency in the foreign exchange market. What happens to the monetary base, the FFR, and the money stock M1?
6. Suppose that the Fed has announced its intention to raise interest rates over the next eight quarters. What happens to the term structure of interest rates?

## NOTES

1 See the Bank of Canada *Backgrounder on Inflation and Price Stability*, at: www.bankofcanada.ca/wp-content/uploads/2010/11/inflation_price_stability.pdf
2 Tao Wu, "Understanding Deflation," Federal Reserve Bank of San Francisco *Economic Letter*, April 2, 2004, at: www.bus.indiana.edu/davidso/corefall04/S12Wudeflationf04.pdf
3 Fed Governor Frederic S. Mishkin, "Comfort Zones, Shmumfort Zones," a lecture at Washington and Lee University, at: www.federalreserve.gov/newsevents/speech/mishkin20080327a.htm
4 e.g. Mishkin, at: www.federalreserve.gov/newsevents/speech/mishkin20080327a.htm
5 John Judd and Glenn D. Rudebusch, "The Changing Goals of US Monetary Policy," Federal Reserve Bank of San Francisco *Economic Letter 1999–04*, January 29, 1999.
6 "2006: A Year of Transition at the Fed," at: www.frbsf.org/publications/economics/letter/2006/el2006-01.html
7 "Enhancing Fed Credibility," at: www.frbsf.org/economic-research/publications/economic-letter/2006/march/enhancing-fed-credibility

8 "Would an Inflation Target Help Anchor US Inflation Expectations?," at: www.frbsf.org/economic-research/publications/economic-letter/2006/august/would-an-inflation-target-help-anchor-us-inflation-expectations

9 Several central banks around the world practice inflation targeting. Among them are the ECB, the Bank of England, the Swedish Riksbank, and the Central Bank of Chile. Inflation targets are typically around 2 percent annually.

10 "Inflation Targets and Inflation Expectations: Some Evidence from Oil Price Shocks," at: www.frbsf.org/economic-research/publications/economic-letter/2006/september/inflation-targets-and-inflation-expectations-some-evidence-from-the-recent-oil-shocks

11 For the US Fed, see www.frbsf.org/publications/federalreserve/monetary/index.html. For the ECB, see www.ecb.int/pub/pdf/other/monetarypolicy2004en.pdf

12 For details of the Fed's reserve requirements, see www.federalreserve.gov/monetarypolicy/reservereq.htm. Since the financial crisis of 2008–9, the Fed and the ECB pay interest on bank reserves. Prior to that, minimum required reserves were akin to a tax on base money held as reserves by banks.

# 5    Fiscal Policy and Aggregate Demand

Fiscal policy refers to the government's use of taxation, spending, and regulatory policies to achieve its economic and political goals. As with monetary policy, there are many issues and controversies that relate to the use of fiscal policy. Since these issues and controversies play out in the political arena daily, business planners need to pay attention, because the results will come to affect them. Fiscal policies of the past and expected policies of the future can have pronounced impacts on interest rates, spending, profits, exchange rates, and many other aspects of the business environment. This chapter develops the basic terminology, concepts, and theories that relate to fiscal policy. It explains how fiscal policy affects aggregate demand and how the government can use it to counteract business-cycle fluctuation.

Fiscal policy is the other main part of AD policy. Together with monetary policy, the government can use it to stabilize aggregate demand, trying to avoid recessions and booms. One point to emphasize from the beginning is that, while monetary and fiscal policies often aim at the same short-term goals, they are very different. They are conducted by different parts of the government: Fiscal policy is determined by the legislative branch (e.g., parliament or congress) and the executive branch of government; monetary policy is determined by the central bank. Furthermore, the tools and procedures for their implementation are very different. Sometimes fiscal policy seems to reinforce the central bank's monetary policy; at other times, they seem to clash and may at least partially offset each other. Fiscal policy generally changes less frequently than monetary policy and is, therefore, less flexible than the latter. Nevertheless, it continues to be used to control aggregate demand in countries around the world and it frequently has both positive and negative impacts that we all deal with.

Fiscal policy evolves around the government's annual budget. The budget, a law passed by the legislature and approved by the executive branch, determines the annual levels of taxation and spending. When taxes change, this impacts spending by companies and families. Government spending does the same. Thus aggregate demand is impacted by both of these elements of fiscal policy.

Impacting the nation's macroeconomic performance is only one of many goals and missions governments pursue. Among them are justice, defense, security, transportation, communication, healthcare, education, income security, caring for the elderly and for economically disadvantaged people, caring for the environment, and just distributions of income and wealth. Government activities directed at all of these goals and missions involve spending money, and, therefore, touch on fiscal policy. Whenever public funds are scarce and government spending must be reduced, fiscal policy involves choices among these goals.

The levels of taxes and spending affect aggregate demand directly and these are what this chapter deals with. A third, more microeconomic part of fiscal policy is dubbed regulatory policy. Regulatory policy sets and changes the rules under which businesses operate. These rules determine what businesses are allowed to do in the marketplace, e.g., what kind of products may be produced and sold, how they may be produced, or in what quality, and the conditions under which firms can hire and dismiss workers. These rules have important macroeconomic effects through the supply side of the economy. We will return to them in Chapter 7.

Chapter 5 begins with an introduction to government spending and taxation. Spending and tax revenue hardly ever are equal and so we learn that government budgets usually have either deficits (spending larger than revenue) or surpluses (revenues larger than spending). We then draw the relationship between annual deficits/surpluses and a nation's national debt. It is these budget imbalances that impact the economy and we define how they come to influence aggregate demand and the economy. Differences of opinion about these effects are highlighted and evaluated. International and domestic applications are explored.

## 5.1    Macro Concepts and Analysis

Fiscal policy is the responsibility of the government. *Government* in this context consists of the executive (president or prime minister) and the legislative (congress or parliament) branches. There are different levels of government, i.e., national, state/regional, and local, each of which have their own fiscal authorities and powers.

Figure 5.1 shows the revenues of the total US government sector, of the US federal government, and the combined revenues of US state and local governments from 1980 to 2017. Because total amounts are not very informative in economic terms, fiscal variables are commonly expressed in terms of percentages of GDP. The figure shows that, during these almost thirty years, government revenues from taxes never exceeded 30 percent of GDP; generally they hovered around 26 percent of GDP. Taking a longer time perspective would confirm the impression that the US government seems to be unable to generate more than 30 percent of tax revenue out of annual US economic activity. The federal government has the largest share of taxes among the three levels of government; in terms of GDP, federal tax revenues

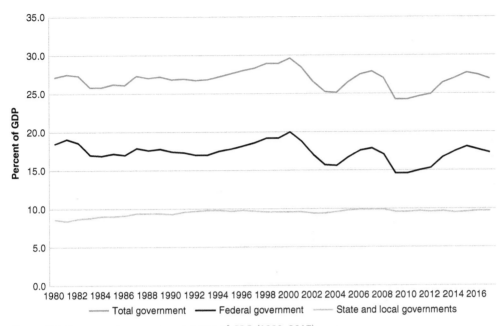

**Figure 5.1** Government revenues as percent of GDP (1980–2017)
*Source*: own calculations based on data from the Office of Budget Management.

have hovered around 17.5 percent. State and local taxes combined are generally very close to 10 percent of GDP.

Figure 5.2 shows the annual expenditures of the total US government sector, the US federal government, and the combined US state and local governments, again as percent of GDP. For the state and local governments, we report expenditures financed from own resources, i.e., state and local taxes and borrowing, only. Federal government spending includes grants to the state and local governments which account for another 2.5 to 3.0 percent of GDP. Except for a brief period in the late 1990s, total government expenditures have been above 30 percent of GDP. They peaked at 37 percent in the Great Recession in 2009 and gradually declined from there, but were still relatively high in 2016 and 2017. Once again, the federal government accounts for the largest part of total government expenditures. Federal spending generally declined in terms of GDP from 22.8 percent in 1983 to 17.6 percent in 2001. During the Great Recession it peaked at 24.4 percent of GDP. Combined state and local spending has trended upward somewhat over these almost three decades, from a little under 10 percent to 11 percent in 2017.

The *government budget balance* is the difference between government revenues and expenditures. Figure 5.3 shows the total, federal, and state and local government budget balances for 1980 to 2017. Total balances have been negative during most years, the exceptions being 1999 and 2000. Figure 5.3 shows that the large swings in the total government balances during this period were driven by large swings in the federal budget balance (–2.5) percent in 1981; (–5.8) percent in 1983;

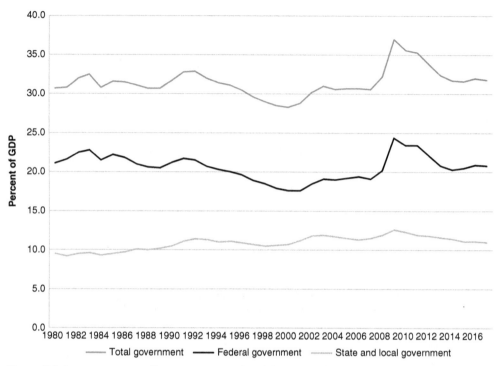

**Figure 5.2** Government expenditures as percent of GDP (1980–2017)
*Source*: own calculations based on data from the Office of Budget Management.

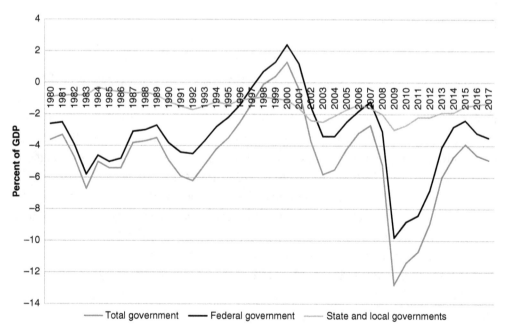

**Figure 5.3** Government budget balances as percent of GDP (1980–2017)
*Source*: own calculations based on data from the Office of Budget Management.

2.4 percent in 2000; (–3.4) percent in 2004; (–9.8) percent in 2009; (–2.4) percent in 2015. Given the size of US GDP, these are huge changes in absolute amounts, and Figure 5.3 shows that the federal budget bears the brunt of macroeconomic management by fiscal policy in the US. State and local governments combined generally had small negative balances between −1.0 and –3.0 percent of GDP.

### 5.1.1   International Application: Is the US Government Large?

We all like to complain about *big* government. But is the US government really big? One way to look at this question is to compare the US with other countries. This is what we do in Figure 5.4. Recall from our national accounts that government consumption is what the government spends on wages and salaries for its own employees who provide public services like defense, security, etc., and on purchases of goods and services from private enterprises. We saw in Chapter 1, section 1.1 that in addition to government consumption, the government spends money on various types of social transfers such as pensions and social security. When we look at the size of government, it is very informative to separate these two types of expenditures.

Figure 5.4 reveals two things. First, the US government is actually relatively small when compared to the governments of other countries. In Sweden, the size of government reaches almost 50 percent, in Germany 44 percent. Second, the

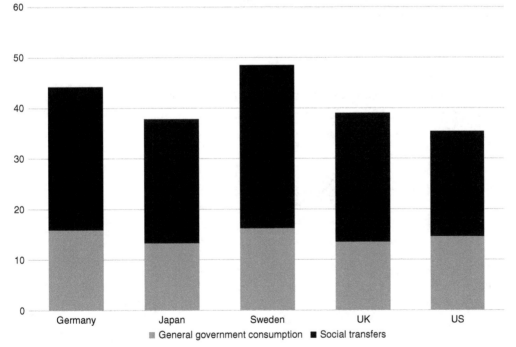

**Figure 5.4** Government size in selected countries (2016)
*Note*: Expenditures in percent of GDP.
*Sources*: IMF and European Commission, AMECO Database.

differences in general government consumption are very small across countries, ranging from 13.3 percent in Japan to 16.2 percent in Sweden. The large international differences in the size of government result from differences in the size of government transfers and this reflects differences in the generosity of social policies. Sweden and Germany are both European welfare states that redistribute about one-third of GDP among their citizens. The US does much less in this regard; its government redistributes about one-fifth of GDP.[1]

## 5.1.2    Working with Data: Fiscal Policy Tools

Most of the focus of fiscal policy is on government's ability to spend and tax. A good source of detailed background information about how the US government taxes and spends is the Congressional Budget Office (CBO) Budget Outlook. CBO reports on US government spending and tax revenues in accordance with the federal government's unified budget, which relates to the government's fiscal year from October 1 to September 30. This is different from government revenues and spending according to the NIPA framework, which relates to the calendar year and is compiled and published by the BEA.

Another important distinction is that the NIPA figures include actual government expenditures and revenues during a given year, whereas the unified budget includes expenditures and revenues budgeted for the same year. Some government revenues and expenditures are not included in the budget. Some are budgeted, but they are executed in a later period. Therefore, national accounts data and budget data are generally not identical.

## 5.1.3    Federal Government Revenues

Table 5.1 reports the composition of federal government revenues in 1934 and in 2017. In 1934, the federal government took in a total of almost USD 3 billion in revenues. It was mainly financed by excise taxes (taxes on goods and services)

**Table 5.1** Composition of federal government revenues by source

| Fiscal year | 1934 | | 2017 | |
|---|---|---|---|---|
| | Mill. of USD | % | Mill. of USD | % |
| Individual income taxes | 420 | 14.2 | 1,587,120 | 47.9 |
| Corporate income taxes | 365 | 12.3 | 297,048 | 6.5 |
| Social insurance and retirement receipts | 30 | 1.0 | 1,161,897 | 35.0 |
| Excise taxes | 1354 | 45.8 | 83,823 | 3.2 |
| Other | 788 | 26.7 | 186,294 | 3.5 |
| Total | 2,955 | 100.0 | 3,316,182 | 100.0 |

*Source*: Office of Management of the Budget.

and other revenues (such as fees, tariffs). Taxes on personal and corporate income accounted for a very small share of total revenues, and social insurance and retirement receipts for just 1 percent.

In contrast, in 2017 the federal government took in USD 3.3 trillion in revenues and 47.9 percent of that came from personal income taxes, and 35.0 percent from social insurance and retirement receipts. Since these are also linked to wages and salaries, over 80 percent of federal government revenues today comes from charges on personal incomes. Corporate income tax accounts for merely 6.5 percent of federal revenues, excise taxes for only 3.2 percent.

### 5.1.4   Federal Government Spending

As shown in Table 5.2, the US federal government spent about USD 4 trillion in 2017. Federal government spending excluding interest payments is called *primary spending*. Primary spending consists of *mandatory spending, national defense spending,* and *nondefense spending*. Mandatory spending is *mandatory* in the sense that it is determined by legislation which is passed outside the annual budget process. It refers to what we earlier called *entitlement programs*, such as social security, Medicare, or Medicaid. Such programs can be changed in principle, but it is very hard to do that because of the strong political groups supporting them. The remaining part of the budget is called *discretionary spending*, which is divided into national defense and nondefense spending. But national defense spending can also not be changed easily because of its high priority. Table 5.2 thus illustrates that a president of the United States has more or less 15 percent of the overall budget that he can allocate according to his wishes. How much fun is that? The fun of USD 610 billion!

Figure 5.5 shows the development of the share of federal mandatory spending and its main components in total federal spending from 1980 to 2023. Health and Medicare includes spending on Medicaid. Income security includes earned income,

**Table 5.2** Federal government spending 2017

| Total (USD trillions) | 4.01 |
| --- | --- |
| Net interest (%) | 6.7 |
| Mandatory (%) | 63.3 |
| National defense | 14.7 |
| Nondefense | 15.3 |
| Selected nondefense items | |
| *Education, training, employment, social services* | 3.6 |
| *Physical resources* | 3.3 |
| *General science, space, technology* | 0.8 |
| *Administration of justice* | 1.5 |

*Source*: Office of Management of the Budget.

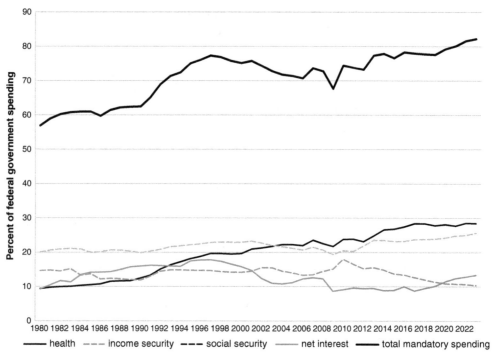

**Figure 5.5** Federal mandatory spending (1980–2023; % of total spending)
*Source*: own calculations based on data from the Office of Budget Management.

child, and other tax credits, food programs, unemployment compensation, family support, and retirement programs. Figure 5.5 shows the rising trend in the share of mandatory spending over the past three decades. It increased from 50 percent to 70 percent. This trend was mainly driven by health and Medicare spending. In contrast, income security programs have generally declined. Combined with the insight that there seems to be an upper limit to taxation in the US economy, Figure 5.5 suggests that there is a limit to the future expansion of health-related spending programs.

Table 5.2 also shows the shares of some selected nondefense items in the total federal budget. In 2017, the federal government allocated 3.6 percent of its spending to education and related programs and 3.3 percent to *physical resources*, which includes energy, natural resources and environment, commerce and housing credit, transportation, and regional and community development. Of the total budget, 0.8 percent went to general science, space, and technology; 1.5 percent to the administration of justice.

### 5.1.5    Who Is Paying Federal Taxes?

Table 5.3 shows the individual income tax contributions by income groups for 2015. Households with an income of USD 100,000 or less contribute to 19.5 percent of

**Table 5.3** Individual income tax statistics by adjusted gross income (2015)

| Adjusted gross income | Share of all returns filed (%) | Share of all income taxes paid (%) | Average effective tax rate (%) |
|---|---|---|---|
| USD 2 million or more | 0.1 | 20.4 | 27.5 |
| USD 500K to < USD 2 million | 0.8 | 17.9 | 26.8 |
| USD 200K to < USD 500K | 3.6 | 20.6 | 19.4 |
| USD 100K to < USD 200K | 12.3 | 21.7 | 12.7 |
| USD 50K to < USD 100K | 21.8 | 14.1 | 9.2 |
| USD 30K to < USD 50K | 17.6 | 4.0 | 7.2 |
| Less than USD 30K | 43.8 | 1.4 | 4.9 |

*Note*: For each income group, the "average effective tax rate" is the ratio of total income tax paid to total adjusted gross income on returns with tax liability. Shares do not add up to 100% due to rounding.
*Source*: Pew Research Center analysis of IRS data.

overall income tax revenues, while households with incomes between USD 200,000 to 500,000 contribute 42.3 percent. Households and individuals with less than USD 30,000 adjusted gross income, which accounted for 43.8 percent of all returns filed, contributed only 1.4 percent to total federal income tax receipts. Their average tax rate was 4.9 percent. In contrast, households and individuals in the highest income bracket of USD 2 million or more, which were 0.1 percent of all returns filed, contributed 20.4 percent to total receipts. So, while overall marginal income tax rates in the US have been low relative to many other developed countries, the system has been rather progressive having higher income household contributing most of the government revenues from individual income tax. Households and individuals with adjusted gross incomes between USD 50K and 500K, paid the majority of all income taxes (56.4 percent), but that is due to the fact that there are so many of them. Their average tax rates are lower than the rate in the highest income bracket.

### 5.1.6 Government Deficits and Debt

A government deficit is defined as a negative government budget balance, i.e., government expenditure exceeding government revenues. Since the US federal government in 2017 spent a total of USD 4.01 trillion and had revenues of about USD 3.3 trillion, it incurred a budget deficit in the region of USD 700 billion. That sounds like a lot of money. But, to put it in perspective, we measure it in terms of GDP, in the same way as one measures the size of one's borrowing relative to the size of one's income – the *one* being the whole economy in this case. Thus, in terms of nominal GDP, the 2017 federal budget deficit was 3.5 percent. We saw in Figure 5.3 that this was actually relatively small compared to recent US history.

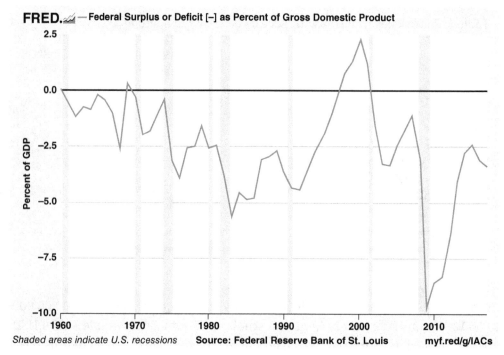

**Figure 5.6** Federal government budget balance (1960–2017)

*Source*: Federal Reserve Bank of St. Louis and US Office of Management and Budget, Federal Surplus or Deficit [−] as Percent of Gross Domestic Product, retrieved from FRED, October 14, 2018.

Figure 5.6 shows the evolution of the federal government budget balance in terms of GDP since 1960. During the 1960s and 1970s, there was a general downward trend, which bottomed out at −5.7 percent in 1983. Following that, we have seen some fifteen years of deficits getting smaller (and turning into surpluses around the turn of the century). After 2000, deficits reemerged, and the largest deficit occurred in 2009 with about 10 percent of GDP.

Another clear message from Figure 5.6 is the correlation between increases in the deficit (surpluses falling) and recessions of the US economy. We see that clearly in the recessions of/starting in 1960, 1970, 1975, 1980, 1981, 1990, 2000, and then the Great Recession, 2008. This shows the interaction between aggregate demand and fiscal policy, an issue to which we return below.

Annual budget deficits add to the total gross debt the federal government has incurred over time, while annual federal government budget surpluses subtract from it. For example, if the federal government had a deficit of USD 100 billion one year and then a surplus of USD 100 billion in the following year, its total debt would rise and then fall. Over time, therefore, persistent deficits lead to an accumulation of debt.

Figure 5.7 shows the evolution of gross federal debt in terms of GDP since 1960. Although the federal government generally ran deficits during the period from

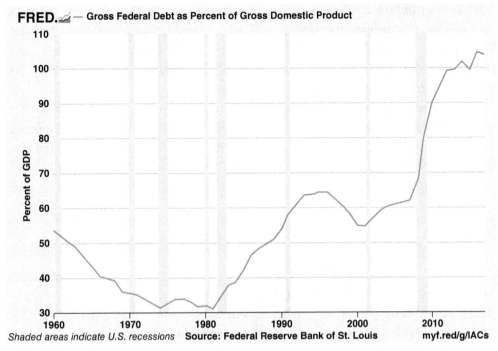

**Figure 5.7** Gross federal debt (1960–2016)

*Source*: Federal Reserve Bank of St. Louis and US Office of Management and Budget, Gross Federal Debt as Percent of Gross Domestic Product, retrieved from FRED, Federal Reserve Bank of St. Louis; October 14, 2018.

1960 to 1980 (see Figure 5.6), the ratio of federal debt to GDP generally fell, because nominal GDP was rising faster than federal debt. That changed dramatically, however, under the Reagan and Bush senior administrations, under which the federal debt-to-GDP ratio almost doubled from 31 percent in 1981 to 58 percent in 1991. The federal debt-to-GDP ratio fell under the second Clinton administration, but then increased again rapidly under the Bush junior and the Obama administrations. At the end of 2017, it stood at 105 percent of GDP.

Much of the federal government debt is held by other government agencies, predominantly the social security trust fund. In 2017, that was the case for 27 percent of total federal government debt. The debt issued by the federal government and not held by other government agencies is called *federal government debt held by the public* or *federal government net debt*. But that is a bit misleading, because a sizeable part of that is held by the Federal Reserve who acquired it through its open market purchases. In 2017, this was another 12.2 percent of total federal government gross debt. Since the Fed is part of the government sector, this means that, in 2017, 39 percent of total federal gross debt was held by parts of the federal government itself. That means that 39 percent of the interest paid by the federal government on its debt actually remains in the government sector.

It follows from these calculations that 60 percent of the federal government gross debt was held by private individuals and institutions, both domestic and foreign. This amounts to 63.6 percent of 2017 GDP. About half of that was held by foreign and international investors, implying that about one-third of the interest paid by the federal government on its debt goes to foreigners.

US *national debt* includes the debt of the federal government, the states, and municipalities, and excludes the federal debt held by government agencies. According to the US Debt Clock, it amounted to about USD 21 trillion at the end of 2017, corresponding to about 105 percent of US GDP, or USD 64,600 per capita.[2]

## 5.2   Fiscal Policy and AD Policy

Until the Great Depression of the 1930s, it was generally thought that governments had little responsibility for correcting macroeconomic developments and fluctuations. Policymakers, business managers, and economists believed that something like Adam Smith's *invisible hand* would operate at the macroeconomic level, meaning that undesirable changes in aggregate demand would be self-correcting and temporary. The experience of the Great Depression gave rise to a new way of thinking, sometimes called *Keynesian economics* after its leader, John Maynard Keynes. Keynesian economics established the idea that aggregate demand might not be self-correcting, and that it is the responsibility of government to use its fiscal tools to correct AD imbalances. Since at least the early 1960s, governments around the world have used changes in taxes, spending, and regulation on several occasions to impact aggregate demand.

### 5.2.1   Fiscal Policy in the Short Run

To explain the short-run impact of fiscal policy on aggregate demand, we return to our macroeconomic equilibrium analysis from Chapter 3. Consider a situation in which aggregate demand is deemed too low relative to potential output. In order to stimulate aggregate demand, the government could engage in a *fiscal expansion* in one of the following ways:

* Buy more goods and services. This directly increases spending and aggregate demand.
* Increase transfer payments to households. This would increase disposable income and if households behave normally, the increase in disposable income should increase spending.
* Reduce tax rates on household income. This would increase disposable income and if households behave normally, the increase in disposable income should increase spending.

- Reduce taxes or change regulations that might increase business income.
- Increase business spending but the size of the increase would depend on many other factors (including business confidence).

Either way, the government would generate additional aggregate demand, meaning that the AD curve shifts out as shown in Figure 5.8 by the blue arrow. As in the case of monetary policy, the shift of the AD curve induces a movement along the short-run AS curve, indicated by the black arrow and leading to a rise in output and the price level or an acceleration of inflation. Output would rise from the actual level to potential output and the price level from $P_0$ to $P_1$.

Conversely, a cut in government expenditures including transfers or an increase in taxes would shift the AD curve to the left and lead to lower output and a lower price level or a deceleration of inflation. This is shown in Figure 5.9. We start from actual output and the price level $P_0$. The fiscal contraction induces a leftward shift of the AD curve indicated by the blue arrow and a move along the AS curve indicated by the black arrow. The new macroeconomic equilibrium would be at potential output and the price level $P_1$.

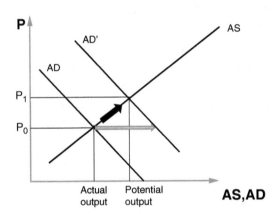

Figure 5.8 Fiscal expansion to increase aggregate demand

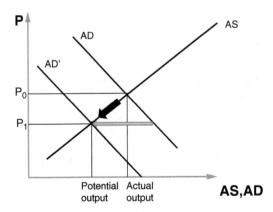

Figure 5.9 Fiscal contraction

Fiscal expansions and fiscal contractions generally translate into rising or declining government budget deficits. One might be tempted, therefore, to interpret changes in the deficit as an indicator of the government's reaction to current macroeconomic developments. But, here is a caveat: Deficits are a two-way street! Changes in government deficits impact the economy, but the reverse is true, too – changes in the economy cause changes in the government deficit.[3] This is because the levels of government spending and taxes change, when the country's income changes. For example, when the economy enters a recession and incomes are falling, people pay fewer taxes and fewer contributions to social security and other social insurance programs. People who become unemployed may pay much less in taxes. Also, in a recession the government pays out more in transfer payments since more people are eligible for unemployment insurance and poverty assistance. So the general rule is:

A stronger economy produces smaller government deficits or larger surpluses.

A weaker economy produces larger government deficits.

So, we need to be careful with interpreting government deficit data, because, in any given year the deficit might change because of policy or because of the impact of macroeconomic developments. For example from 2001 to 2002, the US government deficit swung from a surplus of USD 47 billion to a deficit of USD 254. Some of that swing was caused because the government pursued a specific AD policy to increase the government deficit. The rest of it was caused by a recessionary economy. Unfortunately, we cannot tell exactly how much of an observed change in the government deficit is from policy and how much is from economic developments. We have to use statistical estimates to tell the two apart.

As mentioned above, personal and corporate income taxes and contributions to social insurance programs fall when the economy is weak and rise when the economy is strong. This means that these taxes react *automatically* to macroeconomic fluctuations in the sense that changing the amounts collected does not require a discretionary government action. Since these taxes tend to be progressive, i.e., the average tax rate rises with rising income and falls with declining income, the automatic adjustments have the property of counteracting the decline in aggregate demand resulting from an economic downswing and the rise in aggregate demand resulting from an economic upswing. Thus, they *stabilize* aggregate demand in the same way a legislated tax rate cut would do in a recession and a tax rate hike would do in a boom. Therefore, these automatic reactions of taxes and social insurance contributions are called *automatic stabilizers*. On the expenditure side of the budget, unemployment compensation and similar programs have a similar property: They rise in economic downswings and decline in economic upswings and, thus, counteract the effects of such fluctuations on aggregate demand. How large the effects of automatic stabilizers are on government tax revenues, spending and budget balances depends on the design of the relevant tax and spending rules and differs substantially across countries.

Using statistical estimates of the reaction of tax revenues and government spending to fluctuations in GDP gives rise to the computation of *cyclically adjusted* or *structural* revenues, expenditures, and budget balances. For example, the *primary structural government balance* is the primary balance (revenues minus primary spending) corrected for the impact of macroeconomic fluctuations on taxes and spending. Conceptually, this is the primary balance that would result from current tax and spending policies if real GDP was equal to potential GDP. The *cyclical primary balance* is the difference between the observed primary balance and the structural primary balance. It reflects the impact of current macroeconomic fluctuations on the primary balance.

We illustrate these concepts in Figure 5.10, which uses US data for the years of the Great Recession and thereafter, 2007–15. Gray bars indicate the structural primary balance, black bars the cyclical primary balance. In 2007, the structural primary balance was a deficit of 2 percent of GDP, while the cyclical part was a

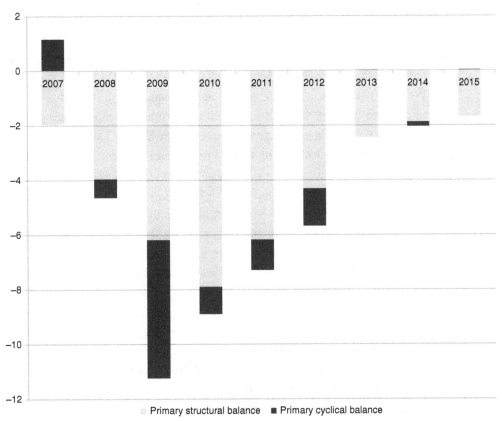

**Figure 5.10** US structural and cyclical primary balances (2007–15; % of GDP)
*Sources*: IMF, WEO Database.

surplus of 1 percent, resulting in a total primary deficit of 1 percent. The government increased the structural primary deficit already in 2008 and in 2009 and 2010. In 2008, the cyclical component turned negative and very much so in 2009. That year, the total primary deficit stood at 11.2 percent of US GDP; 6.2 percent of that was due to the structural primary deficit; and 5.1 percent to the cyclical primary deficit. In the years that followed, the structural part remained fairly large, while the cyclical part of the primary deficit vanished quite rapidly.

### 5.2.2 Macro Magic? The Government Expenditure Multiplier

Here is an extra bonus from macroeconomics. Remember the economic circuit we looked at in Chapter 1. It says that aggregate demand must, in equilibrium, equal aggregate income. Assume that private consumption is a fixed proportion of private income, e.g., households on average spend 80 percent of their current income and save 20 percent. Here is the trick: An additional dollar of government spending must translate into an additional dollar of business revenues which translates into an additional dollar of household income in the form of wages, profits, interest, or rent. Now, this additional dollar of income increases household consumption by another 80 cents. Thus, aggregate demand is now USD 1.80 higher than before. The increase in consumption by 80 cents increases revenues and then income by 80 cents and leads to an increase in consumption by yet another 64 cents. Going through these calculations, we come to the conclusion that an additional dollar of government spending increases aggregate demand by $USD(1/(1 - 0.8) = 1/0.2 = 5$! Quite a bang for a buck! We call this mechanism the government spending multiplier.

Sounds too good to be true? Maybe! Remember that the story does not say that GDP goes up by USD 5 if government spending goes up by USD 1. There are changes in interest rates and the price level to be taken into account to figure out the effect on real GDP. How large the multiplier is with regard to real GDP remains a contested issue among economists. Guesses range from 0.5 to 5.

To understand that debate, go back to our graphical illustration in Figures 5.8 and 5.9. The government expenditure multiplier is the impact of an increase in government spending or a reduction in taxes on aggregate demand. This impact is represented by the length of the light-blue arrows in these figures, i.e., the amount by which the AD curve is shifted to the right or to the left. The impact on real GDP is represented by the black arrows and it is smaller than that. Figure 5.11 compares two scenarios with the same fiscal expansion, i.e., the shift in the AD curve (the length of the blue arrow). In the first scenario, the AS curve is relatively steep. The shift in the AD curve leads to the new short-run equilibrium output $Y_1$. In the second scenario, the AS' curve is relatively flat. It leads to the new short-run equilibrium output $Y_2$. Obviously, the fiscal expansion is more effective in increasing output and less harmful in raising the price level, when the AS curve is flat. Recall from Chapter 3 that the AS curve describes the reaction of aggregate output to changes

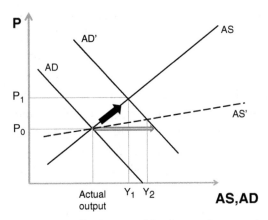

**Figure 5.11** Effectiveness of fiscal expansions: supply side

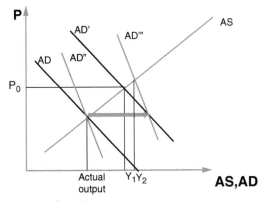

**Figure 5.12** Effectiveness of fiscal expansions: demand side

in the price level from the supply side. A flat AS curve means that it does not take much of a price increase to incite firms to hire additional workers to produce more, and it does not take much of a wage increase to make workers work more. This is a situation when there is a lot of idle capacity in firms and there are many people willing to work at current wages, i.e., a lot of unemployment. Thus, from the supply side, we can say that fiscal policy will be more effective increasing aggregate output when there is relatively much idle capacity and unemployment – a typical description of a recession.

Figure 5.12 similarly compares two scenarios of the same fiscal expansion, but with different slopes of the AD curve. The black AD curves (AD and AD') are flatter than the blue AD curves (AD" and AD'"). When AD and AD" are shifted outward by the same amounts (to AD' and AD'", respectively), the new short-run equilibrium output is smaller for the flatter AD curves ($Y_1$) than for the steeper AD curves ($Y_2$). Fiscal policy is more effective in increasing output when the AD curve is steeper; however, in that case it is also more harmful in terms of pushing up the price level. Recall from Chapter 2 that the AD curve gives us the relationship between increasing prices and output from the demand side. Increasing prices lead to a larger demand for money which, given the money supply, leads to a rise in the interest rate, and the rise in the interest rate reduces aggregate investment. A steep AD curve means that the price level can rise substantially without a large negative impact on aggregate demand. A flat AD curve means that a small rise in the price level can have a large negative impact on output. The AD curve will be steep, if a rise in the price level does not lead to a strong increase in the interest rate. This will be the case either if the central bank tries to keep interest rates down or if the economy is washed with liquidity. The first is typical for modern central banks with regard to short-term interest rates, while the latter is typical for recessions. Thus, fiscal policy is more effective if investment demand depends mostly on short-term interest rates or if we are in a recession.

Therefore, we can expect fiscal expansions to be more powerful in pushing up aggregate output in times of recessions than in times of boom. Debates about the size of the government multiplier and the effectiveness of fiscal policy for macro-economic management come down to debates about the current stance of the economy and about the interaction between monetary and fiscal policy.

### 5.2.3   Uncertainties about Short-Run AD Policies

These short-run stories are pretty straightforward: The economy has an apparent AD deficiency, the government increases the budget deficit, and that causes aggregate demand and the economy to expand. But things are never as simple as they seem. There are several issues connected to the implementation of fiscal policy and to trade-offs between increasing output and achieving other policy goals which make things more complicated. As you consider the following points, think about being someone about to commit USD 100 million to a new program and how this impacts your view of the future economic environment:

- *Inside lags* refers to the time it takes for the political process to recognize that an AD deficiency exists and to legislate the appropriate solution. Some experts believe that by the time the government goes about doing something about the problem it is often too late. Thus, we may get an AD remedy after the problem is gone. The design of tax and spending programs with effective *automatic stabilizers* can overcome the problem associated with these lags.
- *Outside lags* refers to how long it takes for a government policy to impact the economy. The outside lag differs for various forms of fiscal policy. For example, it is possible to change disposable income very quickly with an income tax change. We may not pay our taxes until April, but most of us have automatic withholding each month. So the government could be getting more money into our hands within a month or two after the legislation is signed. That contrasts greatly with a decision to build more roads or nuclear reactors. It could take a

very long time before a contractor is found and does enough work to warrant being paid.

- The *apparent persistence of the output gap* is very important for the policy response. The world is full of uncertainty about the future. When a negative real GDP gap becomes highly noticeable, there is always a question of how long it will last. If it is the result of a very temporary factor and will vanish in the next six months, then it doesn't make sense to enact a policy – it will be gone by the time the policy starts to impact the country. The inherent persistence of any real GDP gap is an arguable matter. Inasmuch as there is a wide difference of opinion about the durability of the problem, there may be a wide difference of opinion about whether it should be the subject of a new fiscal policy.

- Expectations about future policies come into play, too. If households expect future tax hikes, they may start saving more today to pay part of the future tax liabilities from their savings. If that is true, a current increase in the government deficit may induce households to expect future tax hikes and reduce current consumption. David Ricardo, a British economist from the nineteenth century, believed that, as a result, the impact of an increase in the current deficit might be nil. For example, suppose the government tells you they are going to reduce your taxes by USD 100, expecting you to go and spend most of that amount. But, as Ricardo argued, people might save all of it, because they would understand that this tax reduction will cause higher taxes in the future. So, one day the government would give you USD 100 and then the next day they would take USD 100 plus interest away. Foreseeing this, it would be best for you to just hold on to the USD 100 and put it in a savings account where it earns interest. In the end, how strong such expectations effects are is a matter of empirical debate.

- *Inflation trade-offs* interfere with any fiscal policy decision. For example, there may be a difference of opinion about the size of the GDP gap. Those who believe it is very small would worry that an aggressive expansionary fiscal policy would create too much inflation. They might resist voting for such a policy if inflation at the time seemed more of a problem than the real GDP gap.

- *Investment and durable goods trade-offs* are a further worry with fiscal deficits. Consider what happens when the government is selling bonds to finance a deficit. This active selling of bonds can cause interest rates to rise. Any interest-sensitive spending could be impacted if interest rates rise enough. That means that the demand for cars, appliances, houses, plant, and equipment might be reduced or *crowded out*. It is ironic that a tax cut or government spending policy designed to increase national domestic spending and aggregate demand might end up causing some specific sectors of national domestic spending to decline. If the country feels that continued strength of these interest-sensitive sectors is critical, they might not want to support a given fiscal policy.

- *International trade-offs* can also interfere with the passage of legislation. For example, larger government deficits can impact the exchange rate and the country's exports and imports. Here is the simple story. Recall that government deficits mean the government must sell bonds. If foreigners buy those bonds in large numbers, this means they need to buy large amounts of dollars in foreign exchange markets. This activity might cause the value of the dollar to increase. The latter makes a country's exports less competitive and steers both domestic and foreign buyers away from US markets to other ones. Thus a policy aimed at raising the domestic component of aggregate demand could end up reducing net exports – and reducing the foreign part of aggregate demand.
- There is also the question of the *right amount of fiscal policy*. While economics does offer analysis that can help the government determine how much to change the deficit when faced with a USD 100 billion GDP gap, it is possible that the government will not legislate the correct amount. The economists might have been wrong in their analysis. Or the politics might have interfered. Whatever the case, if the deficit is too small, then the program may continue. If the deficit is too large, it may create other problems.

That leaves a lot of planners with plenty of uncertainty about fiscal policy and aggregate demand.

## BOX 5.1 DIFFERENCE OF OPINION: THE TRUMP TAX REFORMS

The tax reforms enacted by the Trump administration in 2017 reduced marginal tax rates on personal income as well as for corporations. The marginal income tax for high-income earners (USD 500,000 for single households) decreased from 39.6 to 37 percent, and most other income levels saw decreasing marginal tax rates. The corporate tax rate was significantly reduced from 35 to 21 percent.

A marginal tax reduction targets the incentives for supplying factors of production, incentives to work and corporations to invest to expand production. Hence, the additional supply of labor and capital should increase real GDP growth and the overall welfare of the economy. The higher economic output results in higher government revenues from income and corporate taxation. While the reductions for the corporate taxes are firm, after 2025 personal income taxes will rebound to previous levels.

Tax reductions cause a decrease in revenues for the government. So the question is: Will tax reductions pay for themselves, or will they negatively affect the government budget (revenues minus expenditures) and increase the overall government debt, which is entirely financed by the issue of treasury securities?

The Congressional Budget Office (cbo.gov), a bipartisan think tank, advises the US Congress on the stance of the economy and consequences of policy changes. CBO has a rather skeptical view about the outcomes of these tax reforms. It mentions three concerns why the outlook for US government finances might be on the negative side.

First, the tax decreases might not be cost neutral. The US economy in 2018 was already running at its full potential, or even growing above potential output growth. The unemployment rate with around 4 percent is very low, capital investment by corporation is solid and strong. An additional AD stimulus is not needed. The effect of the tax relief will be minor with around one-tenth of 1 percent per year until 2022. Therefore, the tax reforms will increase the budget deficit and contribute to further rising debt levels. Hence, the Fed will most likely increase interest rates to ensure price stability. Higher-interest rates tend to decrease household consumption as well as corporate investments. In other words, the fiscal stimulus and the monetary contraction might contradict each other. The fiscal stimulus might come at a time when the economy is already running above potential economic growth.

Second, higher market interest rates caused by raising federal government issues of treasury bonds will increase the cost for financing the existing government debt of more than 100 percent of GDP. This might add to fiscal deficits and higher federal debt levels.

Third, so-called federal entitlement programs such as Medicare, Medicaid, and social security are significantly underfunded and will contribute to a further increase in budget deficits and government debt. If a government absorbs a higher portion of national savings to finance the government debt, interest rates will increase and corporate investment will decrease. So, the overall effect of the tax reforms might bring the opposite, not an increase, but a decrease in potential output growth of the economy. As a result, the ratio of government debt to GDP might increase further; the CBO estimates that net federal debt might rise from today's 80 percent to 90 percent of GDP by 2028. Such a rising trend could be *unsustainable*, an issue we return to in Chapter 6.

## 5.2.4  International Application: Fiscal Reactions to the Great Recession

Fiscal policy generally became less important as an instrument to control aggregate demand in most parts of the global economy after the early 1980s. On the one hand, experiences during the 1970s with fiscal policies counteracting incipient recessions had not been very positive in many countries: The effect on aggregate demand did not seem very strong, it often came later than needed because of time lags in the implementation of such policies, and governments were left with high levels of government deficits and debt that were difficult to rein in because of political pressures. As a result, fiscal policy had fallen into disgrace as a tool of short-run macroeconomic policy among governments. Monetary policy, which could act quickly and effectively, seemed so much more attractive for macroeconomic stabilization.

This changed dramatically at the onset of the Great Recession in 2008. Central banks were now busy dealing with banking and financial market crises and drove down interest rates quickly to deal just with that. As aggregate output and employment began to fall, most economies around the world moved into recession, global trade collapsed, and the world economy seemed to be on the verge of a meltdown. Fiscal policy action was called for in a way not seen for more than twenty years.

However, using fiscal policy to counteract a recession affecting many countries at the same time poses a new problem. A government can take measures to increase aggregate demand in its country. Part of that increase, however, will fall on the demand for imports and stimulate aggregate demand in other countries. In an open economy, there is a *leakage effect* of fiscal policy, meaning that part of the effect of government policy flows to the RoW and benefits other economies. The more open an economy, the greater is this leakage and the less effective is domestic fiscal policy to increase domestic aggregate demand. Another way of saying this is that the government spending multiplier is the smaller, the larger is the share of imports in domestic consumption and investment.

This leakage effect creates a strategic problem among governments. Suppose that a group of countries is affected by the same recession. The government of each country could engage in a fiscal expansion, but each government knows that the other countries will benefit from that expansion and that its own economy will benefit from the fiscal expansions of the others. This gives each government an incentive to sit still and wait for the others to act: If they do, the economy will recover without the government spending money on the effort. But if all governments go through the same reasoning, the fiscal policy reaction to the common recession will be too weak to avail much. As a result, the recession will be deeper than each government desires.

Overcoming this problem requires an effort to coordinate fiscal policies among the governments of the countries affected by the recession. In late 2008, the US government together with the governments of the other G7 countries and the help of the IMF called upon the group of the G20 to coordinate fiscal policies in the face of the incipient Great Recession. Until then, the G20 had not played a big role in global economics; since then it hasn't done so, either. But in that particular moment, it turned out to be an effective device for policy coordination. Meetings of the G20 finance ministers were called and agreed on a coordinated fiscal stimulus program to fend off the global recession. For details on the G7 and G20, see Chapter 9, section 9.3.5.

Table 5.4 shows the main contributors to the joint G20 response to the Great Recession both in terms of absolute amounts and in terms of national GDP. As the world's largest and leading economy, the US spent the largest amount of financial resources to combat the recession. This was to be expected, as was the fact that Germany and Japan would play a major role in the effort. Less expected, however, is that China would spend the second largest amount of resources on the joint fiscal expansion, and this despite the fact that the recession hit the Chinese economy less than others. This was the first time that China assumed a role of responsibility for the global economy.

Table 5.4 also shows the size of the fiscal stimulus programs in terms of national GDP. This is interesting because it shows that Saudi Arabia also made a strong effort to contribute to the joint policy.

Fiscal stimulus can be implemented in the form of increased expenditures or tax cuts. Increased expenditures especially on infrastructure projects have the disadvantage of taking a relatively long time to be realized. Tax cuts have the advantage of being realized quickly but the disadvantage of being difficult politically to reverse once the need for stimulus is over.

Table 5.5 shows that the share of tax cuts in the total fiscal stimulus ranges all the way from zero to 100 percent.

**Table 5.4** Main contributors to G20 stimulus program (2009–10)

| Stimulus in USD billions | | Stimulus in terms of national GDP (%) | |
| --- | --- | --- | --- |
| USA | 841.2 | Saudi Arabia | 9.4 |
| China | 204.3 | USA | 5.9 |
| Germany | 130.4 | China | 4.8 |
| Japan | 104.4 | Spain | 4.5 |
| Spain | 75.3 | Germany | 3.4 |

*Source*: Eswar Prasad and Isaac Sorkin, "Assessing the G20 Stimulus Program – A Deeper Look" (working paper, Brookings Institution, March 2009).

**Table 5.5** Composition of G20 stimulus programs: share of tax reductions (%)

| Russia | 100 | France | 7 |
| --- | --- | --- | --- |
| Brazil | 100 | Argentina | 0 |
| Indonesia | 79 | Mexico | 0 |
| UK | 73 | Italy | 0 |
| Germany | 68 | China | 0 |

*Source*: Eswar Prasad and Isaac Sorkin, "Assessing the G20 Stimulus Program – A Deeper Look" (working paper, Brookings Institution, March 2009).

Was the G20 coordinated fiscal stimulus successful? This is a difficult question to answer. Certainly, the fiscal stimulus had a positive short-term impact. The global economy recovered quickly and growth resumed already in 2010. This is much faster than in the case of the Great Depression in the 1930s.

But the large fiscal expansions left the economies with a huge increase in the public debt burden and, therefore, more vulnerable to negative aggregate demand and financial market shocks than before. Euro-area economies were hit by the European debt crisis soon afterwards and had little room left for fiscal adjustment and response. The very high debt-to-GDP ratios resulting from the fiscal stimulus may have contributed to the persistently slow growth in Europe since 2009. Thus, answering the question involves a judgment of what would have been better: A very deep contraction followed by a resumption of normal growth, or a less deep contraction followed by a long period of shallow growth as we have seen it?

Furthermore, the large debt burden resulting from the stimulus made central banks very reluctant to bring interest rates up to normal levels once the recession was over. A decade after the Great Recession, central bank interest rates are still zero in the euro area. Thus, the fiscal stimulus resulted in a protracted period of negative interest rates that may have caused distortions in investment. It is still too early to assess the long-run consequences of this long period of negative real interest rates for financial markets and normal output.

## 5.3   SUMMARY

Changes in government revenues and spending are an important tool of macroeconomic management for the government. They affect aggregate demand both directly and indirectly, and they impact the price level, real interest rates, aggregate output, and employment. They also involve choices between policy goals in other areas and have consequences for the distribution of income. Because fiscal policy is the outcome of a political process involving both the legislative and the executive branches of government, it is not a very flexible tool for short-term macroeconomic management. Automatic stabilizers built into tax and spending rules can help overcome some of those rigidities.

In this chapter, we have reviewed US fiscal policy in the past twenty-five years in terms of spending, taxes, and deficits. We have introduced the concept of the government spending multiplier which amplifies the effect of changes in government spending and taxes on the economy. We have also discussed the uncertainties surrounding the use of fiscal policy for AD management and looked at the example of the fiscal stimulus program following the Great Recession.

Using fiscal policy for AD management can also have long-term consequences through its impact on government debt and aggregate investment. We will consider those long-term aspects in Chapter 6.

## 5.4 REVIEW QUESTIONS

1. Why are governments in European countries so much larger relative to GDP than the US government?
2. Which part of the population is paying the largest share of income taxes in the US? What does that imply for tax reforms?
3. Why is the government expenditure multiplier larger than one?
4. What are the main sources of uncertainty surrounding the use of fiscal policies to stimulate aggregate demand?
5. Suppose that the government increases spending. What happens to the real interest rate and private investment?
6. Under what conditions on the supply side of the economy is fiscal policy most effective to increase real GDP and why?
7. Under what conditions on the demand side of the economy is fiscal policy least effective to increase real GDP and why?

## NOTES

1 You may have noticed that the total US government expenditure is 35.4 percent of GDP in 2016 according to Figure 5.4 and only 32 percent according to Figure 5.2. The difference between these numbers comes from different accounting conventions and from excluding transfers between different levels of government in Figure 5.2.
2 www.usdebtclock.org
3 See the article by Carl Walsh, "The Role of Fiscal Policy," Federal Reserve Bank of San Francisco *Economic Letter*, September 6, 2002, for a good explanation of these issues.

# 6 Monetary and Fiscal Policy in the Long Run

In the previous chapters, we have discussed the *short-run* performance of the macroeconomy and the effects of monetary and fiscal policies in the *short run*. Now, we turn to the *long run*. This does not necessarily mean that we turn from monthly and quarterly time horizons to several years, although that is often the case. In the context of economic policies, short and long run are analytical concepts with no fixed analogy in time. The *long run* is the time horizon over which firms can vary all those things that lead to fixed costs in the short run, such as their stocks of capital, the location of their activities, and their production technologies. The long run is also the time horizon over which wages fully adjust to price level movements.

Why do we care about the long run? Doesn't life happen here and now, in the short run? This thought seems to underlie the dictum of one famous economist, John Maynard Keynes: "In the long run, we are all dead!" However, responsible policymakers should care about the long run. The reason is that monetary and fiscal policies that have desirable effects in the short run often have very undesirable effects in the long run. For example, we have seen that, in the short run, monetary policy can reduce the rate of unemployment by raising the rate of inflation. In the long run, however, this is impossible, as you will see in this chapter and it would take ever higher-inflation rates to maintain the same desired rate of unemployment. More generally, long-run considerations constrain the extent to which AD policies should be used.

With regard to fiscal policy, another long-run consideration arises from the fact that using government budget deficits to stimulate aggregate demand over an extended period of time results in the accumulation of large amounts of public debt. On the one hand, this may call into question the ability of the government to service its debt and undermine the government's ability to raise further debt. The dire consequences of government debt crises have become visible recently in some European countries such as Greece, Portugal, and Spain. On the other hand, excessive government debt has been regarded as a cause of slow economic growth, implying that it impoverishes a nation in the long run. Business leaders should keep the long run in mind to know what to expect from the government's monetary and fiscal policies.

In this chapter, you will first see how macroeconomic equilibrium is different in the long run compared to the short run. Next, you will understand the long-run effects and consequences of monetary and fiscal policies. Finally, you will learn about certain institutional arrangements aiming at keeping monetary and fiscal policies in line with long-run exigencies.

## 6.1  Macroeconomic Equilibrium in the Long Run

The crucial difference between the short and the long run lies in the behavior of the supply side of the economy and, in particular, in the behavior of wage setters and how they respond to changes in the general price level. The short run is defined by the assumption that wages do not respond fully to changes in the price level. Wages are rigid (or *sticky*) because of contractual agreements, transaction costs, imperfect information, and other causes. This implies that a change in the price level beyond the expected change causes *real* wages to fall, making it profitable for firms to employ more labor and produce more output. This means that the AS curve is positively sloped: The price level and real GDP move in the same direction. With a positively sloped AS curve, shifts in the AD curve caused by monetary or fiscal policies have output effects and these are what makes these policies effective in terms of impacting the levels of output and employment. In terms of the Phillips curve, wage rigidity implies that the Phillips curve is negatively sloped. An inflation rate exceeding expected inflation reduces the rate of unemployment.

Clearly, such positive co-movements of the price level and real output can be observed in practice, as can be negative co-movements of the rates of inflation and unemployment. But in thinking about these, remember that they reflect a kind of mistake wage setters made when setting their dollar wages in the first place. Dollar wages are set with an idea of what their purchasing power should be – what an hour of work is worth in terms of consumer goods and services. When the price level rises by more than expected after dollar wages have been set, this implies that workers will later on realize that they did not receive as much in terms of consumer goods and services per hour of work as they had anticipated. It is reasonable to expect that they will demand compensation for that in the next round of wage setting. Ultimately, therefore, dollar wages will adjust fully to the initial movement in the price level. When that has happened, the economy has reached its long run. The long run is defined by the absence of any correlation between the real wage and the price level. This implies that, in the long run, shifts in the AD curve have no impact on the levels of output and employment.

How long does it take in time to move from the short run to the long run? The answer depends very much on the labor market institutions and wage-setting habits of an economy and these, in turn, depend on the macroeconomic environment. For example, in the low-inflation environment of the 1960s, when inflation rates averaged around 1 percent annually, it was common in Germany to observe union wage agreements extending over several years. When inflation rates became higher and more volatile in the 1970s, the duration of such agreements shrank to a year and sometimes less. In the 1960s, therefore, the long run was reached only after several years, whereas it was reached within a year in the 1970s. In high-inflation environments like Italy in the 1970s and 1980s or Argentina in the 1960s to 1980s, wages were *indexed* to price level data published on a weekly or monthly basis, i.e., they were fully adjusted to price level changes within that period of time. Thus, the long run was reached almost instantly. An important policy implication of this argument is that an excessive use of AD policies to achieve high levels of output and employment eventually undermines its own basis by inducing more frequent dollar wage adjustments and shortening the period during which such policies are effective.

The distinction between the short run and the long run does not affect the AD curve qualitatively; so for our purposes we shall assume that it is the same as before. However, the distinction makes the AS curve look very different. If output does not move with the price level in the long run, the long-run aggregate supply is vertical as shown in Figure 6.1.

As indicated in Figure 6.1, the equilibrium is now the price level corresponding to the intersection between the long-run AS curve and the AD curve.

What happens if the AD curve shifts to the right due to, say, a fiscal expansion, as indicated by the blue arrow in Figure 6.1? In the long run, output does not respond to the change in aggregate demand. The level of real GDP remains at real $GDP_0$. The only lasting effect is the increase in the price level from $P_0$ to $P_1$. In that sense, we can say that the levels of output and employment are determined by the AS side in the long run. Aggregate demand serves to determine the price level. It follows that AD policies can, in the long run, only change the price level. Any gain in the levels of output and employment by expansionary monetary or fiscal policies in the short run will come at the cost of a higher price level in the long run. AD policies, therefore, always involve weighing desirable short-run against undesirable long-run consequences.

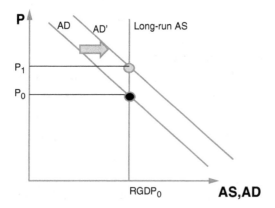

**Figure 6.1** Long-run macroeconomic equilibrium

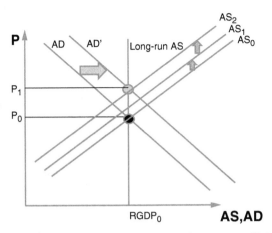

**Figure 6.2** Moving from short-run to long-run equilibrium

Still, we know from our earlier discussion that real GDP does respond to price level changes initially. So how does the economy get from the short run to the long run? Figure 6.2 illustrates the argument.

Here we start from a macroeconomic equilibrium given by output level real $GDP_0$ and price level $P_0$, the black dot in Figure 6.2. The long-run AS curve is vertical but the corresponding short-run AS curve, $AS_0$, is upward sloping. Recall that $AS_0$ is defined by nominal wages not adjusting to changes in the price level. An expansion of AD shifts the AD curve and moves the economy to the intersection between the AD curve and the $AS_0$ curve. This is the first short-run equilibrium. In the next round of wage negotiations, however, employees will demand compensation for the higher price level they are facing. As nominal wages rise, the short-run AS curve moves to the left to $AS_1$, reflecting a rise in the real wage. This is indicated by the gray arrows in Figure 6.2. As the economy moves to the new short-run equilibrium in the intersection between the $AS_1$ curve and the AD curve, output falls and the price level rises further. Nominal wages respond to that in the next round of wage negotiations. Eventually the short-run AS curve ends up as the $AS_2$ curve, where its intersection with the AD curve is the same as the intersection of the long-run AS curve and the AD curve.

These arguments imply that, in the long run, the economy can grow only if long-run aggregate supply grows and the long-run AS curve shifts outward as shown in Figure 6.3. This is possible in a number of ways. The workforce may grow. The capital stock may increase. Technologies may improve implying greater productivity of labor and capital. We will look at these issues in more detail in Chapter 7.

We go through the following argument in detailed steps to make it very clear. As indicated in Figure 6.3, the rightward shift in the long-run AS curve makes real GDP increase from real $GDP_0$ to real $GDP_1$. At a given AD curve, macroeconomic equilibrium would move from the black dot down along the AD curve. As a result, the price level falls.

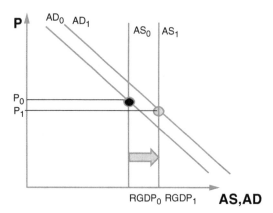

**Figure 6.3** Growing aggregate supply

At this point, however, we have to remember that aggregate demand cannot remain the same in this process. This follows from the economic circuit we came to know in Chapter 1. The economic circuit implies that, as aggregate output increases, aggregate income must also increase. And if aggregate income increases, aggregate demand must also increase. This means that the economic growth caused by an outward shift in the AS curve induces an outward shift in the AD curve. This is shown in Figure 6.3, where the AD curve moves from $AD_0$ to $AD_1$.

Can we say anything about the extent to which the AD curve shifts relative to the AS curve, or what happens to the price level in the process? The answer is yes. Recall, again from the economic circuit, that the money supply, or the stock of money provided by the central bank, times the velocity of money must equal real GDP times the price level, or the volume of transactions per period. For a given money supply and velocity of money, this implies that the price level must fall as real GDP rises. The new macroeconomic equilibrium will be the blue dot in Figure 6.3, where real $GDP_1$ corresponds to $P_1$.

Now consider an economy growing consistently over time. Figure 6.4 illustrates such a process by a movement from $AS_0$ to $AS_1$ and on to $AS_2$ with corresponding shifts of the AD curve from $AD_0$ to $AD_1$ and $AD_2$, and an expansion of real GDP from real $GDP_0$ to real $GDP_1$ and then to real $GDP_2$. The previous argument implies that a growing economy would experience a falling price level or deflation.

This, however, does not need to happen, and this is where skillful AD management comes in again. The previous argument hinges on the assumption that the money stock remains constant. Another way of saying this is that a policy holding the money stock constant exerts a contractionary impact on the economy. In order to avoid that, the central bank should increase the money supply in line with the expected growth in real GDP. In a growing economy, a monetary policy aiming at a stable price level must allow an appropriate expansion of the money supply.

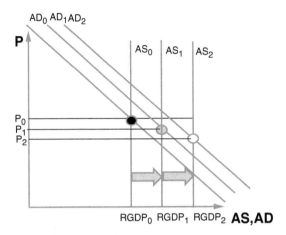

**Figure 6.4** Prices and output with consistent economic growth

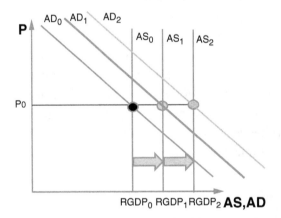

**Figure 6.5** Macroeconomic growth with accommodating monetary policy

This idea is illustrated in Figure 6.5. The expansion of aggregate supply and real GDP is the same as before. However, the shifts of the AD curves are larger than before due to a monetary policy accommodating the economic growth in an appropriate way. As a result, the sequence of long-run macroeconomic equilibria comes with a stable price level.

In Chapter 3, we learned that we can frame the concept of a macroeconomic equilibrium also in terms of the Phillips curve, the negative relationship between the rate of inflation and the rate of unemployment. Since wage negotiations embed inflation expectations, an inflation rate exceeding the expected rate of inflation leads to a decline in real wages, an increase in employment, and a decline in the rate of unemployment. Conversely, a rate of inflation below expected inflation leads to an increase in the rate of unemployment.

Figure 6.6. recapitulates the argument. In a long-run equilibrium, the actual and the expected rates of inflation must coincide. To assume otherwise would imply that

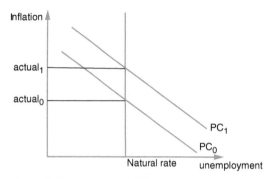

**Figure 6.6** The long-run Phillips curve

wage setters never learn about the true rate of inflation and that is implausible. The initial long-run Phillips curve is represented by $PC_0$. The initial long-run equilibrium occurs at the point where the expected rate of inflation equals the actual inflation rate $actual_0$ and the rate of unemployment equals the natural rate. There is a trade-off between inflation and unemployment in the short run.

Now, suppose that the central bank fixes the rate of inflation permanently at the rate $actual_1$. Initially, the unemployment rate will fall strongly. However, as wage setters get used to the higher-inflation rate and begin to expect it, the Phillips curve shifts upward to $PC_1$ and the unemployment rate rises back to the natural rate. In the long run, therefore, there is no trade-off between inflation and unemployment. The long-run Phillips curve is just the vertical line above the natural rate.

## 6.2   Monetary Policy in the Long Run

The previous section has shown that monetary policy cannot impact real GDP, employment, and unemployment in the long run. However, monetary policy is still important to provide a stable, low-inflation macroeconomic environment. This is the most important macroeconomic task of a central bank in the long run.

### 6.2.1   Conducting Monetary Policy in the Long Run

In the long run, persistent and volatile inflation has adverse macroeconomic consequences. One is that it leads to a redistribution of wealth by reducing the real value of nominal assets such as money, government securities, or corporate bonds. Since households with low levels of wealth tend to save predominantly in such types of assets because of their greater liquidity and lower risk of incurring capital losses, inflation hurts households with low levels of wealth more than rich households. To the extent that welfare payments and pensions are not fully adjusted to the rate of inflation, it also hurts low-income people more than high-income people. At the same time, the decline of the real value of government debt due to inflation means that it reduces the government's debt burden. Governments, therefore, benefit from unanticipated inflation and have a reason to welcome it. This is one important reason why modern central banks are designed as politically independent institutions.

Another adverse, long-run consequence of inflation is that it distorts savings and investment decisions. By reducing the real return on nominal assets such as money, bank deposits, and government securities, inflation induces households to save less than they would otherwise, thus reducing the amount of savings available for financing real private investment. Furthermore, households have an incentive to invest their savings into real estate to avoid the inflation-induced loss of value. This makes more savings flow into housing and less into fixed capital investment, again reducing the productive capacity of the economy.

If high inflation is bad in the long run, what rate of inflation should the central bank aim at? On the one hand, deflation is also bad, because it increases the real debt burden of firms and the government. Furthermore, with a falling price level people tend to hold back consumption of durable goods such that aggregate demand falls and this reinforces the tendency of falling prices. A stable price level seems desirable, because it facilitates long-term nominal contracting of wages and loans and, therefore, reduces transaction costs in labor and financial markets. But there is no magical number for the rate of inflation in the long run. Most central banks in developed economies today aim at long-run inflation rates around 2 percent annually. The argument is that in a growing economy with continuous improvement of product quality, price level measurement is biased upward: Part of all measured price increases is actually due to improved quality. Taking that into account, price level stability can be equated with a measured inflation rate of 2 percent annually.

The problem with implementing a policy aiming at stable and low inflation is that it inherently creates a temptation for policymakers to destroy it. Suppose that the central bank announces a low and stable inflation rate. Wage setters believe it and base their wage negotiations on it. When that has happened, even a small rise in the actual above the expected inflation rate can achieve a nice reduction in the rate of unemployment which may seem desirable for a government especially shortly before elections, when the government's time horizon is too short to take the long-run consequences of its monetary policy into account. It is, therefore, likely that the government gives in to the temptation of raising the inflation rate. Knowing about this temptation, however, and anticipating it in the first place, wage setters will not believe the announcement of a low-inflation policy. They will expect a higher rate of inflation. And, if that is the case, it is advantageous from the government's perspective to deliver a higher-inflation rate to avoid the higher unemployment otherwise implied by the Phillips curve.

This dilemma between what is a desirable monetary policy in the long run and what can be implemented based on wage setters' expectations is called the *credibility problem* of monetary policy. Solving that problem calls for arrangements that make the announcement of a low-inflation policy credible. A traditional way of doing that is to tie the exchange rate to a low-inflation currency (see Chapter 8). Alternatively, a country's central bank may be given a legal charter mandating it to keep inflation low and making it *independent* in the sense that it does not take instructions from the government concerning the conduct of monetary policy. Since the 1990s, *inflation targeting* has been introduced by many countries around the world as a way to improve the credibility of low-inflation policies. Under this concept, the central bank publicly announces the rate of inflation it wishes to achieve. This means that the public can hold the central bank accountable for actual inflation developments, and, fearing to come under public criticism, the central bank will try its best to achieve the announced target.

A similar consideration comes from servicing public debt. A government with a given stock of debt outstanding would like to face a low nominal interest rate in order to be able to refinance its debt at low cost. A low and stable expected rate of inflation is an important condition for achieving that. Yet, the government also faces the temptation to use surprise inflation to reduce the real value of its debt and, anticipating that, investors purchasing government debt will demand a correspondingly higher nominal interest rate. Again an institutional arrangement such as a fixed exchange rate, an independent central bank, or inflation targeting can serve to solve that credibility problem.

## 6.2.2   International Application: Central Bank Independence

We all know that government decisions are full of political compromises. Those who prefer that central banks be independent do not want those kinds of political compromises guiding monetary policy. The history of central banking shows that the worst cases of inflation and hyperinflation have come when monetary policy was captured by government policies. Governments that wanted to spend more than they were willing to tax their citizens ordered the central bank to print money and hand it over to them to finance their expenditures. Central bank independence is supposed to break that nefarious link between politics and monetary policy, such that short-sighted governments cannot interfere with a monetary policy aiming at low and stable inflation.

Central banks are generally set up by an act of government. The parliament or congress passes a piece of central banking legislation that establishes a central bank and fully describes its goals, structure, and operating procedures. Since this is a national law that sets up an institution, we generally think of the central bank as part of the government. But that does not imply that the central bank's decisions are determined by politicians elected to run the government. That is, it is possible to write a central bank charter that sets up an institution that is largely independent of the government. Of course, it is also possible to set up a central bank that does receive regular input and guidance from one or more members of the current government. Such a bank would not be independent.

Most important central banks today are independent. This includes the Fed, the ECB, the Bank of Japan, and the Bank of England. But, even in these cases, the public is not always happy about that state of affairs. There have been many times when the public, or the elected government, or both disagreed with central bank policy and were quite vocal in their wishes that the central bank's policies were more in line with those of the government. In the US when the Greenspan Fed began tightening monetary policy in the late 1990s there was a fear that Fed policy was not compatible with continuing strong economic growth. The "pro-growth" crowd criticized Greenspan for what they perceived as an overly tight monetary policy. Many European politicians suffering through slow growth after 2001 felt that the ECB policies should have been more in line with government desires to see strong aggregate demand and real GDP growth. Similar disgruntlement was aimed at the Bank of Japan. Thus we see that short-term political orientation of a government can put plenty of pressure on central banks.

Central bank independence has several dimensions:[1]

- *Policy independence*: The government does not give the central bank orders regarding the formulation and implementation of its monetary policy, including the choice of policy goals, strategy, and instruments. Members of the government do not attend central bank council meetings or vote on policy issues and, hence, have no direct control over monetary policy. The central bank's budget is independent of government financing decisions, such that the government cannot put the central bank under economic pressures.
- *Personal independence*: Members of the central bank's decision-making bodies serve long terms with no or limited possibility of being reappointed. Therefore, they have no personal reasons to cater to political interests.
- *Financial independence*: The central bank does not have to finance government expenditures directly or indirectly through loans or by buying newly issued government bonds.

In practice, central bank independence comes by degrees. No central bank is totally independent of the government. Measuring the independence of central banks is difficult, because it involves translating legal codes into numerical gauges. Numerous attempts at doing this have been made.[2] The classic study in this field measured central bank independence of many countries in the late 1980s and correlated it with the average rate of inflation over the 1980s.[3] Figure 6.7 shows the result for nineteen industrialized countries.

At the time, central bank independence varied from 0.69 (Germany) to 0.17 (Belgium). The Fed scored 0.48 and ranked fifth among the group of countries. Figure 6.7 suggests a negative association between the rate of inflation and central

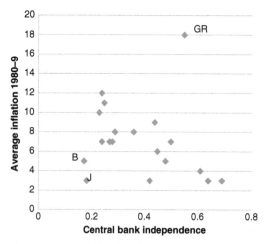

**Figure 6.7** Central bank independence and inflation

bank independence. It is even stronger when three outliers are taken into account, namely Greece (GR), Belgium (B), and Japan (J). Belgium may have been special because the country achieved low inflation by tying its currency to Germany's DM during that period. Japan's government may have had a strong preference for achieving low inflation that needed no support by central bank independence, while in Greece even relatively strong legal independence of the central bank did not suffice to reach low inflation. Overall, one can see a tendency of countries with high degrees of central bank independence showing better inflation performance than countries with low degrees. This has been generally confirmed by other empirical studies.

## BOX 6.1 DIFFERENCE OF OPINION: SHOULD THE US RETURN TO THE GOLD STANDARD?

In 1879, the US Congress officially set the US dollar on a *gold standard* meaning that the dollar price of gold was fixed. Many other countries did the same during this period and this implied that the exchange rates between the main currencies of the world were very stable for long periods of time. This is because the exchange rate between any two currencies on a gold standard is simply the ratio of their respective gold prices.

With a gold standard, US monetary policy was reduced to maintaining a stable price of gold. The number of dollars the government could issue was limited by the gold reserves it had in its vaults. New currency could only be issued by buying additional gold in the gold market. When the price of gold began to rise in the gold market, the government would sell gold and this would reduce the amount of currency circulating in the economy. When the price of gold began to fall, the government bought gold and this would increase the amount of currency circulating.

The great advantage of the gold standard was that it delivered a very high degree of price stability over long periods of time. Recall from the discussion above that a stable price level in a growing economy requires that the money supply grows in line with real GDP. Under the gold standard, this means that the government's gold reserves grow in line with real GDP. This is, in fact, what happened. As the economy grew faster than the gold reserves, the price level would fall and, with a constant dollar price of gold, that made gold production more profitable. Eventually, therefore, the supply of gold in the market would go up, and the government would buy gold, increase its reserves, and issue new currency. But since the gold supply did not react immediately, the gold standard did see frequent periods of a falling price level followed by periods of a rising price level. Long-run price stability was maintained on average only.

The global gold standard broke down during World War I, because many governments were no longer able and willing to follow its rules. After the war, the US and other countries tried to restore the gold standard internationally, but with limited success. The Great Depression and then World War II brought further turmoil in international currency relations. The US officially ended the gold standard in 1971.

Ever since then, there have been numerous voices calling for a return to the gold standard. Advocates of such a return, often referred to as *gold bugs*, argue that this would liberate the US from secular inflation and restore long-run price stability. A recent and prominent example is Texas Senator Ted Cruz who was quoted during the 2015 presidential campaign as saying: "I think the Fed should get out of the business of trying to juice our economy, and simply be focused on sound money and monetary stability, ideally tied to gold."[4]

It is clear, however, that this would come at a high price. Recurrent periods of falling prices carry the risk of businesses and households going bankrupt as the real value of their debts becomes too large. More importantly, a return to the gold standard implies that the Fed would give up its ability to counteract fluctuations in aggregate demand, output, and employment and this would impose excessive hardship on workers and their families.

## 6.3    Fiscal Policy in the Long Run

Long-run aspects of fiscal policy are similar to those of monetary policy as far as shifts in the AD curve are concerned. Based on the analysis in section 6.2, it is clear that the real output and employment effects of an expansionary fiscal policy are wiped out in the long run by increases in the price level. Again, there is a trade-off involved between desirable short-run effects and undesirable long-run effects.

In the case of fiscal policy, however, an additional concern arises. This comes from the fact that, as government spending increases, the real interest rate must increase in order to maintain the equality of aggregate income and aggregate demand; see Chapter 2, section 2.3. The rise in the real interest rate causes real private domestic investment to fall. This is called the *crowding-out effect* of fiscal policy. With lower real private domestic investment, the private capital stock will be lower in the long run than it would be otherwise, and this may reduce the economy's level of potential output. The result would be a leftward shift in the long-run AS curve and a lower level of long-run output than otherwise.

Whether or not that happens depends critically on the type of spending the government undertakes during the expansion. If the expansion goes entirely into government consumption, it is not likely to add to the economy's productive capacity and will result in long-run output losses. If, however, the expansion goes into real government investment such as infrastructure, it may well increase the productive capacity and increase long-run output.

### 6.3.1   The Long-Run Government Budget Constraint

It is one thing for a government to have a temporary government deficit. A temporary deficit might arise and peak within a couple of years – and then go away. It might have large impacts, but if the source of the impacts stops, then the impacts should diminish over time. It is another thing for a government to have sustained or persistent deficits. In this case we have to deal with other complications that might arise. Persistent deficits pile up to large levels of government debt. The *long-run government budget constraint* relates to the question of how much debt a government can raise.

The long-run government budget constraint says that, in the long run, the present value of all current and future expenditures cannot exceed the present value of all current and future government revenues. Thus:

The sum of all discounted current and expected future expenditures ≤

The sum of all discounted current and expected future revenues.

We can restate this condition as saying that the current level of government debt outstanding cannot exceed the present value of all future government budget surpluses:

The current amount of government debt ≤

The sum of all discounted future government surpluses.

Suppose that this is not the case. Then it must be true that the government will not be able to ever pay back its debt. But it is unreasonable to expect that investors will lend their money to a government if they think that they will never be paid back. Note that this condition must only hold over a long time horizon, because as long as it does that, the government will be able to roll over its debt from old to new investors. The long-run government budget constraint does not require that government budget deficits be reversed within a short period of time. Any judgment of the question whether or not a government currently operates within its long-run budget constraint involves expectation about future revenues, expenditures, and, hence, budget surpluses. On the one hand, this allows policymakers to run budget deficits today and promise future surpluses. This is often politically convenient, because the policymakers can reap the short-run benefits of a fiscal expansion and leave the burden of adjustment to future policymakers. On the other hand, this makes any assessment of the long-run budget constraint controversial, because future economic conditions and fiscal policies are necessarily uncertain and people will disagree over assumptions regarding them.

Expectations regarding future economic conditions and fiscal policies are affected by a variety of factors:[5]

- The types of expenditure financed with the debt issued by the government under consideration. Governments financing transfer payments by issuing debt are in a more critical situation than governments financing infrastructure investments that raise the production capacity of their countries.
- The long-term growth prospects of the economy. Fast-growing countries can afford higher debt levels than slow-growing countries, because they can expect faster increases in tax revenues to service that debt.
- This includes a consideration of demographics. Countries with declining or aging populations face a decline of their workforces and, hence, a decline in their productive capacities.
- The scope for generating new government revenues. This includes a look at the tax burden. Countries with already large tax burdens usually find it harder to raise additional tax revenues than countries with low tax burdens.
- The scope for cutting expenditures. Countries with a large proportion of welfare and other transfer programs in total public spending find it politically harder to cut spending to rein in deficits and debt.
- The currency in which the debt was issued. Foreign currency debt is more risky for governments, because its value is subject to exchange rate risk and the government cannot print money to pay its lenders and inflate away the value of the debt.
- Political constraints. Weak governments may not have the political power to pass the legislation necessary to cut expenditures or raise taxes.

Debt-rating agencies use these kinds of criteria to assess the quality of governments as sovereign lenders, and the higher their rating, the lower the interest rate these governments end up paying.

A government's debt or, more generally, its public finances, are called *sustainable*, if the government can be reasonably expected to be able to service its debt in the future, that is, if its future revenues are expected to be sufficient to pay interest and repay its debt to its creditors. In the broadest sense, this is the case if the government operates within its long-run budget constraint defined above. Judging the sustainability of a government's debt is a complex and difficult task and, therefore, subject to much discussion and disagreement. To make the notion of sustainability operational, we usually look at the size of government debt relative to the size of the economy, i.e., GDP. Research done at the IMF suggests that the debt-to-GDP ratio should not exceed 50 percent for emerging market economies in order to be considered sustainable. But there are countries that have defaulted on debt at lower ratios, while others have fared well with higher ratios.[6]

The rules of the European Monetary Union fix a ratio of public debt to GDP of 60 percent, beyond which public debt may not be sustainable. Nevertheless, several countries have experienced much higher debt levels in the wake of the Great Recession without too much difficulty refinancing their debt. The same IMF research suggests that, on average over twenty-three mature industrialized countries, the maximum sustainable public debt-to-GDP ratio is close to 200 percent. Table 6.1 shows some examples. The most extreme one is Japan, whose debt ratio peaked at 242.1 percent of GDP in 2014 and yet there was no sign of concern in financial markets about its sustainability. The debt ratio of the US has consistently increased since 2008 and reached 108.1 percent in 2017. There was no concern about its sustainability, either. Italy's debt ratio steadily increased to 133.0 percent and the country did experience some increase in the interest rate it pays on its government debt, reflecting growing concern among investors about the sustainability of Italian public finances. In order to allay such concerns, the ECB promised to effectively bail out European sovereign debtors, promising that it would buy government bonds in unlimited amounts, if their yields increased by too much. France, Germany, and the UK kept more moderate debt-to-GDP ratios, but even these were much higher than 60 percent.

**Table 6.1** Government debt-to-GDP ratios (%)

| Country | 2008 | 2009 | 2010 | 2011 | 2012 | 2013 | 2014 | 2015 | 2016 | 2017 |
|---|---|---|---|---|---|---|---|---|---|---|
| France | 68.0 | 78.9 | 81.6 | 85.2 | 89.5 | 92.3 | 94.9 | 95.6 | 96.3 | 96.8 |
| Germany | 65.1 | 72.6 | 81.0 | 78.7 | 79.9 | 77.5 | 74.7 | 70.9 | 68.1 | 65.0 |
| Italy | 102.4 | 112.5 | 115.4 | 116.5 | 123.4 | 129.0 | 131.8 | 132.1 | 132.6 | 133.0 |
| Japan | 191.3 | 208.6 | 215.9 | 230.6 | 236.6 | 240.5 | 242.1 | 238.1 | 239.3 | 240.3 |
| United Kingdom | 50.2 | 64.5 | 76.0 | 81.6 | 85.1 | 86.2 | 88.1 | 89.0 | 89.3 | 89.5 |
| United States | 73.6 | 87.0 | 95.7 | 100.0 | 103.4 | 105.4 | 105.1 | 105.2 | 107.1 | 108.1 |

*Sources*: IMF, WEO data set 2017.

When a country's public debt exceeds the level deemed compatible with sustainability, it often has to pay a risk premium in the form of a higher interest rate in order to keep investors willing to hold its debt. This interest rate premium means higher outlays on interest and possibly a larger deficit, and even larger debt. Therefore, a high risk premium can itself contribute to undermining debt sustainability; more on this in section 6.4.2. This creates a risk of self-fulfilling expectations: Investors expect that the debt is not sustainable, demand a risk premium, and thereby increase the likelihood of the debt being unsustainable. This can lead to a vicious circle ending with government default. The government debt risk premium typically also affects the interest international investors charge on corporate debt issued by firms in the same country. Therefore, business leaders typically dislike excessive levels of government debt.

The experience of the euro-area countries that went through public debt crises between 2010 and 2015 illustrates the point. Table 6.2 shows the debt ratios of Greece, Ireland, Portugal, and Spain from 2008 to 2017. Greece started the period with a high debt ratio of 109.4 percent already. In the course of the crisis, the ratio climbed to 180 percent. Both Ireland and Spain started out with the lowest debt ratios in the euro area at the time – around 40 percent. As the crisis hit, however, their ratios climbed very quickly to over 100 percent. Their experience shows that a low debt ratio does not necessarily protect a government against a debt crisis. Portugal started from an intermediate position – not much above Germany's debt ratio in 2008 – and saw its ratio climb to 130 percent in the following years.

Figure 6.8 shows the ten-year bond yields for these countries and Germany as a benchmark over the same period. All five countries started out with yields just above 4 or just below 5 percent in 2008. Their interest rates stayed close to each other through the financial crisis that set off the Great Recession in 2008. Interest rate divergence began in early 2010, when investors began to doubt the sustainability of Greek public debt and such doubts spread to the other countries. In the summer of 2012, Greek ten-year rates reached almost 30 percent, Portuguese rates almost 14 percent. Irish rates had peaked a year before at almost 13 percent. The figure reveals the effect the ECB's bailout announcement in 2012 had on interest rates. By

**Table 6.2** Government debt ratios in euro-area crisis countries

| Country | 2008 | 2009 | 2010 | 2011 | 2012 | 2013 | 2014 | 2015 | 2016 | 2017 |
|---|---|---|---|---|---|---|---|---|---|---|
| Greece | 109.4 | 126.7 | 146.3 | 172.1 | 159.6 | 177.9 | 180.9 | 179.4 | 181.6 | 180.2 |
| Ireland | 42.4 | 61.5 | 86.1 | 110.4 | 119.7 | 119.6 | 104.7 | 77.1 | 72.9 | 69.3 |
| Portugal | 71.7 | 83.6 | 96.2 | 111.4 | 126.2 | 129.0 | 130.6 | 129.0 | 130.4 | 125.7 |
| Spain | 39.4 | 52.7 | 60.1 | 69.5 | 85.7 | 95.5 | 100.4 | 99.8 | 99.4 | 98.7 |

*Sources*: IMF, WEO data set 2017.

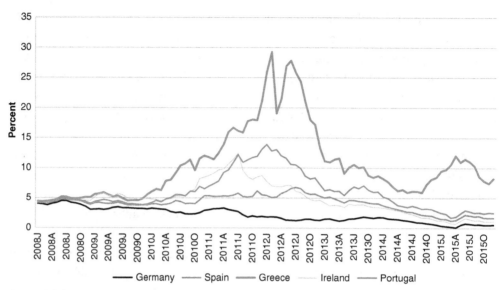

**Figure 6.8** Ten-year bond yields in the euro area
*Source*: ECB.

the end of 2015, interest rates of all countries but Greece had come down close to Germany's level again.

When public debt becomes unsustainable, a government can no longer readily meet its obligations and faces the risk of having to default on its bonds, i.e., to stop paying interest and service and reduce their face value either unilaterally or in negotiations with its creditors. To avoid that, the government would have to reduce spending and raise tax revenues but it cannot or is unwilling to do so because of internal political or economic constraints. Politically, the government may not have the strength to impose the burden of fiscal adjustment on its own population. Economically, the government may find itself in a steep downturn with the result that tax revenues are low and the need for welfare spending is high. Default means that the burden of adjustment is put on the bond holders, and it usually involves losing access to further credit for the government and the private sector. Investors' anticipation of government default will make them pull their money out of the country, thus exacerbating the problem and accelerating the process leading to default. As the Argentine debt crisis of the early 2000s and the Greek, Irish, Portuguese, and Spanish debt crises of the early 2010s have shown, such situations can cause severe economic crises and disruptions in the financial system, resulting in high unemployment and deep recessions.[7] Finally, such crises often lead to political turmoil in fiercely contested elections or revolutions that remove the government from office and create additional uncertainty.

One way to resolve the problem is to ask for emergency loans from other countries or from international organizations like the IMF. If such aid cannot be obtained, governments may try to use the money printing press to reduce the real value of their debts. But this, obviously, works only if government debt is denominated in the issuing government's own national currency. Here is another credibility problem: Knowing that governments can use the printing press to reduce the value of their debts denominated in their currencies, lenders are wary of buying such bonds except those issued by governments with long and proven records of being first class debtors with stable currencies. Most countries in the world do not enjoy that privilege. Those who do are a relatively small group consisting mostly of OECD countries. It includes the US, the UK, France, Germany, Japan, and Switzerland. Such countries must take great care to preserve their high credit reputation.

In the US there is today little concern about the sustainability of its public debt, but some experts look beyond securitized government debt and include pension liabilities in their concept of public debt. They ask how the US will get through the years after the baby boomers have reached retirement age. In the 2016 Trustees Report, we find a very conservative estimate, which puts the net unfunded liabilities of the US social security system for the next seventy-five years at about USD 11.4 trillion. To see the size of the problem, note that the same report estimates that, if the current social security legislation remains in place, the payroll tax rate insured persons pay as social security contributions would have to rise by 2.58 percentage points to 14.98 percent immediately *and* current and future benefits would have to be reduced by 16 percent to keep the Social Security Fund from defaulting.[8] For large numbers of future retirees, this would mean a lot of hardship. Rising costs of the healthcare system and various other uncertainties about the future add to the problem. This is a serious issue even for a rich country like the US. Both political parties seem interested in finding solutions, but progress is impeded by a lack of consensus about how the necessary burden of adjustment should be distributed over the different groups of voters in the electorate.

## 6.3.2  Working with Data: Debt Sustainability Analysis

As discussed above, sustainability of government debt or public finances is a complex issue and, therefore, difficult to ascertain. A practical approach starts from the idea that a minimal requirement for debt to be sustainable is that the debt-to-GDP ratio does not grow infinitely. From this perspective, sustainability requires that, with no policy change and no unforeseen developments, the debt ratio converges to some constant value over time. This gives rise to a straightforward assessment criterion which is used, among others, by the IMF in its monitoring of fiscal policies:

If the growth rate of GDP exceeds the rate of interest paid on government debt, the debt is sustainable.

If the interest rate paid on government debt exceeds the growth rate of GDP, the debt is sustainable only if the government budget-surplus-to-GDP ratio is larger than the interest-rate–GDP-growth-rate differential multiplied by the debt-to-GDP ratio.

## BOX 6.2 Formal Analysis: Fiscal Sustainability Conditions

We start from the following accounting identity: The amount of debt outstanding at the end of year t, $B_t$, equals the amount outstanding at the end of the previous year, $B_{t-1}$, plus the interest paid on that amount, $i_{t-1}B_{t-1}$, minus the primary budget surplus in period t, $S_t$.

$$B_t = B_{t-1} + i_{t-1}B_{t-1} - S_t \text{ or } B_t = (1 + i_{t-1})B_{t-1} - S_t$$

Dividing both sides by GDP, $Y_t$, this gives, with some rearrangement of terms, an approximate expression for the debt ratio in year t given the debt ratio in year t−1 and the primary surplus ratio,

$$\frac{B_t}{Y_t} \approx (1 + i_{t-1} - g_t)\frac{B_{t-1}}{Y_{t-1}} - \frac{S_t}{Y_t}$$

To derive this expression, divide the equation by $Y_t$ and apply the link between $Y_t$ and $Y_{t-1}$, $Y_t = (1 + g_t)Y_{t-1}$, where $g_t$ is the growth rate of GDP. The approximation, indicated by $\approx$, comes from writing $(1 + i_{t-1})/(1 + g_t)$ as $(1 + i_{t-1} - g_t)$ which is approximately true if the interest rate and the growth rate are small numbers.

Suppose that the government pursues a constant deficit-ratio policy, such that $S_t/Y_t = -x$, where x is some positive number. Then, if the interest rate is smaller than the growth rate of GDP, the debt ratio will ultimately converge to

$$\frac{B}{Y} = \frac{x}{g_t - i_{t-1}}$$

Thus, as long as the economy grows sufficiently fast, sustainability is compatible with any constant deficit ratio. But note that a rising interest rate can undermine sustainability. If $i_{t-1}$ exceeds the growth rate $g_t$, sustainability requires a sufficiently large primary surplus, namely

$$\frac{S_t}{Y_t} > (i_{t-1} - g_t)\frac{B_{t-1}}{Y_{t-1}}$$

Otherwise, the debt ratio will grow without bounds. The fiscal effort to rein in the debt represented by the primary surplus ratio must be the larger, the larger the debt ratio inherited from the past and the larger the interest-growth rate differential. Practitioners call the term $(1 + i_{t-1} - g_t)(B_{t-1}/Y_{t-1})$ the *snowball effect*, because, when the interest rate is too high, the debt ratio keeps growing all by itself unless the government achieves a sufficiently large primary budget surplus.

Table 6.3 applies this analysis to the US on average over the period 2004 to 2012 and then annually from 2014 to 2017, where the data for 2016 and 2017 are IMF forecasts from 2015. The average interest rate on US government debt is calculated as the total interest payments divided by the amount of debt outstanding. The first three columns show positive interest-growth rate differentials. Therefore, sustainability would have required primary surpluses, albeit small ones, when in fact the US government ran primary deficits. On this criterion, US government debt was not sustainable in 2004–12, 2014, and 2015. In 2016 and 2017, in contrast, the projected interest-growth rate differential was negative and sustainability was compatible with primary deficits.

Table 6.4 applies the same analysis to Japan. Again, we see a positive interest-growth rate differential in the first column covering the period from 2003 to 2011. Sustainability would have required a primary surplus of 3.1 percent of GDP, which the Japanese government did not achieve. During that period, Japanese public debt was unsustainable.

In the following years, GDP growth recovered and the interest rate fell to very low levels, so that sustainability was regained.

**Table 6.3** Debt sustainability analysis: USA

|  | 2004–12 | 2014 | 2015 | 2016 | 2017 |
|---|---|---|---|---|---|
| Debt/GDP $(_{t-1})$ (%) | 0.79 | 1.042 | 1.062 | 1.073 | 1.079 |
| GDP growth (%) | 3.9 | 3.9 | 2.3 | 4.4 | 4.6 |
| Interest rate (%) | 4.0 | 3.9 | 2.5 | 2.0 | 2.4 |
| (interest–growth differential) $*$ debt/GDP | 0.001 | 0.0 | 0.002 | −0.015 | −0.039 |
| Primary surplus–GDP ratio | −0.05 | −0.028 | −0.024 | −0.021 | −0.016 |

*Sources*: IMF Fiscal Monitor April 2015 and US Art. IV Country Report July 2015.

**Table 6.4** Debt sustainability analysis: Japan

|  | 2003–11 | 2013 | 2014 | 2015 | 2016 |
|---|---|---|---|---|---|
| Debt–GDP ratio | 1.95 | 2.39 | 2.43 | 2.43 | 2.43 |
| GDP growth (%) | −0.6 | 0.9 | 3.0 | 2.7 | 2.7 |
| Interest rate (%) | 1.0 | 0.6 | 0.8 | 0.8 | 1.0 |
| (interest–growth differential) $*$ debt/GDP | 0.031 | −0.0072 | −0.054 | −0.046 | −0.041 |
| Primary surplus–GDP ratio | −0.061 | −0.074 | −0.063 | −0.050 | −0.038 |

*Sources*: IMF Fiscal Monitor April 2015 and Japan Art. IV Country Report July 2014.

### 6.3.3   International Application: the EU's Stability and Growth Pact

During the 1990s, when the EU countries prepared themselves for the introduction of the euro, governments felt very strongly about the risk of unsustainable public debt in one of the member states of the future European Monetary Union. People in the countries with relatively low levels of debt in particular were worried that other countries might run into fiscal troubles which might eventually undermine the stability of the new common currency. As a result, the Maastricht Treaty, which was signed in 1992 and established the monetary union and the procedures for countries to become members of it, set a limit of 60 percent for the debt-to-GDP ratio as a condition for countries to enter the monetary union. The governments also agreed to keep their government deficits below 3 percent of GDP. Countries exceeding these limits would be subject to a monitoring and assessment process by the European Commission which could result in public reprimand and even financial penalties. In 1998, however, when the countries to form the monetary union were selected, too many countries exceeded the 60 percent limit on debt, the 3 percent limit on deficits, or both. This included Germany which, as the economic center of the EU, could not be excluded from a sensible monetary union. As a result, the debt limit was discarded and the deficit limit was sufficiently softened to allow eleven countries to adopt the euro. To enforce fiscal discipline at the national level the Maastricht Treaty also includes a *no-bailout rule* that forbids any member state and the EU as a whole to assume the liabilities of any other member state.

In the late 1990s, the EU governments also agreed on the *Stability and Growth Pact* (SGP). This Pact commits the member states to keep their budgets *close to balance or in surplus* in the medium run and effectively makes zero deficits the target of fiscal policy, while the importance of the debt ratio was deemphasized. The SGP called for a quicker and more automatic assessment process than the Maastricht Treaty. However, many governments proved unwilling or unable to abide by the rules of the SGP. The focus on numerical limits induced governments to play tricks with accounting concepts and practices and hide deficits from the public view, an experience which is not unlike that of states in the US whose governments are subject to numerical fiscal constraints. In 2001, Germany and several other countries grossly violated the fiscal limits and refused to take the necessary steps for adjustment, partly because their economies were in recession, partly because they were facing elections. The 2005 reform of the SGP made the agreement more "flexible" by introducing many excuses governments can make for running large deficits.

The weaknesses of the SGP became obvious in the wake of the Great Recession of 2008–9, when all European governments ran large budget deficits and piled up new, large amounts of public debt. Several of them faced outright fiscal crises. In May 2012, the EU passed the *Fiscal Compact*, an agreement to strengthen again the rules of the SGP and to make it more *forward-looking* in the sense of preventing high deficits instead of merely reacting to them. The Fiscal Compact requires the member states to submit medium-term fiscal programs to the European Commission for approval and to coordinate their annual budget calendars such that the European Commission can give its approval of the underlying macroeconomic forecasts before the annual budget law is passed. In addition to the 3 percent deficit limit and the close-to-balance-or-in-surplus commitment, the Fiscal Compact requires the governments to keep their *structural budget deficits* below 0.5 percent of GDP in the medium run. The structural budget deficit is the budget deficit corrected for the influence of the business cycle and of so-called *one-off* or extraordinary measures. Governments violating these limits must subject medium-term fiscal plans to the European Commission explaining how they intend to come back to compliance with them. The Compact also strengthened the role of the debt-to-GDP ratio by requiring governments in excess of that limit to reduce the debt ratio by at least 5 percent of the difference between the actual ratio and 60 percent on average every year. In 2013, the EU passed further legislation requiring all euro-area countries to set up politically independent *fiscal councils*, which have the task of monitoring the countries' fiscal performance and commenting on it publicly. In addition to these new rules, the EU also created the European Stability Mechanism, an international financial organization which in future crises will be able to act as a lender to governments in financial difficulties. It is financed by capital contributions from the member states.

The experience with the Fiscal Compact so far is not promising. Concepts like *medium term*, *structural*, and *one-off measures* are vague in practice and invite all sorts of efforts to interpret the actual data and make it look like conforming to the set limits. The European Commission every year comments extensively on the fiscal programs submitted by the governments and its criteria and definitions for declaring what is structural and what is not seem quite opaque and arbitrary.

The experience with the SGP shows the dilemma of a framework for fiscal discipline based on numerical rules among a group of sovereign nations. On the one hand, the group desires rules assuring fiscal discipline in order to prevent the kind of debt crises that the euro area experienced after 2010. On the other hand, neither the group nor the European Commission has the power and instruments to enforce such rules. Compliance, therefore, ultimately depends entirely on the willingness of the individual governments to follow the rules, which is there in easy times but dissipates quickly in difficult times when doing so would impose some economic hardship on the national electorate. Furthermore, the framework would obviously lose its credibility if too many countries officially violate the rules too often, and the desire to not let that happen has made the European Commission very lenient in its process of monitoring the member states.

### 6.3.4 International Application: the Greek Debt Crisis

Like other euro-area countries, Greece was hit hard by the Great Recession of 2008–9. In October 2009, shortly after a national election, the new Greek government under George Papandreou announced that its deficit for that year would reach 12.6 percent of GDP instead of the previously posted 3.7 percent. Eventually, the 2009 deficit would be revised again to 15.5 percent of GDP. This not only represented a breach of Greece's commitments under the SGP in the euro area, it also fully exposed the weakness of the country's fiscal position as it came out of the financial crisis. In the weeks and months that followed, yields on Greek government bonds increased both in level and volatility, making the government's finances increasingly unsustainable. On May 2, 2010, the EU together with the IMF decided to grant the country a USD 146 billion loan to avoid a government default. The loan came with a three-year program to reachieve sustainable public finances and improve its competitiveness. It required the Greek government to reform the country's tax system and public administration, cuts in public sector employment and pensions, and privatization of government-owned assets. In May 2010, the ECB announced that it would buy government bonds of euro-area countries in financial distress to avoid interest rates climbing too high. The financial conditions of the rescue program were loosened in July 2011, when the EU and the IMF granted Greece an extended repayment schedule and a lower interest rate.

On February 21, 2012, the EU and the IMF decided to bail out the Greek government a second time, with a new, USD 172 billion loan. The new bailout program included permission for the Greek government to partially default on privately held government bonds by cutting their face value by 53.5 percent. The total value of this *haircut* amounted to 65 percent of Greek GDP, the largest operation of that kind in modern history. The bailout program required Greece to cut public spending and raise additional revenues in order to bring its debt-to-GDP ratio down from 160 percent to 120.5 percent by 2020. In November 2012, the timeline of the program was revised, allowing Greece to have a debt-to-GDP ratio of 124 percent in 2020 and substantially below 110 percent by 2022. These promises notwithstanding, Greek public debt stood at 180.2 percent of GDP at the end of 2017.

Parliamentary elections held in May 2012 did not yield a viable government and had to be repeated in June. The new government under Antonis Samaras affirmed its commitment to the requirements of the bailout program. In the next national elections, however, which were held in February 2015, an extreme left-wing government under Alexis Tsipras came into power. It had promised voters to end the fiscal adjustment program and to write down Greek's debt unilaterally. By that time, however, most of the debt was held by EU governments and official institutions who would have suffered severe financial losses as a consequence. The European governments, therefore, opposed Tsipras's proposals. At the end of June 2015, Greece missed a payment according to the bailout program. The European Commission and the IMF immediately stopped their financial support, leaving Greece in an acute liquidity shortage. The Greek government imposed capital controls to prevent its citizens from taking their money out of the country, and bank holidays to stop runs on Greek banks. In a showdown between Tsipras and Germany's finance minister

Wolfgang Schäuble at a European leaders' meeting in July, Tsipras backed down and agreed to continue playing by the rules of the bailout agreement. Commentators later reported that Schäuble had made Tsipras look into hell – he explained to him what would happen if Greece was abandoned by its international lenders. Against his earlier promises, Tsipras pushed new measures for cutting expenditures and raising taxes through parliament. The EU and the IMF responded with a third bailout program worth USD 94 billion to be extended over the next three years. Following a warning in early 2017 by the IMF that Greek public debt could again become unsustainable, the EU agreed to grant Greece more lenient conditions on that loan.

As shown in Table 6.5, Greece's general government revenues fell from 40.7 percent of GDP to 38.9 percent in the recession of 2008–9 and then climbed again due to the fiscal adjustment programs. They reached 49 percent in 2013, then fell again and reached 50.2 percent in 2016. Half of Greece's economic activity is now devoted to the government. Primary expenditures, i.e., general government spending excluding interest payment, increased to 49 percent of GDP in response to the recession of 2008–9. Despite the adjustment measures taken by the government, they climbed to 58 percent in 2013 and came down afterwards, but never below pre-crisis ratios of GDP. The reason is that GDP during this period fell faster than government spending. Interest spending peaked at 7.3 percent of GDP in 2011, and then came down thanks to the ECB's commitment to bring government bond yields down. The Greek primary deficit peaked at 10.1 percent in 2009 and again at 9.1 percent in 2013. In 2016, the country recorded a sizeable primary surplus of 3.7 percent of GDP for the first time since the beginning of the crisis.

Table 6.6 records the country's economic performance during the debt crisis. Real GDP fell by a total of 23.5 percent during the years from 2010 to 2016, GDP per capita fell by 21 percent. The output gap fell from 4.3 percent of potential GDP to −8.6 percent in 2013 and continued to be negative through 2016. Gross investment nearly halved as a percentage of GDP, indicating that a large part of the Greek capital stock has been lost, while the unemployment rate reached 27.5 percent in 2013 and stood at 23.6 percent in 2016. Between 2009 and 2016, employment fell by 20 percent. The economic cost of the crisis and the hardship it inflicted on the Greek population are obviously huge.

**Table 6.5** Greek general government data (2008–16; % of GDP)

|                  | 2008  | 2009  | 2010  | 2011  | 2012 | 2013  | 2014 | 2015 | 2016 |
|------------------|-------|-------|-------|-------|------|-------|------|------|------|
| Primary surplus  | −5.4  | −10.1 | −5.3  | −3.0  | −3.8 | −9.1  | 0.4  | −2.1 | 3.7  |
| Total revenues   | 40.7  | 38.9  | 41.3  | 43.8  | 46.5 | 49.0  | 46.6 | 48.1 | 50.2 |
| Primary spending | 46.0  | 49.0  | 46.6  | 46.8  | 50.3 | 58.1  | 46.2 | 50.2 | 46.5 |
| Interest spending| 4.8   | 5.0   | 5.9   | 7.3   | 5.1  | 4.0   | 4.0  | 3.6  | 3.2  |
| Total surplus    | −10.2 | −15.1 | −11.2 | −10.3 | −8.4 | −13.1 | −4.4 | −5.7 | 0.5  |

*Sources*: European Commission, AMECO Database 2017.

**Table 6.6** Greek economic performance (2008–16)

| | 2008 | 2009 | 2010 | 2011 | 2012 | 2013 | 2014 | 2015 | 2016 |
|---|---|---|---|---|---|---|---|---|---|
| Real GDP growth | −0.3 | −4.3 | −5.5 | −9.1 | −7.3 | −3.2 | 0.4 | −0.2 | 0.0 |
| Real GDP per capita | 22,591 | 21,554 | 20,328 | 18,465 | 17,174 | 16,742 | 16,919 | 16,989 | 17,108 |
| Output gap | 11.1 | 8.0 | 4.3 | −2.9 | −7.7 | −8.6 | −6.5 | −5.5 | −4.9 |
| Gross investment (% of GDP) | 24.5 | 18.3 | 17.0 | 15.1 | 12.8 | 11.6 | 11.8 | 9.8 | 10.5 |
| Unemployment rate (%) | 7.8 | 9.6 | 12.7 | 17.9 | 24.4 | 27.5 | 26.5 | 24.9 | 23.6 |
| Employment (millions of people) | 4.6 | 4.6 | 4.4 | 4.1 | 3.7 | 3.5 | 3.5 | 3.6 | 3.7 |

*Sources*: IMF, WEO Database 2017.

The Greek crisis and its huge economic cost demonstrate the value and importance of fiscal discipline. Furthermore, it proves that a commitment not to bail out members of a monetary union when they reach the brink of government default, which is enshrined in the Maastricht Treaty, is not credible when it is not backed up by a set of rules for an orderly default. When the Greek crisis hit, the governments preferred acting openly against EU law, because they had no game plan for the alternative. In 2010, this was the greatest weakness of the euro area. It continues to be so, since the EU governments have stubbornly refused to learn any lessons from the episode.

An orderly default procedure would contain provisions for debt restructuring, for providing bridge liquidity to the defaulting government, and for protecting the banking sector against a crisis arising from the government default. Instead, the EU decided to set up a permanent emergency lending facility for governments in financial troubles. Knowing that such a facility exists reduces the incentives for individual governments to assure that their debts are sustainable and thus creates a new moral hazard problem.

### 6.3.5   Public Debt and Economic Growth

The link between rising public debt and long-run economic growth is ambivalent. One the one hand, it is clear that the ability for a government to borrow can promote economic growth. Borrowing allows the government to go beyond the limits of current tax resources to finance productive government expenditures like infrastructure investment. The logic is similar for governments and for private enterprises. In the early stages of economic development in particular, governments should borrow and invest in growth-promoting projects which will later on provide the resources to pay back the debt. But the same logic remains true for more mature economies.

On the other hand, public debt may put a brake on economic growth if it grows too large and too fast. Such concerns have been voiced especially after the large increase in public debt in OECD countries following the Great Recession, and they contributed to the strong efforts at fiscal consolidation in the middle of the continuing recession especially in Europe.[9] Above, we have already mentioned the problem of government deficits crowding gross private investment spending and reducing the growth of the private capital stock. Another negative impact of high debt on economic growth might work through increasing real interest rates on government bonds reflecting rising risk premiums that investors demand in compensation for the risk of government default. As such premiums tend to spill over to interest rates paid by private enterprises, this also reduces gross private investment. Similar arguments can be made with respect to the outlook of higher taxes to pay back higher debts. Rising economic uncertainty and the likelihood of severe economic disruptions following a government default cause further reductions in economic growth.

Empirical evidence concerning this link between public debt and economic growth, however, remains tenuous. There does not seem to be a unique threshold of the ratio of public debt to GDP for all countries from which public debt exerts a negative influence on growth. Every country and government seems to be special in this regard. Governments are well advised to be concerned about this issue and maintain fiscal discipline, but there are no exact guidelines. The US seems no exception. As the debt-to-GDP ratio remains stubbornly high, concerns are growing that this could put a brake on the country's future growth perspectives.

## 6.4   SUMMARY

In this chapter, we have studied the long-run macroeconomic equilibrium. The long run does not refer to calendar time. It is the time horizon necessary for wage setters to adjust nominal wages to unexpected changes in the price level and for firms to adjust their stock of capital. How long this is in terms of calendar times depends on a country's labor market institutions and inflation environment.

The defining characteristic of the long-run macroeconomic equilibrium is that the AS curve is vertical: Aggregate supply does not react to changes in the price level. This implies that changes in aggregate demand do not lead to changes in aggregate supply in the way they do in the short run. An equivalent way to look at the long run is that the long-run Phillips curve is vertical, meaning that changes in the rate of inflation do not affect the unemployment rate.

AD policies are ineffective to change real GDP, employment, and unemployment in the long run. They change the price level, but there is no trade-off between desirable output and undesirable price level effects as in the short run. Governments must keep that in mind when they use AD policies. They can be used to counteract macroeconomic fluctuations and shocks at business-cycle frequencies, but they should not be used to achieve long-run targets for output, employment, and unemployment in order to avoid excessive long-run effects on the price level. Such targets should be pursued by means of AS policies.

In a growing economy, monetary policy should be accommodative in the sense that the money supply grows in line with real GDP to avoid a lasting deflation.

Putting fiscal policy into a long-run perspective has two aspects. On the one hand, fiscal policy affects aggregate demand and, therefore, has no long-run effects on real output, employment, and unemployment. This statement must be qualified, however, by considering the possibility of government spending crowding out real gross private domestic investment through its effect on the rate of interest, and the potential negative effect this has on the economy's capital stock and productive capacity. On the other hand, fiscal policy operates under a long-run constraint, namely the long-run government budget constraint which says that, in the long run, government debt cannot exceed the present value of future budget surpluses.

This brings us to the concept of the sustainability of public debt and public finances more generally. Unsustainable government debt can have very negative macroeconomic consequences. The European Monetary Union has created its own, rules-based framework to preserve the sustainable public finances of its member states, but the framework is not very strong, reflecting a lack of commitment on the part of the member states and a lack of enforcement power on the part of the monetary union. Most importantly, it has not prevented full-fledged public debt crises in several of the member states, namely Cyprus, Greece, Ireland, Portugal, and, to a lesser extent, Italy, and Spain. The Greek debt crisis of the 2010s demonstrates the huge economic costs and political disruptions caused by such crises. Business managers should carefully monitor the sustainability of government debt in the countries they operate in.

## 6.5  REVIEW QUESTIONS

1. What is the difference between the "short run" and the "long run"?
2. What is the slope of the long-run AS curve and why?
3. What are the main elements of central bank independence?
4. Why is central bank independence useful to keep inflation low?
5. What is a government's intertemporal budget constraint?
6. What is the "sustainability of public debt"?
7. How would you assess the sustainability of the public debt of Uruguay?
8. You just learned that the public debt of a country you do business with is not sustainable. How will that affect your business expectations?

## NOTES

1 See Sylvester W. Eijffinger and Jakob de Haan, *The Political Economy of Central Bank Independence*, Special Papers in International Economics 19 (Princeton: International Finance Section, Princeton University, 1996).

2 A recent article presenting such measurements is Ana Carolina Garriga, "Central Bank Independence in the World: A New Data Set," *International Interactions* 42(5) 2016.

3 Alex Cukierman, Stephen B. Webb, and Bilin Neyapti, "Measuring the Independence of Central Banks and Its Effects on Policy Outcomes," *World Bank Economic Review* 6(3) (1992): 353–98. The countries included in Figure 6.7 are Australia, Austria, Belgium, Canada, Denmark, Finland, France, Germany, Ireland, Italy, Japan, the Netherlands, New Zealand, Norway, Spain, Sweden, Switzerland, the UK, and the US.

4 CNBC, "Ted Cruz Calls for Gold Standard," www.cnbc.com/2015/10/28/ted-cruz-calls-for-the-gold-standard.html, October 28, 2015.

5 See the IMF's 2003 *World Economic Outlook* for an interesting discussion of these issues, at: www.imf.org/external/pubs/ft/weo/2003/02/pdf/chapter3.pdf

6 See IMF's *World Economic Outlook* (2003), ch. 3; Jonathan D. Ostry, Atish Gosh, Jun I. Kim, and Mahvash S. Qureshi, *Fiscal Space*, IMF Staff Position Note 10/11 (Washington, DC: IMF, 2010).

7 See Anne O. Krueger, "Crisis Prevention and Resolution: Lessons from Argentina," www.imf.org/en/News/Articles/2015/09/28/04/53/sp071702

8 Board of Trustees of the Federal Old-Age and Survivors Insurance and Federal Disability Insurance Trust Funds, *The 2016 Annual Report of the Board of Trustees of the Federal Old-Age and Survivors Insurance and the Federal Disability Insurance Trust Funds* (Washington, DC, 2016), p. 6.

9 An important contribution to the recent public debate was Carmen Reinhart and Kenneth Rogoff, "Growth in a Time of Debt," *American Economic Review* 100(2) (2010): 573–8, who claim that public debt slows down economic growth when it exceeds 90 percent of GDP. The paper stirred a lot of debate and further empirical analysis, but the results are as yet ambiguous.

# 7 Economic Growth

In this chapter, we turn to economic growth, meaning the long-run *development* of the economy over time. Previously, we have focused on the *level* of economic activity during a given period of time and on how that level is affected by changes in policies and other factors along with the price level, employment, and unemployment. Now we study how that level moves over long periods of time. Another way of saying this is that we are interested in the *trend growth rate* of economic activity.

Economic growth is about trends, not year-on-year changes. It is true that we often get caught up in short-run developments and think that what happens between now and next year is all that matters. It is not. Compared with what happens over ten- or fifteen-year horizons, year-on-year changes are usually quite small and insignificant. In the longer run, a company's performance depends much more on growth than on the business cycle. Therefore, recognizing growth opportunities and spotting the places where fast growth happens is an important task for business managers.

The idea that economic improvement is possible for all people of all parts of society and that our children will be better off than we are today is a central tenet of the *American dream* that has given hope to generations of Americans and motivated them to work hard, save for a better future, and send their kids to college.[1] James Truslow Adams, who coined the term American Dream, called it America's greatest gift to the world.[2] But is it possible for all or almost all Americans to achieve that dream, generation after generation? And is it possible for people outside the US to live the same dream? Economic growth is the key to answering such questions. In an economy that grows over long periods of time, the answer is yes. As aggregate income grows faster than population, per-capita incomes can rise for everybody. In a growing economy, social problems can be addressed by distributing society's extra income to those in need. In an economy with zero or low growth over long periods of time, the answer is no. As aggregate income grows at a rate lower than population growth, per-capita income falls. Some people can still experience economic improvement for themselves and their children, but only at the cost of others experiencing economic decline. An economy with no growth functions like Monopoly, the board game in which you win by bankrupting your fellow players.[3] Another way of putting this is that, in a zero-growth economy, every social conflict is a zero-sum game: You win what I lose and vice versa. It is hard to imagine that the type of democracy Western countries have enjoyed for the past century is possible under such circumstances. In fact, history offers no examples of such democracies in no-growth economies.

We begin this chapter with a discussion of the future growth prospects for the world economy and for individual countries and regions. We will then discuss economic policy approaches to promoting economic growth. Following that we will look at the most astounding case of economic growth in the last sixty years: the case of China. Next, we will look at the historical record of economic growth around the world. We will see that growth is a relatively young phenomenon, at least if we take into account the record of the past 2,000 years. We will then consider the factors driving economic growth. Finally, we will discuss the limits to economic growth, or the question whether or not our economy can continue to grow forever.

## 7.1    Growth Prospects for the World Economy

Economic growth means economic change. As we will see below, economic growth is driven by technological development creating new products, improving production techniques, reducing cost, and thus affecting competitiveness. Successful business leaders must know the growth prospects of the economy they operate in to master the competitive challenges of technological progress. Furthermore, the composition of AD changes as per-capita incomes grow. With growing incomes, consumers tend to appreciate product quality and sophistication more than mere quantity and availability. Successful business leaders must be aware of such trends in order to anticipate changing consumption patterns.

Economic growth varies across countries. Market size and purchasing power increase faster in fast-growing economies than in economies with sluggish growth. Successful business leaders must have an understanding of the growth prospects of different countries in order to know which markets have the largest future potential and establish a presence there. Table 7.1 illustrates the point. The table has actual and projected levels of real GDP in USD for the years 2014 and 2050. The data have been adjusted for actual and projected differences in the purchasing power of money, i.e., the fact that a dollar buys more goods in poor countries than in rich countries because the price level is lower.

## 7.2    Economic Policies to Promote Growth

When we talk about growth properly, we talk about trend, not actual changes in real GDP. Growth is what drives potential output. Consider the following statement from

**Table 7.1** Projected real GDP in 2014 and 2050

| Rank | Country | Real GDP 2014 | Country | Real GDP 2050 |
|---|---|---|---|---|
| 1 | China | 17,632 | China | 61,079 |
| 2 | US | 17,416 | India | 42,205 |
| 3 | India | 7,277 | US | 41,384 |
| 4 | Japan | 4,788 | Indonesia | 12,210 |
| 5 | Germany | 3,621 | Brazil | 9,164 |
| 6 | Russia | 3,559 | Mexico | 8,014 |
| 7 | Brazil | 3,073 | Japan | 7,914 |
| 8 | France | 2,587 | Russia | 7,575 |
| 9 | Indonesia | 2,554 | Nigeria | 7,345 |
| 10 | UK | 2,435 | Germany | 6,338 |
| 11 | Mexico | 2,143 | UK | 5,744 |
| 12 | Italy | 2,066 | Saudi Arabia | 5,488 |
| 13 | South Korea | 1,790 | France | 5,207 |
| 14 | Saudi Arabia | 1,652 | Turkey | 5,102 |
| 15 | Canada | 1,579 | Pakistan | 4,253 |
| 16 | Spain | 1,534 | Egypt | 4,239 |
| 17 | Turkey | 1,512 | South Korea | 4,142 |
| 18 | Iran | 1,284 | Italy | 3,617 |
| 19 | Australia | 1,100 | Canada | 3,583 |
| 20 | Nigeria | 1,058 | Philippines | 3,516 |
| 21 | Thailand | 990 | Thailand | 3,510 |
| 22 | Egypt | 945 | Vietnam | 3,430 |
| 23 | Poland | 941 | Bangladesh | 3,367 |
| 24 | Argentina | 927 | Malaysia | 3,327 |
| 25 | Pakistan | 884 | Iran | 3,224 |

*Note*: USD billions purchasing-power adjusted. *Source*: pwc, *The World in 2050. Will the Shift in Global Economic Power Continue?* February 2015, www.pwc.co.uk/economics

the World Bank's 2018 *Global Economic Outlook* about the growth of the world economy:[4]

> Despite a recent acceleration of global economic activity, potential output growth is flagging. At 2.5 percent in 2013–17, post-crisis potential growth is 0.5 percentage point below its longer-term average and 0.9 percentage point below its average of a decade ago. The decline has been even steeper in emerging market and developing economies.

The World Bank warns us not to confuse the strong business-cycle performance of the world economy in 2016–17 with a strong trend. In this particular instance, trend growth is considerably weaker than actual growth. The Bank continues with the following outlook:

This slowdown mainly reflects weaker capital accumulation. It is also evidence of slowing productivity growth and demographic trends that dampen labor supply growth.

These forces will continue and, unless countered, will depress global potential growth further by 0.2 percentage point over the next decade. Policy options that could slow or reverse this trend include steps to lift physical and human capital, encourage labor force participation, and improve institutions.

Note that the Bank does not recommend doing anything to boost aggregate demand. Since output already accelerates faster than potential output, any further policies stimulating AD policies would result mostly in more inflation. Instead, the Bank's diagnosis is that there is not accumulation of productive capital, that the growth of the labor force is slow, and that productivity growth is lackluster. These are all AS factors which should be addressed by supply-side policies. In line with this, the Bank recommends that

A combination of additional investment, better educational and health outcomes, labor market or business climate and governance reforms could stem or even reverse the expected decline in potential growth over the next decade.

Policies to promote growth are policies that improve the economy's human and physical resources. Obviously, policies to improve the education and health of the labor force take time until they show the desired results. The same is true for reforms of labor market institutions aiming at higher rates of labor market participation especially of women, and reforms of the legal business environment (e.g., better enforcement of contracts) and governance (e.g., reduction of corruption) for a more investment-friendly economic climate. Policies for growth involve long time horizons and require patience and tenacity on the part of policymakers and business leaders.

## 7.3   International Application: Sixty Years of Growth in China

At the end of World War II, China was a country stricken by poverty. The economy was predominantly agricultural, but with low productivity, the supply of food and other agricultural goods was among the lowest in international comparison. The socialist Chinese government under the leadership of Mao Zedong engaged in a policy of forced industrialization promoting heavy industries and pursued a strategy of economic independence from other countries. The country experienced some moderate growth, but, as large parts of the rural population migrated to the cities to find jobs, agricultural development was neglected.[5] Government taxes, prohibitions, and regulations and a dire lack of infrastructure created massive obstacles to economic growth. Two large government policy programs, the *Great Leap Forward*

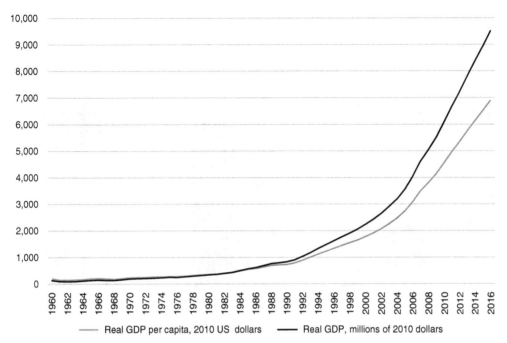

**Figure 7.1** China's economic growth (1960–2016)
*Source*: own calculations based on World Bank data.

from 1958 to 1962 and the onset of the *Cultural Revolution* that the government launched in 1966 caused the Chinese economy to shrink massively.[6]

Figure 7.1 illustrates the growth experience of the Chinese economy since 1960. Measured in USD and prices of 2010, China's real GDP amounted to USD 128 billion in 1960, and real GDP per capita stood at USD 192 annually, roughly half a dollar a day in 2010 prices. The country experienced some moderate growth until the late 1970s. Figure 7.2 shows that the average growth rate of Chinese real GDP was just above 4 percent annually, while the growth rate of real GDP per capita stood at just above 2 percent.

In 1978, the Chinese government under Deng Xiaoping introduced a program of reforms liberalizing the economy and introducing elements of market and capitalist systems. Figure 7.1 shows that the economy soon embarked on a path of faster growth. As Figure 7.2 indicates, the average growth rate between 1978 and 2000 amounted to almost 10 percent for the whole economy and a little above 8 percent on a per-capita basis. As a reminder, twenty years of growth at a rate of 8 percent means that per-capita real GDP increases by a factor of 4.7. In the subsequent sixteen years, the average growth rate of per-capita real GDP was 8.9 percent, implying another increase by a factor of 4.6.

Figure 7.3 shows the ratios of gross domestic fixed investment and private household consumption for China from 1960 to 2015. Household consumption

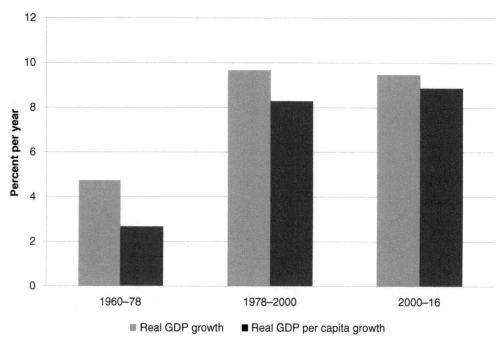

**Figure 7.2** China average real growth rates
*Source*: own calculations based on World Bank data.

**Figure 7.3** China shares of private consumption and investment in GDP
*Source*: World Bank.

accounted for 50 percent of Chinese GDP in 1960 and peaked at 71 percent in 1962. Since then, the consumption ratio has fallen to reach 36 percent in 2015. Despite the falling share of consumption, however, real private consumption has increased rapidly. Measured in 2010 USD, real per-capita consumption increased from 206 to 2,586 between 1990 and 2016. This corresponds to an average growth rate of 10 percent annually. Gross domestic fixed investment rose from 16 percent in 1962 to 44 percent of GDP in 2015. The Chinese growth model since the late 1970s has been one of continuously increasing the capital stock.

So far, so good, but who benefits? Critics of the Chinese experience argue that it has caused growing income inequality, a continuous widening of the gap between the rich and the poor. China's Gini coefficient rose from 0.3 in 1978, peaked at 0.53 in 2010 and stood at about 0.5 in 2014.[7] The Gini coefficient is a widely used measure of income inequality which is zero with perfect equality and 1 with complete inequality, when one person earns all income. A rise from 0.3 to 0.53 indicates a significant increase in inequality. This is also illustrated by the fact that the ratio of the average income in the highest 10 percent of all incomes and the average income in the lowest 10 percent increased from 8.7 in 1995 to 19.1 in 2014. Furthermore, the share of the 10 percent lowest incomes in total income has continuously declined in China between 1995 and 2014. According to World Bank data, this share stood at 2 percent in 2012.

Does this mean that the poor have not benefitted from China's spectacular growth in the past forty years? Only if one is concerned with relative magnitudes. In contrast, China's rural head count ratio of poverty has fallen by 94 percent from almost 100 percent in 1980 to around 5 percent in 2015. This is the number of rural people living in poverty according to China's official poverty line divided by the total rural population. The number of people living in poverty in China has come down from 770 million people in 1978 to 55.8 million in 2015, or from 81 to 4.1 percent of the total population.

Four factors have contributed to the reduction in poverty.[8] First, mass migration of people from rural areas to the cities. Between 1978 and 2015, the share of nonfarm in total employment increased from 29 to 70 percent. As people found jobs in the cities, they began to send money to the families they had left behind and this helped reduce rural poverty. Second, a relatively equitable distribution of land ownership allowed the poor rural population to benefit from state programs aiming at agricultural development. Third, the increased availability of social services such as education and medical services to rural populations. Fourth, targeted poverty reduction programs implemented by the government. Poverty reduction remains an issue in China, but it would be wrong to say that economic growth has not benefitted the poorest groups in society.

## 7.4    The Record of Economic Growth

What is the long-term record of economic growth around the world? In this section we take a very long-run perspective – 2,000 years – to answer that question. This is not easy, because producing economic statistics for national accounting is a relatively young industry that started only in the 1920s. Therefore, it is difficult to measure economic growth over long periods of time. Luckily, some economic historians have used whatever other data is available to construct long time series of data giving us a view of the economic history of the world.

### 7.4.1    Two Thousand Years of Global Economic Growth

Figure 7.4 shows the (estimated) development of the global population over the past 2,000 years. Here is the most astonishing fact: World population was roughly constant for the first 1,200 years. In year 1, global population was about 226 million people, of which 75 percent lived in Asia, 11 percent in Europe, 7.5 percent in Africa, 0.3 percent in what is now the US. In the year 1000, global population was

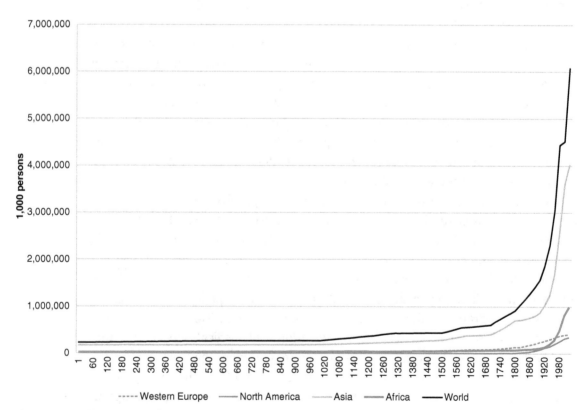

**Figure 7.4** World population growth

*Source*: own calculations based on Angus Deaton, "Historical Statistics of the World Economy", 1–2008.

about 267 million people, most of the population growth over the preceding 1,000 years had occurred in Africa. Global population began to grow slowly but significantly in Asia after the year 1200. Asia's population increased from 217 million in 1200 to 708 million in 1800, and to 4 billion in 2009. In Europe and Africa, population grew from 35 million and 37 million people respectively in 1200 to 131 million and 72 million respectively in 1800, and 402 million and 990 million respectively in 2009. US population reached 307 million people in 2009. Global population reached 6.8 billion people in 2009, more than double the size of 3.0 billion in 1960. Today, 60 percent of the world's population live in Asia.

Figure 7.5 shows the development of real GDP per capita over the same 2,000 years. Remember that these are rough estimates expressed in dollars at 1990 prices. Real GDP per capita was roughly constant and equal throughout the world until about 1700. This means that the average person on this globe in 1700 was about as well off economically as the average person in the year 1000 and the average person in year 1. In the first millennium, per-capita incomes ranged between USD 400 and USD 450 (in 1990 prices) in Europe, Asia, Africa, and Latin America with practically no growth in per-capita terms everywhere.[9] Figure 7.5 shows that significant economic growth in per-capita terms only started in the second half of the seventeenth century. It is, therefore, a relatively recent phenomenon in world history. For

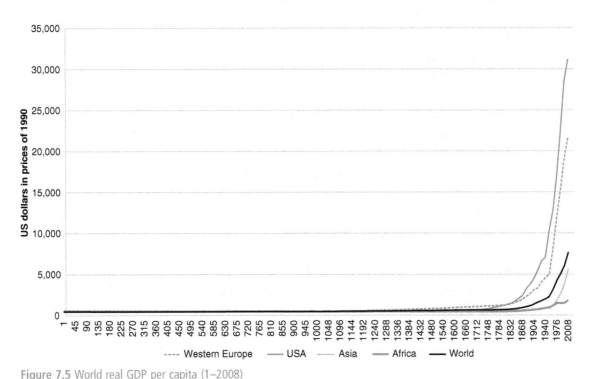

Figure 7.5 World real GDP per capita (1–2008)

*Source*: own calculations based on Angus Deaton, Historical Statistics of the World Economy, 1–2008 (see www.rug.nl/ggdc/historicaldevelopment/maddison/releases).

the longest part of history, each generation was about as well off as the previous one. This does not, of course, exclude the possibility that individual regions saw temporary increases in their prosperity. Such increases, however, were reversed over time due to increases in population as higher prosperity tended to lead to rising birth rates, falling mortality rates, and immigration. Similarly, temporary declines in the prosperity of a region would lead to reductions in population through falling birth rates, increasing mortality, and emigration. On average over time, therefore, the world seemed to be the same forever. Furthermore, the regional distribution of income was fairly equal over time. This does not, of course, exclude the possibility of individual persons and families becoming very wealthy. With no economic growth, however, a person could only become wealthy by making other people poor.

Sustained economic growth in per-capita terms first started in the second half of the seventeenth century in Western Europe and in the US. In Asia, per-capita real GDP began to grow in the late nineteenth century, mainly driven by the economic development in Japan and only lately by the economic surge of the Chinese economy. Africa remains the continent with the slowest economic growth and the lowest level of per-capita real GDP.

The large differences in economic growth have caused large differences in the world income distribution. Table 7.2 reports the evolution of the global income distribution over the past two centuries.[10] Incomes are measured in constant 2011 USD adjusted for cross-country differences in purchasing power, ranging from USD 0.2 to 500 a day. For this data, the UN's definition of extreme poverty is an income of USD 1.90 per day.

Table 7.2 shows that the share of people living on less than USD 2 a day has declined strongly over those 200 years, from 89.6 percent in 1800 to 9.3 percent in 2015. In 1900, the median income was still no more than USD 1 a day. In 1800, 98 percent of the world's population was living on less than USD 5 a day. In 2015, that was true for 53.5 percent of the world's population. Overall, the share of people with very low incomes has declined, while the share of people with high incomes has increased. Thus, while it is true that the gap between the people with very high and the people with very low incomes has widened, very low incomes today apply to a much smaller share of the population than in the past. Has economic growth increased economic inequality? The answer is clearly *yes* if you think of inequality in terms of the range of incomes observed. But the answer is much more difficult if you take into account the shares of people having low, medium, and high incomes.

Table 7.2 also reports the income distributions for several large regions of the world economy, i.e., Africa, the Americas, Asia, and Europe. It shows that all four regions went through similar changes in their income distributions. However, there are noticeable differences across these regions. Median incomes are still only slightly above USD 2 a day in Africa, up from USD 1 in 1950. Median incomes are between USD 5 and USD 10 in Asia and between USD 10 and USD 20 in the

**Table 7.2** Global income distributions

| USD | \multicolumn{10}{c}{Percent of population living on daily incomes of less than:} |
|---|---|---|---|---|---|---|---|---|---|---|
| | 0.25 | 0.50 | 1.00 | 2.00 | 5.00 | 10.00 | 20.00 | 50.00 | 100.00 | 200.00 |
| Year | | | | | | World | | | | |
| 1800 | 0.26 | 25.9 | 67.2 | 89.6 | 98.0 | 99.5 | 99.9 | 100 | 100 | 100 |
| 1850 | 0.20 | 22.8 | 62.5 | 86.8 | 97.2 | 99.3 | 99.9 | 100 | 100 | 100 |
| 1900 | 0.11 | 16.2 | 50.1 | 75.2 | 90.8 | 96.7 | 99.2 | 99.9 | 100 | 100 |
| 1950 | 0.19 | 16.7 | 42.8 | 60.4 | 77.7 | 89.2 | 96.4 | 99.7 | 100 | 100 |
| 1975 | 0.06 | 11.3 | 36.7 | 54.1 | 65.9 | 75.4 | 87.7 | 98.4 | 99.7 | 100 |
| 2015 | 0.02 | 1.8 | 6.1 | 14.3 | 53.5 | 57.7 | 76.5 | 94.2 | 98.8 | 99.8 |
| | | | | | | Africa | | | | |
| 1950 | 0.19 | 18.2 | 49.6 | 74.4 | 92.2 | 97.6 | 99.3 | 99.9 | 100 | |
| 2015 | 0.08 | 9.3 | 28.7 | 49.5 | 73.1 | 87.8 | 96.1 | 99.6 | 99.9 | 100 |
| | | | | | | Americas | | | | |
| 1950 | 0.00 | 1.7 | 7.6 | 19.6 | 46.6 | 63.8 | 84.9 | 98.6 | 99.1 | 100 |
| 2015 | 0.00 | 0.5 | 2.0 | 5.7 | 17.3 | 33.3 | 53.2 | 82.9 | 94.9 | 99.1 |
| | | | | | | Asia | | | | |
| 1950 | 0.31 | 27.6 | 68.1 | 88.3 | 97.0 | 99.1 | 99.8 | 100 | 100 | 100 |
| 2015 | 0.00 | 0.3 | 2.0 | 9.3 | 35.5 | 63.4 | 84.2 | 97.5 | 99.5 | 100 |
| | | | | | | Europe | | | | |
| 1950 | 0.01 | 1.1 | 5.2 | 17.5 | 50.9 | 79.0 | 94.6 | 99.7 | 100 | 100 |
| 2015 | 0.00 | 0.0 | 0.0 | 0.2 | 3.5 | 13.8 | 35.4 | 97.9 | 99.9 | 100 |

*Source*: gapminder.org (www.gapminder.org/tools/#_state_marker_opacityRegular:0.96;;&ui_presentation:true;& chart-type=mountain&locale_id=en).

Americas. While there was still considerable poverty in Europe in 1950, it had practically disappeared from that region in 2015.

## 7.4.2  Intensive versus Extensive Economic Growth

So far, we have talked about economic growth as if it was always one and the same thing. In fact, it is not. Economic growth can be *intensive* or *extensive* growth. Intensive growth occurs when an economy produces ever more of the same goods and services. Early industrial development was marked primarily by intensive growth. Production methods were improved, economies of scale were realized, larger and larger firms could produce larger and larger quantities of output at falling unit costs.[11] Henry Ford's invention of mass production of automobiles is a good example: Ford was able to produce large quantities of Model T's – which all looked the same – making automobiles affordable for a much larger number of consumers than before.

*Extensive* growth occurs when an economy produces either a growing variety of goods and services, or goods and services of increasing quality, or both. Because consumers like variety, the value added produced by an economy (its real GDP) increases, when it produces goods in greater variety. For example, as the economies of scale in producing simple models like Model T were exhausted, car makers realized that their consumers wanted cars in different shapes, colors, etc. Because consumers value quality, real GDP also increases when goods of greater quality are produced. Extensive growth also includes the development and sale of new products which did not exist before, such as PCs, mobile telephones – and more recently virtual reality headsets, fiber optic cables, etc. Because, as we saw in Chapter 1, developed economies like the US are very much service-oriented economies, extensive growth also includes the production of new services such as medical services, financial services, childcare, or care for the elderly.

Table 7.3 illustrates the concept of extensive growth by showing the features of newly built homes in the US over a time span of forty years. It reminds us of the fact that many features we take for granted today did not exist or were available only in luxury homes sixty years ago. The same source reports that the median size of a new home was 1,150 square feet in 1956 and 1,950 square feet in 1996. Homes have become more comfortable and larger. Another example comes from the automobile industry: In 1970, only 50 percent of all new cars had air conditioning, 20 percent had power windows, and 15 percent had power locks. Antilock brakes and airbags that increased driver safety significantly only came in the late 1980s. The fact that the construction industry and the car industry grew over this period does not simply mean that they produced ever more homes and cars of the same type. Their products became more valuable, because they were of better quality and had more differentiated features, and each product contributed more to real GDP than before.

Today's model of growth in North America, Japan, and Europe is predominantly extensive growth. Economic growth in these economies does not mean that we consume ever larger quantities of the same stuff. Instead, it means that many of the

**Table 7.3** Quality improvements in new homes

Percentage of newly built homes equipped with:

|  | 1956 | 1996 |
|---|---|---|
| Two or more bathrooms | 28 | 91 |
| One or more fireplaces | 35 | 62 |
| Insulation in the walls | 33 | 93 |
| Storm windows | 8 | 68 |
| Central heating and air conditioning | 6 | 81 |
| Range | 1 | 94 |
| Dishwasher | 11 | 93 |
| Garage door opener | 1 | 78 |

*Source*: *Time Well Spent*, 1997 Annual Report, Federal Reserve Bank of Dallas, S. 6 (www.dallasfed.org/~/media/documents/fed/annual/1999/ar97.pdf).

things we consume are of better quality than in the past or that they are things we did not even imagine twenty years ago. Yet, with admirable foresight, James T. Adams, in his 1931 book *The Epic of America* wrote that the future paradigm of economic improvement would have to be better quality rather than bigger quantity.[12] Shortly after that, psychologist A. H. Maslow argued that there is a hierarchy of human needs beginning with basic needs of food and clothing and rising to higher needs that require more sophisticated goods and services to be satisfied. Maslow's conjecture provides the underpinning of Adams's idea from the demand side: With growing income, people demand more quality rather than quantity of the things they consume.[13]

A final caveat remains: In the early stages of economic development, economic activities often move from the subsistence sector, where people produce goods and services only for themselves and their families, to the market sector. Because we measure economic activity in terms of GDP, which excludes the subsistence sector by definition, *measured* economic growth in developing economies to some extent reflects the move of economic activities into the market system rather than an increase in the volume or quality of goods and services produced. Growth statistics can, therefore, exaggerate true economic growth in such economies.

### 7.4.3 Sources of Economic Growth: Labor, Capital, Technological Progress

Where does economic growth come from and what can we do to promote it? There are three basic factors driving economic growth, namely population growth, capital deepening, and technological progress. We have already looked at population growth in the previous section. Larger populations mean larger markets and, therefore, a greater scope for a finer division of labor leading to increased productivity. Such was the view of classical economists like Adam Smith. Based on this view, one would expect that declining population growth and, even more so, declining populations put a limit on economic growth. Alvin Hansen, one of the great American economists of the first half of the twentieth century, argued just that.[14] Hansen thought that the prospect of declining population growth would lead to an era of *secular stagnation* with high rates of unemployment. Hansen's views have regained prominence recently in view of the stagnating and declining populations of many Western and Asian countries. Hansen concluded that the industrialized economies would have to find a new paradigm of economic growth, in which *per-capita* economic growth would be facilitated by improvements of technology.

If we are interested in growth in real per-capita GDP, the two other factors remain. Capital deepening occurs when the capital–labor ratio – the amount of equipment, machinery, buildings etc. available on average to each worker – increases. In the early stages of economic growth, capital deepening is the main source of economic growth. A well-known example is the observation that, from the mid-seventeenth century onward, European weavers who traditionally worked with handlooms in their homes were driven out of existence by factories using mechanical looms. This is but one instance of the process of industrialization. China's experience of a very high investment ratio in the past forty years is another instance of growth driven by capital deepening. A rising capital–labor ratio increases labor productivity, or real GDP per worker, and thus reduces the unit cost of output.

Can a rising capital–labor ratio be a source of sustained economic growth? Generally, the answer is no! Recall from Chapter 3 that production technologies exhibit *declining marginal products* of labor. We now extend the same argument to capital, arguing that production technologies exhibit *declining marginal products of capital*, too. This means that, with a constant labor force, adding more capital to an existing capital stock leads to more output, but the increments in output become smaller and smaller as the capital stock grows. You can extend this argument by saying that increasing the capital stock per worker leads to more output, but the increments in output become smaller as the amount of capital per worker rises.

Is it reasonable to assume that technologies exhibit declining marginal products of capital? There are three empirical observations at least suggesting that the answer is yes.

- If the marginal product of capital is increasing, larger firms necessarily produce at lower unit cost than smaller firms. This implies that small firms have no chance of survival and all markets are monopolies for technological reasons. This is not what we observe in the process of economic development.
- Declining marginal products of capital imply that capital yields higher returns in capital-poor countries than in capital-rich countries. If capital can move across borders, we should observe capital to flow from capital-rich to capital-poor countries. This is consistent with empirical observations.
- Capital-poor countries should exhibit higher rates of per-capita growth than capital-rich countries, implying a process of economic convergence. Again, this is consistent with empirical observations.

Let's assume, then, that technologies exhibit declining marginal products of capital. Now remember that the capital stock is partially used up in the process of production due to wear and tear or technical depreciation. Assume for simplicity that the rate of depreciation is constant, i.e., some fixed percentage of the capital stock is used up in production every period. Unless the depreciated part of the capital stock is replaced, the capital stock will fall.

It is now easy to see that the amount of depreciation per period grows larger and larger as the capital stock grows larger and larger. The additional output, however, becomes smaller and smaller. Putting these two tendencies together implies that, if we let the capital labor ratio grow larger and larger, there will be a point at which all output must be used to replace depreciated capital. But this is impossible since there would be no output left for consumption and workers would starve to death. It is, therefore, impossible to achieve sustained economic growth only by letting the capital labor ratio grow. Still, capital deepening can make a significant contribution to historically observed economic growth before that limit has been reached and it is an important driver of growth in developing and emerging economies. Capital deepening can be stimulated by policies that increase firms' return on capital such as lowering corporate income taxes and low and stable costs of borrowing.

Let us now turn to technological progress as a source of growth. An economy's *technology* describes in what quantities capital and labor must be combined in order to produce a given amount of output efficiently, i.e., with the least cost possible. An economy's *total factor productivity* (TFP) is the level of output it produces with an efficient combination of given amounts of capital and labor. *Technological progress* occurs when TFP increases. It is the result of the development of better machinery and equipment and better production techniques. Technological progress is the main force driving economic growth in mature economies such as the US or Western Europe. Empirical studies suggest that it accounts for about two-thirds of the observed growth in OECD countries between 1960 and 2000. This is illustrated in Table 7.4.

By definition, the contribution of capital deepening to total economic growth is 100 minus the TFP share. By way of comparison, note that the share of TFP growth in China's spectacular real GDP growth since 1978 has been estimated to be 54 percent, which is considerably lower than the OECD average.[15] This means that the contribution of capital deepening was relatively large in China which is in line with China's very high investment rates we observed in section 7.3.

Technological progress is the result of R&D, the production of new technological knowledge and the development and implementation of more efficient technologies from that new knowledge. R&D activities are costly. Firms need to employ people who are skilled in such activities, buy equipment for them to try out new ideas, and have patience when apparently promising ideas fail. Governments can stimulate TFP growth by increasing the returns firms reap from R&D activities. One important policy tool here is patent protection. The purpose of patents is to make new technological knowledge produced by one firm available to others – since patents are published – and yet allow that firm to get a return on it in the form of license income. Another important tool is to give tax reductions for the cost of R&D. Finally, public universities engage in similar activities though often more fundamental than applied and make the result available to the business sector at no cost. In more mature economies, such policies become more important than those aiming at promoting capital formation and capital deepening.

The critical difference between capital deepening and technological progress is that physical capital depreciates in the process of production while technological knowledge does not. We can think about the stock of knowledge at a certain point

**Table 7.4** Average real GDP growth and TFP growth in OECD countries

| Country | Growth rate | TFP growth | TFP share (%) |
| --- | --- | --- | --- |
| Australia | 1.67 | 1.26 | 75 |
| Austria | 2.99 | 2.03 | 68 |
| Belgium | 2.58 | 1.74 | 67 |
| Canada | 1.57 | 0.95 | 60 |
| Denmark | 1.87 | 1.32 | 70 |
| Finland | 2.72 | 2.03 | 75 |
| France | 2.50 | 1.54 | 62 |
| Germany | 3.09 | 1.96 | 64 |
| Greece | 1.93 | 1.66 | 86 |
| Iceland | 4.02 | 2.33 | 58 |
| Ireland | 2.93 | 2.26 | 77 |
| Italy | 4.04 | 2.10 | 52 |
| Japan | 3.28 | 2.73 | 83 |
| Netherlands | 1.74 | 1.25 | 72 |
| New Zealand | 0.61 | 0.45 | 74 |
| Norway | 2.63 | 1.70 | 72 |
| Portugal | 3.42 | 2.06 | 60 |
| Spain | 3.22 | 1.79 | 55 |
| Sweden | 1.68 | 1.24 | 74 |
| Switzerland | 0.98 | 0.69 | 70 |
| UK | 1.90 | 1.31 | 69 |
| US | 1.89 | 1.09 | 58 |
| OECD average | 2.41 | 1.61 | 68 |

*Source*: P. Aghion and P. Howitt, "Capital, Innovation, and Growth Accounting," *Oxford Review of Economic Policy* 23(1) (2007): 79–93, S. 83.

of time as a stock of knowledge capital. New knowledge adds to this stock and makes it larger. But knowledge does not deteriorate when it is being used. Quite the opposite, actually! Using it in different contexts can produce additional knowledge and add to the existing stock.

Technological progress has repercussions also for human labor and employment. In modern industries, physically exhausting jobs and jobs requiring monotonous and repetitive human activities have often been replaced by machinery and are now being replaced by robots. This has caused some people to lose their jobs and forced them to seek new ones resulting in economic difficulties and hardship. Yet, such difficulties are easier to overcome in a growing economy and it is possible in principle at least for governments to assist individuals in such situations. At the same time, comparing survey data from the late 1960s and early 2000s suggests that working conditions and job satisfaction have generally increased over time as jobs become less physically demanding due to technological change.[16]

At the same time, working with more sophisticated technologies demands new and better skills of the labor force, or, to use a concept first introduced by Nobel laureates Theodore Schultz and Gary Becker, more *human capital*.[17] The idea is that it is not sufficient to consider labor as an input into production simply by counting the number of people who work. Each worker brings his own *human capital* into the production process. It consists of the knowledge and skills which he has acquired during his education, training, and work experience. Human capital is human because it is inseparably connected with individual human beings. It is capital in the sense that it can be accumulated over a lifetime.

Human capital can be considered as another factor of economic growth. Specifically, better education and training of a nation's workforce increases labor productivity and the ability to adopt new technologies. The concept of human capital moves learning and education into the focus of policies promoting economic growth. Time spent in education is time not spent working and earning wages. Hence, the decision to get education is an investment decision, in which current cost (including income forgone) must be weighed against future pay-offs in the form of higher wages. Governments can improve long-term economic growth by subsidizing education and training of the workforce. However, if human capital empirically exposes declining marginal products similar to physical capital, the effect on human capital on growth and the desired stock of human capital will be limited. Empirical studies suggest that the growth of human capital explains between 12 and 14 percent of long-term economic growth.[18]

## 7.4.4  Working with Data: US Labor Productivity Growth

If a country's economy grows faster than its labor force, the average worker produces more output than before, i.e., his or her average productivity has increased. In terms of work time (not necessarily individual incomes), this must imply that he or she can afford more goods and services. The following tables illustrate the point. Table 7.5 shows that an average worker in the US had to work 463 hours to buy a dishwasher in 1913. In 1997, he had to work 28 hours to afford a (much improved) dishwasher. In 1916, an average worker in the US had to work 3,162 hours to buy a refrigerator, almost a year at 10-hour workdays. In 1997, he or she worked 68 hours to buy a (much better) refrigerator, a week and a half at eight hours a day. But note that the average number of hours required to work for a new home did not come down that much between 1920 and 1996. This is most likely due to the fact that construction has remained relatively labor intensive. In other words, when you buy a new home, you mostly exchange the work time of the builders for your own work time. In contrast, the making of a dishwasher today involves a lot more capital and a lot less labor than a hundred years ago.

To avoid the obfuscation caused by the quality improvement of the appliances considered, one can also look at the cost of food items in terms of minutes of work

**Table 7.5** The cost of home appliances in average hours worked

Dishwasher

| 1913 | 1954 | 1970 | 1997 |
|------|------|------|------|
| 463  | 140  | 69   | 28   |

Refrigerator

| 1916  | 1958 | 1970 | 1997 |
|-------|------|------|------|
| 3,162 | 333  | 112  | 68   |

Clothes washer

| 1911 | 1956 | 1970 | 1997 |
|------|------|------|------|
| 553  | 138  | 72   | 26   |

New homes (hours per sq. ft.)

| 1920 | 1956 | 1970 | 1996 |
|------|------|------|------|
| 7.8  | 6.5  | n.a. | 5.6  |

*Source*: *Time Well Spent*, 1997 Annual Report, Federal Reserve Bank of Dallas, S. 8 (www.dallasfed.org/~/media/documents/fed/annual/1999/ar97.pdf).

required to afford them. Table 7.6 gives a few examples. In 1919, it took an average worker 101 minutes of work to earn 3lb of tomatoes. In 1997, that number had fallen to eighteen minutes. Once again, we observe that an hour of labor is worth a lot more consumption goods today than a hundred years ago.

Figure 7.6 plots an index of the average labor productivity in the US nonfarm business sector from 1947 to 2017, with the 2009 level normalized to 100. Productivity is measured as the ratio of output to total hours worked. Nonfarm business output is measured as US real GDP less the output of the general government sector, private households, nonprofit institutions, and the farm sector. The figure shows that productivity has generally been on the rise over those seventy years, but with some fluctuations in the growth rate. The total increase between 1947 and 2017 amounted to 433 percent. At the same time, real hourly compensation, which is total labor cost divided by hours worked and corrected for price changes using the CPI, increased by a total of 284 percent. This is a comprehensive measure of gross hourly real wages in the nonfarm business sector. If hourly real wages grew in line with productivity, real unit labor cost would remain constant. Figure 7.6 indicates that in fact real unit labor cost fell by 34.5 percent over the total period. This indicates that labor productivity has grown faster than real wages.

Since total real output equals labor productivity multiplied by hours worked, we can decompose the growth of output into labor productivity growth and the growth of total hours worked. Figure 7.7 shows this decomposition for several sub-periods since 1950. The 1960s had the strongest productivity growth in the US with an annual average of 2.46 percent, up from 1.95 percent in the 1950s. Productivity growth slowed down considerably in the 1970s and 1980s, with average growth

**Table 7.6** The cost of food items in minutes of work

|  | 1919 | 1997 |  | 1919 | 1997 |
| --- | --- | --- | --- | --- | --- |
| Tomatoes, 3lb | 101 | 18 | Milk, half-gallon | 39 | 7 |
| Eggs, 1 dozen | 80 | 5 | Ground beef, 1lb | 30 | 6 |
| Sugar, 5lb | 72 | 10 | Lettuce, 1lb | 17 | 3 |
| Bacon, 1lb | 70 | 12 | Beans, 1lb | 16 | 3 |
| Oranges, 1 dozen | 68 | 9 | Bread, 1lb | 13 | 4 |
| Coffee, 1lb | 55 | 17 | Onions, 1lb | 9 | 2 |

*Source*: *Time Well Spent*, 1997 Annual Report, Federal Reserve Bank of Dallas, S. 8 (www.dallasfed.org/~/media/documents/fed/annual/1999/ar97.pdf).

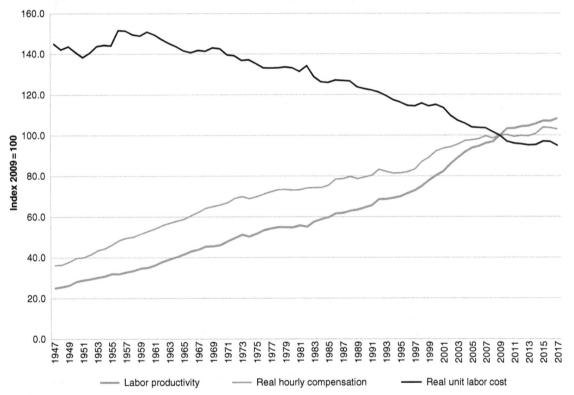

**Figure 7.6** US labor productivity and unit labor cost
*Source*: BLS Labor Productivity and Costs Measures for Business and Nonfarm Business Sectors, www.bls.gov/lpc/#tables, February 1, 2018.

rates of 1.35 and 1.48 percent, respectively. In contrast, the 1990s and the 2000s saw a strong recovery of productivity growth with average rates of 2.0 percent and 2.28 percent annually, but productivity growth slowed down to 0.78 percent annually following the Great Recession. With the exception of the 1950s and the period after the Great Recession, increases in hours worked contributed between 1.7 and

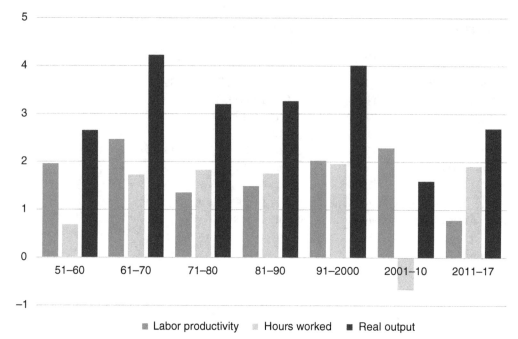

**Figure 7.7** Average growth rates of labor productivity, hours worked, and output
*Source*: BLS Labor Productivity and Costs Measures for Business and Nonfarm Business Sectors, www.bls.gov/lpc/#tables, February 1, 2018.

1.9 percent to total output growth. From 2007 to 2010, the number of hours worked in the US economy fell by almost 10 percent.

## BOX 7.1 DIFFERENCE OF OPINION: PRODUCTIVITY AND EMPLOYMENT

At this point some might question the argument that greater productivity leads to more employment. We are all aware of many situations where individual companies buy better and more machines as a way to *replace* labor. Thus, many of us associate higher productivity with less employment. This might in fact be true for individual firms and periods of time, but it does not go far enough when considering the entire macroeconomic situation over the longer run. Firms that displace the labor are not doing this to reduce output or profits. They adopt higher productivity so that they will be more competitive and sell more output. Some of the increase in output can be done without more labor. But as higher productivity facilitates lower prices and more competitiveness, the extra output will eventually require more labor. In most countries we observe that this latter positive impact on employment swamps the displacement impact. In most countries the evidence is quite compelling. The late 1990s in the US is one such period in which both productivity and national employment were rising at very strong rates.

But in the time periods following the 2001 and the 2008–9 recessions, employment did not snap back as quickly as many people had hoped. Productivity did continue to rise rapidly and there were many stories of companies that closed in the US, leaving unemployed workers as they found locations in other countries. This worry that higher productivity leads to less employment resurfaced after 2001 and continues as an economic and political issue. This issue resurfaced again after 2007 and was a key part of the presidential election of 2012.

## 7.5  Limits to Economic Growth?

Can economic growth continue forever? The question has been raised almost from the beginning of the growth process in Europe that started in the second half of the seventeenth century and there has been no scarcity of writers arguing that it cannot. Three types of limits to economic growth have been pointed out so far: population growth, the limited availability of mineral resources, and climate change.

### 7.5.1  Limit 1: Population Growth

In 1798, the Rev. Robert Thomas Malthus, an Anglican pastor who later became professor of history and political economy at Haileybury College, published his *Essay on the Principle of Population*, in which he claimed that economic growth could not be sustained for a long period of time.[19] Malthus argued that unhindered population growth would be exponential (i.e., with rising increments), while the growth of food supply could be linear (i.e., with constant increments) at best. The former is true in all biological populations. The latter argument rested on the notion that food supply could grow only by cultivating more land with more people. Combining these two growth principles immediately implies that population growth leads to declining per-capita food supply. Malthus further argued that rising per-capita food supply would increase birth rates and reduce death rates, while falling per-capita food supply would reduce birth rates and increase death rates. An economy might go through a period of rising prosperity, but this would lead eventually to higher birth and lower death rates and, therefore, population growth, which would result in a decline in prosperity. An economy exhibiting these characteristics would find itself in a *Malthusian equilibrium* characterized by constant standards of living over long periods of time – a conclusion consistent with most of economic history and experience in the centuries before Malthus. Malthus concluded in particular that government efforts to improve the living conditions of the poor were vain – they would only lead to more poor people.

Malthus's ideas had great influence on many writers and thinkers following him, including the authors of modern science fiction dystopias such as *Soylent Green*

(1973), and *Blade Runner* (1982), two of many movies that illustrated the supposed consequences of overpopulation. In 1968, Stanford University professor Paul R. Ehrlich published his *Population Bomb* which made a very similar argument.[20] His prologue begins like this:

> The battle to feed all of humanity is over. In the 1970s and 1980s hundreds of millions of people will starve to death in spite of any crash programs embarked on now. At this late date, nothing can prevent a substantial increase in the world death rate . . . We are today involved in the events leading to famine and ecocatastrophe; tomorrow we may be destroyed by them. (p. xi)

Ehrlich called for policies promoting population control not only in the US but also in the developing countries of Africa and Asia to make sure that their growing populations would not come and eat up the wealth of the US. Inspired by his and similar arguments, governments in many developed countries began to make the payment of development aid money to poor nations conditional on the enforcement of population control there.

Despite Ehrlich's dire predictions, the earth today feeds more than twice the number of people it did in the 1960s and yet there is, according to UN statistics, no food shortage in the world. The UN's Food and Agricultural Organization (FAO) evaluates global food supply by comparing dietary energy requirements with dietary energy supplies.[21] Dietary energy requirements are the number of calories individuals need to maintain a healthy life. Taking individual dietary energy requirements and multiplying by the number of people in a population results in that population's dietary energy requirement. Different types of food are evaluated based on the average amount of calories they provide. This gives rise to the calculation of annual dietary energy supplies. Dividing total dietary energy supply by total dietary energy requirements gives a measure of average dietary energy supply adequacy, which the FAO publishes for periods of three years.

Table 7.7 shows that the world today produces 20 percent more food than needed to feed all people adequately. In Europe and North America, food supply surpasses requirements by 46 percent and 38 percent respectively, but in no continent in the world is there a food shortage in principle. Differences between country groups, however, reveal that there are countries with significant food shortages. The fact that there are today 815 million people, or 11 percent of the global population, suffering from hunger is a consequence of an inadequate distribution of food, not of the inability of the earth to feed its population as Malthus and Ehrlich claimed.[22] Those who starve are denied access to food by those who have more than enough. What neither Malthus nor Ehrlich expected was the enormous increase in agricultural productivity due to better production and cultivation techniques and the breeding of more resilient and productive crops.

**Table 7.7** FAO dietary energy supply adequacy (2014–16)

| Region | Dietary energy supply adequacy (%) | Country group | Dietary energy supply adequacy (%) |
|---|---|---|---|
| World | 120 | Least developed | 95 |
| Africa | 106 | Landlocked developing | 103 |
| Asia | 120 | Small island developing | 96 |
| Latin America and Caribbean | 124 | Low-income | 88 |
| Oceania | 119 | Lower-middle-income | 113 |
| Northern America | 138 | Low-income food-deficit | 105 |
| Europe | 146 | | |

*Source*: FAO, Food-Security Indicators 25–10–2017 (www.fao.org/economic/ess/ess-fs/ess-fadata/en/#.XRZarI_RZPY).

## 7.5.2   Limit 2: Non-Renewable Resources

In 1865, British economist William Stanley Jevons published *The Coal Question*, in which he argued that economic growth in the UK was not sustainable.[23] Jevons's main point was that the UK economy relied on coal as its main source of energy. Jevons wrote: "Day by day it becomes more evident that the Coal we happily possess in excellent quality and abundance is the mainspring of modern material civilization" (I.1). He also wrote that:

> The present rate of increase in our coal consumption is then ascertained and it is shown that, should the consumption multiply for rather more than a century at the same rate, the average depth of our coal mines would be 4,000 feet, and the average price of coal much higher than the highest price now paid for the finest kinds of coal. (I.19)[24]

The fact that coal is a limited, non-renewable resource, Jevons argued, implied that the prosperity of the UK would necessarily come to a halt.

In 1972, a book presented by the Club of Rome, a global think tank (www.clubofrome.org), shocked politicians and the general public around the world. The Club of Rome had asked a team of scientists to study Jevons's problem at the global level, namely the question whether the world economy could go on growing as it had done in the previous century or so. The report, entitled *The Limits to Growth*, focused on the problem of non-renewable resources and the pollution of the world's air and water reserves. It presented a dramatic forecast, concluding that, without major changes in the patterns of production and consumption around the globe, the world economy would sooner or later reach a point of collapse.[25] Depending on the scenario analyzed, "sooner" would mean by the turn of the century; "later" would mean well before the year 2100. For example, at the then prevailing growth rate of oil consumption, technologies, and known oil reserves, the world would run out of oil by 1992.

The main points of the book are summarized as follows:

Our world model was built specifically to investigate five major trends of global concern – accelerating industrialization, rapid population growth, widespread malnutrition, depletion of nonrenewable resources, and a deteriorating environment. [p. 21]

Our conclusions are:

1. If the present growth trends in world population, industrialization, pollution, food production, and resource depletion continue unchanged, the limits to growth on this planet will be reached sometime within the next one hundred years. The most probable result will be a rather sudden and uncontrollable decline in both population and industrial capacity.

2. It is possible to alter these growth trends and to establish a condition of ecological and economic stability that is sustainable far into the future. The state of global equilibrium could be designed so that the basic material needs of each person on earth are satisfied and each person has an equal opportunity to realize his individual human potential.

3. If the world's people decide to strive for this second outcome rather than the first, the sooner they begin working to attain it, the greater will be their chances of success. [pp. 23–4]

. . . The industrial capital stock grows to a level that requires an enormous input of resources. In the very process of that growth it depletes a large fraction of the resource reserves available. As resource prices rise and mines are depleted, more and more capital must be used for obtaining resources, leaving less to be invested for future growth. Finally investment cannot keep up with depreciation, and the industrial base collapses, taking with it the service and agricultural systems, which have become dependent on industrial inputs (such as fertilizers, pesticides, hospital laboratories, computers, and especially energy for mechanization). For a short time the situation is especially serious because population, with the delays inherent in the age structure and the process of social adjustment, keeps rising. Population finally decreases when the death rate is driven upward by lack of food and health services. The exact timing of these events is not meaningful, given the great aggregation and many uncertainties in the model. It is significant however, that growth is stopped well before the year 2100. [p. 125]

. . . We can thus say with some confidence that, under the assumption of no major change in the present system, population and industrial growth will certainly stop within the next century, at the latest. [p. 126]

The authors concluded that, in order to survive, humankind must stop population growth and the accumulation of capital per worker. The world economy would then converge to an equilibrium with constant real GDP per capita. The book fueled the then fledgling ecological movement. It provided the impetus for regulation protect-ing the environment and saving resources, such as by recycling. In that, it was useful.

Nevertheless, it shared a number of severe methodological flaws with Jevons's book. The main one was to neglect the role of market prices in guiding economic decisions. Prices of non-renewable resources rising relative to the general price level provide incentives for producers to switch to technologies economizing on such resources and to develop new technologies for exploring resource deposits and making them economically usable. For example, as oil became much more expen-sive in the 1970s, new technologies were invented that reduced the amount of oil needed in industrial production. Furthermore, new drilling techniques were developed that facilitated the exploitation of offshore oil fields in depths that no one imagined in the early 1970s. For minerals such as copper, rising relative prices have also provided incentives for more recycling. As a result, relative prices of mineral resources generally came down again after some time.

Figure 7.8 illustrates that argument. It shows the relative prices of several mineral raw materials from the early or mid-nineteenth century until 2014. These relative

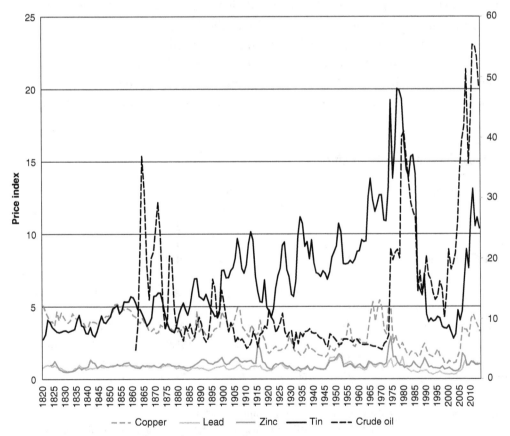

**Figure 7.8** Relative prices of mineral raw materials

*Source*: Martin Stuermer, "150 Years of Boom and Bust: What Drives Mineral Commodity Prices?" *Macroeconomic Dynamics*, published online September 9, 2016.

prices are calculated by dividing the British pound prices – for which long data series exist – by the UK producer price index in the case of copper, lead, zinc, and tin and by an international producer price index in the case of crude oil. The resulting series can be interpreted as the relative prices of the respective raw materials and a standardized British or international tradable manufactured good. The relative price of crude oil is on the right-hand scale, the other relative prices are on the left-hand scale.

The figure demonstrates that, over long periods of time, these relative prices do not exhibit increasing trends. Upswings of relative prices are followed by downswings. This refutes the Jevons/Club of Rome hypothesis that the prices of mineral raw materials increase signaling the soon-to-be-expected end of economic growth.

Table 7.8 reports several energy consumption statistics for OECD countries. Energy efficiency is the amount of real GDP in USD 1,000 at prices of 2005 produced per unit of energy measured in tons of oil equivalents. For the OECD as a whole, energy efficiency increased by 84 percent between 1973, the year of the first *oil price shock*, and 2014. In the US, energy efficiency increased by 127 percent and in the European OECD countries by 100 percent. Table 7.8 shows that energy efficiency increased only slightly in the years after 1973. Larger gains were realized after 1990.

Industrial energy efficiency considers the volume of industrial production per unit of energy. Table 7.8 indicates that efficiency gains have been larger in industry than in the economy as a whole. This reflects the fact that industrial producers are

**Table 7.8** Measures of energy use and efficiency

| Aggregate energy efficiency | 1973 | 1980 | 1990 | 2000 | 2010 | 2014 |
|---|---|---|---|---|---|---|
| OECD | 4.17 | 4.55 | 5.56 | 6.25 | 7.14 | 7.69 |
| US | 2.94 | 3.33 | 4.35 | 5.00 | 6.25 | 6.67 |
| OECD Europe | 5.00 | 5.56 | 6.67 | 7.69 | 8.33 | 10.00 |
| Per-capita energy consumption | 1973 | 1980 | 1990 | 2000 | 2010 | 2014 |
| OECD | 4.07 | 4.13 | 4.22 | 4.58 | 4.36 | 4.12 |
| US | 8.16 | 7.92 | 7.66 | 8.05 | 7.15 | 6.91 |
| OECD Europe | 3.15 | 3.23 | 3.34 | 3.29 | 3.13 | 2.96 |
| Industrial energy efficiency | 1973 | 1980 | 1990 | 2000 | 2010 | 2013 |
| OECD | n.a. | 55.87 | 75.92 | 85.94 | 100.00 | 106.73 |
| US | 41.34 | 45.45 | 68.74 | 84.35 | 100.00 | 115.51 |
| OECD Europe | 49.49 | 56.80 | 74.82 | 87.72 | 100.00 | 106.25 |

*Source*: International Energy Agency, *Energy Balances of OECD Countries* (2015).
*Notes*: Aggregate energy efficiency is measured as real GDP in thousands of 2005 USD adjusted for differences in purchasing power divided by the total primary energy supply in tons of oil equivalents; per-capita energy consumption is measured as total energy supply in tons of oil equivalent divided by total population; industrial energy efficiency is measured as the index of industrial production divided by the index of industrial energy consumption (2010 = 100).

more sensitive to relative prices of energy than private households and the government. Finally, Table 7.8 shows that energy consumption per capita of the population has increased slightly in the OECD between 1973 and 2014, but it has decreased both in the US and the European OECD countries. Overall, these data indicate that the oil price movements of the 1970s have triggered adjustments that were not foreseen by the Club of Rome report and have caused a more economical use of energy.

Technological progress in natural resource extraction has increased both the level of proven reserves and unproven reserves of mineral resources. *Reserves* are known resource deposits which are economically recoverable with given technologies. For oil, these would be oil fields that are known and can be exploited with current drilling techniques. *Unconventional reserves* are known deposits which are not economically recoverable with given technologies. A few years ago, oil sands would have been considered as unconventional reserves. When oil prices rose in the early 2000s, however, technologies were developed to exploit such reserves and they have now been turned into *reserves*. Finally, one may also consider estimates of *geological deposits* that are estimated to exist in the earth's crust, although their location is not known today. Based on those distinctions, Table 7.9 gives estimates of the availability of several mineral resources in terms of current annual consumption. Note that the estimated availability of crude oil now extends to 2068, much later than the date of exhaustion predicted by the Club of Rome report.

Technological progress has moved unconventional reserves into reserves, and geological deposits into unconditional reserves. Thus, it increases the reserves available to the global economy. The implication is that the point of exhaustion at given rates of production and usage is pushed out in time.

With this in mind, the Club of Rome's conclusion that world population growth and global economic growth have to be stopped quickly is difficult to maintain.

**Table 7.9** Estimated reserves and deposits of selected minerals

| Mineral | Reserves/annual consumption | Unconventional reserves/ annual consumption | Geological deposits/ annual consumption |
|---|---|---|---|
| Copper | 43 | 189 | 95 million |
| Iron | 78 | 223 | 1.35 billion |
| Coal | 129 | 2,900 | Combined 1.4 million |
| Crude oil | 55 | 76 | |
| Natural gas | 59 | 410 | |

*Source*: Martin Stuermer and Gregor Schwerhoff, "Non-Renewable But Inexhaustible – Resources in an Endogenous Growth Model" (working paper, University of Bonn, 2013).

### 7.5.3   Limit 3: Climate Change

The third potential limit to sustained economic growth is the threat of climate change due to global warming. Global warming is caused by the accumulation of greenhouse gases in the atmosphere, which are a by-product of the use of fossil fuels to produce energy.

In 2006, former World Bank chief economist Sir Nicholas Stern published the *Stern Review on the Economics of Climate Change*, a study commissioned by the British government.[26] In the executive summary (p. vi), Stern writes:

> Using the results from formal economic models, the Review estimates that if we don't act, the overall costs and risks of climate change will be equivalent to losing at least 5% of global GDP each year, now and forever. If a wider range of risks and impacts is taken into account, the estimates of damage could rise to 20% of GDP or more.

In 2016, world GDP equaled USD 75.6 trillion; 5 percent of that would be USD 3.8 trillion, 20 percent would be USD 15.6 trillion. These are truly enormous costs. But there is an important fallacy here. Those costs make for a level effect, not a growth effect. Since most of the economic costs estimated by the *Stern Review* occur over a time horizon of 200 years and more, one must keep them in perspective against the prospective growth of the world economy. If the world economy keeps growing at an average annual rate of 2.5 percent over the same time horizon, it will have increased by a factor of 139.6 at the end. Subtracting 20 percent from that still leaves a global economy larger than today's by a factor of 111.7.

The cost estimates presented by the *Stern Review* and the uncertainty associated with them have come under substantial critique.[27] There is agreement, however, that the underlying issue, greenhouse gas emissions, constitutes a massive market failure. Energy producers have been allowed to pollute the atmosphere with greenhouse gases without consideration of the adverse effects this has on the climate and the damage it causes to the global economy. Since the earth's atmosphere is a free good which can be used by anybody at no charge, there is no price mechanism forcing energy suppliers to take these effects and damages into account. This means that producers have no economic incentive to reduce greenhouse gas emissions.

There are, in principle, two solutions to this problem. One is direct government intervention. Governments could limit the amount of permissible greenhouse gas emissions and fine producers for exceeding those limits, or governments could impose *carbon taxes* on the use of fossil fuels making them more expensive and less economically attractive. Alternatively, governments could create property rights that can be traded among producers. Following the example of $SO_2$ emissions, the government would issue permits to use fossil fuels which would then be tradable and have a price indicating the economic value of greenhouse gas emissions. Either way, energy producers would feel the cost of greenhouse gas emissions and that would create incentives for investment in more greenhouse gas-efficient technologies and their development.

The effects of such policies on economic *growth* are rather ambiguous. On the one hand, raising production costs by making fossil fuels more expensive and by new government regulation is likely to reduce economic growth. On the other hand, it would make a large part of the global capital stock less economically valuable and stimulate growth in new, more atmosphere-friendly capital. This, together with the related R&D activities to develop new technologies, would stimulate investment. Furthermore, climate change will make economic activities in some regions of the world impossible, namely those that would be affected by rising sea levels, while facilitating economic activities in other regions. Climate change will, therefore, require additional investment linked to the relocation of people and their economic activities. This again would accelerate world economic growth. The net effect of climate change on economic growth could, therefore, very well be positive.

One important aspect of climate change is the risk of policy failure in addition to market failure. Since climate change is a global issue, it requires policy action at the global level, i.e., global cooperation of governments. No country has an incentive to do something about it, since it is too small to achieve significant results for the earth's atmosphere and the effects of its own policies would dissipate globally. For the same reason, every country has an incentive to tacitly cheat on global climate treaties assuming that all other countries will comply, hoping to get a competitive advantage for its own industries. Government cooperation, therefore, suffers from a collective-action problem. Even if one or a group of countries musters sufficient leadership to get all governments to sign a climate agreement, it is not clear how such an agreement would be enforced.

## 7.6   SUMMARY

Economics Nobel laureate Robert Lucas of the University of Chicago once said that economists should stop worrying about business cycles and think about economic growth instead, because this is what really matters for a nation's wellbeing. History clearly proves that he was right. Over long periods of time, economic growth or the lack of it are the most important macroeconomic facts. Business cycles make us nervous or excited, growth makes us happy or unhappy. We have seen that the most important part of economic growth is productivity growth that comes from technological progress. Capital accumulation cannot sustain growth of per-capita real output for a long time, and the contribution of human capital to economic growth seems rather limited, too. Therefore, the forces of technological progress are the most important determinants of a nation's wellbeing in the long run.

The past 200 years have seen repeated arguments claiming that economic growth will and must come to an end, soon, because the earth's resources are limited and its population is growing too large. Such arguments raise a host of ethical questions that are difficult to solve in free democratic societies: Who decides which human beings are allowed to have children and how many? Who decides how long human beings are allowed to live? Who sets the level of consumption that is made available to each person? The Rev. Malthus at least was honest about this and recommended ending policies assisting the poor. It did not make him popular in his time.

So far, however, these arguments have turned out to be wrong. The experience of the past 200 years shows that population growth has long been decoupled from economic growth. As economies have grown richer, birth rates have fallen and population growth rates with them. This is in part at least a response to economic incentives. During this century, world population growth will probably turn negative.

Furthermore, prices have created the right incentives to overcome resource scarcity. When a resource becomes scarcer, its price goes up relative to other resources, and this stimulates investment in the development of new technologies that make new quantities of the resource available or reduce the need for that resource by replacing it with others. Creating the right price and cost incentives stimulating technological progress and investment to counteract climate change remains a big challenge.

Can technological progress continue as an engine of economic growth forever? This is perhaps more a metaphysical than an economic question. R&D, invention, and innovation are the products of human imagination and creativity. With a skeptical view of the human mind, you may think that there will be a point in time when human imagination and creativity will have been exhausted. There will be no new ideas to be conceived any more. With a positive view, you may think that there is no limit to human creativity and imagination. Only time will tell which view of humankind is the right one.

## 7.7   REVIEW QUESTIONS

1. What is the difference between intensive and extensive economic growth?
2. What is your response to the following statement: Economic growth does not benefit the poor?
3. What are the main drivers of economic growth?
4. Can economic growth continue forever?
5. What can governments do to promote economic growth?
6. How will the global economy be different in 2050 compared to today?

## NOTES

1 See Lawrence R. Samuel, *The American Dream: A Cultural History* (Syracuse, NY: Syracuse University Press, 2012).

2 James Truslow Adams, *The Epic of America* (Boston, MA: Little, Brown, and Company, 1931), p. viii.

3 As Samuel points out, *The Epic of America* came out around the same time that Charles B. Darrow invented Monopoly (1933), the former being an optimistic and the latter a pessimistic interpretation of the US experience of the Great Depression, a decade of low and even negative growth and high unemployment (*American Dream*, ch. 1).

4 "Highlights from Chapter 3," at: www.worldbank.org/en/publication/global-economic-prospects

5 See Ding Dou, "Can China Eradicate Poverty?," East Asia Forum, at: www.eastasiaforum .org/2016/07/30/can-china-eradicate-poverty; and the discussion there.

6 Anton Cheremukhin, Mikhail Golosov, Sergei Guriev, and Aleh Tsyvinski, "The Economy of the People's Republic of China from 1953" (NBER working paper 21397, Cambridge, MA: NBER 2015).

7 Daniel J. Mitchell, "A Lesson from China on Poverty Reduction and Inequality." Fee Foundation for Economic Education, at: https://fee.org/articles/a-lesson-from-china-on-poverty-reductions-and-inequality (posted June 23, 2017); Ravi Kanbur, Yue Wang, and Xiaobo Zhang, "The Great Chinese Inequality Turnaround" (IFPRI Discussion Paper 01637, May 2017).

8 Guobao Wu, "Four Factors That Have Driven Poverty Reduction in China." World Economic Forum (October 21, 2016), at: https://weforum.org/agenda/2016/10/four-factors-that-have-driven-poverty-reduction-in-China

9 Oded Galor, *Unified Growth Theory* (Princeton, NJ: Princeton University Press, 2011).

10 The data used in the table have been constructed based on per-capita incomes for different countries together with data for within-country income distributions. They should be regarded as rough estimates. See Max Roser and Esteban Ortiz-Ospina, "Income Inequality" (2017). Published online at OurWorldInData.org. Retrieved from: https://ourworldindata.org/income-inequality

11 Economies of scale occur when the average cost of producing a good falls as the quantity produced increases.

12 Adams, *Epic of America*, p. 431.

13 A. H. Maslow, "A Theory of Human Motivation," *Psychological Review* 50 (1943): 370–96.

14 See "Alvin Hansen on Economic Progress and Declining Population Growth," *Population and Development Review* 30(2) (2004): 329–42.

15 See https://fred.stlouisfed.org/series/RTFPNACNA632NRUG

16 Report of Special Task Force to the US Secretary of Health, Education, and Welfare, *Work in America* (Boston, MA: MIT Press, 1973); James O'Toole and Edward E. Lawler III, *The New American Workplace* (New York: Palgrave Macmillan, 2006).

17 Gary S. Becker, *Human Capital* (New York: Columbia University Press, 1964); Theodore W. Schultz, *The Economic Value of Education* (New York: Columbia University Press,

1963) and *Investment in Human Capital: The Role of Education and Research* (New York: Free Press, 1971).

18  Bas van Leeuwen, "Human Capital and Economic Growth in India, Indonesia, and Japan: A Quantitative Analysis 1890–2000" (dissertation, Utrecht University, 2007, googlebooks, table 2.1).

19  Robert Thomas Malthus, *An Essay on the Principle of Population As It Affects the Future Improvement of Society, with Remarks on the Speculations of Mr. Goodwin, M. Condorcet and Other Writers* (1st edn, London: J. Johnson, in St. Paul's Churchyard, 1798).

20  Paul R. Ehrlich, *The Population Bomb* (New York: Ballantine, 1968).

21  www.fao.org/ag/agn/nutrition/Indicatorsfiles/FoodSupply.pdf

22  FAO, IFAD, UNICEF, WFP, and WHO, *The State of Food Security and Nutrition in the World 2017: Building Resilience for Peace and Food Security* (Rome: FAO).

23  William Stanley Jevons, *The Coal Question* (London: Macmillan, 1865).

24  Quoted from www.econlib.org/library/YPDBooks/Jevons/jvnCQ.html

25  Donella and Dennis L. Meadows, Jay W. Forrester, Jorgen Randers, and William W. Behrens III, *The Limits to Growth: Report to the Club of Rome* (New York: Universe Books, 1972).

26  Nicholas Stern, *The Stern Review on the Economics of Climate Change* (London: HM Treasury, 2006), at: http://webarchive.nationalarchives.gov.uk/20100407011151/www .hm-treasury.gov.uk/sternreview_index.htm

27  See e.g. Ian Byatt, Ian Castles, Indur M. Goklany et al., "The Stern Review: A Dual Critique Part II: Economic Aspects," *World Economics* 7(4) (2006): 199–232.

# 8  International Trade, Exchange Rates, and Capital Flows

Two World Wars were sufficient to create a large void in international trade for about forty years. While a cold war and various hostilities prevailed after the late 1940s, international trade and capital flows resumed and grew remarkably. The fall of the Berlin Wall, symbolic of the end of the Cold War, intensified interest and growth in trade in the early 1990s and we find us now in a world where almost all countries feel quite free to trade with any of the others. We trade anything and everything. We trade old and new goods. We trade each other's financial assets and we open up factories, stores, and offices almost any place we want.

As tourists we enjoy the freedom to go to places that once were taboo behind the Iron Curtain as well as old haunts like Rhine castles in Germany and vineyards in France. Many US cities beckon and enjoy the throngs of foreign tourists who come and enjoy seeing the US. Many business executives see the whole world as their opportunity and foreign firms among their main competitors. There is hardly any domestic business any more that is free from competition from foreign firms.

In today's world of international trade, business planners embrace a larger knowledge set. Companies like General Electric have activities in most countries of the world. Many companies see international trade as offering all kinds of benefits from importing, exporting, outsourcing, foreign partnerships, wholly owned foreign subsidies, and more. Whether you are a human resource manager, a product manager, or operate in a finance function, it is likely that your firm is engaged or wants to be engaged in foreign activities. Because of changes in the global economy, you may want to change where you operate the different links of your supply chain. Because of changes in global capital markets and interest rates, you may find that the company's investments need to be deployed in different countries. Changes in trade barriers might mean new and better places to send your exports. Of course, you may be a company that does none of the above, but is greatly affected by imports of goods or services from other countries. You compete in the global marketplace despite your best intentions!

One conclusion from the above is that your knowledge set has already widened and promises to continue to do so. Country information becomes more important for international business decisions. How do you decide where to locate that new foreign factory unless you acquire a lot of information about China, Singapore, Brazil, or South Africa?

You also need to acquire what we might call international macroeconomic information, that is, information about the global economy, global trends of output, employment, and prices, and the global business cycle. Such information is important to understand and analyze the international environment in which you are doing business and is, therefore, crucial for you to pinpoint your specific global business decisions. Will next year be a good year for international trade and investment? Should you be moving away from importing to thinking more about exporting? Will the value of your currency be rising or falling next year? Will next year be a year in which national policymakers have big positive or negative effects on our ability to conduct trade abroad?

From the US standpoint, we do not begin this discussion from a neutral point of view. The US situation has been volatile and controversial. The value of the dollar has bounced around a lot. In the summer of 2001, one could ask for €100 from any ATM in Europe and it would have cost you a little more than USD 80. In the summer of 2008, the same amount of euros cost over USD 155. In December 2015, USD 1.06 bought €1, while in early 2018, it took USD 1.25 to buy €1 (we will call this "the USD equivalent" notation of the exchange rate). These are large swings – they made European goods sometimes quite cheap and sometimes very expensive for people paying for them in dollars – and it made US goods sometimes very expensive and sometimes quite cheap for people paying for them in euros. Was the dollar too highly valued in 2001 and again in 2015? Was it too low in 2008? Should the Fed or the ECB do something about these exchange rates? These exchange rate issues go well beyond the US and Europe. Any multinational company that, for example, produces goods in Japan and sells them in Australia would be very interested in the exchange rate of the yen versus the Australian dollar. Business planners whose companies are impacted by exchange rates must think about these kinds of questions.

The value of dollar is not the only interesting issue confronting US business executives. For many years, the US has been experiencing large international trade deficits. Along with this trade deficit has come a very large and rapidly growing negative international net investment position – the US is a net debtor against the RoW. Large trade imbalances between the major countries and regions around the world have become the focal points of international conflicts and created a risk of currency wars and trade conflicts.

Some people think these facts indicate problems that should be addressed by government policy. Are they really problems, and, if so, why? If they are problems, can governments find good ways to address them? How would these policies impact households, workers, business costs, business sales, and business profits? These are the kinds of question we address in this chapter. As we will see, answering them requires information not only about domestic monetary and fiscal policies, but also about monetary and fiscal policies in other countries and about how governments conduct international trade and exchange rate policies.

This chapter and the next are largely a primer on international trade, exchange rates, and international capital flows. We begin with a discussion of how countries measure trade, making sure that you are acquainted with important terms like *trade deficit, current account, capital account, financial account,* and *international investment position.* We link these concepts to forecasting and policy issues that confront most firms. We then move to defining concepts relevant to understanding exchange rates, such things as *bilateral exchange rates, multilateral exchange rates, nominal,* and *real exchange rates.* Exchange rates are like prices that relate different currencies to one another. To understand the cause of exchange rate changes, we build a simple supply-and-demand model that helps us better understand the causes of exchange rate changes. In Chapter 9 we end the book and this excursion into international macroeconomics with a discussion of free trade and protectionism.

## 8.1   Macro Concepts and Analysis

All economic transactions between the US and the RoW during a given year (or quarter) are reported in the balance of payments of the US. Such transactions arise mainly from international trade in goods and services and from international trade in financial and other assets. A country's balance of payments is a complete record of the flows of goods and services, flows of incomes, and flows of financial assets between that country and the RoW. It requires detailed data from the customs offices, businesses, and financial institutions. The balance of payments is based on a residence principle. For example, a US resident is a person or institution whose main economic activity is located in the US, regardless of that person's or institution's nationality. A non-US resident is a person or institution whose main economic activity is located outside the US.

The balance of payments follows the principle of double-entry bookkeeping: For every transaction, one entry records the item entering or leaving the US (such as a car in international trade in goods or a government bond in international trade in assets) and the other entry records the corresponding payment. The US balance of payments is prepared and published by the Bureau for Economic Analysis (BEA).

Balance-of-payments statistics are produced under international conventions defined by the UN to make them comparable and these conventions can change over time. Similar to the national accounts we saw in Chapter 1, compiling the balance of payments involves processing data from various sources and a lot of complex estimates. Therefore, it is never fully accurate; instead, there is always a statistical discrepancy. The BEA releases an early version of the balance of payments for a given year during the spring of the following year and marks it with a *p* for preliminary. The statistics then get revised several times (marked with an *r*) to increase accuracy.

Table 8.1. shows the US balance for the years 2015 to 2017. It consists of three main parts, the *current account*, the *capital account*, and the *financial account*. Of

**Table 8.1** The US balance of payments (USD billions)

| Current account | 2015 | 2016 | 2017 |
|---|---|---|---|
| **Exports of goods and services and income receipts (credits)** | 3,173 | 3,157 | 3,408 |
| Exports of goods and services | 2,264 | 2,208 | 2,331 |
| Goods | 1,511 | 1,456 | 1,550 |
| Services | 753 | 752 | 780 |
| Primary income receipts | 783 | 814 | 926 |
| Secondary income (current transfer) receipts | 126 | 135 | 149 |
| **Imports of goods and services and income payments (debits)** | 3,606 | 3,609 | 3,874 |
| Imports of goods and services | 2,764 | 2,713 | 2,900 |
| Goods | 2,273 | 2,713 | 2,361 |
| Services | 492 | 505 | 538 |
| Primary income payments | 606 | 641 | 709 |
| Secondary income (current transfer) payments | 241 | 255 | 264 |
| **Capital account** | | | |
| Capital transfer receipts and other credits | 0 | 0 | 0 |
| Capital transfer payments and other debits | 0 | 0 | 0 |
| **Financial account** | | | |
| Net US acquisition of financial assets excluding financial derivatives (net increase in assets/financial outflow (+)) | 194 | 348 | 1,212 |
| Direct investment assets | 311 | 312 | 424 |
| Portfolio investment assets | 160 | 41 | 589 |
| Other investment assets | −271 | −6 | 200 |
| Reserve assets | −6 | 2 | −1 |
| Net US incurrence of financial liabilities excluding financial derivatives (net increase in assets/financial inflow (+)) | 502 | 741 | 1,587 |
| Direct investment liabilities | 506 | 479 | 348 |
| Portfolio investment liabilities | 214 | 237 | 837 |
| Other investment liabilities | −218 | 25 | 402 |
| Financial derivatives other than reserves, net transactions | −25 | 16 | 26 |
| Statistical discrepancy | 102 | 74 | 92 |
| **Balances** | | | |
| Balance on current account | −435 | −452 | −466 |
| Balance on goods and services | −500 | −505 | −568 |
| Balance on goods | −762 | −753 | −811 |
| Balance on services | 261 | 248 | 242 |
| Balance on primary incomes | 181 | 173 | 217 |
| Net lending (+) or net borrowing (−) from financial account transactions | −333 | −378 | −114 |

*Source*: BEA.

these three, the current account and the financial account are the most important ones. The current account reports all international transactions related to trade in goods and services and income payments between the US and the RoW.

The financial account relates to the flow of payments generated by the transactions reported in the current account and to trade in financial instruments and assets between the US and the RoW. When a US exporting firm receives payments from a foreign customer, the payment is recorded in the financial account, while the value of the goods is recorded in the current account. If the payment is from the customer's bank account in the US to the exporter's bank account in the US, it is recorded as a decrease in US liabilities. This is because a foreign-owned bank account in a US bank is a liability of the US to the RoW. If the payment is from the customer's bank account in his home country to the exporter's bank account in the same country, it is recorded as a US acquisition of financial assets. This is because a US-owned bank account in a foreign country is a US foreign asset. When a Chinese resident buys US government T-bills from a financial institution in the US, the purchase is recorded as an incurrence of liabilities. How the corresponding payment is recorded in the US financial account depends again on whether it is made from a Chinese-owned bank account in the US or to a US-owned bank account in China.

The capital account relates to changes in US international assets and liabilities which are not linked to trade in goods, services, and financial assets. Examples are disaster-related losses of assets, international debt forgiveness benefitting poor countries, or private bequests. Since the capital account is typically very small for the US, we will neglect it from now on. Note that in previous terminology, which you still find in older books and reports, the financial account was called the capital account.

## 8.1.1 The Current Account

Positive entries in the current account (credits) relate to exports of goods and services and income receivables earned abroad, negative entries relate to imports (debits) of goods and services and income payables. The current account has four subcategories: Trade in goods, trade in services, primary incomes, and secondary incomes. An *export* is a sale of a good or service by a US business to a foreign customer. An *import* is a purchase of a good or service by a US business or household from a foreign producer.

---

### BOX 8.1 **Terminology for Trade in Services**

Recall that the balance of payments is based on a residency principle. For example, when a Mexican citizen residing in the US receives a haircut from a Mexican hairdresser residing in Mexico City, the transaction constitutes a service import from the point of view of the US balance of payments and a service export from the point of view of the Mexican balance of payments. When the same Mexican citizen residing in the US receives a haircut from a Mexican hairdresser residing in Los Angeles, it is neither an export nor an import, simply a domestic transaction.

If an American resident travels to Paris as a tourist and rides the metro there, this is an import of services (debit) from the point of view of the US balance of payments. Obviously, such an import is impossible to be recorded statistically. However, the fact that the tourist bought euros when entering France to pay for such services will be recorded in the balance of payments. The resulting gap between imports recorded and financial transactions recorded is one source of the statistical discrepancy in the balance of payments.

Trade in services includes financial services, business services such as consulting, transportation, and travel-related services. Royalties and license fees relating to the use of intellectual property are reported under trade in services.

Primary income receipts include compensation of employees residing in the US by firms residing outside the US and investment income earned by US residents on their foreign assets. American residents (corporations and private households) own assets abroad such as companies, stocks, bonds, deposits, and real estate. The income derived from these assets such as profits, dividends, rents, and interest is reported as income receivables (credits) in the primary income balance. Conversely, primary income payments include compensation of employees residing in a foreign country by firms residing in the US and investment income earned by foreigners on their US assets. Secondary income transactions are payments made without any immediate reciprocation. International donations and foreign aid paid by the US government to a foreign country are examples. Another example is the remittance of incomes by Mexicans working in the US to their families in Mexico.

Table 8.1 shows that exports and imports in goods account for the largest part of the current account. The bottom of the table reports various concepts of balances from the balance of payments. It shows that the US had a current account deficit of USD 466 billion in 2017. This means that the total amount of US revenues earned by the US economy by selling goods and services to foreign countries and as primary and secondary incomes fell short of the total expenditures of the US economy on foreign goods and services and as primary and secondary incomes paid. In other words, the US borrowed from the RoW in 2017.

The balance of trade in goods and services is commonly referred to as the US trade balance. The US had a trade deficit of USD 568 billion in 2017. The deficit in goods trade was even larger and amounted to USD 811 billion, while the balance of services was in surplus with USD 242 billion. The primary income showed a

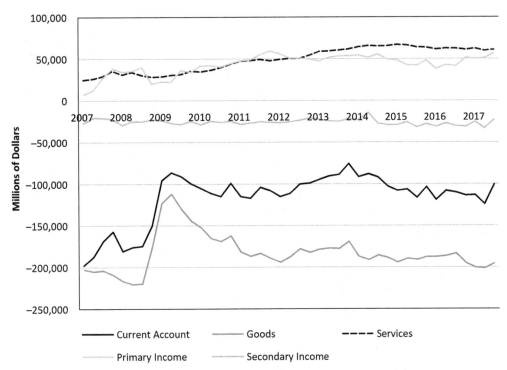

**Figure 8.1** The US current account balance and sub-balances (2007–2017)
*Source*: own calculations based on BEA data.

surplus of USD 217 billion. The secondary income balance showed a deficit of USD 114 billion in 2017, which should be expected for a wealthy, mature economy such as the US.

Figure 8.1 plots the current account balance together with the sub-balances for goods, services, primary income, and secondary income.

Some things are to be noted here: The US current account deficit is largely the result of a deficit in goods plus a deficit in secondary income. The balances on services and primary income are positive. The current account has generally been in deficit. After shrinking strongly during the Great Recession, it has hovered around USD 110 billion each quarter. In 2016, the annual current account deficit of USD 452 billion represented 2.38 percent of GDP, which is moderate compared to the beginning of the twenty-first century.

## 8.1.2   The Financial Account

The first broad category of transactions in the financial account is net changes in US-owned assets abroad, or net US acquisition of financial assets excluding financial derivatives, which are recorded separately. Because it is a net entry, it can be positive when US residents buy more foreign assets than they sell, or negative when US residents sell more foreign assets than they buy. A positive value represents a financial outflow (capital outflows in older terminology). The financial account distinguishes between three types of US residents owning foreign assets: The Federal Reserve System, the remainder of the US government sector, and the private sector (corporations and households). Foreign assets owned by the Federal Reserve are called US official reserve assets. They include gold reserves, claims on the IMF, and foreign currency reserves. The Fed could use these to influence the value of the dollar in terms of other currencies. US government assets other than official reserve assets are foreign assets held by other branches of the US government. US private assets include foreign direct investment assets, portfolio investment assets, and other investment assets. Formally, direct investment occurs when the investor acquires a share in a foreign business exceeding 10 percent of its capital. The idea is that such investments aim at gaining some influence over the foreign business. Portfolio investments include equity and debt instruments bought with the purpose of exerting control. Other investment assets include currency and bank deposits used to make payments related to foreign transactions as well as bank loans, insurance reserves, and trade credit and advances.

In 2016, the US reported a net financial outflow of USD 348 billion. The increase in foreign direct investment assets amounted to USD 312 billion. In the same year, US net portfolio investment abroad was USD 41 billion. Acquisition of other investment assets was negative USD 6 billion. These include holdings of foreign cash and bank deposits, trade credit and advances, and loans. US reserve assets did not change by very much.

The second broad category of transactions in the financial account is net US incurrence of liabilities excluding financial derivatives, or increases in foreign-owned US assets. In 2016, these amounted to USD 741 billion. This includes foreign direct investment liabilities, portfolio investment liabilities, and other investment liabilities. In 2016, net direct investment liabilities changed by USD 479 billion. Thus, foreigners acquired more direct investment assets in the US than US residents abroad. Portfolio investment showed a net inflow of USD 237 billion, which was also larger than US acquisitions of foreign portfolio assets. Other investment liabilities changed only marginally.

The third broad category is trade in financial derivatives. This is separated from the other assets and liabilities based on the idea that derivatives trade is secondary to trade in financial assets. A positive entry indicates net US cash payments resulting from derivatives contracts. The table shows a net outflow of roughly USD 16 billion.

The overall balance on the financial account is the difference between net financial outflows and net financial inflows, or the sum of the net US acquisition of assets plus the net outflows from financial derivatives minus the net US incurrence of liabilities. A positive balance indicates that the US acquired more foreign assets net than it incurred foreign liabilities net, or that net US foreign wealth increased. In contrast, a deficit indicates that US net foreign debt increased. This overall balance showed a deficit of USD 378 billion in 2016.

### 8.1.3    The Statistical Discrepancy

Finally, the balance of payments includes a *statistical discrepancy*, USD 74 billion in 2016. The sources of this discrepancy include the fact that there is often a time gap between the transactions recorded in the current and the financial accounts, as well as underreporting of incomes earned on and trade with financial assets and services such as tourism.

### 8.1.4    Accounting Identities

By the principles of double-entry bookkeeping, the overall balance of payments must always equal zero. That is, the sum of the current account balance plus the capital account balance minus the financial account balance must, in principle, be zero. Thus:

Current Account Balance plus Capital Account Balance minus Financial Account Balance equals 0.

In practice, we have to account for the statistical discrepancy and we can neglect the capital account balance, because it is so small. Thus, we have:

Current Account Balance plus Statistical Discrepancy minus Financial Account Balance equals 0,

or:

Current Account Balance equals Financial Account Balance minus Statistical Discrepancy.

If a country has a current account surplus, it has, in value terms, exported more than it has imported. This implies that it has acquired net financial assets abroad. Its net foreign wealth has gone up. If a country has a current account deficit, it has, in value terms, exported less than it has imported. This implies that it has incurred net financial liabilities abroad. Its net foreign wealth has declined or its net foreign debt increased.

The accounting relationship between the current and the financial account balances essentially says that a current account deficit is financed by financial inflows, while a current account surplus leads to financial outflows that must be allocated in foreign capital markets and financial systems. Now, for later purposes, we can separate the financial flows into changes in central bank reserve assets and the rest, i.e., net private and government financial inflows and outflows, where "government" means the domestic government sector excluding the central bank and the government sectors of foreign countries including their central banks. We are already familiar with central bank reserve assets from Chapter 4: These are the international assets on the central bank's balance sheet which contribute to changes in the monetary base. Thus we have:

Financial account balance = net private and government financial outflows
            − net private and government financial inflows
            − change in net official reserves.

Taking these statements together and ignoring the statistical discrepancy, we can say:

Current account balance
        − net private and government financial outflows
        + net private and government financial inflows
                = change in net official reserves

This says that, if the central bank keeps its official reserves unchanged, current account transactions and private and government net financial flows must adjust such that they sum up to zero. As we will see later, exchange rate adjustments will cause a tendency toward such an equilibrium. For example, if the current account is in deficit and net private and government financial flows are not sufficient to finance that deficit, there will be a tendency for the exchange rate to depreciate. The central bank can prevent that from happening by selling official reserves of foreign currency to the private sector.

## BOX 8.2  Change in US Methodology

In the spring of 2014, the BEA changed its methodology for the balance of payments, specifically for the financial account. The change was in accordance with revised UN statistical conventions. The idea behind it was to simplify the understanding of the balance-of-payment statistics and to bring them in line with the SNA.

Until 2014, if an American resident purchased foreign assets, this was recorded as a debit (−) entry in the financial account. If a foreign resident purchased an asset in the US, this was recorded as a credit (+) entry. Consequently, for the US, having a negative current account (a debit), the financial account was positive (a net credit), which represents a net inflow of capital. In net terms non-residents have increased their claims against the US.

In other words, in the old methodology:

Current account balance plus capital account balance plus financial account balance equals = 0.

In the spring of 2014 the previous debit entry in the financial account was changed into "increase in foreign assets," and when non-residents purchase American assets it is an "increase in liabilities," and thus, the new methodology is as explained above.

Before spring 2014, the financial account distinguished between private and official financial flows, where the latter mostly corresponds with purchases by central banks of foreign currency. The new methodology still shows the change in net foreign reserves for the Federal Reserve System, but bundles the change in liabilities, private and official other than the Fed in one item. An additional BEA table, dubbed *US International Financial Transactions for Liabilities to Foreign Official Agencies* provides the additional information. Table 8.2 shows the relevant data for 2015 to 2017.

**Table 8.2** US international financial transactions for liabilities to foreign official agencies (billions of dollars)

|  | 2015 | 2016 | 2017 |
|---|---|---|---|
| Net US incurrence of liabilities to foreign official agencies | −115 | −241 | 185 |
| Portfolio investment liabilities | −223 | −301 | 206 |
| Other investment liabilities | 108 | 60 | −20 |

*Source*: BEA.

Table 8.2 shows that, in 2015 and 2016, foreign central banks sold USD reserves and thereby decreased their claims against the US (decrease of liabilities for the US point of view). In 2017 this changed and foreign central banks again purchased USD reserves in order to avoid an appreciation of their domestic currencies against the USD. While Table 8.2 shows the activities of all foreign central banks in foreign exchange markets against the USD, the data are dominated by selling and buying through the Chinese central bank, the People's Bank of China. Later in this chapter we will discuss in more detail the motivation of central banks buying USD denominated assets and the possible consequences for the US economy.

## 8.2 Methodology in Other Countries

Some countries do not report changes in official reserves as an entry in the balance of payments. Instead, net financial inflows and outflows only include private sector transactions. In that case, the overall balance of the balance of payments is equal to the change in official reserves.

## 8.2.1   US Net Investment Position

As mentioned above, current account surpluses lead to increases in the country's net foreign wealth, current account deficits to decreases in net foreign wealth or increases in net foreign debt. Table 8.3 shows the US net international investment position resulting from the accumulation of past current account surpluses and deficits. It consists of the difference in value of all foreign assets owned by US residents and the value of all US assets owned by non-residents. At the end of 2016, US foreign assets amounted to USD 23.849 trillion, while US foreign liabilities stood at USD 32.168 trillion. That is, the US was in significant debt (USD 8.318 trillion) to the RoW. How big is this? It amounts to 44 percent of US GDP in 2016.

It is interesting to observe, however, that the balance on international investment incomes received and paid was positive in 2016 despite this significant net debt. In fact, it has been consistently positive in recent years (see Figure 8.2). This implies that US assets abroad must have earned much higher yields than US assets have yielded to their foreign owners. The average rate of return US residents earned on their foreign assets (calculated as investment income received from the current account divided by US foreign assets from Table 8.3) in 2016 was 3.4 percent, while the average rate of return foreigners earned on their US assets (calculated as investment income paid from the current account divided by US foreign liabilities from Table 8.3) was merely 1.9 percent. This suggests that non-residents are willing to invest in the US although they earn lower returns than they could in their own

**Table 8.3** US international investment position (end of period; USD billions)

|  | 2015 | 2016 | 2017 |
|---|---|---|---|
| US net international investment position | −7,493 | −8,318 | −7,846 |
| US assets | 23,352 | 23,849 | 27,633 |
| Direct investment at market value | 6,999 | 7,375 | 8,863 |
| Portfolio investment | 9,570 | 9,879 | 12,443 |
| Financial derivatives other than reserves | 2,428 | 2,209 | 1,622 |
| Other investment | 3,971 | 3,979 | 4,254 |
| Reserve assets | 0 | 0 | 0 |
| US liabilities | 30,846 | 32,168 | 35,786 |
| Direct investment at market value | 6,700 | 7,569 | 8,871 |
| Portfolio investment | 16,646 | 17,352 | 19,504 |
| Financial derivatives other than reserves | 2,372 | 2,148 | 1,594 |
| Other investment | 5,127 | 5,099 | 5,509 |

*Source*: BEA.

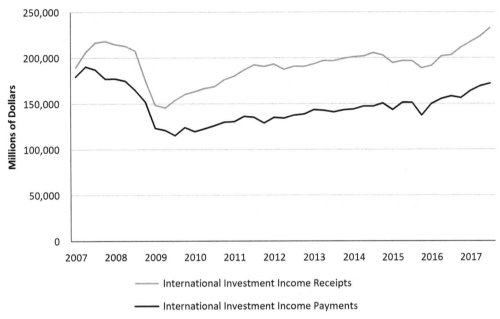

**Figure 8.2** US international investment income receipts and payments
*Source*: own calculations based on BEA data.

countries. This reflects the privilege US assets enjoy as safe-haven investments. It is due to the fact that the US is still the biggest economy in the world, has the most developed financial markets, and a stable political system. Only very few countries around the world enjoy a similar position, Germany, Switzerland, and the UK being among them. At the same time, US investors seem to be willing to take relatively risky positions in foreign countries successfully, resulting in higher returns.

## 8.3   International Application: Current Account Balances in the G7

Not all countries have current account deficits – in fact, if some countries have deficits, other countries must have surpluses. World current account balances must sum up to zero, since the world as a whole does not export from anywhere else (in practice, though, there is a statistical discrepancy). So do world current accounts.

Figure 8.3 shows the current account balances of some of the main industrial countries in terms of percentages of GDP. That way it is easier to compare across countries – because the country sizes can be so different. The US current account deficit was 4 percent of GDP at the beginning of this century. It increased to 6 percent of GDP by 2006 and then shrank during the Great Recession. Since then, it has remained between 2 and 3 percent of GDP.

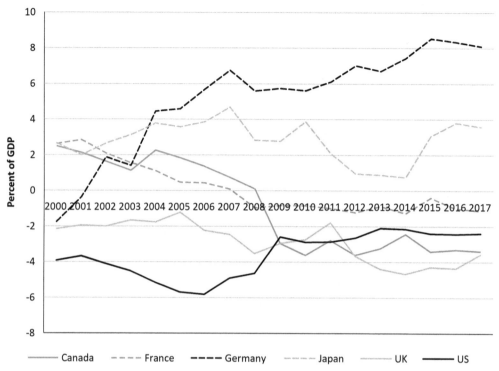

**Figure 8.3** Current account balances (% of GDP)
*Sources*: IMF, WEO Database.

The UK is another country that has had current account deficits every year since 2000. In terms of GDP, its deficits were initially smaller than those of the US, but after 2011, the UK current account deficit has stood consistently at around 4 percent of GDP.

Figure 8.3 shows that there are also countries which have current account surpluses consistently. Germany is most noteworthy for this. Germany's current account surplus reached 8 percent of GDP in 2017 and was even larger than that the years before. Japan's current account surpluses were between 2 and 4 percent in most years since the beginning of the century. Canada switched from moderate surpluses in the early years of the 2000s to moderate deficits.

## 8.3.1   Trade Deficit Issues

Figure 8.4 gives a larger time perspective of the US current account and trade balances. Both balances started going into sizeable deficits in 1982. After that there was a string of deficits peaking at 3 percent of GDP in 1986. Both deficits shrank subsequently and the US experienced one very small current account surplus in 1991. During the 1990s and early 2000s, both deficits increased rapidly to reach 6 percent of GDP in 2006.

The emerging trade and current account deficits coincided with the emergence of large federal government budget deficits under the Reagan administration. This

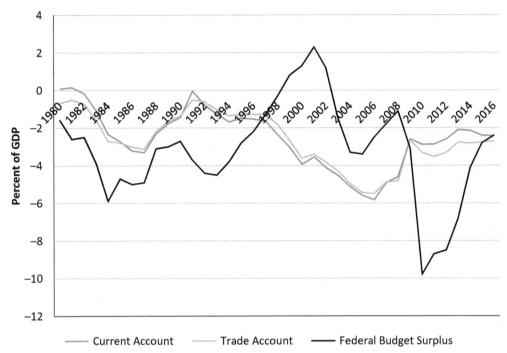

**Figure 8.4** US current account balance and trade balance and government surplus (% of GDP)
*Source*: own calculations based on BEA data.

coincidence has sometimes been interpreted as a story of *twin deficits*, with growing government budget deficits causing growing trade and current account deficits. However, the figure suggests that the story is not that simple. It is true that the current account, the trade, and the federal budget deficit all moved in the same direction in the early 1980s. In later years, however, they often went in opposite directions. In the late 1990s, for example, private households reduced their saving considerably and the current account deficit remained despite increasing government saving (more on that relationship below). During the Great Recession and the years following it, the federal government had the largest peacetime deficits ever, but both the trade deficit and the current account deficit decreased.

Some take this deficit/debt performance as a sign of economic weakness. Others see it as the opposite. Which is it? It could be either. If trade deficits result from importing goods or technology that make the economy more productive and stronger, then perhaps trade deficits aren't so bad. The resulting foreign debt can be serviced and repaid from a larger GDP subsequently. Second, the answer to this question depends on what is causing what. Large current account deficits as in the 1990s are the mirror image of massive financial inflows from abroad. What caused foreigners to desire to invest in the US? Most likely it was a combination of poor investment projects abroad and the thriving markets in the US resulting from the IT revolution and very strong economic growth. Why would this cause a trade deficit – isn't this all about the financial account? There are two parts to this answer. The first is the accounting identity between current account deficits and financial account surpluses we saw above.

The second is that the great demand for US assets meant that many foreigners were buying dollars in foreign exchange markets – they were buying dollars as a prelude to buying US bonds and stocks. This drove the value of the dollar up. When the dollar appreciated enough, it cut into US exports and increased imports – causing a current account deficit. Why is this story important? Because it shows how apparently "bad things" can be caused by good things. The US had a strong economy. It sucked in the world's capital. The dollar appreciated and the trade deficit widened. Do Americans want to get rid of this problem? Probably not.

Notwithstanding the above, trade deficits do lead to a further negative international net investment position. If the international debit gets too large, a real problem might arise. If foreign investors eventually begin to believe that the US is not such a good place to invest any more compared to Europe, Asia, and other places, they might decide to pull their investments out of the US. This would trigger a reverse process: The dollar would fall in value, US imports would decline and exports rise, moving the current account to a surplus. If done in an orderly fashion, this would not be a terrible thing. But if it is done in a chaotic panic, it could be highly disruptive to international trade and financial markets. This is a good reason to pay attention to this problem.

Finally, there is a "psychological" reason to pay attention to trade deficits. People think a lot of things about trade deficits. For one thing, many people are very nationalistic and simply don't like the thought that foreign persons or institutions are buying domestic assets. They also don't like the idea that these entities may be controlling more and more of their economy. Anti-globalization protesters, for example, declare that the US controls too many coffee plantations in South America. The US wouldn't want French control over the Statue of Liberty and the French would resist a US takeover of Air France. Such nationalistic feelings tend to swell up whenever a country starts to have a larger trade deficit. They could, under the right conditions, lead to political trends that promote protectionist policies. One way to defend against extreme and unproductive policies is to find better ways to address the problems before they get out of hand.

## BOX 8.3 DIFFERENCE OF OPINION: TRADE AND JOBS

A common notion is that importing more than you export costs the country jobs. The logic behind the argument is as follows. An exported good requires someone to produce it. So, more exports create more jobs. An import is something that is produced elsewhere. It could have been produced at home. So an import displaces labor. If imports are greater than exports, then the labor displacement must be greater than the labor increase. This seems pretty clear. Unfortunately, it is wrong. This is because jobs are created by supply (expanding capacity), not by demand. The trade balance reflects the net demand for goods and services from international trade. A rise in the trade balance does not automatically translate into an increase in the demand for domestic output and more jobs. For example, the trade balance could rise because imports fall while exports remain the same. No increase in the demand for domestic goods would occur. Alternatively, the trade balance could rise because imports fall by more than exports. In that case, the demand for domestic output falls and so does employment. Even if the trade balance increases due to increasing exports, the rise in the demand for domestic output might just cause higher inflation. In sum, there simply is no direct link between trade balances and the number of jobs.

## 8.4   The Balance of Payments and the System of National Accounts

In this section we discuss the balance of payments as part of the overall SNA and aim to explain how current account surpluses or deficits are linked to domestic savings and investment. In Chapter 1, we saw that, in a *closed* economy, domestic savings (S) must equal gross domestic investment (I).

In an open economy, domestic savings can be used to acquire foreign assets and a shortfall of domestic savings over gross domestic savings can be compensated by financial inflows from abroad. More generally, domestic savings do not have to equal gross domestic investment. Instead, we have the following accounting identity:

Domestic savings = gross domestic investment plus the current account balance.

If domestic savings are just equal to gross domestic investment, the current account balance will be zero. If domestic savings fall short of gross domestic investment, the current account balance will be negative. The country finances part of its invest-ment by foreign financial inflows. If domestic savings exceed gross domestic investment, the current account balance will be positive. The country uses part of its savings to acquire foreign assets.

Recall that domestic savings has two components: private savings and govern-ment savings. Private savings consist of personal savings (disposable household income less consumption expenditures) and undistributed profits. Government savings consist of government revenues less expenditures. Call this the government budget surplus.[1] We can now rewrite the above identity as:

Private savings plus government budget surplus = gross domestic investment plus the current account balance.

Now we can see why people talk about *twin deficits*. Assuming that private savings and gross domestic private investment remain unchanged, a decline in the government budget surplus must lead to a decline in the current account balance. But this, of course, is pure accounting. There is no good reason to assume that private savings and gross domestic private investment remain unchanged, when the government runs a larger deficit. Furthermore, a decline in private savings can lead to a current account deficit, even if the government budget surplus increases, provided that gross domestic private investment does not fall by too much – this is the story of the late 1990s mentioned above.

More generally, policies changing the government budget surplus will affect aggregate income, interest rates, and exchange rates, and these effects will lead to adjustments in private savings, gross domestic investment, and the current account. In section 8.5, we will look at these adjustments in more detail.

While the overall US current account is moderate in percentage of GDP, several bilateral trade deficits are significant. While the US has a trade deficit with all major trading partners, the net imports from China reached USD 375 billion in 2017, mostly in goods and not services. As you can see from Table 8.4, the trade deficit with China has increased year by year. With most other countries the deficit remained relatively stable. With Canada net trade even turned into a small surplus.

**Table 8.4** US net trade balance with ten major trading partners (USD billions)

|  | 2013 | 2014 | 2015 | 2016 | 2017 |
|---|---|---|---|---|---|
| China | −318.7 | −344.8 | −367.3 | −347.0 | −375.2 |
| Canada | −31.7 | −36.5 | −15.4 | −10.9 | −17.6 |
| Mexico | −54.6 | −54.7 | −60.2 | −64.3 | −71.0 |
| Japan | −74.3 | −67.6 | −69.0 | −68.8 | −68.9 |
| Germany | −67 | −74.7 | −74.8 | −64.7 | −64.2 |
| UK | −5.4 | −0.8 | −1.8 | 1.0 | 3.2 |
| South Korea | −20.7 | −25.0 | −28.3 | −27.6 | −22.9 |
| France | −13.9 | −15.8 | −17.7 | −15.6 | −15.3 |
| India | −20.0 | −23.8 | −23.3 | −24.4 | −22.9 |
| Italy | −21.9 | −25.4 | −27.9 | −28.5 | −31.6 |

*Source*: www.census.gov/foreign-trade/balance/c5700.html

## BOX 8.4 DIFFERENCE OF OPINION: SAVING AND EMPLOYMENT

In the October 20, 2004, *New York Times*, Ronald McKinnon argued that US government budget deficits are a primary contributor to a long-term savings shortfall and reduction in manufacturing employment.[2] He argues that without persistent government budget deficits, national saving would have been higher and manufacturing employment would have been 4.7 million higher in 2003. He ends this article with the following words: "The proper way of reducing protectionism pressure and relieving anxiety about US manufacturing is for the government to consolidate its finances and move deliberately towards running surpluses – in short, to eliminate the US economy's saving deficiency."

It is clear now that McKinnon's point is valid in a closed economy: Rising government deficits absorb domestic savings and *crowd out* domestic investment by causing the real interest rate to rise. But in an open economy, McKinnon's point vanishes. A rising real interest rate will attract foreign financial inflows and provide the financing for domestic investment. Why the capital stock and, ultimately, employment, should fall remains unclear.

If a large and persistent trade deficit is due to a large and persistent imbalance between domestic savings and investment, an obvious way to reduce the trade deficit is to increase national savings. Why are governments reluctant to do that?

A first point is that the obvious way for governments to increase domestic savings is to reduce the government budget deficit. This requires spending cuts or higher taxes or a combination of both. We know from Chapter 5 that reducing the government budget deficit reduces aggregate demand and, in the short run, leads to lower output and employment. Unless the economy is booming and the labor market tight to begin with, so that reducing the budget deficit brings about a welcome cooling of the economy, governments are often reluctant to adopt such policies for fear of losing voters' support.

A related point is that spending cuts and rising tax rates typically affect some groups in society more than others. Governments may reduce public employment, which will meet the opposition of labor unions in the public sector. Alternatively, governments may reduce welfare spending, which will meet the opposition of the poorer parts of society. Governments may increase income tax rates, which will make the richer parts of society especially angry. Or governments may increase taxes on consumption and raise the ire of the less well off, who are most affected by such taxes since consumption is a larger part of their disposable incomes than for people with higher incomes. The new federal sales tax President George W. Bush proposed in 2004 and the strong opposition it met is an example of that. Policies to cut budget deficits are notoriously unpopular, which is why governments try to avoid them.

Alternatively, governments could try to persuade people to spend less on consumption and save more. But this is easier said than done. Private households may have good reasons for maintaining a high level of consumption even if the government thinks otherwise. For example, C. Alan Garner suggested in an article written for the Kansas City Fed that private saving is not measured well and may not be as deficient as the published data suggests.[3] "There are reasons to think that the NIPA estimate of personal saving might be revised upward in the future . . . to the extent that American households have correctly anticipated future gains in productivity and labor income and incorporated these expectations into their spending plans, any future adjustments in consumption spending need not be wrenching." Regardless of whether or not Garner was right, the point here is that private households may have a different perception of their own situation than government politicians and, therefore, may not be susceptible to government persuasion.

What other policies could governments use to correct a high and persistent trade deficit? If a high value of the domestic currency against other currencies causes the trade deficit, why not focus policy directly on lowering the exchange rate? The central bank could do that by lowering interest rates (more on how that reduces the value of the currency below) and this would even boost the economy rather than slow it down. The problems with this idea are twofold. First, the exchange rate is a symptom, not a cause of trade deficits. Trade imbalances come from the interactions between domestic savings and investment; not from exchange rates. Focusing policy on the symptoms of a problem isn't always a terrible thing. Exchange rate policies can alleviate a trade deficit problem for a while, as a weaker currency makes domestic exports less expensive abroad and imports more expensive at home, inducing consumers to buy more domestic and less foreign goods. But, sooner or later, easing monetary policy will lead to higher inflation with the result that the relative price of domestic and foreign goods rises and consumers start buying more imported goods again. Exchange rate policies can buy some time, but dealing with symptoms should not detract attention from looking at the true causes of the problem. The second problem with this idea is that foreign governments will not necessarily accept the strengthening of their own currencies implied by this policy. They may retaliate by cutting interest rates, too, such that the intended exchange rate effect does not materialize. This suggests that only small countries which are not considered to be sufficiently important for foreign governments to engage in retaliation can get away with exchange rate policies to address a trade deficit.

Finally, could a current account deficit be reduced by prohibiting or taxing imports? Assume that the government directly reduces imports through trade restrictions like tariffs or quotas. Imports will decline and the trade deficit shrink. But this means that there are now fewer financial inflows from abroad available to finance gross domestic investment. Given the increased scarcity of financing, domestic interest rates will rise to attract more foreign capital and this will increase the value of the currency. Exports will fall due to the stronger exchange rate, and investment will fall due to the higher-interest rate. In the end, any reduction in the trade deficit would be bought at the cost of a weakening of the economy. So far, this is not unlike the effects of a reduction of the government budget deficit discussed before. Using trade policy instruments, however, will attract the attention and arouse the ire of foreign governments much more than using domestic policy instruments. Foreign governments will complain against such measures, because they directly affect their own economies, and they may retaliate by imposing quotas and higher tariffs on imports. Again, only small countries can get away with such policies, larger ones would risk international trade conflicts. For more on that, see Chapter 9.

In the end, the trade deficit problem comes back to saving and investment. It is hard to escape from this macro fact.

## 8.5   Exchange Rate Concepts

The *external value of a currency* is measured by the exchange rate of that currency against another currency or other currencies. Exchange rates come in two notations. First, we can say that, for example, 3 Brazilian reals buy USD 1. This *quantity* or *real per dollar* notation is the answer to the question: How many units of foreign currency buy one unit of domestic currency? Second, we can say that one-third of a USD buys 1 Brazilian real. This is the *price* or *dollar equivalent* notation and it is the answer to the question: How many units of domestic currency do I need to buy one unit of foreign currency? Obviously, the *per dollar* or *quantity* notation is the inverse of the *dollar equivalent* or *price* notation. To say that USD 1.20 buys €1 is the same as saying that €0.833 buys USD 1. Central banks of the largest currencies, the USD, the euro, the GBP, and the yen use the quantity notation for their official exchange rate announcements.

When the value of a currency changes, we speak of a currency *appreciation* or *depreciation*. An appreciation means that the value of the currency rises, while a depreciation means that it falls. In the quantity or per-dollar notation, an increase of the exchange rate corresponds to an appreciation of the domestic currency. One gets more units of foreign currency for a unit of domestic currency. A decrease corresponds to a depreciation. In the price or dollar-equivalent notation, the opposite holds: An increase in the exchange rate stands for a depreciation of the domestic currency dollar. One needs more units of domestic currency to buy one unit of foreign currency. Therefore, when interpreting exchange rate movements, be sure that you know which notation is used. We also say that the domestic currency becomes *stronger* when it appreciates, and *weaker* when it depreciates, against other currencies. Since an exchange rate is a relative price, an appreciation of the domestic currency implies that the foreign currency or currencies depreciate and vice versa.

A *currency index* relates the value of a currency to the values of several other currencies. For example, the US *major currency index* is an average of the exchange rates of the dollar against the currencies of its major trading partners. It shows how the dollar performs on average against the currencies of the main trade partners instead of focusing on a single one of them. The Fed publishes a *trade-weighted US dollar index* for the currencies of the seven main trading partners of the US, which together make up a little over half of US international trade. It includes the euro, the Canadian dollar, the Japanese yen, the British pound, the Swiss franc, the Australian dollar, and the Swedish kroner. All exchange rates are taken in quantity notation for the dollar (or as the dollar prices of foreign currencies): A rise in the index indicates an appreciation of the dollar.[4] The *broad index* is a trade-weighted average of the exchange rates of the twenty-six most important trade partners of the US including the seven main ones, again in quantity notation. These twenty-six countries combined account for over 90 percent of US international trade.

Figure 8.5 shows the swings in the value of the dollar since January 1997. The dollar first appreciated against the currencies of the main trading partners, then

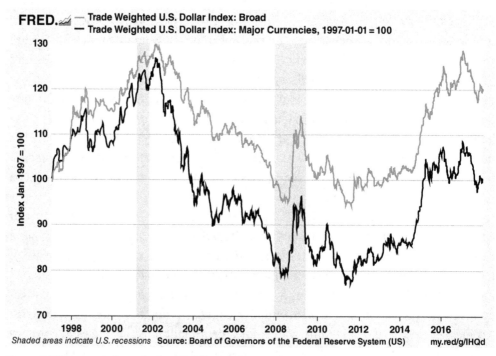

**Figure 8.5** Currency indexes for the US dollar

*Source*: Board of Governors of the Federal Reserve System, Trade Weighted US Dollar Index Major Currencies, and Trade Weighted US Dollar Index Broad, retrieved from FRED, Federal Reserve Bank of St. Louis; October 23, 2018.

depreciated until the beginning of the Great Recession, then gradually appreciated again. The figure also indicates that the movements in the dollar exchange rates against the currencies of the major trading partners have been stronger than against the larger group of countries.

While exchange rates are important, we are often more interested in the relative purchasing power of one currency compared to another. The exchange rate tells us how many units of one currency buy a unit of another currency. We sometimes call this the *nominal* exchange rate. The *real value of a currency* is its *purchasing power* compared to the purchasing power of another currency. Recall from Chapter 1 that we compute the real value of things denominated in units of money (such as money itself or government bonds) by dividing them by the price index. Thus, the real value or the purchasing power of a dollar is $1/P$, where P is a price index for the US economy such as the CPI. It tells us how many units of the basket of consumption goods underlying the CPI one can buy with a dollar. If the CPI rises, the real value or purchasing power of a dollar declines; if the CPI falls, the real value or purchasing power of a dollar increases. Similarly, if P* is the CPI for a foreign economy, $1/P^*$ is the real value of that economy's currency. The *real exchange* or *real value* of the dollar tells us how many units of foreign goods a dollar buys compared to the units of domestic goods. We can express the real exchange rate as the nominal exchange rate in quantity notation multiplied by the ratio of the price levels, $P/P^*$. A rise in the real exchange rate corresponds to a *real appreciation* of the domestic currency. Equivalently, we can express the real exchange rate as the nominal exchange rate in price notation times the ratio of the price levels $P^*/P$. A rise in the real exchange rate in this notation corresponds to a *real depreciation* of the currency.

Since the price level or the purchasing power of a currency is measured by an index whose level is arbitrary, we commonly use these concepts to express relative changes over time. Thus, we say that the *real value* of a currency rises, if the relative (percentage) increase in the exchange rate (quantity notation) plus the domestic rate of inflation minus the foreign rate of inflation is greater than zero. Equivalently, the real value of a currency rises, if the relative (percentage) increase in the exchange rate (price notation) plus the foreign rate of inflation minus the domestic rate of inflation is less than zero.

Either way, it means that a unit of the currency under consideration buys more foreign goods relative to domestic ones. For example, on January 1, 2017, it took USD 1.05 to buy €1. On January 1, 2018, it took USD 1.1993 to buy €1. The nominal exchange rate (quantity notation) *of the euro* appreciated by 13.62 percent during the course of 2017. The average CPI inflation rate in the euro area was 1.5 percent in 2017, while the average rate of inflation in the US was 2.13 percent. Thus, the *real value of the euro* increased by 13.62 + 1.50 − 2.13 = 12.99 percent. A real appreciation of the euro and a real depreciation of the dollar.

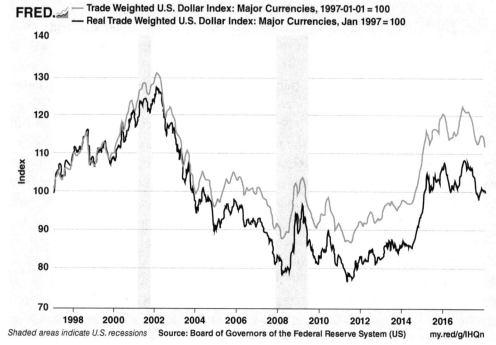

**Figure 8.6** Nominal and real exchange rate indexes for the US dollar and seven major currencies
*Source*: Board of Governors of the Federal Reserve System, Trade Weighted US Dollar Index and Real Trade Weighted US Dollar Index: Major Currencies retrieved from FRED, Federal Reserve Bank of St. Louis; October 23, 2018.

The difference between nominal exchange rates and real exchange rates is pretty small when the currencies of countries are considered that, like the US, have relatively low and stable rates of inflation. This can be seen in Figure 8.6, which plots the nominal and real exchange rate indexes for the seven main trading partners of the US from 1997 to 2017. By and large, the two indexes follow the same movements over time. Sizeable differences only occurred in the mid 1980s, when the nominal exchange rate of the dollar appreciated more than the real exchange rate, and after 2005, when the nominal exchange rate depreciated more than the real exchange rate.

This is very different when countries are considered which have larger and more volatile rates of inflation. In Figure 8.7, we show the nominal and real exchange rate indexes for the US dollar and the currencies of the nineteen main trading partners of the US other than the seven largest ones. This group is called *other important trade partners*.[5] Figure 8.7 shows that the dollar consistently and steadily appreciated against these currencies between 1973 and 2005. After that, the value of the dollar fluctuated but with no clear trend. In contrast, the real value of the dollar against this group of currencies had no trend at all during 1973 to 2005, nor afterwards. While there were large swings up and down, differences in the rates of inflation

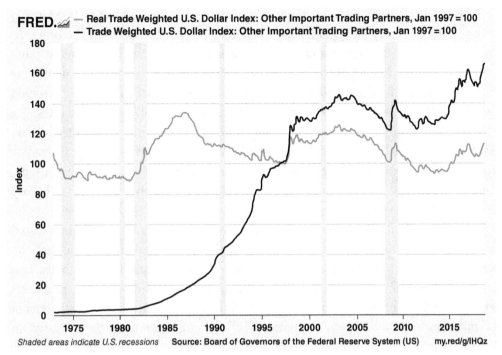

**Figure 8.7** Nominal and real exchange rate indexes for the US dollar and nineteen other important trade partners

*Source*: Board of Governors of the Federal Reserve System, Trade Weighted US Dollar Index and Real Trade Weighted US Dollar Index: Other Important Trading Partners, retrieved from FRED, Federal Reserve Bank of St. Louis; October 23, 2018.

compensated for the changes in the nominal exchange rates. The figure shows that looking at nominal exchange rates alone can be very misleading when one is interested in emerging and developing economies.

### 8.5.1    Exchange Rate Parity Conditions

As business planners, you may want to know where the exchange rate of the dollar against another currency will move in the future. Should you expect a depreciation of the foreign currency, making exports to that country harder, or an appreciation, making exports easier? Foreign exchange market analysts and practitioners often use two important *parity conditions* to answer such questions. The *purchasing power parity (PPP) condition* predicts exchange rates based on inflation differentials. It is useful in the long run, but not in the short run. The *interest rate parity condition* predicts exchange rates based on interest rate differentials. It is most useful in the short run.

PPP assumes that differences in the rates of inflation between two countries will be compensated over time by an equal adjustment of the nominal exchange rate. Thus, according to PPP, the relative change in the exchange rate (euros per dollar) equals the euro-area rate of inflation minus the US rate of inflation.

This implies that the real exchange rate between the two countries is relatively stable. If one country persistently has a higher rate of inflation than the other, its exports lose competitiveness and imports would become cheaper. This would cause a net demand for foreign currencies and cause the domestic currency to depreciate until equilibrium is reached again. In other words, countries with higher inflation should see their currency depreciate against countries with lower inflation rates. The PPP does not imply that the real exchange rate is a constant. For example, differences in the rates of productivity growth between countries are likely to lead to changes in their real exchange rates. However, PPP does imply that, in the long run, the real exchange rate is independent of inflation and, therefore, of monetary policies in the two countries.

Several factors diminish the forecasting power of the PPP. First, goods produced in different countries might not be perfect substitutes and, therefore, trade flows do not react quickly to changes in relative prices of domestic and foreign goods. This might be due to a market structure of monopolistic competition, giving producers some pricing power. Second, many goods and services included in the measurement of inflation are not traded internationally, and are, therefore, not exposed to international price competition. Third, tariffs and subsidies exist that distort free trade. Finally, international foreign exchange markets are dominated by financial players and not by real trade. Nevertheless, Figure 8.7 shows that the assumption of a stable real exchange rate is not all that bad for forecasting exchange rates over longer time horizons.

The interest parity condition looks at the short run and focuses on capital flows. Assume that two countries have currencies with the same quality as store of value (no currency risk) and also assets with identical quality (no default risk). Both countries have well-developed capital markets and capital is perfectly mobile between them, i.e., investors are free to place their funds wherever they bring the higher return. An example could be the US and Japan or the US and Germany. Under these assumptions the expected dollar returns on assets of the same quality and maturity should be the same in both countries.

Obviously, the dollar return on dollar-denominated assets is simply the nominal interest rate. Let's call it $i_{USD}$. In contrast, the expected dollar return on a foreign-currency-denominated asset has two components. The first is the nominal interest rate paid on that asset. Call it $i_{FC}$. Since an investor holding dollars must first purchase foreign currency to acquire that asset, and then, at the end of the asset's maturity, must sell foreign currency to repatriate his dollars, the second component is an expected capital gain on foreign currency during the holding period. This expected capital gain is equal to the expected relative change in the nominal exchange rate in price notation (dollars per unit of foreign currency).[6] Thus, the dollar return on the foreign-currency-denominated asset in foreign currency is equal to the nominal interest rate in foreign currency plus the expected rate of change in the exchange rate.

## BOX 8.5 **The Interest Parity Condition**

We consider a US-dollar-denominated asset and a foreign-currency-denominated asset of equal asset quality and maturity. Let the exchange rate between the two currencies (foreign currency per US dollar) at the time of maturity of both assets be $e_{+1}$ and the current exchange rate at the time of purchasing the assets be e. Since the exchange rate at maturity is not known, investors must form an expectation about it using all information they currently have. We call this expectation $Ee_{+1}$.

The gross return on the dollar denominated asset is $1+i_{US}$.

The gross return on the foreign currency denominated asset in foreign currency is $1+i_{FC}$.

For a US investor, what matters is the gross return on the foreign-currency-denominated asset in terms of USD. This includes the expected capital gain $(Ee_{+1}/e)$.

Equal returns on both assets requires that

$$(1 + i_{US}) = \frac{Ee_{+1}}{e}(1 + i_{FC}) = \left(1 + \frac{Ee_{+1} - e}{e}\right)(1 + i_{FC})$$

Assuming that nominal interest rates and the expected change in the exchange rate are very small numbers and, therefore, multiplying them yields even smaller numbers, we can approximate this condition as

$$i_{US} = \frac{Ee_{-1} - e}{e} + i_{FC}$$

Under interest parity, the domestic interest rate must equal the expected rate of change in the exchange rate plus the foreign interest rate.

With this, the interest rate parity condition says that the nominal interest rate on dollar assets, $i_{USD}$, equals the nominal interest rate on foreign-currency assets, $i_{FC}$, plus the expected rate of change in the nominal exchange rate.

We can turn this statement around to say: The expected rate of change in the nominal exchange rate = $i_{US} - i_{FC}$.

All you need to do to get a good forecast for the change in the nominal exchange rate is to look at the interest rate differential, which you can find in the newspaper every day for the main currencies.

To see why this makes sense, suppose that the parity condition is violated such that the expected rate of change in the nominal exchange rate exceeds the interest rate differential, $i_{US} - i_{FC}$. This implies that the expected dollar return on foreign assets exceeds the expected dollar return on dollar-denominated assets. Investors will sell their dollar-denominated assets and buy foreign currency to buy foreign assets. Thus, the demand for foreign currency goes up and the foreign currency appreciates, i.e., the current exchange rate increases. Given the expected future exchange rate, this means that the expected rate of change declines until the parity is restored.

Keep in mind, however, that differences in the quality of assets and international capital market frictions can limit the usefulness of the interest rate parity condition to predict exchange rate movements.

## 8.5.2  Exchange Rate Changes and Policy

We use the supply and demand for internationally traded currencies to discuss the external value of a currency. We use the dollar in our example, but we could have equally used any currency. We simplify the analysis by assuming only two countries – the US and the RoW. What we are describing here might be called the foreign exchange (FX) market. The interaction of the supply of internationally traded dollars and the demand for internationally traded dollars will determine the value (price) and quantity of dollars traded.

Traders in the FX market are predominantly financial institutions such as banks or brokers acting on behalf of their customers or as part of their own business. They count for about 93 percent of a total daily turnover of more than USD 5 trillion. In an FX transaction, there are always two currencies involved; one is traded for the other. The USD is the dominating international currency, and it is used in 44 percent of all FX transactions, followed by the euro with a market share of around 16 percent. The most traded currency pair is USD against euro, followed by USD against the Japanese yen.

Private people and businesses buy and sell foreign currency for three basic reasons. The first is international trade. For example, a foreigner who wants to import US-produced goods or services to his or her country needs dollars to pay for them and, therefore, needs to sell his or her own currency for dollars. Conversely, a US resident who wants to buy foreign goods must sell dollars and buy foreign currency to pay for his or her imports. Thus, when US exports or foreign imports of US-produced goods and services increase, the demand for dollars rises in the FX market. Conversely, when US exports or foreign imports of US produced goods decline, the demand for dollars in the FX market declines. Similarly, when US imports of foreign goods or foreign exports to the US increase, the supply of dollars in the FX market rises; the supply of dollars falls when US imports of foreign goods or foreign exports to the US decline.

The second reason for trading in the FX market is linked to international capital flows. A foreigner who wants to buy a US Treasury security or some IBM stock needs to acquire dollars in the FX market to pay for them. A US resident who wants to buy foreign assets needs to buy foreign currency and sell dollars in the FX market. Conversely, if a foreigner sells his or her US assets to repatriate his or her capital, he or she will sell dollars in the FX market and buy foreign currency. If investment in US assets becomes more attractive to foreigners, the demand for dollars increases in the FX market. If investing in foreign assets becomes more attractive, the supply of dollars will rise.

The third reason for trading in the FX market is currency speculation. Speculators buy dollars for foreign currency expecting that the value of the dollar will rise above its current value, and they sell dollars for foreign currency expecting that the value of the dollar will fall below its current value. Given an expected future exchange rate (foreign currency units per dollar), their demand for dollars falls when the current exchange rate rises.

Apart from private people and businesses, central banks participate in these markets too. Some central banks wish to keep the exchange rate between their currencies and the dollar fixed or within a more or less narrow range of values. In order to *peg* their currencies to the dollar, they must buy or sell dollar reserves to counteract changes in the demand and supply of dollars from the private sector.

As in the case of other markets, we can think of the FX market in terms of the interaction of demand and supply. This is illustrated graphically in Figure 8.8, which brings together these supply-and-demand concepts into a model of exchange rate determination:

In Figure 8.8, we plot the quantity of dollars traded against foreign currency on the horizontal axis and the exchange rate (units of foreign currency per dollar) on the vertical axis. The supply of dollars increases in the exchange rate, because, when the exchange rate rises, all other things being constant,

- foreign goods become cheaper in the US and imports rise;
- investing in foreign assets becomes more attractive and investing in US assets becomes less attractive for international investors;
- speculating on an increase in the exchange rate becomes more profitable.

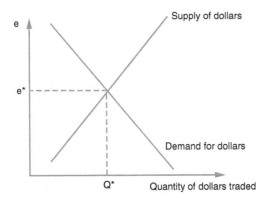

**Figure 8.8** The foreign exchange market

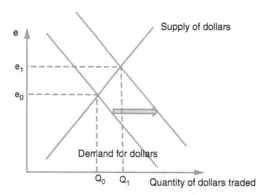

Figure 8.9 A rise in the demand for dollars

Similarly, the demand for dollars falls when the exchange rate rises, because

- US goods become more expensive abroad and foreign imports decline;
- investing in US assets becomes more attractive and investing in foreign assets becomes less attractive;
- speculating on an increase in the exchange rate becomes less profitable.

As in other markets, an FX market equilibrium is a situation where the exchange rate is such that the supply and demand for internationally traded dollars are equalized.

We use this framework to understand what causes change in the exchange rate. Consider Figure 8.9. The figure shows that, when the demand curve for internationally traded dollars shifts outward, the equilibrium exchange rate will rise. This may happen, if

- the foreign economy grows faster than the US economy, leading to a strong increase in the demand for US exports;
- US exporting industries become more competitive in foreign markets relative to foreign industries;
- US interest rates rise relative to foreign interest rates, making investment in dollar-denominated assets more attractive;
- speculators expect a higher exchange rate in the future and buy dollars today to benefit from the expected increase.

In Figure 8.10, we consider a situation where the supply of internationally traded dollars rises in the FX market. As a result, the exchange rate of the dollar falls. This may happen, if

- the US economy grows faster than the foreign economy, leading to a rise in US imports;
- foreign industries become more competitive in US markets relative to US industries;

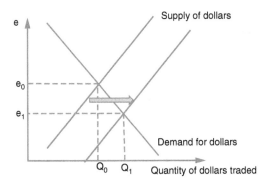

**Figure 8.10** A rise in the supply of dollars

- US interest rates fall relative to foreign interest rates, making investment in foreign-currency-denominated assets more attractive;
- speculators expect a lower exchange rate in the future and sell dollars today.

### 8.5.3   International Application: Currency Pegs

Many countries in the world peg (or manage) their currency values to the dollar. Some fix it exactly, while some allow for a band around a mean value (a managed float). Some keep that mean value constant for long periods of time, while some let the mean value change gradually. Some countries have what is called a currency board, which means that the central bank can only create domestic money by buying foreign currency. This is tantamount to a completely fixed exchange rate. For example, Estonia fixed its kroon to the German DM and then the euro before entering the European Monetary Union. Some countries give up their own currencies and replace it with dollars – this is called *dollarization*. For example, Ecuador uses the US dollar as legal means of payment.[7]

Central banks maintain pegged exchange rates in order to provide more stable trading environments for export and import markets and to stabilize the expectations of international investors who, by bringing in and out large amounts of hot money, might create turmoil in domestic financial markets otherwise. But sometimes they just can't keep up the peg. Why? Because something happens that makes the world have less confidence in this country. The government might have larger fiscal deficits that become very difficult to pay back. Maybe the government has a scandal. Maybe the new government isn't trustworthy. Whatever the case may be – if world investors withdraw their funds, the currency will depreciate. The country can try to stop this by using their foreign reserves to buy their own currency in FX markets – but they usually have limited foreign reserves and once they start to dwindle, the problem gets even worse. So, people watch these foreign countries with exchange rate pegs like hawks watch rabbits in the field. As soon as a country shows signs of weakening, the chances of the peg failing start to increase.

**Figure 8.11** China exchange rate and real exchange rate
Note that the real exchange rate provided by the Federal Reserve Board is defined as dollars per yuan. Here we use the inverse to make it consistent with the nominal rate.
*Source*: Board of Governors of the Federal Reserve System, China/US Foreign Exchange Rate, and OECD, Real Effective Exchange Rates Based on Manufacturing Consumer Price Index for China, retrieved from FRED, October 23, 2018.

China is an example of a country that has pegged its currency tightly to the US dollar. Figure 8.11 shows an index of the exchange rate (Chinese yuan to a dollar) setting the 2010 average at 100. It shows that, from mid 1995 until mid 2005, the exchange rate was literally fixed. From June 2005 until August 2008, the People's Bank of China allowed the yuan to gradually appreciate against the dollar. Between August 2008 and July 2010, the exchange rate was almost fixed again. From July 2010 until early 2014, the yuan again appreciated somewhat against the dollar. Since then, the People's Bank has moved it up and down in relatively small steps.

China has often been accused of maintaining an exchange rate peg to keep the value of its currency artificially low and give its export industries a competitive advantage in US markets. From the analysis above, one would indeed expect that the currency of a country experiencing large current account surpluses over long periods of time would appreciate against the currencies of its main trading partners, unless there are continuous, large private capital outflows from that country to others. This is because a large current account surplus means that there is a large excess demand for its currency in the FX market.

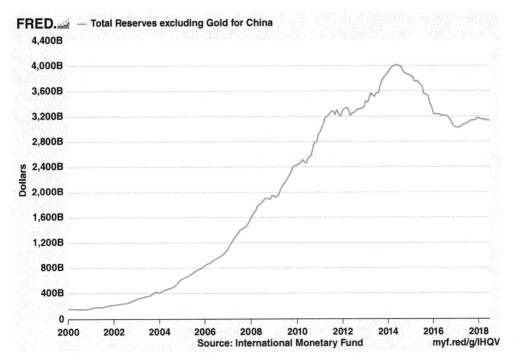

**Figure 8.12** People's Bank of China foreign currency reserves

*Source*: IMF, Total Reserves excluding Gold for China retrieved from FRED, Federal Reserve Bank of St. Louis, October 22, 2018.

In the absence of capital outflows, that excess demand has to be absorbed by the central bank if it is to keep the exchange rate constant. In that case, the central bank would accumulate foreign currency reserves. Figure 8.12 shows that this was indeed the case for China between 1998 and 2014. The international reserves (mostly dollar reserves) of the People's Bank rose from USD 144 billion to 4.0 trillion. Since then, China's foreign currency reserves have declined to about USD 3.1 trillion, indicating that the central bank did not keep the value of its currency artificially low.

In an economy with relatively liberal financial markets, one expects that such a rise in the foreign currency reserves of the central bank will eventually translate into a rise in the money supply – recall from Chapter 4, that the money stock created by the central bank has the bank's foreign currency reserves among its balance sheet counterparts. Accumulating foreign currency reserves creates liquidity in the domestic financial markets and it would take tight controls on interest rates and private credit to keep that liquidity outside the domestic private sector. Therefore, a long period of keeping the value of a currency artificially low should eventually lead to domestic inflation as the supply of money grows too fast. When that happens and inflation begins to exceed foreign inflation, the *real* exchange rate should appreciate and this would eventually eat up the trade advantage the central bank sought for its domestic industries. Figure 8.11 shows the yuan–dollar real exchange rate based on the CPIs of manufactured goods, the kind of goods dominating Chinese exports to the US. The figure shows that, in the late 1990s and until 2001, the yuan indeed mostly appreciated against the dollar in real terms. Thus, although the yuan–dollar exchange rate was still kept relatively high (the value of the yuan low), its real value increased. Following a period of real depreciation until 2005, the People's Bank seems to have managed the exchange rate to keep the yuan's nominal and real exchange value in line with one another, but since 2014, the yuan has again mostly appreciated in real terms against the dollar.

## 8.5.4    International Application: Dollarization

Most countries have their own currencies. Having a national currency can have high symbolic value and be a matter of pride. When the Baltic countries regained their freedom from the Soviet Union, these small countries decided to drop the Russian ruble and replace it with Latvian lats, Lithuanian lits, and Estonian kroons. This added an extra layer of transactions for these countries, but that seemed to be a small price to pay to restore their status as independent countries.

Other countries have gone the other way – replacing their own national currencies with other ones. The euro is a recent example since there are nineteen countries that have introduced the euro as their common currency. Using a common currency saves a lot of transaction costs and makes economic sense in the tightly integrated European single market, where all participating countries have adopted largely the same regulations and trade and capital flows are completely free. However, the introduction of the euro was also seen as a great symbolic step toward the creation of a politically unified Europe.

Replacing your national currency with the dollar is called *dollarization*. Dollarization helps a country in several ways. First, since the dollar is the dominant currency in international trade, it reduces transaction costs. Second, the dollar is known to be more stable than other currencies, so using it reduces risk involved with currency trades and promotes financial and monetary stability. Third, the dollar is often stronger in value than other currencies and lends benefits to countries that might encounter risk of a rapidly declining currency.

Countries have adopted the dollar as their currency in various ways. Ecuador, El Salvador, and East Timor use the dollar as their only means of payment. Panama uses the dollar as legal means of payment along with its existing national currency. Palau, the Federated States of Micronesia, and the Marshall Islands chose the dollar instead of introducing their own national currencies when they gained political independence. Two former British colonies, the British Virgin Islands and Turks and Caicos Islands, adopted the dollar when they became independent from Britain, while Bonaire, Sint Eustatius, and Saba adopted the dollar after the dissolution of the former Netherlands Antilles. After the collapse of its own currency the

Zimbabwe dollar, in a hyperinflation, Zimbabwe adopted the US dollar alongside the euro, pound sterling, the pula, and the South African rand.

While these are cases of official dollarization, the adoption of a foreign currency as medium of exchange can also occur spontaneously by the private sector when people lose trust in their national currency. In many socialist countries in the 1970s and 1980s, the dollar or the deutsche mark were commonly accepted in shops and used for large purchases of valuables or assets. During the economic crises of Mexico, Argentina, and Venezuela, a large part of business transactions were made in dollars rather than national currency.

## 8.6 SUMMARY

The balance of payments provides a record of trade in goods and services and capital flows between the domestic economy and the RoW. It allows us to track trade deficits and current account deficits and identify imbalances in trade and capital flows. Issues in international trade are often controversial. It is important, therefore, to understand how they are linked to broader issues in macroeconomics such as imbalances between domestic saving and investment. In today's environment of large, global financial markets, traditional trade policies are often no longer adequate.

Changes in foreign exchange rates are driven by fluctuations in the supply and demand of internationally traded domestic and foreign currencies in the foreign exchange market. The balance of payments provides the background for understanding such fluctuations and, ultimately, changes in exchange rates. Central banks can – and do – intervene in these markets to manipulate the value of their currencies, leading to changes in their stocks of foreign currency reserves. Such interventions can contribute to more stable trading environments, but when they fail, they can cause major disruptions in financial markets. It is, therefore, important for business executives to keep an eye on balance-of-payment developments of the countries they operate in to correctly anticipate exchange rate movements and the policies governments and central banks might take to correct them.

## 8.7 REVIEW QUESTIONS

1. What is the relationship between the current account balance and the financial account balance?
2. What is the relationship between national savings, investment, and the current account balance?
3. Does the current account deficit necessarily rise when the government budget deficit increases?

4. The US is a net foreign debtor and yet receives positive net foreign asset income. How is this possible?

5. The ECB announces it is going to lower euro interest rates. What are the likely consequences for the US financial account balance and the US dollar–euro exchange rate?

6. What is the meaning of purchasing power parity? Is it a useful concept to forecast exchange rates?

7. What happens to the yen–US dollar exchange rate, if the Bank of Japan unilaterally increases its interest rate?

## NOTES

1 It is an approximation to the budget surplus because of accounting differences between national accounts and the government budget.
2 "American Savings Shortfall Is Hurting Workers," https://aparc.fsi.stanford.edu/news/americas_savings_shortfall_is_hurting_its_workers_mckinnon_asserts_in_oped_20041021
3 C. Alan Garner, "Should the Decline in the Personal Savings Rate Be a Cause of Concern?" Federal Reserve Bank of Kansas City *Economic Review*, Second Quarter 2006, pp. 5–28.
4 See "Indexes of Foreign Exchange Value of the Dollar" (prepared by Mike Loretan), *Federal Reserve Bulletin* Winter 2005, pp. 1–8.
5 These countries are Argentina, Brazil, Chile, China, Colombia, Hong Kong, India, Indonesia, Israel, Korea, Malaysia, Mexico, Philippines, Russia, Saudi Arabia, Singapore, Taiwan, Thailand, and Venezuela.
6 Strictly speaking, the two assets become equal in quality only if investors eliminate exchange rate risk by using forward contracts over the relevant holding period. With perfect forward currency markets and risk-neutral traders, the forward rate will be equal to the future spot rate.
7 See the IMF's *Annual Report on Exchange Arrangements and Exchange Restrictions* for a classification and an overview, www.imf.org/en/Publications/Annual-Report-on-Exchange-Arrangements-and-Exchange-Restrictions/Issues/2017/01/25/Annual-Report-on-Exchange-Arrangements-and-Exchange-Restrictions-2016-43741

# 9  Free Trade and Protectionism

In the new world of international trade, the playing field is hardly level. The richer countries have relatively low trade barriers for most goods and commerce, but cling to protection for selected sectors of the economy, especially their farmers, services, and their airlines. These countries enjoy the trade advantages of having high-quality transportation and communication networks, the best technology, and the most educated workers. Developing countries, in contrast, seek to achieve equality in infrastructure, capital, and labor, but know it will take decades to catch up. In the meantime, they also feel the need to protect many of their young industries from the full force of the industrial nations, while demanding access to the markets of those countries for their agricultural and food products.

The World Trade Organization (WTO) and various other world organizations attempt to move the whole world toward freer trade, but the process is slow and uneven. Much progress has been made in the last fifty years, but there is still much to do. Countries use regional trade agreements, bilateral agreements, as well as unilateral policies as they try to get the benefits of freer trade. Like domestic competition, international trade is tumultuous – it rewards the winners generously and requires that the losers either improve or move aside. Governments see many important manufacturing companies moving offshore to take advantage of new global opportunities. They see how the Internet allows for outsourcing of even high-value-added services to foreign countries. They sometimes use social policies to mitigate the harshest impacts on their companies and citizens. And sometimes they interfere with the process of international trade through policies that protect their citizens – things like tariffs, quotas, standards, and currency manipulation.

There was probably a time when businesspeople mostly used local resources and workers to produce goods and services for people who lived within the community – or at least within a day's ride on a horse. While there might still be remote villages where such local trade dominates the minds of business managers, the typical experience of an executive today involves one or more cross-border implications. We don't have to think about Procter & Gamble to see the growing importance of international transactions. My local dry cleaner might service mostly townsfolk who drive at most a few minutes to pick up their newly pressed garments, but this company is heavily involved with international trade. For one thing, some of his employees are immigrants. For another, some of the dry-cleaning chemicals are imported from around the world – for example, US dry-cleaning companies import millions of pounds of tetrachloroethylene each year. While we have not seen any foreign competition for dry-cleaning services in my community, we all know it is possible that a chain of such cleaners from Europe or Asia could set up and operate in any town in the US. You can run, but you can't hide from international business and competition.

When a government puts a 100 percent tariff on imported washing machines to protect a US appliances worker, this policy action affects the playing field for US and foreign countries.

When a European government makes it harder for an immigrant to move and work in Europe to protect the jobs of local citizens, this impacts the business outcomes of many firms in Europe – and could lead to companies moving from Europe to other parts of the world.

If an Asian government gives subsidies to foreign manufacturing firms locating facilities in Asia, this subsidy impacts decisions about where companies want to operate. This will also impact where many other firms will want to import or export their own goods.

The upshot is that every country has policies that directly or indirectly affect a wide variety of cross-border transactions – and these policies are changing all the time. If many companies are impacted by international trade, then it behooves them to learn as much as they can about these policies.

This topic took on even greater significance after Donald Trump became President of the US in 2017. His "America First" trade policy correlated US trade deficits with economic weakness and difficulties for US workers. Trump argued that existing trade agreements were not working out for America – that trade is neither free nor fair to the US. As such, he resorted to reopening existing FTAs (like the North American Free Trade Agreement) and postponing or denying new ones (like the Trans-Pacific Partnership). Additionally, in 2017 Trump threatened to impose tariffs on imported steel to protect US steel workers. There was also a discussion of tariffs on imports of appliances from Asia.

There is much discussion and debate about Trump's international policies and we will shed light on these issues in this chapter. One way to look at this issue is to understand America's changing role in the world economy. After World War II, many countries were challenged by rebuilding both economic systems and governments. The US saw a great opportunity to help – help that was both humane and selfish. But time has passed, and America is just one of the world's economic powers. Additionally, the US has major economic challenges and a large national debt. Thus, its role in pulling the wagons is evolving as it becomes just one of the horses. Reevaluating its role among nations is neither wrong nor unexpected.

Yet there remains the question of why trade is part of a macroeconomics book. There are three key reasons why trade impacts macroeconomics. First, trade is the way for a country to enlarge its markets. Suppose a country is very good at producing a new, amazing orphan drug. But the number of people who might benefit from that drug in that country is too small for its companies to gain real productive efficiency. Exporting that good is a way to enlarge the market and the amount produced will facilitate business efficiencies that help to keep the drug more affordable. Second, international trade allows for a country to avoid supply bottle-necks. Perhaps there are short-term events that interrupt a domestic supply chain. Diversifying the source of materials and other productive inputs means that a company need not be shut down by local conditions that prevent a smooth flow of operations. Third, countries follow different business cycle timing. The US might be up when Japan is down. Diversifying the demand for one's goods across regions gives local companies a way to reduce the risk of a downward change in the demand from any single country or part of the world.

Recall that a key component of aggregate demand is net exports. As exports and imports of final goods and services rise and fall, the world has a way of impacting the aggregate demand of any country. But net exports and aggregate demand are only part of the macroeconomic story. Flows of workers across countries impact the amounts and prices of labor. Different monetary policies can affect real interest rates across countries that impact where funds move. These changes in funds and interest rates impact financial markets but also affect a broad array of decisions in housing markets as well as the demand for plant, equipment, cars, and so on. In short, very few countries are insulated from the rest of the world. Macroeconomics is global.

Chapter 9 starts by defining free trade and discussing why trade is desirable. We next turn to protectionism, explaining its roots and examining to what extent it is harmful. This good/bad story sets up the idea that government policy is part and parcel of any discussions about trade and macroeconomic policy. Trade might enlarge markets, but it also could harm domestic workers when firms are free to locate abroad or when companies import goods and services rather than buying them at home. The policy question is how we can obtain the benefits of trade while minimizing its harmful effects. We are not naive enough to think that major opportunities can be had without some economic or social cost. Thus, international trade policies are an important part of the full set of macroeconomic policies.

The remainder of the chapter explores international trade policy by examining trade disputes, the role played by FTAs, and international trade organizations including the WTO. We believe the general trend is for free trade to continue to increase but the precise timing and geographical locations of the changes will be as difficult to predict as ever. There will likely be almost as many steps backward (toward protectionism) as forward. The implication is that business planners will have to cast wider and more complex information nets. They will have to deal with the uncertainty of difficult-to-predict swings between freer and less free trade.

## 9.1   Macro Concepts and Analysis

Free international trade is a lot like free beer and brats. They don't really exist except in somebody's mind. Like pure or perfect competition, free trade is a polar state that has very desirable properties and its extreme form probably never did nor ever will exist. But that doesn't mean that we can't think about freer trade. We can ask the very practical question – can we or should we try to bring about freer international trade?

### 9.1.1   What Is Free Trade?

International trade implies an exchange is being made between two parties – whether it involves people, goods, services, real capital, financial capital, foreign currencies, cuckoo clocks, or anything else exchanged between parties in two or more different countries. Free trade further means that there are no artificial or "constructed" obstacles to that trade. If two willing parties of an exchange lived 10,000 miles apart, the distance might provide hurdles to overcome, but we would call that an inherent cost of distance rather than a lack of free trade. For free trade to be lacking, we think of some form of power that is exerted to reduce or prevent the trade. More will be said about specific barriers that impede free trade below.

A world of perfectly free trade would be totally free of all such barriers. Most people think that such an extreme is impossible to achieve – sort of like finding the Holy Grail. The more realistic goal, therefore, is to move toward "freer" trade – implying some reduction in the barriers to free trade.

Another way to understand free trade is to note that transactions are guided by free market principles. This wording connects international free trade to our notions about competitive market economies. Recall Adam Smith's notion of the *invisible hand*. The invisible hand is a way of saying that there is some inherent force of nature in an unfettered market economy that brings about good results. Competition is crucial for that to happen. It implies that, apart from assuring competitive market conditions, there is no need for a *visible hand* of the government to solve most economic problems. There is no need for the government to regulate prices or wages. There is no role for tariffs on imported goods other than providing the government with tax revenues similar to other taxes, and no rationale for quotas that limit cross-border trade in specific goods.

While we generally believe that competitive markets work well, we also know that there are limits to that and admit that there is an economic role for governments.

For example, we do not consider it a trade barrier when the government enacts and enforces anti-trust or anti-corruption regulations aimed at firms that cheat. Most people agree that some form of government social policy is necessary to bring about better solutions for poverty and unemployment. The role of governments in pollution control and education is often lauded.

When it comes to various forms of government intervention, there is often disagreement about whether an action is a necessary reaction to a market failure or whether it is an unnecessary intervention that reduces national welfare. Despite this lack of consensus, however, it is probably true to say that most economists favor freer competition both domestically and in international trade. What they don't always agree on is how best to accomplish that.

### 9.1.2 Why Is Free Trade Desirable?

The WTO is an international organization charged with the governance of international trade. The WTO offers its views on ten benefits of a WTO trading system.[1] These are benefits derived from more countries participating in a system whose main objective is freer trade. The ten benefits of the WTO trading system are to

1. cut living costs and raise living standards;
2. settle disputes and reduce trade tensions;
3. stimulate economic growth and employment;
4. cut the cost of doing business internationally;
5. encourage good governance;
6. help countries develop;
7. give the weak a stronger voice;
8. support the environment and health;
9. contribute to peace and stability; and
10. be effective without hitting the headlines.

Here is a brief synopsis of the benefits of freer trade. Fewer impediments to trade mean that price signals work more effectively – producers produce what is demanded and less is wasted. That leads to more efficiency. Because obstacles to trade can reduce competition and/or lead to protection for individual firms, that allows them to raise their prices higher than necessary. Thus, free trade makes goods cheaper. When goods and services are cheaper, households can buy more of the same goods or they can buy the same amount as before and have money left over to spend on other things – that leads to the production of even more goods. When a country produces more, the incomes of its citizens increase. If freer trade creates clearer incentives and does not allow for arbitrary impediments against particular goods or services, then it is easier for a greater variety of goods and services to be produced and made available to consumers. Firms may be freer to experiment with (high and low) quality and features and packaging and other aspects.

The issue of trade causing economic growth and job growth is quite controversial. One argument is that free trade and the resulting stronger competition creates more incentive for survival – it brings out the entrepreneurial juices. Some firms in some countries are too weak to compete with other firms. Thus, free trade in those countries hurts companies and reduces incomes. This worry was voiced loudly as Mexico initially approached the North American Free Trade Agreement (NAFTA). This concern was voiced in Mexico, but it was also registered in the US where some US firms felt they could not compete against low-wage Mexican firms. While these concerns have merit, they miss the whole point about the benefits of free trade. Why have a NAFTA if it isn't going to cause change? Won't many US companies be made stronger by having access to cheaper goods in Mexico? Won't Mexico be made stronger by having better access to US technology and capital? From a national standpoint free trade is a win–win situation – despite the fact that some firms will be injured by it.

So why is there a real debate? There are three things to discuss. First is the issue of compensating the losers. There will be companies and persons that are harmed and cannot survive in the new competitive environment. Social policy must find ways to address this without reducing the ability to trade. Second, corruption must be expected, monitored, and eliminated. Too many free trade situations have failed essentially because the spoils went to a few unscrupulous persons in the private and public sectors. Free international trade cannot paper over domestic obstacles to commerce. Third, while it is easy to see why economic growth would increase, the issue over employment is murkier. It is quite possible for companies to increase output without a corresponding increase in labor input. It is very likely that new and higher levels of competition will lead to higher productivity – but productivity is a double-edged sword for employment.

The first edge of a productivity increase involves the cutting of jobs. But the second one finds that countries with strong productivity and economic growth tend to have increasing employment. Why is that? It is because when many companies want to increase output, they generally need to increase employment. This is the usual story of productivity growth – each year many jobs are destroyed as competition rewards winners and penalizes others. But the process of "most" companies seeing their outputs rise by 2 percent to 3 percent per year tends to "pull" the total level of employment upward. Consider the US experience. Both President Reagan and President Clinton bragged that employment in the US increased by about 18 million jobs during each of their eight-year terms in office. That's a total of 36 million jobs in 16 years – an average of 2.25 million jobs per year! Over that time many people lost jobs – many manufacturing jobs declined and went overseas, some jobs just ceased. So while productivity appears to be a double-edged sword – one edge is a lot bigger than the other one. Productivity growth tends to lead to much more employment – not less.

### 9.1.3   International Application: Why Globalization Works

Arvind Panagariya wrote an excellent summary of a book by columnist Martin Wolf, *Why Globalization Works*. He summarizes the case for free trade as follows:[2]

- Critics say that globalization has not created faster economic growth. Wolf argues that India and China are shining examples of opening up their economies to free trade and faster economic growth.
- Almost all cases of growth "miracles" between 1961 and 1999 involved rapid trade growth. In contrast, countries that had declining per-capita incomes tended to have dismal trade growth.
- Freer trade did not always produce growth miracles – when other aspects of good governance were missing. For example, stifling industrial licensing that used to typify India held back economic growth despite freer trade. Poor transportation facilities didn't help either.
- Wolf adds, "Poor performers have corrupt, predatory or brutal governments or, sometimes even worse, no government at all, but rather civil war among competing war lords."
- Panagariya adds that while Latin America did try free trade reforms, they also borrowed too much and made themselves more subject to financial crises. Chile was the counterexample. It opened its economy to trade, grew rapidly, moderated its borrowing, and maintained macroeconomic stability.
- Wolf notes that while developing countries will gain by having more access to other countries, the largest improvements will come from their own liberalization.
- Wolf points out that multinational companies generally have not exploited local workers – in fact his evidence shows that they pay the workers more and treat them better than local firms.
- Some critics worry that when firms and jobs leave the US for foreign countries or when US firms outsource, this leads to lower wages in the US; Wolf counters that the US is a major recipient of inbound capital investment and insourcing. This tends to balance the impacts on employment and wages.

### 9.1.4   What Is Protectionism?

Protectionism is anything that creates a "protection" from the impact of international competition. One very interesting aspect of protectionism is that it usually bestows large benefits to a small number of firms that can be spread out as costs to a large number of households. That is interesting because it shows that the politics might favor the legislation or implementation of various kinds of protectionism. Consider the vigor and enthusiasm and resources that local steel mills might have to devote to the passage of a high tariff on imported steel. These few companies might exert considerable pressure on government to obtain this end. Consider also that while this tariff might increase the price of steel in the home country, the extra amount that each household or each voter might have to pay could be a few bucks – perhaps not even enough to notice. If government can convince the voters that the cost to each person is negligible and the gain to a local industry is worth millions of dollars and could save jobs – then the chances are it will be able to pass this legislation. This underscores how politics do not necessarily stand in the way of growing protectionism. It also emphasizes how difficult it is to stop it.

An article published by the Heritage Organization nicely illustrates the point.[3] Because of US protection of the sugar industry, Americans paid 6 cents more than the average world price for a pound of raw sugar in fiscal year 2013. That seems like a small number, but it amounts to a total of USD 1.4 billion extra cost to American consumers and USD 310,000 extra revenue for the average sugar beet or sugar cane farm. The article cites a US International Trade Commission estimate that abolishing US sugar protection would create a net annual welfare gain of more than USD 1 billion per year. But how much sugar do you buy every week? Probably not too much. Therefore, your individual benefit from lifting that protection would be small. In contrast, the gains enjoyed by the individual producer are huge and this explains why sugar producers spend a lot of money on lobbying for their case and on campaign donations.

How does a nation protect itself against international competition? The answer is that there are both subtle and obvious ways to protect domestic producers from outside competition. The most obvious ways have been the use of tariffs and quotas. Tariffs are taxes imposed on imports or exports. A high tariff on an imported item gives a local producer a great advantage. A quota is a quantity constraint that limits the amount of imports of a certain good to a country. For example, a quota might say that a country can import only so many bananas, pounds of sugar, or textile garments. While this does not add directly to the price of the imported good, it does leave the domestic producers with a larger share of the market and allows them to charge higher prices.

Anti-dumping duties and safeguards can be another form of protectionism. They are levied against countries that violate the spirit of fair trade by taking what they cannot sell at home and selling it at lower-than-bargain-basement prices in other countries – that is, they sell them at prices that are below their costs of production. This might be justified from the standpoint of the dumping company facing a temporary slump in domestic demand for its product – why let goods collect dust in a local warehouse when you could sell them for a penny more than transportation costs to another country? But if it becomes a lasting practice, it is perceived to be an unfair trading strategy to gain larger market shares and drive out competitors in foreign markets.

Clearly, countries ought to be able to react against such unfair practices. But it is hardly ever so clear. The problem is that it isn't always easy to prove that a foreign company is selling below its costs. It might just be selling at a very low price at home and everywhere because it has a better technology and lower input prices. Since costs of production are usually private affairs within companies, it takes a lot of work to determine if dumping is occurring. Most countries know that and they can at least temporarily fend off competition by using anti-dumping duties.

Safeguards allow a country to protect itself from any kind of significant but largely unpredictable wave of new imports that threatens an industry. The perpetrator need not be dumping. The safeguards give the local industry some time to adjust to the new competition. More is said about the steel safeguards below. In November 2017, Whirlpool of the USA asked for a new tariff and protection from competition from Korean washing machine companies LG and Samsung. They cited eroding market share as the reason for the need for protection.

Other, more subtle forms of protectionism may occur in conjunction with some very legitimate goals of government that relate to public health, safety, information, certification, and environment. One recent example has to do with genetically modified organisms (GMOs). US farms had a considerable first-mover advantage. US companies found that by genetically modifying seeds, they could make them more resistant to disease. There have been no studies to link any specific health hazards to GMO corn or other products, but we all share some concern that something negative could occur in the longer term. The US is studying these problems but is allowing GMO products to be sold. Some other countries, however, do not want GMO corn sold in their markets and prohibit it on the grounds of health issues. Is this a legitimate health issue – or is this simply a way to protect local corn producers from US corn?

Varied customs regimes among the twenty-five countries of the EU were viewed as a trade barrier by the US in 2004. Dealing with up to twenty-five different tariff regimes raised the knowledge requirement and costs for foreign companies wanting to export to various parts of the EU. This is an interesting case. Notice that the US was not lodging a similar complaint against the countries of South America or Africa. Why? The answer is that these continents do not advertise or have goals to create a common and free economic space. It might be a free unimpeded marketplace for the twenty-five countries within the EU – but having to deal with up to twenty-five different trade regimes for everyone else could be considered unfair. The EU reacted by saying that if the US had a problem with Europe, they should have brought it directly to them. This raises the question of whether trade problems should be dealt with bilaterally – or by the whole world.

### 9.1.5  International Application: Safeguards and Chinese Textiles

The *Financial Times* reported that US textile and clothing companies asked the US government to impose new quotas on Chinese imports – mostly trousers, shirts, cotton shirts, and other products.[4] The European Commission had recently reported they were investigating rising imports of similar products in Europe. US industries complained of a loss of 350,000 jobs in four years. Textile associations from fifty-four countries joined US textile companies as they urged the US to act on their petitions.

### 9.1.6   Is Protectionism Bad?

Paul Krugman, in *The Age of Diminished Expectations*, said that the negative aspects of protectionism are exaggerated.[5] While Krugman does not argue that protectionism is a good thing, he does explain why he thinks that the case against protectionism is less clear than most economists are willing to admit. Consider some of Krugman's points.

- While some economists point to the *Smoot–Hawley tariffs* as contributing to the severity of the Great Depression, Krugman comments that Smoot–Hawley didn't cause the Great Depression. These tariffs were designed by Herbert Hoover to help US farmers against foreign competition at the outset of the Great Depression in 1930 and led to retaliation by other countries. In the end, world trade decreased by about 66 percent between 1929 and 1934. While Krugman is right that these tariffs didn't cause the Great Depression, not many economists ever said they did. But they did, no doubt, have a very negative impact on most countries during a very bad time. It is correct to worry that protectionism can bring harmful retaliation and is therefore a threat to economic wellbeing. While protectionism elicits retaliation the result is not simply in the form of tariffs. Escalating tariffs have their own negative impacts but compounding the problems are when retaliations take other forms. For example, a country can respond to a tariff by devaluing its currency. The effect is intended to be similar – increasing the home country's exports at the expense of exports of its trading partners. Thus, a trade war can elicit currency wars. Such wars have been common during and after major recessions.
- Krugman's better point is that neither trade deficits nor protectionism hurt a country's job situation. His logic is that employment is determined by supply-side factors – not by the composition of demand. He likens protectionism to something that would simply divert foreign demand to domestic demand. But adding a protective tariff to an imported good – especially an input like a part or capital good – simply increases the cost of production. This kind of negative impact on jobs became very apparent with the steel safeguards in the US. Some economists noted that the protection for any one steel job in the US put in jeopardy a multiple of jobs for workers in the steel-using industries.
- Krugman says that the "real harm" from protectionism is really very small. He acknowledges that protectionism causes inefficiency and loss of opportunities of

scale, but then says that these losses are estimated to be less than 0.5 percent of GDP. He says the US savings and loan (S&L) crisis loss was much bigger. That might be true, but the S&L crisis was a very big problem that thankfully does not come along every year. But protectionism is with us every year. This GDP loss −0.5 percent – continues each year. If this loss can be translated into dollars, it means roughly USD 100 billion per year. If a job averages USD 40,000 per year, then that is equivalent to more than 2 million jobs per year.

- Krugman says that some people see protectionism as a bargaining tool to pry open foreign markets for exports. Krugman says this won't work. US goods aren't kept out of markets by government policies in large amounts (except agricultural products) and even if they were, most governments have protectionist policies for very strong domestic political reasons. Bullying won't get very far.

- Krugman says there is a case to be made for protectionism – the *new view*. While much trade is based on the comparative advantage of nations, much is also done because of historical accident or first-mover advantage that led to scale economies. In short, why can't countries without comparative advantage create their own "historical accident" by subsidizing or investing in industries that could become trade champions (with government help and protection)? One example is high-tech, high-value-added industry development. Krugman's most persuasive argument is that other countries are heavily involved with subsidies aimed at developing new industries. If they can create first-mover advantages by offsetting very large fixed costs, it is possible that a temporary subsidy could go a long way. The potential for technology developments that have spillovers into other industries broadens the appeal of these subsidies. If the US doesn't play at this game, then we might lose out. The problem with this line of reasoning is that it leaves out the risk involved with "picking winners." There are plenty of examples of government attempts to subsidize industries that didn't succeed. Looking at this in a planning sense, how do governments make good decisions about which promising new developments are worth subsidizing and which ones are not? What if the government had spent billions developing 8-track music players in the 1970s just around the time that people decided they preferred the cassette technology? How many of these kinds of "duds" can a government afford? How many failures can be justified for each blockbuster?

Krugman might be correct on some facts, but he isn't correct enough if one interprets his meaning to imply that increased protectionism would be a good thing. One final lament of those who would seek more protectionism is that small or low-income countries simply cannot and never will be able to survive and compete. A look at a country like Haiti might draw sympathy for this worry, but even for impoverished Haiti opening the country to foreign trade makes sense. Consider the following statement of the World Bank:[6]

> As the Peruvian development expert, Hernando de Soto has persuasively argued, the lack of effectively enforced property rights in poor countries, together with opaque and inefficient legal and judicial systems, prevents the extension of credit and economic growth. Moreover, excessive bureaucracy is a recipe for corruption by allowing unscrupulous officials to exact tribute from businesses wishing to transverse the passes of regulation they guard so closely . . . Many of the policies that are needed do not require a lot of money to implement . . . improving the climate for doing business is, as the bank's report says, a marathon rather than a sprint . . . a process rather than an event . . . nor is it one size fits all . . . policies must fit local conditions. But the overall direction of policy is clear. Poor countries' economies are strangled by red tape and blinded by uncertainty. They should be freed from both.

### 9.1.7    International Application: the Steel Safeguards and Employment

Gary Hufbauer and Ben Goodrich of the Institute for International Economics commented on the job losses in the steel-using industries.[7] While the press bandied about estimates as high as 200,000 jobs lost, Hufbauer and Goodrich conclude their analysis with the following quote:

> These figures (meaning estimates in the range of 15,000 to 25,000 jobs lost) are in the range of an earlier CITAC estimate of 15,000 jobs dislocated in steel-using industries (narrowly defined) as a result of proposed tariff remedies. Whether steel-using firms discharged 15,000 or 26,000 workers or 52,000 workers because of safeguard tariffs, a lot of unnecessary misery was created. The misery is especially hard to justify when there was little pickup in employment among steel-producing firms.

Why did President Bush adopt "safeguards" for steel? Safeguards, unlike dumping cases, do not require a proof of below-cost pricing – they simply require a large harm to an important industry that needs temporary protection. Bush explained the safeguards in a speech announcing their end as follows:[8]

> Today, I signed a proclamation ending the temporary steel safeguard measures I put in place in March 2002. Prior to that time, steel prices were at 20-year lows, and the US International Trade Commission found that a surge in imports to the US market was causing serious injury to our domestic steel industry. I took action to give the industry a chance to adjust to the surge in foreign imports and to give relief to the workers and communities that depend on steel for their jobs and livelihoods. These safeguard measures have now achieved their purpose, and as a result of changed economic circumstances it is time to lift them.

An interesting sidelight of the steel "safeguards" is that President Bush withdrew them shortly before countries could retaliate against them. The WTO found that the US "safeguards" were illegal. "Safeguards" are available to countries as a means to legally protect their companies and workers in specific cases – after unpredictable import surges that caused direct harm. The WTO panel disputed the facts in the US steel case. As a result, President Bush withdrew the "safeguards" shortly before other countries would have been able to legally retaliate. While the president noted that the "safeguards" gave steel producers some time to reorganize and adjust, one cannot come away from this experience with a good feeling about the benefits of protectionism.

### 9.1.8    International Application: Job Losses and the Outsourcing of Jobs

Outsourcing of service jobs has attracted much attention and concern for US employment. For many years we have dealt with manufacturing plants moving abroad to take advantage of being closer to foreign markets, lower wages, and other benefits. More recently, however, we find US companies outsourcing many services to foreign countries. A lot of attention has been paid to Indian call centers, but we are finding that more and more business services can be outsourced to foreign countries.

Why business services? Largely because technology now makes it easier to do business. Faster computers with better software hooked up to the Internet mean it is possible that a trained draftsman half-way around the globe can be working on architectural drawings for a US architect as the latter sleeps and dreams about lower costs. Bookkeepers, consultants, tax specialists, investment bankers, medical doctors, and many other workers abroad can learn the US system and provide rapid, higher-quality, low-cost services.

Whereas the threat to even high-paid US jobs seems obvious, the truth is that not many US jobs have been replaced by these kinds of outsourcing. C. Alan Garner studied the phenomenon and reported his conclusions in, "Offshoring in the Service Sector: Economic Impact and Policy Issues."[9] He concludes that (p. 29), "offshoring should not permanently lower the nation's employment or production. It is likely to improve the average living standard if displaced workers are retrained and moved into new jobs with higher value added." He then focuses on national policy:

> Laws protecting a particular service industry will likely raise the costs of services to consumers and other businesses, hurting overall welfare. Instead policymakers should ease the movement of resources from sectors that are losing to international competition toward sectors that are gaining. Improved educational systems, better trade adjustment programs, and international negotiations to open foreign markets and guarantee intellectual property right can improve national welfare.

## BOX 9.1 DIFFERENCE OF OPINION: CONSERVATIVES AND FREE TRADE

A decade ago or longer, I thought that conservatives favored free trade, while modern liberals and progressives did not. You could count on Democrats to be against FTAs as part of support for labor and environmental issues. Republicans in contrast liked the efficiency and growth that came from expanding capitalism beyond one's borders. But those simple differences evaporated. Knowing one's party does not guarantee a position about free trade and FTAs. The first thing to note is that free trade suffers from the same language inadequacy as say, free markets and free internet. In all three cases there is no such thing as "free." In the latter case building and operating an internet takes labor and capital and ingenuity. So someone has to pay for it. In the case of free trade and free markets, they only exist in the minds of economists and are less a real event or outcome and more a desirable though unattainable goal.

Free trade sounds terrifying to some people. Some say that Haiti cannot compete against the US. If we ask Haiti to reduce tariffs on corn, beans, or wheat, you will hear the protests all the way to Washington. But please explain why the world has been moving toward freer trade since World War II. The WTO now has 161 members that agreed on major reductions in import tariffs and on other policies designed to reduce protectionist trade barriers. Or maybe you want to talk about the EU's twenty-eight members who operate in a virtually single market zone where once there was a complex of trade impediments and tariffs. Freer trade and competition work and countries vote for it.

Every country has a long list of goals that include ways that government intervenes and promotes growth, security, fairness, environmental quality, poverty, and many more. In the real world we recognize the benefits of freer international trade but have to compare those advantages to gains coming from pursuing other goals. It is no secret that the WTO has been working without agreement on its latest round of negotiations since 2001. The closer we get to reducing remaining trade barriers, the more we seem to encroach on other national goals. It does not help that the world's economy has been weak since 2008 – struggling countries care less about gains from trade and more about keeping the food on the table.

It is easy to see why an FTA is so controversial today. Free trade is the right thing to do but it appears to jeopardize other goals. Some politicians will see an opportunity to accept a watered-down trade agreement if it gives them the chance to advance other policies. Witness the 2,000-plus pages and thirty chapters of the latest proposed agreement (TPP). It is ironic that those who often hate FTAs are so willing to sign one now. Equally ironic is that those who usually love FTAs see what is going on and don't want to be part of it. It seems that the truth of the matter as it relates to free trade is what is contained in those thirty chapters and 2,000 pages and if the trade-offs are worth each ounce of free trade advanced. It is okay if free trade Republicans decide that this agreement does pass muster.

*Source*: https://larrydavidsonspoutsoff.blogspot.com/2015/11/conservatives-and-free-trade.html (November 24, 2015).

## 9.2   Global Trade Policy

At the global level, these issues of free trade and protectionism are being played out within the framework of the WTO which is charged with the governance of international trade. WTO is a *multilateral* framework involving all member countries. In contrast, regional trade agreements are frameworks for free trade among select groups of countries. Trade disputes arise mainly between pairs of countries when one accuses another of violating the WTO rules to gain unfair trade advantages. The WTO provides a framework for settling them.

### 9.2.1   The WTO

The WTO was founded in 1995 as the successor organization to the General Agreement on Tariffs and Trade (GATT, founded in 1947) and is headquartered in Geneva, Switzerland. It is a relatively small organization with a staff of approximately 650, but it currently has 164 member countries.

Following the breakdown of international trade relations during World War II and the onset of the Cold War, GATT was created under the leadership of the US and the UK to rebuild international trade and liberalize it. Between 1947 and 1994, GATT sponsored several *GATT Rounds* of negotiations for more liberal world trade, each one leading to reductions in tariffs. The *Uruguay Round*, which began in 1986, led to the creation of the WTO in 1995. While GATT was dealing with international trade in goods only, WTO has several parts: GATT, the General Agreement on Trade in Services (GATS), Trade-Related Investment Measures (TRIMS), and Trade-Related Aspects of Intellectual Property Rights (TRIPS). An agreement signed in Singapore in 1996 also set up rules for government procurement assuring that foreign firms can bid for governments' projects, rules for labor market standards making it harder to gain competitive advantages based on cheap labor, and standards for national environmental regulations. These additional rules were pushed through by the developed countries and perceived to make it harder for developed countries to compete internationally.

WTO (and formerly GATT) is based on two principles of non-discrimination:

- Non-discrimination among the member countries is enshrined in the principle of *most-favored nation (MFN) treatment.* This means that all WTO members grant each other the best trading conditions they grant to any other country. In a multilateral system, MFN facilitates negotiations about tariff reductions. For each item, the countries with the highest and the lowest import tariff for a specific good negotiate a tariff reduction. The result will benefit all members, but not all have to be involved in the negotiations.
- Non-discrimination between domestically produced and imported goods and services is enshrined in the principle of *national treatment.* This means that members cannot have tax and regulatory systems in place that discriminate between domestically produced and foreign products. For example: Medical drugs are subject to the same regulations regardless of whether or not they have been made at home or in another GATT country. But note that each country is free to choose its own regulatory rules.

Non-discrimination reduces the power of the bigger economies to pick favored trading partners, and it reduces the scope to protect domestic industries by setting higher product and regulatory standards for imports. There are, however, two exceptions to these principles. First, developing countries can obtain special and differential treatment. This exception aims at taking into account that developing countries have greater difficulties competing in international trade. Second, countries are allowed to enter into regional trade agreements that reduce trade barriers beyond what WTO has achieved for all. Regional trade agreements must be notified with WTO.

WTO rules also limit the scope of trade policy instruments member governments can use. Governments should abolish export and import quotas, and other discriminatory schemes, and use tariffs only for trade policy. The idea is that tariff mechanisms are more transparent as their price effects are relatively easy to compute. Export subsidies and dumping are prohibited for all members.

WTO serves as the platform for trade negotiations with the aim to reduce barriers for trade among all its member states. Trade negotiations are organized in "rounds," named after the city of the opening meetings. The *Doha Round* is the latest one. It was initiated in November 2001. Conflicting interests of the developed economies like the US and the EU, who seek to protect their agricultural sectors, and developing economies like Brazil and India, who like to preserve current levels of tariffs for manufactured goods and services, have caused a stalemate in the negotiations.

### 9.2.2  WTO Trade Disputes

Each year the WTO participates in resolving trade disputes – or apparent violations of existing agreed-upon WTO trade rules. Below is a passage taken from the WTO Annual Report, 2004:[10]

The central work of the WTO's dispute settlement system continued throughout the year. During 2003, the DSB (Dispute Settlement Body) received 26 formal requests for consultations. It established panels to deal with 19 new cases, received Notices of Appeal in 5 cases, and adopted panel and/or Appellate Body reports in 15 cases. The year 2003 saw the number of disputes initiated under the dispute settlement system since its creation less than nine years ago pass the 300 mark. This compares to the roughly 300 disputes brought to its predecessor, the GATT during its existence of almost 50 years. This figure emphasizes two important points: firstly, that Member governments have confidence in the WTO dispute settlement system; and, secondly, that the WTO system of agreements, and, therefore, Members' rights and obligations, are far more extensive than was the case under GATT. This has led to a great deal of dispute settlement activity under the new system.

The WTO's Annual Report for 2017 reports that, during 2016, the DSB received seventeen formal requests for consultations and established eight new panels. The number of disputes initiated under the dispute settlement system since its creation was slightly larger than 520. Two-thirds of the WTO member states had participated in a dispute settlement.

Consider some examples of actions brought to the WTO:

- Honduras complained that the Dominican Republic was unfairly preventing the importation of Honduran cigarettes. Imports from Honduras were being treated less favorably than other imports.
- South Korea complained about EU and US countervailing duties against Korean D-Rams (computer chips).
- The US complained about Mexico's anti-dumping regulations against US beef and rice.
- The US, Canada, and Argentina complained against the EU food import and marketing moratorium on biotech products.
- Antigua and Barbuda complained about US barriers preventing the importation of gambling and betting services into the US.
- Mexico complained about US anti-dumping measures against Mexican cement.
- Canada complained about US anti-dumping restrictions on Canadian soft-lumber.
- The EU complained about unfair subsidies given by the government to Korean ships and other commercial carriers.
- China led the field in a number of exporters that had two or more actions against them – forty-two between July 2002 and June 2003. The EU, South Korea, Chinese Taipei, India, the US, Thailand, and Japan each had ten or more actions against them.
- In 2016 alone, we had the following actions:
  - Brazil launched three requests for consultations – against Indonesia, Thailand, and the United States.

- Canada requested consultations with the United States concerning the impos-ition of countervailing measures on super calendered paper.
- China initiated two disputes, one with the EU and the other with the United States.
- The EU requested consultations with China on the export duties imposed on raw materials and with Colombia concerning measures imposed on imported spirits.
- India initiated two disputes with the United States, one concerning non-immigrant visas and another concerning measures relating to the renewable energy sector. Japan also launched two disputes, one with Korea concerning anti-dumping measures on pneumatic valves and another with India regarding measures on imports of iron and steel products.
- Turkey requested consultations with Morocco on anti-dumping measures on hot-rolled steel. This is Turkey's third request for consultations and its first since 2003. Ukraine requested consultations with Russia on certain restrictions.

Trade disputes happen very frequently. A trade dispute is a situation where the government of one country thinks that another country engages in unfair trade practices that harm its own economy. The WTO offers a legal framework to settle such disputes, the *dispute settlement mechanism*. The main characteristics of this mechanism are as set out below.

A WTO member can ask another member for consultations, if it thinks that the latter has violated WTO rules in a way harming its economy. The other member must respond to the request within ten days and negotiations begin within thirty days. If the dispute has not been settled within sixty days, the complaining country can ask WTO to set up a *Dispute Settlement Panel*, typically consisting of three members who are acknowledged international trade experts. Third countries with substantial trade interests in the specific case can become involved in the case hearings. The Panel submits a report to the WTO *Dispute Settlement Board* within six months. The report makes a recommendation for the settlement of the dispute. If the Dispute Settlement Board does not reject the report within sixty days by unanimous vote, it is assumed to be accepted. The respondent is then required to implement the Panel recommendation. Both parties are allowed to submit an appeal to the *Appellate Body*. The *Appellate Body* can confirm, change, or overturn the recommendation. If the respondent country does not implement the decision, the complainant is allowed to take retaliatory action. Such action must be *proportional* to the harm caused, i.e., reasonable in scope and intensity, and must be revoked as soon as the respondent has implemented the decision.

Experience has shown that most trade disputes can be settled timely and effect-ively within that mechanism. By far the most trade disputes involve either the US or the EU as complainant or respondent. This is simply because the US and the EU are the largest players in international trade. China is the third most frequent responder in trade disputes, i.e., it is relatively frequently accused of unfair trade practices.

## 9.2.3  Regional Trade Agreements

Sometimes a group of countries will pursue freer trade outside the global scope of the WTO. It seems easier to make an agreement with fewer than 164 countries. Regional trade agreements are an instrument to achieve that. They are designed to reduce trade barriers among the group of signatory states. FTAs and *customs unions* (CUs) relate to trade in goods between the member states of the agreement. *Enabling clause agreements* cover trade in goods among developing countries. *Economic integration agreements* relate to trade in services among the member states. While regional trade agreements are based on the principle of reciprocity – the members grant trade advantages to each other – there are also *preferential trade arrangements* (PTAs) under which countries unilaterally grant trade advantages to others.

An FTA eliminates tariffs and quotas for trade in goods between the members. However, each country is left to decide its own tariffs with respect to other nonmember countries. FTAs have domestic content regulations that prevent non-members from using one member country as a means to get lower tariffs in another member country. For example, countries A, B, and C form an FTA. Suppose country X trades with A, B, and C. Country A has very low tariffs on X's products, but country C has very high tariffs against X. Without domestic content regulations it would be possible for country X to ship to C by going through A as an entry port. But here is the catch. Domestic content regulations say that the tariff is zero between members A and C only if a threshold domestic production can be proved on the goods. The actual threshold varies from good to good and from FTA to FTA. For example, in the NAFTA agreement, automotive goods must have about 60 percent local content to be eligible for duty-free status. The rule is about 55 percent for footwear. If domestic content regulations are not met, then the good may not enter tariff-free between the members of the FTA.

A *customs union* is an FTA that imposes a common external tariff (CET) to outsiders. If A, B, and C are members, then each of these countries will have the same tariff against the goods of nonmember country X. In a customs union, the CET obviates the need for domestic content regulations – it is impossible for X to enter C with a lower tariff by coming through A. The EU (with twenty-eight members) and Mercosur (Paraguay, Uruguay, Brazil, and Argentina) are examples of CUs.

A *single market* is a customs union combined with a harmonization of all market regulations among the member states.

A *monetary union* is a single market in which all member countries use the same currency.

**Table 9.1** Regional trade agreements

| | |
|---|---|
| Free trade areas | 235 |
| Customs unions | 20 |
| Enabling clause agreements | 49 |
| Regional integration agreements | 151 |
| Total | 455 |
| Preferential trade arrangements | 32 |

*Source*: WTO http://rtais.wto.org/UI/publicsummarytable.aspx

Table 9.1 gives an overview of the existing regional trade agreements reported by the WTO in 2017.[11]

There is a substantial amount of double counting in these numbers, because they count treaties not country groups. For example, a regional trade agreement between a group of countries involving both an agreement in goods and in services trade would be counted twice. The number of physical regional trade agreements was 140 for goods alone, one for services alone, 143 for goods and services, for a grand total of 284. This is up from nineteen in 1990. During the 1990s, the EU concluded a large number of FTAs to bring the countries emerging out of the former Soviet Union and its trading block into the global trading system. In 2000, the number of regional trade agreements had already reached seventy-nine. The further increase in the number of regional trade agreements has been a reaction to the difficulties the WTO has had in promoting further trade liberalization at the global level since the turn of the century. Countries that wanted to intensify their trade relations simply did not want to wait until every WTO member came on board. In 2017, every WTO member had signed at least one regional trade agreement. Many members had signed multiple such agreements with partially overlapping memberships, resulting in an often complicated mesh of trade advantages. Of the total of 284 agreements, 97 involved European countries, 82 East Asian countries, 57 South American, and 42 North American countries.

One might be inclined to think that regional trade agreements promote free trade and are, therefore, welcome additions to the WTO framework. This, however, is not the case. The reason is that regional trade agreements violate the MFN principle. When two or more countries grant each other special trade advantages, those who are not part of the agreement are discriminated against. The very nature of a regional trade agreement is that it creates trade distortions between members and nonmembers. Nevertheless, the WTO allows such agreements if they meet certain criteria. They must reduce or remove trade barriers on substantially all sectors of trade within the group. The exceptions are enabling clause agreements which can be more narrow and restrictive in scope. Nonmembers should not find trade with the group any more restrictive than before the group was set up. WTO will ordinarily allow regional trade agreements, because they also have a number of advantages. First, they might be easier to fashion, because a smaller number of countries is involved. Second, regional trade agreements may pave the way for broader agreements to liberalize trade among all WTO members.

Forming a monetary union is a way of reducing the impacts on trade of changes in exchange rates. It creates the image that these countries are part of the same economic space. The adoption of the euro in Europe is today's most prominent case of a monetary union for the purpose of reducing trade barriers among countries. As of 2017, the euro was used by nineteen countries in the EU. Other monetary unions around the world include the West African Economic and Monetary Union founded in 1945, the East Caribbean Currency Union founded in 1965, and the currency union of the member states of the South African Customs Union (South Africa, Lesotho, Namibia, and Swaziland) founded in 1974.

## 9.2.4   The Doha Round

The WTO's first round of trade negotiations was supposed to start in Seattle in November 1999, but it was met with unprecedented, violent anti-globalization protests and never took off. Trade negotiations were finally opened again in Doha in 2001. The Doha Round has also been called the *Development Round* as it was supposed to address the needs of developing countries in particular. The key issue was the improvement of the access for developing countries to markets in the industrialized countries. While many developing countries today have bought into the message from the industrialized world that competitive markets and international trade are far better for economic development than the traditional approaches of state planning and intervention, they rightfully complain that industrialized countries both in Europe and North America do not give producers in developing countries fair access to their markets. This concerns mostly markets for agricultural and food products, where fair access would have required the cutting of agricultural subsidies governments in the developed countries pay to their farmers to protect them against competition from outside. Furthermore, it would have required cutting subsidies and removing import quotas for low-tech industries such as textiles. The industrialized countries asked the developing countries for better access to their markets for manufacturers' goods, demanding a *level playing field* for their industries in developing countries. Other areas of conflict between the two groups included stronger rules for protecting foreign investments in developing countries and better protection of intellectual property. The fact that WTO membership had by then expanded to over 150 countries, most of them from the developing world and eager to bring home results that would be in their favor, made all negotiations much more complicated than they had been in times past. Many of the developing countries misunderstood what could be achieved and how quickly through the WTO process. They made unrealistic demands for change that the WTO and the industrial countries simply could not accommodate.

The Doha Round first faltered at a ministerial meeting in Cancún in September 2003, when a large group of developing countries essentially walked out, protesting what they considered to be a lack of flexibility on the part of the industrial countries. The meeting showed how deep the rift was between the developing and the developed countries, and it also showed that the latter no longer could push through their agenda without making significant concessions to the former. After Cancún there was considerable disappointment and the likelihood that progress would not be possible.

The text below was taken from the WTO website and quotes Dr. Supachai of the WTO – and the considerable optimism shown in mid 2004 about the Doha Round:[12]

Although the frameworks of that time were not final agreements they do include significant commitments, which Dr. Supachai was able to describe as 'truly historic' achievements. These commitments were negotiated intensively day and night for two weeks, culminating in a grueling, non-stop session involving key ministers and ambassadors, that began at 5 p.m. on Friday 30 July and lasted almost twenty-four hours. During the fortnight, there were several meetings of heads of delegations, intensive consultations, and countless gatherings of various groups, with a number of trade ministers participating. During the General Council meeting many delegates commented that the deadlock of the Cancún Ministerial Conference had been broken. Dr. Supachai shared that view. Afterwards, Dr. Supachai listed the achievements:

- For the first time, member governments have agreed to abolish all forms of agricultural export subsidies by a certain date. They have agreed to substantial reductions in trade distorting domestic support in agriculture.
- As part of this agreement we have achieved a significant breakthrough in cotton trade which offers great opportunities for cotton farmers in West Africa and throughout the developing world.
- Governments have agreed to launch negotiations to set new rules streamlining trade and customs procedures. We have assigned ourselves ambitious guidelines for opening trade in manufactured products and we have set ourselves a clear agenda for improving rules that are of great benefit to developing countries.
- As importantly, WTO governments have sharpened the focus of the Doha round and provided a foundation which will enable negotiators to continue these talks from significantly higher level; greatly enhancing our chances for successful completion of these important talks.
- I fully expect that when negotiators return in September negotiations in these areas and all others will recommence with a high degree of enthusiasm.

Jeffrey Schott of the Institute for International Economics analyzed the failure at the Cancún meeting and speculated in early 2004 about what was needed to produce progress.[13] Schott enumerated the main stumbling blocks to agreement at Cancún:

- Negotiations relating to agriculture failed miserably. The US and the EU could not agree on a proposal until they fashioned a last-minute compromise. The compromise was not what the developing countries were hoping for. Given such little time, these countries could not agree on their own contributions to the reforms. Time ran out and they all agreed to disagree.
- The developing countries seemed very firm that they wanted to focus on a limited set of issues – and wanted to postpone progress on investment issues. The EU, Japan, and South Korea wanted to open up these discussions.

In July 2006, after five years of negotiations, the Doha Round was officially suspended at a meeting in Geneva. Lack of agreement and political will to move forward among the representatives of the US and the EU were the principal reason for the suspension. This was not the first WTO Round to fail, but the suspension is significant not least because it came shortly after the expiration of the US Trade Promotion Act that gave the US president special authority to conclude international trade agreements. Several attempts were made to revive it, and in December 2013 a ministerial meeting was held in Bali, Indonesia, which produced an agreement on the *Bali Package* that aimed primarily at reducing administrative barriers to trade and red tape. As of the end of 2017, however, the Doha Round remains unconcluded and there is very little hope of reaching a significant agreement. In the meantime, however, countries are free to pursue FTAs involving fewer but willing nations.

### 9.2.5   International Application: the Trans-Pacific Partnership

The Trans-Pacific Partnership (TPP, or Comprehensive and Progressive Agreement for Trans-Pacific Partnership) is a trade agreement between Australia, Brunei, Canada, Chile, Japan, Malaysia, Mexico, New Zealand, Peru, Singapore, and Vietnam. Originally signed on February 4, 2016, the agreement was renegotiated after the US withdrew from it.[14] The eleven remaining members reached a partial agreement on November 11, 2017.

The original TPP contained measures to lower both non-tariff and tariff barriers to trade, and to establish an investor-state dispute settlement mechanism. The US International Trade Commission, the Peterson Institute for International Economics, the World Bank and the Office of the Chief Economist at Global Affairs Canada found the final agreement would, if ratified, lead to net positive economic outcomes for all signatories, while an analysis using an unorthodox model by two Tufts

University economists found the agreement would adversely affect the signatories. Many observers have argued the trade deal would have served a geopolitical purpose, namely, to reduce the signatories' dependence on Chinese trade and bring them closer to the US.

## BOX 9.2 DIFFERENCE OF OPINION: IS TRADE GOOD OR BAD?

You don't grow bananas or manufacture your own shirts, and Bill Gates doesn't do his own typing. That's called the benefits of trade. There was a day when people were mostly self-sufficient. Families grew their own crops, chopped wood, made their own clothing, and so on. But we don't do that anymore. True, we are all getting fatter as a result. But we are also getting richer too.

The change from self-sufficiency to trade came gradually, and now we don't think about it. Today is an age of specialization and trade. Most of us are plumbers or accountants or bartenders. We earn incomes at our specializations and use our incomes to buy whatever we need or want. We don't think of it this way but what we are doing is benefiting from the activity called trade.

We benefit from trade mostly because of what some economists call comparative advantage. Bill Gates is really good at what he does for a living. Suppose he is worth USD 1 million a day in the marketplace. Should he do his own typing? I think not. If he spends a day typing, he loses USD 1 million and gains the average wage of an administrative assistant. It wouldn't make sense. And of course, trade doesn't just help Gates. Some people cannot make business decisions and are not valued at USD 1 million a day. Some people are really good at being an administrative assistant. Those people are delighted that Mr. Gates needs their services. They happily trade with Bill Gates.

It is true that the administrative assistant might earn USD 30,000 per year. But that person cannot pawn himself off to a company for more. That person is probably quite happy to find employment for what he is good at. In trade, people willingly enter into agreements, and both parties are advantaged by it. This goes on every day.

We live at a wonderful time when all we have to do is want something and someone else is there to make it or sell it to us. Of course, we have to uphold our end of the bargain and make sure people value what we do, so we can earn the money to buy all those other things.

That's simple. But it all goes haywire when we go from talking about Nathan and Christina to similar trade between the US and Mexico. You see, trade is trade, whether it goes across a national boundary or not. The same principles apply. Nations have always traded. Trade works because a nation can produce and sell things in which it has a comparative advantage and buy things in which it has no advantage. In doing so, all countries benefit.

Back to benefit. Recall Bill Gates and his administrative assistant. Both of them enter into an agreement willingly and gain from it despite the fact that one is a lot richer than the other. Some people believe that some countries are always harmed by trade. These countries are poor and get taken advantage of. That may sometimes be true but what is also true is a country's poorness often gives it great advantages in trade. Think of why we richer nations buy things from places like Vietnam. We buy because they have learned production techniques and combined that mastery with employees who are used to living on very low incomes and wages. It might not seem fair to some of us, but if you are from such a country and a new trade deal makes you more valuable, you are less inclined to envy the rich and more inclined to take advantage of a higher income and standard of living and perhaps better job security.

Trade is good and makes both parties better off even if it doesn't make them equal. The problems come when one or more of the parties to trade receive actual benefits that are less than expected. Unintended effects of trade can occur for many reasons. Some reasons are real and can be addressed. Other problems are made up or simply contrived for political purposes.

For example, Bill Gates might suffer business losses because of a new competitor. He might blame his administrative assistant despite the fact that the assistant was not the real problem. So he reduces the wage of his assistant or fires him. Clearly, if the real problem is a new business competitor, firing the assistant accomplishes nothing and sooner or later we find out the truth of the matter.

In the US today, we are rethinking trade. We have trade deficits with the world and with specific countries. We are about to say, "You are fired!" to these trading partners. How much of these trade deficits are in fact the direct results of freer or unfair trade? How much are caused by ourselves, or at least things out of control of our biggest trading partners?

We don't have all the answers, but we can offer a few. One answer comes from macroeconomics. We in the US love to spend. We love to buy goods and services. Apparently, we can't make enough to satisfy our love of buying, so we have to import. Maybe if we saved more that would help. Furthermore, we find ourselves in a time when the US economy, despite a lumbering pace, looks stronger than many of our trading partners. We have more ability to buy from them than they from us. None of this has to do with cheating, and none of this argument can be solved by US protectionism.

Another answer has to do with a realistic assessment of economic transformation in developing countries. When we made trade agreements with these countries, we made them with the full knowledge that they were transforming. Transformation is neither easy nor quick. When the Soviet Union collapsed, I recall economists kept saying that it would take thirty to forty years for countries like Poland (not in the Soviet Union) and Latvia to approach rich country status.

The problem is that subjecting a country that was centrally planned for decades to the rigors of competition is rough. You can't wave a magic wand and privatize very inefficient companies that have little experience with competitive markets. Likewise you can't overnight liberalize prices of all goods and services when many prices were kept at a very non-economic low.

Rapid privatization of companies can lead to large-scale unemployment and liberalization of prices can cause drastic increases in prices. Any country engaged in these and many other transition policies understands the social/economic upheavals associated with change. Nevertheless, they do it because of the eventual benefits transformation promises.

Richer countries know this, and trade agreements were made with the understanding that many of our important trading partners have government-owned companies and government control over prices, wages, and many other things. To say today that country X unfairly subsidizes its industry Y makes no sense. The word subsidize makes no sense in the context of a transforming nation.

Are we all wrong and are they all right? Maybe we do need to reopen some trade agreements. After all, some of them are old, and times have changed. But in doing this we need to remember a few things. First, some of these problems we bring on ourselves because we probably won't ever produce enough to satisfy our appetite for goods and services. Second, some of the problems will go away when economic growth in other countries returns to something more normal. Third, developing countries are still developing. They have very low incomes. They are in transition.

Putting unrealistic pressures on them only weakens them. We don't gain by weakening the people who we want to buy our goods. Trade is good. Trade agreements can be reopened. But there are clear limits to what can be accomplished without changes in our own domestic policies.

*Source*: https://larrydavidsonspoutsoff.blogspot.com/search/label/Free%20Trade (February 7, 2017).

## 9.3   International Organizations

In this section we discuss the major international institutions dealing with macro-economics and finance, describing their specific role, objectives, and functions. These organizations are the IMF, the World Bank Group, the WTO, the Bank for International Settlements (BIS), the OECD, the G7, and the G20.

### 9.3.1  The International Monetary Fund

The IMF, headquartered in Washington, DC, was created in 1945 together with the World Bank under the Bretton Woods agreement. The Bretton Woods agreement was the last formal global monetary order. It tied the value of the US dollar to the value of gold and featured fixed exchange rates of most other currencies around the world to the US dollar. The IMF served as a supervisory and regulatory agency of that arrangement. The Bretton Woods agreement ended in 1973.

Subsequently, the IMF assumed a new role as lender of last resort for national governments and central banks. Today the IMF has 189 member countries which pay quotas into the fund according to their respective economic seize. The USA has a quota which is lower than what would correspond to the size of its economy, but retains a voting right on all decisions made by the executive board of twenty-four directors, representing single large countries, and groups of countries. Currently, the fund has a staff of 2,400 with representative offices in 147 member countries. The managing director of the IMF historically comes from a Western European country.

The main tasks of the IMF are surveillance, lending, and technical assistance.

Surveillance  Annually or every other year the fund is providing so-called Article IX consultations for member countries. The focus of these consultations is on monetary and fiscal policy, but also the broader economic outlook for the economy. In the Article IV report the fund gives recommendations for policy adjustments.

Lending  The IMF provides emergency lending facilities for countries with balance-of-payment problems. While in the long run a balance of payment must be always balanced, see above, financial flows react much faster than the flows of goods and services and a country might face a shortage in foreign currency to manage the external value of its currency. Lending by the IMF provides time for countries implementing the necessary macroeconomic reforms such as fiscal austerity, to balance international flows of goods, services, and capital.

Technical Assistance and Training  The IMF is providing technical assistance and training for its member countries such as compiling the balance-of-payments statistics, but also developing an appropriate monetary and fiscal policy framework.

As a major player in balance of payment but also broader financial crises, the IMF also plays a pivotal role in international debt restructuring. The "conditionalities" that are coming with IMF lending and debt restructuring have provoked a lot of criticism regarding the role of the IMF handling these crisis scenarios.

### 9.3.2  The World Bank Group

The World Bank Group (aka the World Bank) consists of the International Bank for Reconstruction and Development (IBRD), created in 1945, the International Finance

Corporation (IFC), established in 1956 with the aim of promoting private sector development, and the International Development Association (IDA), created in 1960. The Bank, with approximately 10,000 employees, is led by the Board of Directors, consisting of the president and twenty-five vice presidents. While some funding of the World Bank comes from its 189 member countries, its main source of financing is issuing bonds in international financial markets, currently around USD 29 billion. Due to its status as an international organization, the World Bank can borrow in international markets at much lower rates than many of its member countries, and it passes this advantage on in loans to its members.

The first mandate of the IBRD was to support the financing of the reconstruction of postwar Europe. After the Marshall Plan came into existence in 1947, the IBRD focus shifted to financing developing countries.

The IDA is providing subsidized conditional loans to poorest countries. When a borrowing country reaches a certain threshold in GDP per capita, currently USD 1,725, IDA loans are not further available and new credit lines from the IBRD with higher-interest rates are available.

The World Bank is frequently under criticism for lending overwhelmingly to established emerging economies who already have access to international capital markets and don't need subsidized loans. In addition, World Bank lending often overlaps with lending operations from other institutions such as the IMF, but even more regional development banks such as the Asian Development Bank.

### 9.3.3   The Bank for International Settlements

The BIS, founded in 1930 and headquartered in Basel, Switzerland is the oldest international financial institution. Its original purpose was to manage the German WW I reparation payments. Today the BIS serves as "the central bank of central banks" with sixty member central banks covering 95 percent of world economic output. The BIS is not an operational bank, but rather acts as a facilitator for discussions and collaboration among central banks. It also provides data and research on cross-boarding banking. The BIS serves as a platform for major reforms in banking. The Banking Supervision Committee is drafting best practices for bank regulation, the so-called Basel standards, with currently Basel III discussing and formulating the regulatory consequences of the lessons learned by the banking crisis of 2008. Those best practices are recommendations and need implementation on a national level. In the US, the Dodd–Franks Act is the legislation aiming to implement major elements of the Basel III recommendations.

### 9.3.4   The Organisation for Economic Co-operation and Development

The OECD is headquartered in Paris. It was established in 1961 and currently has thirty-five members, most of them in Europe and North America. Australia, Chile, Japan, Mexico, and New Zealand are also members of the OECD. You can think of the OECD as a club of industrialized nations that agree on certain standards of regulation of their markets. The OECD collects huge amounts of data from their member nations and provides a wealth of studies of economic issues. It seeks to identify "best practices" in many areas including health and education, always with a view toward increasing economic prosperity. An important idea of the OECD's work is that "peer reviews" (reviews of the practices of one country in comparison to other members) can change and improve government policies.

An important mission of the OECD in the 1990s was the review of labor market regulations and the promotion of more labor market flexibility. In the early 2000s, the OECD introduced the "Pisa Studies" of educational achievements in the member nations, pointing to weaknesses of school systems.

### 9.3.5 G7 and G20

G7 and G20 are both governmental political forums. G7 originated in 1975. Its members are the globally most important industrial countries representing about 40 percent of world economic output, Canada, France, Germany, Italy, Japan, the UK, and the US. Russia was invited to join the group in 1997, but it was expelled after the annexation of Crimea in 2014.

G20 was created in 1999 comprising as members Argentina, Australia, Brazil, Canada, China, France, Germany, India, Indonesia, Italy, Japan, South Korea, Mexico, Russia, Saudi Arabia, South Africa, Turkey, the UK, the US, and the EU. The main focus during usually annual meetings is issues of global economic governance. Since the global financial and economic crisis of 2008, the G20 has evolved into the premier leaders' forum for international economic cooperation.

G7 and G20 meetings are called summits. They result in declarations of intention by the member governments. These are not binding policy agreements and it is an issue of debate whether summit declarations actually influence national government policies. Even if they don't, the exchange of views and information is probably useful to maintain peaceful cooperation in the world economy.

## 9.4 SUMMARY

International trade impacts the economy in numerous ways and, therefore, it is apt to end this book with a final chapter integrating trade into the story of macroeconomics. To say that all macro is global macro might exaggerate a bit – but not very much. Trade is good for a country. But like Cognac or Jack Daniel's, the good comes with the bad. And the negative consequences imply a role for policy. This chapter examines the good, the bad, and the role of policy.

The world can be a nasty and unpredictable place. The last sixty-plus years have brought more attention to creating freer and fairer trade. Enforcement of previous agreements and the growing number of FTAs portend a sanguine future for trade. The future promise of freer trade does not, however, tell the business planner enough.

A sanguine future suggests a trend, but one should continue to expect uneven progress over time and over place. A step backwards is sometimes necessary to move forward. At the root of some of the uncertainty is war and security. The war on terror creates strains between Moslem and Judeo-Christian countries. They also produce tensions among countries within these "camps." For example, long-standing trade disputes and differences between the US and Europe have not been ameliorated by their different stances in the Middle East.

But even without such extreme security problems there will continue to be local and regional issues that work against the expansion of free trade. We began this chapter by pointing out how capitalism combines creation with destruction. While we are pleased by the benefits that accrue from the winners' actions, we can't avoid the fact that change involves displacement – loss of jobs and income. Every country and every government within each country must resolve these issues or the political process will make expansion of free trade more difficult. The US and the French want to protect their farmers and low-income workers. China cannot turn its back on millions of workers furloughed from closed government enterprises. Brazil's poor demand better treatment.

This all means that business executives have wide information nets to cast. The world economy promises ever larger rewards for companies that take advantage of its growth and change. But the latter won't announce themselves with blaring horns. The changes will arise abruptly and unexpectedly over time and over space. As in most phenomena, the degree to which these changes are unexpected depends upon how much one invests in learning. Those who pay attention to global economic and business changes will be the ones that best take advantage of the spoils.

In this chapter we define and evaluate trade, free trade, and protectionism. We explore the many ways countries have used to come together to manage trade and the institutions that define these policies. We explore the policies and histories of these institutions and discuss how they will or will not shape the trends of freer trade and protectionism.

## 9.5  REVIEW QUESTIONS

1. What is free trade and why is it a desirable goal?
2. What is comparative advantage and what does it have to do with free trade?
3. Name at least three important benefits of international trade.

4. Why is free trade so controversial?
5. What is protectionism?
6. What is the WTO and what is its role with respect to free trade and protectionism?
7. In addition to the WTO, are there other means for countries to reduce trade barriers and promote freer trade?
8. Name some international organizations that promote better relations among countries.

## NOTES

1  See www.wto.org/english/thewto_e/whatis_e/10thi_e/10thi00_e.htm
2  Panagariya's summary, "The Miracle of Globalization: Free Trade's Proponents Strike Back," appeared in *Foreign Affairs*, September/October 2004, pp. 146–51.
3  www.heritage.org/trade/report/us-trade-policy-gouges-american-sugar-consumers
4  "Chinese Imports to Face Quota Call," *Financial Times*, October 13, 2004, p. 6.
5  Paul Krugman, *The Age of Diminished Expectations: US Economic Policy in the 1990s* (Cambridge, MA: MIT Press, 3rd edn, 1994).
6  Quotes come from an editorial, "Growing Pains," *Financial Times*, September 29, 2004, p. 12.
7  www.citac.info/study/job_dislocation.html
8  www.nytimes.com/2003/12/04/politics/bushs-statement-on-steel-tariffs.html
9  Federal Reserve Bank of Kansas City Economic Review, Third Quarter 2004, pp. 5–37.
10  WTO, *Annual Report 2004* (Geneva: WTO), p. 6.
11  See WTO at www.wto.org/english/tratop_e/region_e/scope_rta_e.htm
12  www.wto.org/english/news_e/news04_e/dda_package_sum_31july04_e.htm
13  www.iie.com/publications/papers/schott0604.htm
14  https://en.wikipedia.org/wiki/Trans-Pacific_Partnership

# Index

CPSIA information can be obtained
at www.ICGtesting.com
Printed in the USA
LVHW020748030822
725072LV00007B/286

9 781108 470858